THE MISKITU PEOPLE OF AWASTARA

PHILIP A. DENNIS

LLILAS New Interpretations of Latin America Series

THE MISKITU PEOPLE
OF AWASTARA

PHILIP A. DENNIS

UNIVERSITY OF TEXAS PRESS, AUSTIN
TERESA LOZANO LONG INSTITUTE OF LATIN AMERICAN STUDIES

First University of Texas Press Edition, 2004

Requests for permission to reproduce material from this work should be sent to Permissions, University of Texas Press, P.O. Box 7819, Austin, Texas 78713-7819

∞ The paper used in this publication meets the minimum requirements of American National Standard for Information Sciences–Permanence of Paper for Printed Library Materials, ANSI Z39.48–1984.

Maps by Yuri Trushin and Jenise Haynes Wooten
Drawings by Wiskat Morales
Photos by Philip A. Dennis

A section of chapter 11 appeared in *Ethnology* (Spring 2003) as "Cocaine in Miskitu Villages." Reprinted with permission.

Library of Congress Cataloging-in-Publication Data

Dennis, Philip Adams, 1945–
    The Miskitu people of Awastara / Philip A. Dennis.
        p. cm. — (LLILAS new interpretations of Latin America series)
    Includes bibliographical references and index.
    ISBN 0-292-70280-9 (alk. paper) — ISBN 0-292-70281-7 (pbk. : alk. paper)
    1. Miskito Indians—History. 2. Miskito Indians—Social life and customs. 3. Auastara (Nicaragua)—History. 4. Auastara (Nicaragua)—Social life and customs. 5. Nicaragua—History—Revolution, 1979. I. Title. II. Series.

F1529.M9D35 2004
972.85004'97882—dc22

2004049463

CONTENTS

LIST OF ILLUSTRATIONS   vi

ACKNOWLEDGMENTS   vii

CHAPTER ONE. Introduction   1

CHAPTER TWO. Who Are the Miskitu People?   23

CHAPTER THREE. The Village of Awastara   42

CHAPTER FOUR. Life in Victor and Plora's Family   73

CHAPTER FIVE. Food and the Search for *Upan*   107

CHAPTER SIX. Turtle Fishermen and Others   127

CHAPTER SEVEN. Working in the Plantations   153

CHAPTER EIGHT. School Days   165

CHAPTER NINE. Miskitu Christianity   181

CHAPTER TEN. Health and Curing   205

CHAPTER ELEVEN. Public Affairs and Community Development   232

CHAPTER TWELVE. Tibang and Concepts of Personhood   273

CHAPTER THIRTEEN. Leaving Awastara   281

MISKITU GLOSSARY   285

REFERENCES CITED   289

INDEX   301

ILLUSTRATIONS

Maps

1. The Miskitu Coast of Nicaragua   2
2. The Awastara region   4
3. The village of Awastara   5

Figures

1. First page of Genesis from new Miskitu Bible   31
2. The Awastara population in 1978 and 2000   44
3. Victor and Plora's family   75
4. Miskitu kinship terms   76
5. Seining at the beach, by Wiskat Morales   116
6. Turtle fishing at the Keys, by Wiskat Morales   139
7. Plantation work, by Wiskat Morales   158
8. Sample page from first-grade reader in Miskitu   168
9. The anthropologist at work, by Wiskat Morales   283

Photographs

1. Victor Renales Kingsman   6
2. Building a house   51
3. Obediah Kingsman   61
4. Changing into city clothes   65
5. Kids playing in front of my house   99
6. Kids eating cashew fruit   123
7. *Duri raskaia* (pulling the boat)   132
8. Husking coconuts   159
9. Harvesting rice with Victor   161
10. Making bread for the Moravian Church conference   193
11. Juan Downs, traditional healer   230
12. Maestra Zulaina presenting community problems   251
13. New house in Sandy Bay   266
14. My Miskitu family   282

ACKNOWLEDGMENTS

In Nicaragua, I would like to thank many friends and work companions: Dra. Myrna Cunningham, Miss Judith Cunningham, Dr. Pablo Cuadra, Lic. Alta Hooker, and Sra. Maira Vargas. All helped me in many ways as well as offering friendship. The Reverend Santos Cleban and the Reverend Norman Bent of the Moravian Church kindly offered encouragement and information about the Moravian faith.

In the United States, I am especially indebted to my old friend and mentor Dr. Arthur J. Rubel, who first interested me in the Miskitu Coast and continues to follow events there closely. I also thank the Moravian Archives in Bethlehem, Pennsylvania, for help with archival research. I thank my colleagues at Texas Tech, Grant Hall, Deborah House, Paula Marshall-Gray, Richard Nisbett, Bob Paine, and Tammy Walter, for their friendship and interest in my work. Thanks also to Lahib Jaddo for visiting me in the field. Thanks to my students, both at Texas Tech University and at the Universidad de las Regiones Autónomas de la Costa Caribe de Nicaragua (URACCAN) in Nicaragua, who have attended endless lectures and slide shows and contributed many good questions and comments. Special thanks to Becky Haskitt for a careful proofreading of the manuscript, and for all of her love and support.

Intellectually, I would like to thank Mary W. Helms and Barney Nietschmann, whose major scholarly works provided my grounding in Miskitu culture. Both have been generous and helpful to me, serving as mentors, to whose work I now add my own contribution. Mike Olien, Karl Offen, and Mark Jamieson also provided much appreciated advice and encouragement. Thanks to Bill Davidson for the Archivo General de Indias reference to Awastara. Scholars of a younger generation also work as colleagues and friends, among them David Brooks, Wolfgang Gabbert, Miguel González, Laura Herlihy, Christopher Kindblad, and Melesio

Peter. Thanks to all of them. Two anonymous manuscript reviewers provided much useful commentary and critique, which I appreciate. Nancy Perkins was extremely helpful with preliminary versions of several figures. Thanks also to Yuri Trushin and Jenise Haynes Wooten at PrinTech for their hard work on the maps. At the Teresa Lozano Long Institute of Latin American Studies at the University of Texas at Austin, Managing Editor Virginia Hagerty provided constant warmth and encouragement, and Heather Teague did outstanding work on the design and layout.

My greatest debt is to Victor Renales and his family in Awastara and to all the other friends and acquaintances from Awastara who appear as the protagonists of this book. Their willingness to accept me as a community member, their kindness and encouragement, and their keen interest in my work all have made Awastara one of my homes. *Man nanira sut tengki pali lukisna.*

My original research on the Miskitu Coast in 1978–79 was sponsored by a National Institute of Mental Health (NIMH) Postdoctoral Traineeship through the Department of Anthropology at Michigan State University. My 1999–2000 research was made possible by a generous grant as a Fulbright Senior Scholar, and also by a Faculty Development Leave from Texas Tech University. At Tech, the Latin American and Iberian Studies program and the Department of Sociology, Anthropology, and Social Work also contributed. I gratefully acknowledge all these sources of support, which made the experience possible.

CHAPTER ONE

Introduction

AWASTARA HOMECOMING

Most anthropologists who have lived among other people for months at a time, struggling to learn their language and understand their way of life, feel a periodic need to go back and see their people again. Fieldwork gives you a stake in the people themselves, memories and relationships that last you the rest of your life. You wonder about the people you've known—if they're still alive, how they have changed, what has happened to their way of life. These people have become part of your own life; and when the time is right, it's important to go back.

May 19, 1997: it has been nineteen years since I did fieldwork on the Miskitu Coast of Nicaragua (map 1). I had been back several times in the 1980s, during the middle of the war, but that was a strange and different experience, hardly a homecoming. I arrive again in Puerto Cabezas, the regional capital. In Creole English the city is called Port, but in Miskitu it is referred to as Bilwi. The three different names indicate the multilingual, multicultural nature of the region. I visit friends and then begin looking for a way up to my village, Awastara. I find out that it isn't any easier to get to than it ever was. I catch a flatbed truck headed to Krukira, almost halfway (map 2), and find myself crammed into the back of the truck with thirty other people as well as their sacks of food and bundles and assorted purchases. Along the way a tire blows out. Everyone out to unload the truck! All of the men jack up the truck by standing on a long, thick mahogany plank wedged under the axle near the tire. The driver mutters something unintelligible under his breath as he loosens the lug nuts and changes the big tire, while the rest of us balance on the plank to keep the axle in the air. I'm back on the Coast!

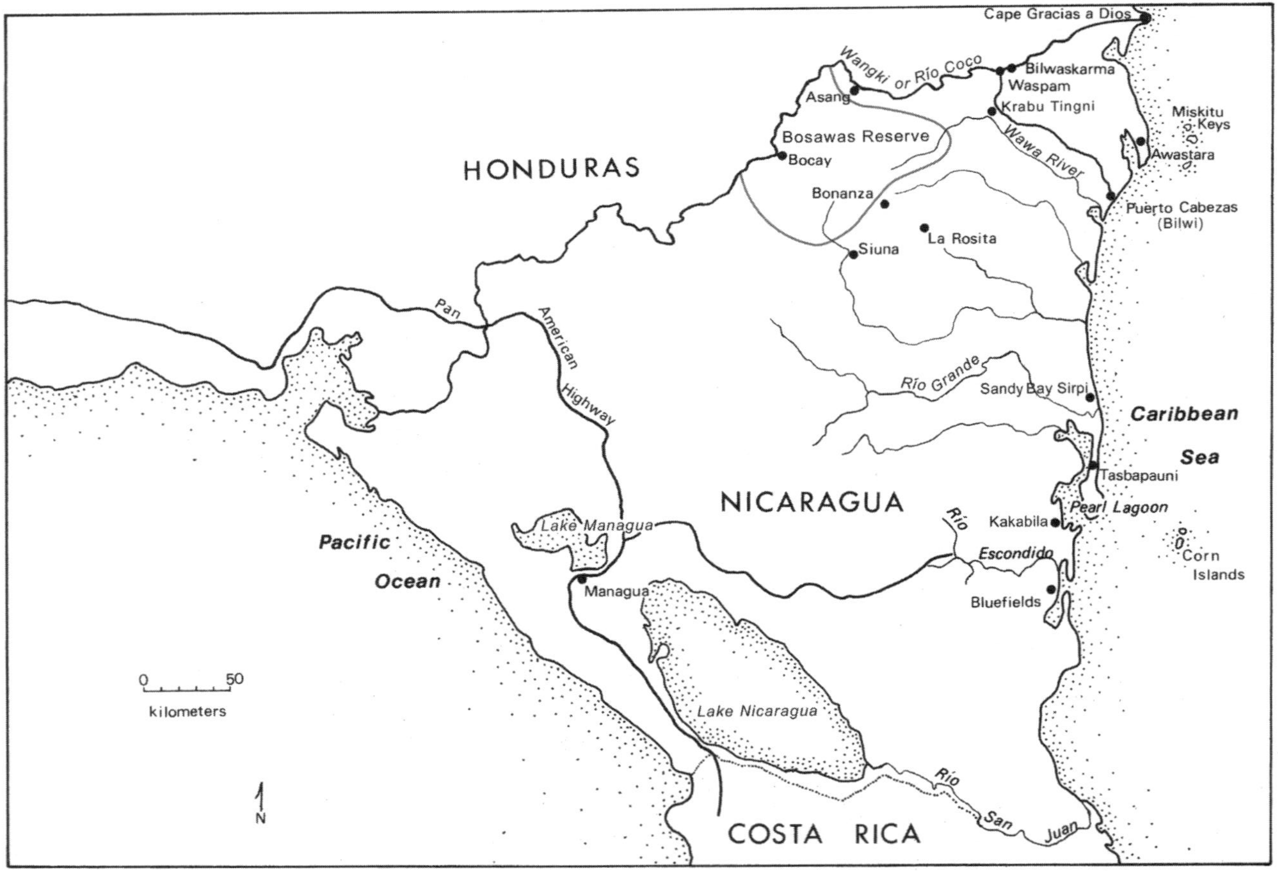

MAP 1. *The Miskitu Coast of Nicaragua*

When we reach Krukira, I run into an Awastara man named Bantan, who recognizes me and calls me by name. "Get in the canoe, Pelipe," he tells me (there is no *f* in the Miskitu language). He hands me a paddle and we put our backs into it, paddling three hours up the river toward the Páhara Lagoon against a stiff headwind. I dip my paddle again and again, hour after hour, my shoulders aching and the blisters starting to form on my tender pink hands, accustomed to office work. Bantan seems to know every twist and turn through the mangrove channels in the river. I comment on how easy it would be to get lost here. "Yes," he replies, and tells me a story about getting lost here once himself. Just before we get to the lagoon, we stop underneath a big tree whose roots spread out into the water. It is a pretty spot, dappled with shade. Bantan uses his cast net to throw around the roots, and when he pulls it back several bright silvery stone bass or *trisu* gleam as they flop in the net. My Miskitu friends are not about to miss a fishing or a food-gathering opportunity, I reflect happily.

As we enter the lagoon, the sun goes down. The sunset is glorious, moments of absolute silence, with shimmering crimson clouds in the west. The dark forest lines the shore and the water is a flat, dark mirror, now completely calm. Thankfully, the strong northeast trade wind has finally died. The still air is filled with birds, an *unki* (great blue heron), a *krasku* (kingfisher), several cormorants, and many others. Bantan takes delight in telling me the Miskitu names of the birds. Far off a *wangki* makes a deep, throaty call in the mangroves. I am filled with joy to be back on the Miskitu Coast, paddling a canoe again with a Miskitu friend. For a moment the silence is so profound, the sunset so beautiful, the mirror of the lagoon so perfect, that it seems a sacrilege to dip our paddles in the water. Then it is gone. The stars come out to accompany us as we paddle the rest of the way up to the trailhead for Awastara.

It is about midnight when we arrive at the trailhead, and the sky is beginning to cloud up. We load all our things on our backs. As usual, I have brought way too much. I have small presents for Victor's family, books, extra clothes, my camera. Bantan shows me how to put the straps on my plastic duffel bag around my shoulders and carry it like a backpack. We start off across the savannah, a two-hour walk to the village. The moon is shining as we set out; but soon it is covered by thick clouds, and we are soaked by a brief, fierce thunderstorm. It is not really cold, probably in the fifties, but it certainly feels cold, with a light breeze blowing and me wet to the skin. By the time we finally reach Awastara, I am soaked, cold, and miserable, and I feel half dead. The Moravian church in the center of town is the easiest place to find in the dark. I knock on the

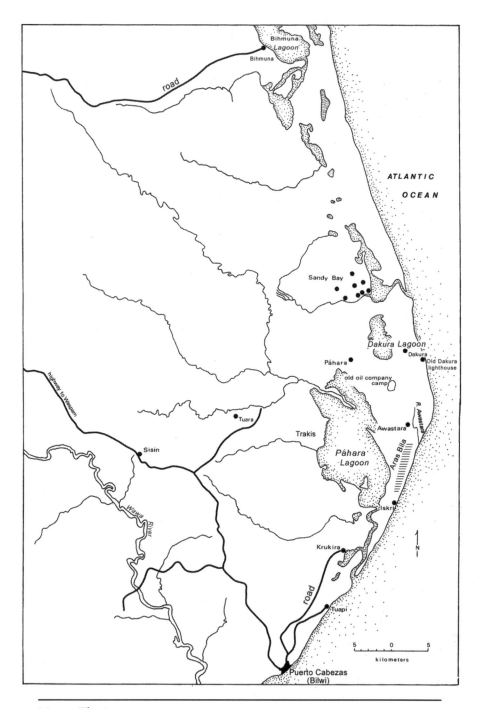

MAP 2. *The Awastara region*

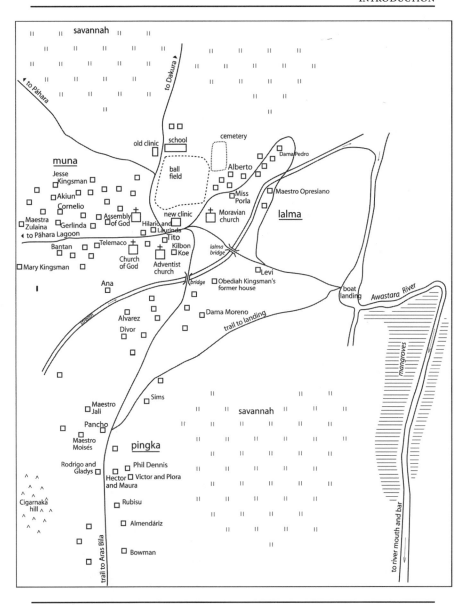

MAP 3. *The village of Awastara*

Moravian preacher's door, and he invites me in. I sink to the plank floor of his house exhausted, stripping off my wet clothes. Before I expire, I remember thinking, "Maybe I'm getting too old for this kind of stuff."

An unworthy thought, of course.

My old friend Victor Renales shows up in the early light to rescue me from the preacher. Somehow the word has already spread that I am back. Photo 1 is one of the few pictures I have of Victor, a gaunt man about six foot four, in his late sixties, with great physical strength. He has a ready smile and a seemingly endless stock of stories and anecdotes. A complex, interesting person, Victor has led a long life and likes to reflect about it. Since I first came to Awastara, he has made it a personal task to teach me about life in the village, taking me to work in his rice fields and out to the Keys to catch turtles and feeding me in his house. Our friendship goes back more than twenty years, although it's been a long time since I've seen him. A devout Christian and a member of the rival Church of God, he usually scoffs at bush medicine and traditional curing in general. The traditional beliefs in spiritual creatures such as the *swinta* and the *liwa mairin* are just foolishness, he often says. Interestingly enough, however, as we become closer, Victor begins telling me his own *swinta* stories from time to time.

Victor befriended me when I first went to Awastara in 1978. In fact, one of his life strategies has been to talk with strangers, put them up in his house, and make friends of them. His early friendships with Cayman Island turtle fishermen helped transform Awastara into a turtle-fishing

PHOTO 1. *Victor Renales Kingsman*

6

village. In recent years he has made friends with a Chinese businessman from Costa Rica, a U.S. marine biologist, and a Dutch expert on alternative technology, as well as with me. This time he tells me about encountering several Jehovah's Witnesses a few months earlier. After a long walk across the savannah carrying a sack of provisions, they were exhausted. Victor thought they were good people and felt sorry for them, and he invited them to his house. They stayed for several days.

Victor takes me over to his house, where I spend the rest of the week. I find the house full of Jehovah's Witness pamphlets! He lectures me severely on coming straight to his place the next time I visit, no matter what the hour, and avoiding the Moravian church like the plague. Victor, I remember, was one of the first members of the Church of God in Awastara. He has strong opinions about many things and is not shy about expressing them.

For the next two weeks Victor's wife, Plora, stuffs me with food: turtle meat and cassava, Johnny cake and sweetened black coffee. I play happily with their dozen or so grandchildren, taking time out to go to school and to the churches (all four of them). I wander all over town, visiting old friends and finding out what people are doing and who has died. It feels wonderful to be back. I find a few brightly painted new houses around town, a strange hint of prosperity. Later I will learn that kilo bricks of cocaine are washing up regularly on the beach and that cocaine use has become a major problem in the community. For some, it has provided a new source of wealth to invest in houses and boats, especially for people in neighboring Sandy Bay.

My ability to speak Miskitu is almost gone; but with lots of patience on the part of my friends, and by reviewing my notebooks at night, it starts coming back. There are brand-new school texts in Miskitu, through the fourth grade. I bring copies back to the United States with me, to keep on studying the language and to use in my Miskitu conversation course. Wandering around the village, I run into one old fellow I barely remember. I tell him I'd like to come back to Awastara again and spend more time. He says, "Of course you can come back. It's your town!" I realize they like having a pet "Miriki" around, to watch and teach how to be human and to provide a constant source of entertainment. They've missed me! And I've also missed them.

I especially love playing with the kids. One little seven-year-old named Jasira falls in love with me, and I with her. With her two missing front teeth and her devilish grin, Jasira is delightful. One evening, as we sit together on the front porch, she lets a big fart. Ever alert to linguistic opportunity, I ask her how you say that in Miskitu. *Tusban krabaia,* she replies. I promptly write it down in my notebook. Curious herself, Jasira asks how you say the same thing in Spanish. "Pedo," I say. "Pedro?" she asks. It strikes me as funny, since we both know an old man in the village, *Dama* (grandfather) Pedro (see the glossary). "No, *pedo*," I emphasize. She works on that for a while but can't get it right. I tell her Grandfather Pedro wouldn't be too happy if he thought his name meant "fart." "Well," said Jasira, "how do you say it in English then?" The answer turns out to be completely unpronounceable in Miskitu, with no *f* and the strange consonant cluster at the end. After a lot of giggling we give up and decide just to say *tusban krabaia*.

On the last day of my visit, as I am saying good-bye to everyone, Jasira announces matter-of-factly, "I'm going home with Pelipe." The "pamily" members all look at me to see if it is true. Miskitu kids are quite independent and are generally allowed to do what they want. They definitely have minds of their own; and if people try to order them around, which they do all the time, they don't pay attention. Control struggles abound. So it is generally thought best to respect children's decisions and then let them deal with the consequences. Had I been able, I would gladly have brought Jasira home with me, along with her little cousin Jaseth, to brighten up things back in Lubbock, Texas.

MY LIFE ON THE COAST

I first went to Nicaragua in 1978, as a postdoctoral student in medical anthropology at Michigan State University. I wanted to study a culture-bound syndrome reported from the Miskitu Coast, called *grisi siknis*, in which victims, mostly women, are possessed by devils, tear off their clothes, run away from their houses, and have to be restrained. Working with the University of Wisconsin health program, I visited about twenty different villages near Puerto Cabezas taking a health survey. One of them was Awastara. There had been over sixty *grisi siknis* victims in Awastara, more than in any other community. It apparently had been the center of an epidemic of this syndrome or disease. My wife and I rented a house in the village and moved in. I had studied the Miskitu language at Michigan State, but my proficiency was very limited. Only a few people in the village spoke Spanish or Creole English. The daily language was and is Miskitu. As I spent each day talking with and interviewing people, keeping a vocabulary notebook, and studying, my proficiency began to grow. By May 1979, when I left Nicaragua, I had very modest competence in

Miskitu. The information from all my notebooks about *grisi siknis* was eventually published (Dennis 1981b, 1985, 1999), but I wasn't satisfied. I still had four large notebooks full of information about other aspects of life—turtle fishing, farming, living in families, folktales (*kisi*), and many other things. For me, experiences in the community had been vivid, larger-than-life events. Miskitu culture fascinated me, and I had enjoyed living in Awastara. I wanted to understand not just *grisi siknis* and health issues but the whole pattern of life in the community, as experienced by local people. I intended to go back and finish my general ethnographic work, but twenty years were to intervene.

In 1979 a revolution was raging in Nicaragua, with the fighters from the Sandinista National Liberation Front trying to wrest power from the Somoza dictatorship, which had held power for sixty years. There was little fighting on the Miskitu Coast, however. The Coast is a completely different region from western Nicaragua, cut off geographically and with a different history and ethnic makeup. Ties always have been with Great Britain and the United States rather than with Spanish-speaking Nicaragua. When the Sandinista government came to power, the new leaders expected the indigenous peoples of the Atlantic Coast to support the popular revolution in the same way that communities with an Indian identity on the Pacific side had supported it (C. Hale 1994: 92–94). The myth of a potentially revolutionary indigenous heritage was an important part of Sandinista ideology, confirmed for them by the spontaneous uprisings against the dictatorship in the communities of Sutiava and Monimbó in the late 1970s (Field 1999: 98, 185–86). This myth was generalized to include indigenous people from the Atlantic Coast, a region the Sandinistas patronizingly called "a giant, about to awaken" (Adams 1981: 16). The Sandinistas regarded the integration of the Atlantic Coast as a major political problem to be tackled (Dennis 1981a).

The Miskitu, however, were profoundly suspicious of "Spaniards," as mestizo Nicaraguans continue to be called. Miskitu leaders formed their own self-determination organization, called MISURASATA (Miskitu, Sumu, Rama, and Sandinista, Asla Takanka, or Working Together) (C. Hale 1994: 2). Tension increased as MISURASATA coordinated a regional bilingual literacy program and eventually presented a demand for indigenous land rights to a large area of the Atlantic Coast. The "separatist" attitudes of the indigenous and Creole *costeños* were suspicious from the Sandinista point of view, and a series of violent incidents occurred. When MISURASATA leaders were arrested, open conflict flared. MISURASATA became a military organization and with U.S. support began a counterrevolution on the Coast. People from the coastal villages were deeply involved in the fighting. Some twenty-one young men from Awastara went off to fight with the Miskitu forces. By the late 1980s, however, peace agreements had been signed, and legal autonomy was granted to the region in 1987. Autonomy included a new regional government, which would supposedly use revenue from the fishing and lumbering industries for the benefit of the region. In the cultural sphere, it provided for bilingual education programs and a new *costeño* university, the Universidad de las Regiones Autónomas de la Costa Caribe de Nicaragua (URACCAN). Unfortunately, during the 1990s the region's "autonomy" proved to be paper thin (González Pérez 1997; Dennis 2000).

I visited the Coast several times during the war years of the 1980s, but only very briefly. In 1985 I accompanied two Miskitu male nurses and several Sandinista soldiers to Awastara to vaccinate children. It was during the middle of the war, with the Miskitu rebel groups controlling much of the countryside and periodically attacking Sandinista military bases. The small Sandinista military base near Awastara had come under attack once, and many young men from the community were off in the bush with the Miskitu rebels. Things were very tense indeed. But I managed to find Victor and spent several hours talking with him. Then it was time to get back in the boat—the soldiers alert, weapons ready—and return to Port.

My own life led me to different places, and it was not until 1997 that I finally managed to return to the Coast and visit Awastara for a week. In 1998 I was able to come back for a whole month and told Victor that I would like to spend another year in the community to finish my ethnographic work. He was very enthusiastic, and we began making plans to build a house of my own near his. After knowing each other for so long, we decided to call each other brother (*moihka* in Miskitu), with all that implies—respect, trust, and closeness. This was not a lightly taken decision. Victor undoubtedly thought he would get tangible benefits out of the relationship, and I thought I would too. Besides that, we had grown to like each other and wanted to cement the tie. I wished to return for a year and live in Awastara and complete this book about the community and the Miskitu people, begun many years before. And I wanted to live with a family, Victor's family. At the same time, I applied for a Fulbright grant to teach medical anthropology at the URACCAN in Puerto Cabezas, to help with the university's new Intercultural Master's of Public Health (MSPI) program. And so, in July 1999, I came back to spend my second year in Awastara.

LIVING IN AWASTARA

After an exhausting sea voyage, it is always a pleasure to row up the Awastara River and see, at long last, the boat landing with the village beyond (map 3). It is a relief to get out of the cramped boat and walk up the path as the children come running. In July 1999 a special treat awaits my arrival. From the landing, I get a glimpse of my own new house in Awastara. When I come close enough, I can see it, set high on posts, looking east over the savannah toward the ocean. It is pretty in its new green and white paint—a place of my own in Awastara!

For a year I have been sending money to Victor each month to have the house built. His son-in-law Casey, a master craftsman, was the carpenter. The house will give me a place to sleep and work and some privacy of my own but still be close to Victor and his family. Having my own house built was actually a suggestion of local people, which reflects the Miskitu value that people should have their own place. *Dama* Pedro tells me: "Living in somebody else's place can be a problem. Suppose you burn it down? Then you've got a problem! But if you burn your *own* place down—well, too bad."

The rhythm of life is slow here in Awastara, with plenty of time to sit and think and write, and fieldwork activities all day long. I spend time talking to the health leader at the community's new health clinic, going to church services, walking all the way out to Rosa's to spend an afternoon listening to the story of her son's murder last year, walking to each corner of the village to search out interesting people and talk with them. People have learned that I want to understand every aspect of their lives, and they always have interesting stories when I come to visit. The role of anthropologist is a welcome one here—someone interested in these people for themselves, without trying to convert them or change them according to some outside agenda. I try to be a good community member too, helping clean the trails, attending church, contributing toward supplies for our local baseball team. Back at Victor's house, I play with the children, spend hours listening to Victor's long stories, and sit in the kitchen talking with the women. I teach a small English class in the afternoon, a couple of times a week, at the request of a group of young people. They seem to like the class and actually do their homework, at least some of the time. I really don't know how to teach English, but I feel good nevertheless about having a teaching job here in the village and become good friends with the schoolteachers, who share their classrooms with me.

If I expect people to tell me their stories, it is obligatory to tell my own story first: where I live, why I returned to Awastara, my two marriages and my children. Soon people begin to talk among themselves, and the Miskitu language gradually eludes me—their voices rising and falling with animation, as my poor mind falters along behind, trying to follow the drift of the conversation. I soon lose the thread but break in every once in a while to ask a question. Somebody then patiently explains to me what the story was about, so I can comment on it: "Terrible! Good grief! May God help us!" and so on. Then I can ask another question.

In general, I enjoy the people. They have been good to me, even Cornelio, the sly ex-headman with whom I never got along, and two current drug dealers that I knew as boys in 1978. I know I will miss this place when I leave for the United States. And Awastara friends tell me, "When you're not here, things are sad."

VICTOR'S HOUSEHOLD

Victor's extended household includes many people (see chapter 4). His grown daughter Pamela still lives in the same house with her parents, her husband, Casey, and their children. This sort of matrilocal residence is the preferred pattern among Miskitu people generally (Helms 1968). Nevertheless, prosperous men like Victor can sometimes arrange for sons to bring spouses home and live patrilocally, in hopes of sharing their father's wealth and eventually inheriting it. Thus Victor's son Adolpo also lives in the main house with his wife, Eliza, and baby Nachalie. Some hundred feet away, Victor's eldest son, Hector, and his wife, Maura, have built a large house of their own and live there with their five children. Victor's son Rodrigo and his wife, Gladys, and their four children have built a house another seventy-five feet away, across the main trail. These people appear many times in the text, as do other Awastara friends and neighbors, referred to either by their own names or by pseudonyms. I regard this book in part as a tribute to these people, and I hope that they will be proud of their contributions to it.

Thus Victor's family becomes my family. Although I have my own house, I eat in Plora's kitchen, buying provisions on every trip into Port, and paying her twenty cordobas a day for meat and daily expenses. I soon realize that I provide the major cash flow in the household. In local terms, my modest income as a visiting professor is a fortune, and I gladly chip in for coffee, laundry soap, and other essentials. I also will give my house to Casey and Pamela to live in and take care of when I leave, so the family will prosper by my stay with them. Victor's life strategy of making friends with strangers has paid off again, I reflect to myself.

The daily routine in Awastara begins very early. Many adults get up around 4:00 A.M., well before sunrise, to go to the plantations to work, to seine for fish at the beach, or to gather firewood. Many of the men in the community are gone for a week at a time, turtle fishing out on the Miskitu Keys. They take their turtles to Port to sell, then come back to Awastara to spend a few days at home with their families and to repair their nets and other gear for another week of turtle fishing. The rhythm of life in the village thus revolves around turtle fishing. Women and men who have gone to the plantations or the beach don't usually come back until mid-morning. But some of the women always stay at home, to start the cooking fires, make breakfast, and get the children ready for school. I have three meals a day in Plora's kitchen, at around 7:00 A.M., noon, and 6:00 P.M. Plora likes to have the last meal over and all the dishes washed before it gets dark, when the kerosene lantern is lit for the evening.

NIGHTTIME

The cool of the evening is very pleasant after the intense heat of the day. I sit on my front porch listening to the short-wave radio and watching the stars. Orion and Canis Major are out in all their beauty. I hear the children playing and shrieking at Maura's house, nearby. They usually quiet down by 7:30 or so. Some nights my neighbors across the way sing church hymns to the accompaniment of a guitar, and the sound carries over the distance. It is peaceful and beautiful at night in Awastara. I reflect on what I have accomplished during the day and on my plans for tomorrow.

With my own children grown, I enjoy Victor's grandchildren, who come to see me all the time. Sometimes they also come to sleep on my floor. "It is too sad to sleep alone," says Plora, who sends the children over. Not every night, but once or twice a week, the grandchildren squabble to see who will come. The first night that Nena (nine years old) sleeps on my floor, she stays up a long time quizzing me about my own family. She wants to know about my mother and father (both dead), my brothers and sisters, my two former wives, and my own children. I tell her as best I can in Miskitu, imagining how her little mind must be translating all this back into her own world. I have a feeling that she is disappointed that my own family is so small, and there is so little to tell, as compared to her own large family. Victor is her grandfather; but her father is far away, so she calls Victor papa. Following kinship logic, she announces that—because he and I are now brothers—she will now call me *rapiki*, "my father's brother."

Nena and Josepa, seven, often come together to sleep at my house. About 6:30, as it gets dark, they climb up my stairs with their *sityapa* (sleeping gear). This consists of a sheet and a pillow each. They throw them down on the board floor inside and come sit on the porch with me to watch the moon and talk. Josepa likes to snuggle up with me in the big chair on the porch. I snuggle with Nena too, but I'm wary of her long, thick black hair, because I noticed her mother Pamela picking lice out of it earlier in the day. The girls talk for a while and then want to sing songs. I agree but warn them: "Only a few." They sing church hymns, one after another, in loud, brassy voices. They obviously have been taught to sing as loudly as they can, without much regard for melody or quality of tone. My Texas grandfather used to sing church hymns in the same tone of voice. I listen for about fifteen minutes and then tell them it's time for bed. *Mahka yapaia!* I say. "Hurry up to sleep!" The little girls take turns going over to the edge of my high porch, where they squat and pee before bed, quite without shame. A little more self-conscious, I wait until they go inside and then walk over to the edge and pee as well.

Once inside, I light the kerosene lantern and hang it up on the rafter to keep the bats away. The girls spread their sheets out on the floor and put their heads on their pillows. I tell them to be really still and I will sing them a song. In earlier times there were Miskitu lullabies, I have learned, but no one seems to know them anymore. So I sing them the ones I know, such as "The Dark-Eyed Sailor," an old English lullaby my own children liked very much. It has many verses and a haunting, happy/sad sort of melody. By the time I finish, both little girls are asleep. I get up and go over to my table, where I work on my field notebooks for a while, finishing the day's notes. Then I plug in my headphones and listen to the British Broadcasting Corporation (BBC) news on my little short-wave radio. I'll get sleepy within an hour myself and lie down on my bed, a few feet above the floor where the little girls are sleeping. I walk out on the porch before retiring. The almost full moon is high in the sky, and the tropical night is beautiful.

There are dangers in the night too, however. They include spiritual creatures that molest people as well as more tangible creatures, such as blood-eating bats. One morning Victor shows me the cuts on his feet and hands where the bats have bitten him. Ten-year-old Melvin has a white rag wrapped around his thumb with dried blood on it. And Nena shows me her nose, which has a very noticeable scar right in the middle where a bat bit her when she was small. Victor says the danger lies in letting your feet or hands poke through the mosquito netting at night or in not having a kerosene lantern burning all night. The bats apparently don't like to come inside a house where a light is shining. I make sure my lantern is always lit at night! The bat bites are painful, but I haven't heard of any cases of their transmitting rabies as they sometimes do in the United States.

BATHING

One of the great pleasures of living in Awastara is bathing. After a few hours in the hot, sticky climate, it feels wonderful to bathe in the water from Victor's well. A few years ago Victor, always progressive, was one of the first people in town to hire a visiting alternative technology specialist to build him an enclosed well. It touted a cover and hand pump, to draw the water up a pipe from the deep well and out through a spigot. It works beautifully, and we have clean, fresh water right in the middle of our cluster of houses.

I draw a big bucket of water from the pump and go into the bathhouse, shut the door, and simply indulge for a few minutes. Bathing also has strong positive value in Miskitu culture. One day Josepa and Jasira, both nine, come by to show me their clean skin and clean clothes. "Look! Our skin is so clean!" they say. "We bathe two times a day! We're not like Juana's daughter. She even comes to school in her dirty clothes. We are really clean!"

The bathhouse is a small stall (about four feet by four feet), with wooden walls and floor. The water simply runs out through the spaces in the floorboards. The makeshift metal door on the bathhouse is not closing completely, so I put a new string on it to satisfy my own sense of modesty. As omnipresent as children are, however, they do not seem to look in at people bathing. Peeping at naked people is not part of the mischievous "rogue" character that many Miskitu kids have. Rather, a strong sense of modesty is learned at an early age.

First I pump a bucket of water at the well. Then, in the bathhouse, I take off my clothes (usually just shorts and a T-shirt) and throw them up over the wall, take a cup of water from the bucket, and pour it slowly over my head, letting the cool, delicious water trickle slowly down my sweaty body. I dip some more and lather up with shampoo and soap, from head to foot. This is sticky, athlete's foot country, so I wash carefully between my toes as well as my crotch and butt, armpits, scalp—

15

everywhere that tiny invisibles might be hiding. Then I pour cool water over my body, cup by cup, washing off all the soap, which I watch run off through the slats onto the ground and away down the gentle slope. I usually have part of the big bucket of water left at the end. I towel off quickly, anxious now to get back up to my porch, where the cool trade wind will be blowing. The coolness of the clean well water on my skin will be one of my enduring memories of Awastara. The well water is also pure to drink, so I don't have to worry about getting it in my mouth as I bathe, as I do in Managua or Puerto Cabezas. Pure, clean, cool well water, in inexhaustible quantities: wonderful!

THE CHANGE OF SEASONS

Here in the tropics, the seasons are strongly marked. It rains about 130 inches a year in Puerto Cabezas (Nietschmann 1973: 66–67), with the rains beginning in late May and continuing through December and January. From January or February through May is the dry season or *mani taim*. By early May the days are long and hot, and the land is parched and dry. The sun beats down mercilessly on the dusty trails, day after day. Even Victor's deep well begins to dry up. After pumping and pumping, only a partial bucket of water comes up, clouded with sediment. In the center of the village, you can see all the houses clustered close to each other. No longer are they hidden by walls of leafy foliage. There is a continual haze in the air from people burning off their plantations. The world is thirsty, just waiting for rain. Life is suspended, it seems, contracted within itself, biding its time until the life-giving water returns.

When the first light rains do begin, large crabs called *kaisni* come out on the savannah in large numbers. Many people go to gather them, grabbing them with a gloved hand to avoid their big pincers, and bringing them home in burlap bags. Each large bag, thrown across the shoulder, is a moving mass of crabs. The small legs are broken off before putting each crab into the bag, and the trail across the savannah is littered with tiny crab legs. After a week or two of light rains, the wet season usually announces its arrival with a torrential downpour. Deep, rumbling thunderbolts shake the sky, one after another. *Alwani puli ba wina mahka li auisa,* they say in Miskitu: "Thunder is playing and soon indeed the rain will come!" It is true: when you hear the thunder (*alwani*) off in the distance, far away on the northeast trade wind, you know the rain will follow soon. In 2000 the rainy season begins in earnest as I teach my English class in the school building. The skies open up and the rain falls in sheets, turning the baseball field in front of the school into a large lake. We have to wait an extra hour in the leaky classroom before we can even step outside.

During the rainy season, I sit on my porch and listen to the deep thunder pealing off in the distance. The big gray rain clouds come rolling in from the northeast, pushed by the strong trade winds. I can see the approaching sheets of rain out on the savannah, near the landing, before they get to my house. All the people in our part of the village scurry to get inside their houses and shut all the doors and wooden window shutters tightly. In a minute the first drops hit, followed by the driving rain, torrents of it. I think of the large catboats, the local Miskitu sailing vessels, out at sea. In such a storm they are tossed wildly around as the Miskitu sailors try to keep control of the sheets and the rudder, and the passengers huddle under a plastic sheet trying to stay as dry as possible. The rain lasts for only five or ten minutes then slows and stops. In Awastara people emerge from their houses into a dripping world. The northeast trade wind blows freely again. But out over the ocean the next cloudbank is already forming.

It rains almost every day during the long rainy season from June through December. Occasionally huge storms come through, bringing incessant rain day after day. The world is drenched, with water dripping from everything. All of Awastara—only about ten to fifteen feet above sea level—becomes a shallow lake several inches deep. The houses, erected on top of tall posts, rise out of the sheet of water that covers the earth. The water soaks quickly into the sandy soil, though, and within a couple of hours people can again walk the village paths. Such storms are most common in July or August. During the rest of the rainy season, the thunderstorms may be intense but are interspersed with hours of bright, sunny weather.

Just before and after a rain the air is filled with flying insects. Asterio, the health leader, tells me they are *usra* (termites). These are the same insects that make large black nests in trees, which are burned and mixed with paint to make caulk or putty for boats. The winged form represents one stage of their life cycle, seen only in the rainy season. The complex natural world here in the tropics, so fascinating to me, is also a topic of intellectual interest for my Miskitu friends. They discuss with great animation the life cycles of different animals, the various species of birds and fish, and the many kinds of plants that can be used as medicine. It is hard to elicit exclamations of beauty, however. A magnificent sunset, a brightly colored bird, the night darkness filled with fireflies, called *tilam*—these things often move me profoundly; but the most I can elicit from my Miskitu friends is an admission that they are *painkira*—just fine. I know there are things that move them too, but here I face a frustrating difference in aesthetics.

Although tropical storms are intense and frequent in the rainy season, the Miskitu Coast has suffered relatively little from the hurricanes spawned in the Caribbean Basin. Bluefields was destroyed by Hurricane Joan in 1988 (Vandermeer, Perfecto, et al. 1991), however, and Awastara was also hit by a major hurricane in 1906. To the south along the coast, in Tasbapauni, older people described the devastation caused by the 1906 hurricane to Bernard Nietschmann (1973: 75). In Awastara Victor's father told him stories of the great *prari* (hurricane) of that year. In those days, there were still spiritual specialists called *prapit nani* who could actually deflect hurricanes, but in spite of their efforts the community suffered terribly that year. In the hours before the storm, people constructed low shelters of logs, close to the ground, into which they could crawl to escape the storm's fury. That year no one was killed; but when people emerged from their shelters after the storm, they found their local world destroyed. All the houses were gone, the large mango and coconut trees were all lying on the ground, the plantations were destroyed, and the village was littered with the carcasses of dead cows and pigs and other animals. There was also a large dead animal from the sea, a kind of creature no one had ever seen before. Perhaps, I think as Victor tells me the story, it was a whale or a giant squid. For a long time people survived by digging palm roots and mashing them up and scavenging whatever they could from the ravaged forest and river bottom. I comment that it was a miracle that no one was killed. "Yes," replies Victor with a grin, "but us Miskitu people are pretty hard to kill."

THE TEXT

Two full-length studies of Miskitu communities already exist. The first is by anthropologist Mary W. Helms (1971) and represents research from the mid-1960s. Helms provides a careful, detailed description of Asang, a village on the upper Wangki or Río Coco (map 1). Her information about kinship and the role of the Moravian Church in the community is especially rich. The second is by cultural geographer Bernard Nietschmann (1973), reporting research from the late 1960s. Nietschmann describes the cultural ecology of Tasbapauni, a village on the south coast near Pearl Lagoon. His data on agriculture, turtle fishing, and food habits and nutrition are extremely valuable. Both works provide a wealth of information about Miskitu people, presented in a traditional social science format. They are essential sources for any student of Miskitu culture. Both are more than thirty years old, however. There is no full-length study of any of the Miskitu communities on the Coast north of Puerto Cabezas, where I worked. Awastara is both similar to and different from Asang and Tasbapauni, and I hope this book will complement those works by providing information about another Miskitu group in a different region. When possible, I try to compare Awastara with Asang and Tasbapauni. I write in the present tense when describing 1997–2000 experiences, to try to let the reader experience life in Awastara along with me.

This book is also written in a different time, and from a different point of view, than the books by Helms and Nietschmann. I lived in Awastara both before and after the war years of the 1980s. From these years emerged a large, often highly politicized literature on the conflict and the Miskitu role in it (Dennis 1993). Serious research about the Coast was also accomplished, however. Charles R. Hale (1994) recounts the Miskitu-Sandinista conflict in great detail. His firsthand information from his fieldwork in Sandy Bay Sirpi (map 1) is especially rich and is crucial for understanding the conflict. Hale and many other colleagues also have published in the new trilingual journal *Wani*, the scholarly organ of the Centro de Investigaciones y Documentación de la Costa Atlántica (CIDCA). *Wani* has come out regularly since 1984, publishing articles in Spanish, English, and Miskitu in many different fields, including history, anthropology, literature, linguistics, and tropical biology. It is a valiant effort in a very poor country. By the late 1990s, however, few researchers remained to study the Miskitu Coast, which had become a backwater in geopolitics, although an important transit area in the cocaine trade from Colombia to the United States.

In the last twenty years concepts of ethnography have changed enormously. Impelled by the postmodern critique of science as a cultural product, not something above culture, interpretive anthropology has insisted on reporting the ethnographer's own interactions with his or her subjects. The ethnographer's voice becomes one among many, and culture itself becomes a latticework of contested codes and representations (Clifford 1986: 2). Dialogue emerges as the subjects of research talk back, argue, and even reject the theories of the anthropologist. It becomes the metaphor for how anthropologists conduct their fieldwork (Marcus and Fischer 1986: 30). Culture is presented as contested, temporal, and emergent. The overly self-confident voices of earlier ethnographers are replaced by more tentative sorts of statements. Revealing partial truths, in all the complexity of their cultural context, becomes a sufficient research goal.

While avoiding imposing outside categories that distort local realities, the ethnographic description itself becomes much more textured and detailed, producing what Clifford Geertz (1973) calls "thick description." The ethnographic text attempts to take the reader into the cultural scene as experienced by the ethnographer, not simply provide an authoritative and "objective" description.

The interpretive ethnography that has been emerging from this critique is rich and fascinating. In *First-Time* (1983) and *Alabi's World* (1990), Richard Price uses texts left by Moravian missionaries and colonial planters and administrators, and the enigmatic information provided by his contemporary Saramaka friends (whose photographs he provides), in constructing a historical tapestry of the Saramaka people of Suriname. Barbara Tedlock's *The Beautiful and the Dangerous* (1992) gives a running account of her interactions with Zuni friends over a number of years, interwoven with her own unfolding understanding of Zuni culture. In *The Taste of Blood* (1991), Jim Wafer lets the spiritual beings in Brazilian *candomblé* emerge as characters in their own right in his ethnography, in the same way that his Brazilian friends and he himself experienced them. In *Mama Lola* (1991), Karen McCarthy Brown describes her long-term relationship and apprenticeship with a Haitian vodou priestess. She provides short stories about Mama Lola's immediate ancestors, who figure so prominently in Lola's life and in her religious worship. Interspersed among the short stories are chapters that provide ethnographic and historical context. Brown writes candidly of her own experiences, including her marriages to two of the most important vodou spirits, and the initiation through which she becomes a devotee herself. Of her participation, she says: "I realized that if I brought less to this Vodou world, I would come away with less. If I persisted in studying Vodou objectively, the heart of the system, its ability to heal, would remain closed to me" (1991: 11).

In *Translated Woman* (1993), Ruth Behar lets her Mexican friend Esperanza tell her own compelling story; Behar herself edits and organizes and occasionally explains (to Esperanza as well as to the reader) what she is doing. Like Brown, Behar enters the text, writing of her own participation in Esperanza's life and of the parallels she eventually begins to draw between her own life and Esperanza's.

Nancy Scheper-Hughes, in *Death without Weeping* (1992), describes her long research on mothering and infant death, among the desperately poor inhabitants of a neighborhood in northeastern Brazil. Through becoming involved in her subjects' lives, she comes to understand the reasons behind the extremely high infant mortality rate. Mothers here use a strategy of triage, selecting among all the infants born those most likely to survive, and nourishing only them.

All of these interpretive ethnographies are vivid and rich, inviting the reader into the cultural worlds experienced by the ethnographer, while allowing the Others to speak for themselves. The ethnographer becomes one of the participants in the interaction described, and Brown goes so far as to describe herself in the third person on occasion. "Karen Brown approached Alourdes' door shortly after ten-thirty" (1991: 262). These postmodern ethnographers rarely pretend to explain everything for the reader's benefit. Partial truths are the best that can be managed, it is assumed. The information that is presented is so richly textured, however, that it speaks for itself.

About earlier, more positivistic anthropology, Mary Louise Pratt (1986: 33) comments: "How, one asks oneself constantly, could such interesting people doing such interesting things produce such dull books?" One certainly could not make this criticism of Price or Tedlock, Wafer or Brown, Behar or Scheper-Hughes. Their work is detailed and compelling, leading the reader deeper and deeper into the cultural worlds they explore. It is richer if not better ethnography. My own efforts are inspired by these works but are much more modest. I am present in the narrative to follow, but I also try to let my Miskitu friends offer their own view of things as much as possible. I quote directly from them, realizing the reader may get lost among all their names but nevertheless wanting to attribute information and points of view correctly to those who provided them. I also allow myself to generalize about Miskitu culture on the basis not only of my own experiences but of my reading of the extensive literature on the Miskitu. I hope the text will be interesting reading for those who know little about the Miskitu people, for general readers as well as specialists. Someday, perhaps, it may be accessible to my Miskitu friends themselves, if it is ever possible to translate it into Spanish and Miskitu. I was delighted when my last article about research on *grisi siknis* was published in these languages for the benefit of *costeños* (Dennis 1999).

This information is taken from about 900 notebook pages of field-notes, roughly half of them from 1978–79 and half from 1999–2000. The notebooks are full of the small stuff that life is made of in this one Miskitu community that I know well. They don't have much pretension of being anything more. At the beginning I try to summarize some basic information about Miskitu history and language to provide context. The book essentially reflects my own life and experiences in Awastara, however: my ongoing friendship with Victor, working in the cassava and rice fields with Pamela and Casey, attending church services with Plora and the children, fishing for *mas mas* with Gladys and the small boys, watching little Nachalie grow up. It depicts a little piece of life, in another place where people live. Life goes along slowly here. I have learned to wait and watch and listen carefully, day after day—and attempt to write it all down, while enjoying the whole process.

CHAPTER TWO

Who Are the Miskitu People?

My friends in Awastara are part of a general Miskitu population of approximately 150,000 people living along the Atlantic Coast of Nicaragua and Honduras. Roughly two-thirds of the people live in Nicaragua, and one-third in Honduras. Most of the villages from Tasbapauni to Cape Gracias a Dios in Nicaragua are Miskitu speaking, as are the forty or so villages lining the Río Coco from Cape Gracias a Dios to Bocay (map 1). The Miskitu population in Honduras is concentrated in La Mosquitia, the easternmost province of the country. Most Miskitu people live by fishing and catching turtles; by raising small plantations of rice, cassava, plantains, and other crops; and by working as wage laborers whenever the opportunity presents itself. Many young men today work as lobster divers, and in earlier years men went off to work in the gold mines near Siuna and Bonanza and La Rosita. The days of good wage work are remembered fondly by older men. The Miskitu people speak their own language and maintain a vigorous hybrid culture of their own, with many elements derived from the indigenous past as well as from Black Creole culture and from the English and North Americans with whom they have interacted for centuries.

At the time of first European contact, the native inhabitants of the Coast were small groups of people speaking languages of the Macro-Chibchan family, related to those along the northern coast of South America (Helms 1971: 14–15). Like their modern descendants, they practiced slash and burn farming and fished and hunted. English buccaneers established friendly relations with these people and fought with them against their common enemy, the Spanish. Today mestizo Nicaraguans are still referred to disdainfully as "Spaniards." Together the Miskitu and their English allies traveled up the San Juan and other rivers to attack the Spanish settlements in western Nicaragua (Floyd 1967: 64–66). The relationship was to the advantage of both sides. The Miskitu obtained arms, metal tools, rum, and manufactured clothing, while the buccaneers and traders got lumber, animal skins, food (including turtles, which the Miskitu were proficient at harpooning), and sexual access to Miskitu women. Intermarriage began early on the Coast.

Awastara itself is an old community. An early Spanish document (Archivo General de Indias 1699) lists it among the coastal villages, mentioning "the mulattos of the pueblo of Aguastara," but there is no additional information. It seems likely to me that the rich agricultural land south of the village along the river bottom and the pine-covered land between the ocean and the lagoon were major attractions for the earliest inhabitants, who founded their community there. Turtles were caught along the Coast itself in earlier days; and the river and lagoon provided fish and oysters and crabs and other marine resources, while subsistence agriculture was carried on in the river bottom. The settlement site, slightly elevated above the ocean, catches the northeast trade winds and is as pleasant a place to live now as it was in 1699.

One possible etymology for the word "Miskito" or "Miskitu," as indigenous scholars themselves now prefer, is the English word "musket." Helms (1971: 16) points out that it was through acquiring muskets that the Miskitu subjugated other indigenous groups and spread up and down the Coast from Cape Gracias a Dios and up the Río Coco. Miskitu hegemony extended as far south as Costa Rica, where some places along the Atlantic Coast, such as Cahuita and Sixaola, continue to bear Miskitu names. Through conflict with the Miskitu, the Mayangna and Ulwa and other indigenous groups were pushed farther into the interior, where remnant groups remain today. These groups, formerly known as Sumu, are struggling today to preserve their lands in the large Bosawas Reserve and to keep their own language and culture. They prefer to be called by their own term for themselves, Mayangna. Cultural and linguistic relatives of the Miskitu, the Mayangna have adopted retreat and seclusion as defensive strategies, rather than the openness and intercultural exchange practiced by the Miskitu. The Mayangna heritage is reflected in some place names along the Coast, such as Bilwi (Puerto Cabezas in Spanish), Bihmuna, and Krukira, which are said to be Mayangna words. Miskitu dominance on the Coast for several hundred years resulted from their successful contacts with the British and from their position as intermediaries in the lively trade that developed between these interior groups and the Coast (Helms 1969).

Karl Offen (1999: 149) suggests a different etymology for the name. "Miskitu," in its various alternative spellings, may have derived from the Miskitu verb *miskaia*, "to fish." Fishing would certainly have been an important activity of the coastal inhabitants at the time when they were first encountered by Europeans. According to Offen, the term "Musketo Indians" first appeared in print in 1671.

Helms (1983) describes an early pattern of raiding between the coastal Miskitu and interior Mayangna groups, which developed into a full-scale slaving operation once there was a market for slaves on the English plantations. Traditional intertribal conflict had included capturing women and children, to be incorporated as wives and productive members of Miskitu communities. When male slaves became valuable to the British and could be traded to them for guns and iron tools and cloth, however, slave raiding took on new dimensions. There was a steady market for Indian slaves on Jamaican sugar plantations; and the Miskitu, with guns provided by their English allies, supplied this market and prospered. Slaving expeditions ventured down the Coast as far as Panama and deep into the interior, and the Miskitu were soon the dominant political group on the Coast. Helms suggests that slave raids had become productive economic ventures, comparable to the hunting or harvesting expeditions of earlier years. She remarks (1983: 191) that in some sense slave raiding was the first of the economic "booms" that the coastal Miskitu were to experience.

Apparently in self-defense against Miskitu raiders, the Mayangna moved farther and farther into their mountain forests and maintained a closed attitude toward relations with strangers, both Miskitu and others, which has persisted until the present. The Mayangna seem to have discouraged intermarriage and attempts to live with them and learn their culture and language, and there is still no full-length ethnography of these people. A 1999 incident illustrates their defensive posture. A journalist published a book about Mayangna culture without permission; outraged, a Mayangna council of elders protested. URACCAN, the new *costeño* university, was co-publisher of the book. Recognizing Mayangna intellectual property rights, URACCAN authorities promptly stopped distribution of the book.

The memory of conflict with the Mayangna is preserved in stories still told by older people in Awastara. For instance, Victor tells a story about one of his grandfathers or great-grandfathers catching "wild Indians" on the south Coast. These people came out to the beach periodically to boil saltwater and make salt, which they carried back to their interior villages. M. W., an anonymous buccaneer who provides one of the first

European descriptions of the Miskitu, describes groups of Indians from the interior coming to the Coast in the dry season to make salt and provides interesting details about the salt-making process (1732: 288). He also gives the Miskitu word for these people as "Alboawinney," which may perhaps represent his rendering of *alba wina,* "from a slave." In Victor's story, the Miskitu men from Awastara made a big pot of *chicha* (home-brewed beer) and left it for the "wild Indians" to find, while they watched from cover. The Indians couldn't resist the *chicha* and drank and drank. When they were completely intoxicated, the Miskitu men fell on them and captured them with nets. They tied some up with ropes but not all of them. In the boats on the way back to Awastara, some of those left untied managed to jump overboard and drowned rather than live as slaves. Victor does not know if any were sold, but some of the survivors were brought back to Awastara to live. The Buik family in particular is said to be descended from these people. They are short and stocky and "look Indian," according to Victor. One interesting aspect of this story is Victor's distinction between "wild Indians" from the interior, who can be caught like animals and enslaved, and the Miskitu people of Awastara, who are neither "wild" nor "Indians."

Relations between the Miskitu and the early British buccaneers and traders were very good. Many English words, concepts, and items of material culture were adopted and permanently integrated into Miskitu culture. Words like *la* (way of doing things, from English "law") and *trausis* (trousers) are easily traced to English, but they are "traditional" Miskitu words today. The flexibility and adaptability of Miskitu culture probably allowed it to survive and prosper. Today it continues to change, with many Miskitu immigrants living in such places as Port Arthur, Texas, and Miami, Florida. The total Miskitu population continues to increase rapidly.

THE SAMBO-MISKITU AND THE TAWIRA

Karl Offen (1999, 2002) describes the importance of the political division between the two early Miskitu-speaking groups, the Sambo-Miskitu and the Tawira. The Sambo population resulted from early intermarriage with escaped African slaves. One large contingent of slaves came from a Dutch slaver that was wrecked off the Coast near Awastara in 1640 or 1641. This event is mentioned in Eduard Conzemius (1932: 17–18), Orlando Roberts (1965: 153), and other earlier sources, but little addi-

tional information is available. According to Offen, the mixed population came to have different political leaders and a different self-identity.
This population stretched from about Awastara north to the cape, up the
Río Coco, and into eastern Honduras. The less mixed, more phenotypi-
cally "Indian" population extended south along the Coast from about
Awastara to Bluefields. These people referred to themselves as "Tawira"
(straight-haired people). C. Napier Bell's classic nineteenth-century book
is in fact titled *Tangweera* (1989). The *ng* spelling represents his attempt
to record the nasalized sound of the initial Miskitu *a* vowel.

According to Offen, conflict between the two Miskitu-speaking groups
culminated in a devastating war in the 1790s. A smallpox epidemic in the
early 1700s may have changed the region's demography, decimating the
Tawira groups, which had less resistance to the Old World disease, and
favoring the Sambo groups, which did have some degree of resistance
(Offen 1999: 185). Relationships between the two groups had always
been uneasy, Offen notes, but war broke out after the murder of the
Tawira governor Colvil Briton by the Sambo king George II, who was
known in Miskitu as Ibihna. The Tawira responded to the murder with
all-out attacks on Sambo communities. Awastara, a Sambo village according to Offen, was attacked, and all the men were tied to the largest
house and burned to death (2002: 325). Eventually the Sambo regained
the upper hand and proceeded to destroy most of the Tawira villages.
Offen is the first scholar to discuss this intergroup Miskitu warfare and
speculate about its consequences. He argues that throughout the colonial
period the Tawira made strategic alliances with the Spanish, thus confronting their enemies the Sambo, who were staunch allies of the British.
The tension between descendants of the two groups persists to the present day, according to Offen. He mentions (2002: 328), for example, that
factional disputes between rival Miskitu groups in the 1980s war against
the Sandinista army may be attributable to underlying Sambo-Tawira
differences.

Offen actually collected some oral history about the Sambo-Tawira
conflict, particularly the dramatic murder of Colvil Briton. In Awastara I
could find no folk memories of these events, although the word "Tawira"
is still recognized. My elderly neighbor *Dama* Rubisu pointed to his long,
straight black hair and says with a laugh that his ancestors were Tawira,
"real Indians."

English-speaking people of African descent are called Creoles on the
Atlantic Coast and continue to be an important part of this multicultural
society. The Creole population centers are mainly in Bluefields, Pearl La-

goon, and the Corn Islands, but Creole people are also found in Puerto Cabezas and local communities to the north. An interesting and flexible ethnic boundary exists between the Miskitu and Creole populations, with many Creoles who live in local communities learning Miskitu and being absorbed into the Miskitu population over time. A number of families in Awastara are descended from recent Creole immigrants who came to live in the community. Conversely, on the south Coast some Miskitu communities have become "Creolized," with Creole English influencing and replacing the local dialect of Miskitu (Jamieson 1998: 718–19). Edmund T. Gordon (1998) has provided a detailed, interesting account of Nicaragua's Creole population, noting their strong identification with Anglo culture and their frequent rejection of their Africanness.

PHYSICAL TYPES

A common pattern over several centuries has been for English, Black Creole, Chinese, and other men to come to the coast, live with Miskitu spouses, and leave behind children who then join the "mainstream" of Miskitu culture. As a result, the diversity of physical types is remarkable, from individuals with straight black hair and coppery skin, to very dark skinned individuals, to people with light hair and eyes. Conzemius (1932: 13) mentions this openness to intermarriage, pointing out that children from mixed unions always grow up speaking Miskitu, their mothers' language. In discussing the mixed racial composition of the Miskitu, Mary Helms (1977: 161) notes that early Spanish sources emphasized their African characteristics. "African" or *zambo* in Spanish was an epithet implying savagery and violence, and it carried the stigma of slavery. Such negative images were reinforced by centuries of Miskitu raids on Spanish settlements to the west. Apart from Spanish sources, though, Helms (1977: 169) concludes that most outside observers have identified the Miskitu population as more "Indian" than "Negro."

Being Miskitu is definitely a cultural category rather than a "racial" one. In earlier centuries, a common term that the Miskitu used in referring to themselves was "Mosquito-men." Offen (2002: 323) suggests that it paralleled the European usage of their friends and allies, who called themselves Englishmen, Scotsmen, Dutchmen, and so on. Today, as Helms observed in Asang (1971: 169), being Miskitu really seems to depend on living in a Miskitu-speaking family and observing proper behavior toward kin, speaking the language, and considering oneself Miskitu. Older people in Awastara speak with pride of their Creole and Anglo ancestors, but they clearly identify themselves as Miskitu people.

THE MORAVIAN CHURCH

For the last 150 years the history of the Miskitu people has been intimately related to the work of the Moravian missionaries, who arrived in Bluefields in 1849 (Wilson 1975). One of their first goals was to learn the Miskitu language and create a writing system for it, to help in the evangelical endeavor. By the late 1800s the missionaries had begun translating the Bible, the hymnbook, and the Moravian prayer book. They also produced the first grammars and dictionaries of the language (Heath 1927; Heath and Marx 1953; Thaeler n.d.; Gray n.d.). These works are still extremely useful for the scholar trying to learn the language. Heath's lexicon (1947) is an especially valuable piece of linguistic ethnography, containing a rich potpourri of Miskitu words and concepts about society and the natural world. Only extracts from it have been published (Heath 1950). Missionaries like the Reverend G. R. Heath were trained in classical scholarly fashion, not in modern linguistics, however, and they tried to cast Miskitu in the mold of Latin grammar. They "found" noun cases and other Latin-like features, and their work contains erudite references to such features as "the apodosis of a conditional sentence" (Thaeler n.d.: 23).

Sentence construction in Miskitu follows rules quite different from Spanish or English, and it seems quite complicated at first. For example, a Miskito sentence often contains a number of inserted clauses not marked by any pauses or commas. This characteristic provoked an early Moravian missionary (Moravian Church, Periodical Accounts 1879: 200, "from Br. Sieborger") to remark: "The grammar is simple and regular, but the construction of sentences singular, reminding one of the remark, that the languages of savages have been concocted in a professor's study."

The most important missionary translation was of course the Bible, now in various editions. A 1974 edition of the complete New Testament or *Dawan Bila* (God's Word) represents the efforts of foreign missionaries. Miskitu friends tell me it is perfectly understandable but sounds unidiomatic. By 1998, however, a joint effort of the Moravian and Catholic churches had resulted in a translation of the complete Bible, done by native speakers of the language. It is entitled *Dawan Bila Aiska* (All of God's Word) and is a monumental work in fluent, idiomatic Miskitu.

Unfortunately for local people, it is not being given away freely, as were earlier editions of the Bible. Few local people can afford a copy. The first page of Genesis from this new edition illustrates for the reader the current written form of the language (figure 1). The Hebrew story of creation sounds as majestic to me in Miskitu as it does in the original King James translation into English.

The missionaries not only reduced the language to writing but also introduced many concepts into it, to be permanently integrated there. Phrases like *pura sunaia* ("to rise above," i.e., to pray) and *tibil briaia* ("to have the table," i.e., communion) occur very frequently in modern Miskitu. Another process has been to build on traditional Miskitu words and concepts and turn them into something Christian. For example, the verb *smalkaia* means "to lecture" or "to preach at" someone. It is easy to imagine this concept or behavior being introduced by the early Moravian missionaries, but in fact it antedates it. Charles Napier Bell was a Scotsman who grew up on the Miskitu Coast in the mid-nineteenth century, speaking Miskitu fluently and living among the people throughout his childhood and youth. Bell's *Tangweera: Life and Adventures among Gentle Savages* may be the most insightful book yet written about the Coast. Regarding the verb *smalkaia*, he says (Bell 1989: 126–27):

> Almost all old Indians, especially headmen of the settlements, have the inveterate habit of what they call *smalkaya* (teaching)—that is lecturing the young people and preaching at them, drawing wise examples and "modern instances" from the news of the day. This serves the same purpose as our Sunday sermons, and the Indians are by no means free from the tendency to exhort and preach, which is often so offensive among Europeans. On analyzing this species of teaching, it is found to be very much the same as that we receive from the pulpit . . . Other than this, these people have no restraint on their conduct.

The missionaries not only used the *smalkaia* concept for teaching the gospel but also created a new social role, the *sasmalkra* or teacher. These individuals were lay pastors trained in Christianity, who lived in the communities and served as local pastors. The word *sasmalkra* is now standard Miskitu and is often shortened colloquially as a term of address to *sasmal*. The social role of the *sasmalkra* is well integrated into local life. He conducts worship services and also actively lectures people about the good life, nowadays defined in Protestant Christian terms. The *sasmalkra*'s wife must be a model of traditional feminine virtue, cooking,

BLASI STURKA 1   2

Tasba paskan sturka ba

1 [1]Gâd kau diara wala nani sut paskras kan ba tâura, kasbrika pura ba bara tasba ba wal pas paskan. [2]Bara tasba ra diara nani ba, ai watlika kat apia kan, bila man kan. Kabu tihuka tara ra tihmia tara nani baman baha purara kan, bara Gâd Spiritka ba li nani purara tauki kan. [3]Bara Gâd bila win: "Ingni ba takbia!" Bara ingni ba takan. [4]Bara Gâd kaikan, ingni ba yamni kan, witin ingni ba tihmia tara ba wina dakbi sakan. [5]Bara Gâd mita ingni ba, "kakna" makan, bara tihmia tara ba, "tihmia" makan. Bara tutni kan ba wina, tihmia aiska titan kat ba, yu kumi kan.

[6]Ba ningkara Gâd bila win: "Li nani ba lilara aihka dakbi sakanka bara kabia; bara li nani mayara ba bara purara ba wal, aihka dakbi sâkbia."

Bara baku takan. [7]Aihka dakbi sakaia ba Gâd daukan. Li nani lilpasra bila kwawanka takan kan, bara li nani purara ba, mayara ba wina baiki sakan. [8]Bara baku Gâd, pura ba nina, "kasbrika pura" makan. Bara tutni kan ba wina, tihmia aiska titan kat, yu wal kan.

[9]Gâd sin win: "Kasbrika purara ba munhtara, li nani bara ba, watla kumira asla prawbia; bara tasba lawan nani bal takbia."

Bara baku takan. [10]Ningkara tasba lawan ba nina "tasba" makan. Bara li nani asla takan ba nina "kabu" makan.

Bara gâd kaikan baha sut ba yamni kan; [11]baha ningkara win: "Tasba ba yaka intawahya sangni nani sâtka sut sâkbia, tasba purara. Inma bani ai saumukka sâtka nani sakbia. Dus ma nani satka bani ba, sin ai saumukka sakan kabia; bara ai saumukka nani ba; ai wina ra bri kabia."

Bara baku takan. [12]Bara tasba ba intawahya sangni sâtka nani bani ba sakan: inma ai saumukka sâtka nani ai wîna wina saki ba, dus nani ai ma sâtka nani saki ba, bara ai saumukka ai wina ra bri nani ba sin. Bara Gâd baha ba yamni kaikan. [13]Bara tutni kan, ba wina tihmia aiska ban titan kat, yu yuhmpa.

[14]Bara tisku kan, Gâd bila win: "Ingni nani bara kabia, kasbrika pura sangnika tara bara, kakna ba tihmia wina aihka lakaia dukyara. Bara Baku tukin nani bara kabia pyua nani ba kulki saki kaia ba dukyara. Yu nani, bara mani nani kulkaia dukyara sin. [15]Bara kasbrika purara, sangnika tara bara; ingni nani bara kabia, tasba purara ingwaia dukyara."

Bara baku takan. [16]Bara ingni tara nani wal ba, Gâd paskan. Ingni kau tara ba, kakna ra ingni daukaia, bara ingni kau ningkara ba, tihmia ra ingni daukaia dukyara. Slilma nani sin paskan. [17]Bara Gâd baha ingnika nani ba, kasbrika purara sangnika tara bara mangkan, tasba purara kakna bara, tihmia ra ingwaia, [18]baku ingni ba tihmia tara ba wina aihka sakaia dukyara sin. Bara Gâd kaikan baha ba yamni kan. [19]Bara tutni kan ba wina, ban tihmia aiska titan kat, yu wahlwal.

[20]Bara Gâd win: "Li nani ba sin yarka daiwan sâtka bani ba sâkbia. Bara tnawira nani sin tasba purara, pasa ra pali tauki kabia."

Bara baku takan. [21]Bara Gâd li daiwra tarkatara nani ba paskan. Bara diara rayaka bri nani bani liura aiaui tauki nani ba sin. Tnawira nani bani ai tnawa brih pâli nani ba sin paskan, ai satka nani kat. Bara Gâd kaikan baha ba yamni kan. [22]Gâd baha nani yamni munan, bara win: "Man nani sahwi ailal pali taki, kabu laya ba bangki dauks. Bara tnawira nani sin, sahwi ailal pali takan kabia tasba purara." [23]Bara tutni kan ba wina ban tihmia aiska titan kat, yu matsip.

[24]Baha ningkara Gâd bila win: "Tasba ba yarka daiwan ai rayaka bri sâtka bani ba sâkbia. Daiwan tara nani sâtka bani, pyuta satka bani bara daiwan wala nani sin ai sâtka bani ba sâkbia."

FIGURE 1. *First page of Genesis from new Miskitu Bible (Sociedad Biblica de Nicaragua, 1998)*

washing, taking care of children, and helping organize women's activities within the church.

THE COMPANY PERIOD

The foreign companies that have come to exploit the region's natural resources have been another major influence on Miskitu culture. Helms (1971: 27–32) and Nietschmann (1973: 39–43) describe the company period of the late nineteenth and early twentieth centuries, when many Miskitu men found work in lumbering, mining, and banana production. Helms's diagram of the various booms (1971: 29) shows them to have been roughly sequential, with rubber as the earliest, followed by gold mining through the 1960s, a banana boom ending about 1940, and lumbering of the pine savannahs since the 1920s. She argues that, although the foreign companies may seem exploitative in retrospect, local Miskitu men felt fortunate at the time to have what they regarded as well-paying jobs. They could return home to their villages when each boom ended, feeling poorer but still able to make a living in traditional ways.

This is certainly true, but it is also true that the foreign companies exploited the natural resources voraciously, without thought for the future. They sent many millions of dollars' worth of profit out of the country, with little concern for the workers' safety or the environmental consequences. Jorge Jenkins Molieri (1986) provides details. For example, between 1945 and 1963 the Nipco Lumber Company clear-cut about 300,000 hectares of pine savannah (1986: 199). Meanwhile, workers in the foreign-owned mines at Siuna, Bonanza, and La Rosita suffered notoriously high rates of silicosis and tuberculosis (1986: 221). Most of the miners were Miskitu. Nietschmann (1973: 242–44) documents the cumulative damage to the environment involved in these enterprises, with each successive boom degrading it further. The most recent boom has been the commercial exploitation of turtles, shrimp, lobsters, and fish, whose depletion directly affects the subsistence resources of the coastal communities.

In the late 1940s an oil company established a large camp between Awastara and Dakura and conducted exploratory drilling. The plan was apparently to run a pipeline straight from the area to the old Dakura lighthouse (map 2) to export the oil. The company employed many men from the neighboring communities. Victor's brother Pancho worked there, and he enthusiastically describes the good food and the good wages they earned. "The American bosses treated people right!" Pancho exclaims. At the same time, since business was so good, a Chinese man named Wong Sau opened a small store in Awastara. He lived with a local Awastara woman and raised a family with her. The company supposedly discovered oil deposits but could not agree on terms with the Somoza government then in power and never began exploitation of the oil. When the company left, Wong Sau also closed his store and moved away to the gold-mining area of Bonanza, taking his Awastara spouse and their children with him. "He was following the money," *Dama* Telemaco tells me.

Many Awastara men also worked in the mines. *Dama* Hilario, for example, worked there for twenty-seven years, saving enough money to build a good house back in Awastara, to which he eventually retired. Victor, however, never went to the mines. He saw other men coming back with tuberculosis and dying, with no money to show for their hard work and sacrifice. Most of them just drank up their money on paydays, the way many lobster divers do now. But at one point he did decide to go to the mines. He and a friend went to Waspam to catch the free airplane to the mines, available to men who had signed up to work. They had never been to Waspam, and first they went off sightseeing along the broad Río Coco. When they came back to the airstrip, the plane had already left. "What luck!" Victor concludes. "If I had gone to the mines I probably would be dead by now, instead of being here at home telling you these stories." Victor's philosophy has been to be his own boss. "I didn't want to work for a company and have someone bossing me around all the time, yelling at me [*palaia*]," he says. "I wanted to build my own boat and make my own money."

THE SANDINISTAS AND THE WAR YEARS

The bloody, destructive war years of the 1980s brought a dramatic interruption to my fieldwork in Awastara. The events leading up to the war years, and the subsequent autonomy law, have been well chronicled (Adams 1981; Diskin et al. 1986; CIDCA n.d.; Dennis 1981a, 1993). Negative images of the "Communist" Sandinistas on the part of *costeños*, naiveté and misunderstanding of the Coast on the part of the Sandinista government, and money and political pressure from the U.S. government to oppose the Sandinista revolution all contributed to counterrevolution on the Coast in the early 1980s. The Miskitu self-determination organization MISURASATA was at first recognized by the Sandinista government. But when it became apparent that the organization might not support the government, the leaders were arrested, provoking a general uprising on the coast. MISURASATA splintered into YATAMA (Yapti Tasba Masrika Nani, or Descendants of Mother Earth) (C. Hale 1994: 241) and other groups. Several years of violence and destruction followed, until peace negotiations finally brought an end to the killing in the late 1980s. An autonomy statute for the Atlantic Coast (appended in C. Hale 1994: 231–39) was enacted by the Sandinista government in 1987, giving legal recognition to Miskitu and Creole hopes for self-rule.

The war affected all the coastal communities. Major battles were fought near Páhara and Sandy Bay, and for several years there was a small Sandinista military base near Awastara. People readily told me stories of those years. Maura's father, Nolan, from Páhara, told me about being held prisoner for three months by the Sandinista soldiers, being left without food for days, and being interrogated about his family and what they were doing. At one point he was hit on the neck with a pistol by an officer and was sure he would be killed. The injury still bothers him. It was a powerful story, told in a quiet, calm way by an unassuming person. Many other people were tortured and killed, he told me. In the battle at Páhara, the YATAMA fighters, mostly very young men, soundly defeated the Sandinista soldiers, killing many of them. The YATAMA commander was a man named Reynaldo Reyes (nicknamed "Ráfaga" or burst of gunfire), from Awastara. He has written a biography, in collaboration with a woman from the United States, relating his war experiences in detail. In the book he describes the Páhara battle (Reyes and Wilson 1992: 102–3) and mentions that the YATAMA forces killed twenty-four Sandinista soldiers. Nolan says that Ráfaga told people not to go near the battlefield for a few days, so the buzzards could pick the bodies clean.

Dama Hilario, in his late sixties, tells me how much he disliked the Sandinistas. Hilario was working in the mines when the revolution occurred. A Creole man named Ralph Moody was the Somocista *diputado* or legislator from La Luz. Hilario said he was a good man, respected by everyone. Hilario watched as the Sandinistas hanged him in the public square then dragged his body around town behind a truck. He says he will never forget seeing that. It was horrible. Hilario concludes bitterly: "The Sandinistas are Communists, good for nothing. They are like the *itimur* termites that eat up your house, a rotten pest."

There was only one battle near Awastara. A YATAMA boy had come back to the village to see his sick mother. But someone in town told the

Sandinistas at the base, who tried to catch the boy. He got away but was shot in the foot. Afterward the YATAMA fighters came and attacked the base, killing the Sandinista commander, who had been liked and respected by many people. A big Sandinista helicopter then came up from Port and dropped three bombs, causing huge explosions. A large crater north of town remains from the explosions, and it fills with rainwater every year. When I visited the village in 1985, the Sandinista soldiers quartered there were all teenaged boys, who seemed scared to death—and for good reason. Victor says they knew little about taking care of themselves in the bush. Ráfaga (Reyes and Wilson 1992: 93) writes that many did not even know how to swim and drowned in the ocean or the rivers trying to escape.

The YATAMA boys came to houses in Awastara at night, to ask for food, and Victor willingly supplied it. It was difficult, he says, because if the Sandinistas found out that you were providing food to the rebels they would arrest you. There were also Sandinista sympathizers in the village who reported YATAMA collaborators to the military base, and some Miskitu boys fought with the Sandinistas. Loyalties were obviously divided. One Creole-Miskitu boy from Tasbapauni stayed for a while in Victor's house. He had fought with YATAMA but later defected to the Sandinistas. When the YATAMA fighters caught him at Victor's house, they killed him on the porch and dragged the body away. It was never properly buried, and Victor's family believes his spirit or *isingni* continues to frequent the house and make people sick.

Like those of many people, Victor's political sympathies are mixed. He says at the beginning he strongly supported the YATAMA cause of Miskitu self-rule. Later he became disillusioned with the leaders, who were interested only in power and money for themselves. He and Miss Porla and others point out, however, that the Sandinistas were the only Nicaraguan leaders who ever cared about poor people. They built a clinic and a new school building in Awastara. A young man from Awastara, Marcos Hoppington, worked with the Sandinista government to try to bring benefits to local communities and was instrumental in getting the school building for his own community. Miss Porla comments that it was the Miskitu who started the war; and if they had not, the Sandinistas would have done many other good things for local people. Victor said they gave him a loan, and Porla said they began providing sheet metal for roofs, something only wealthy people had possessed before. Both sides committed terrible acts of violence against civilians, however, and many of my Awastara friends argued that it was naive to think that one side was better than the other in this bitter civil war. After listening to stories of torture and abuse by both sides, I could only agree with them.

MISKITU SELF-IMAGE

Charles Hale (1994: 83–86) describes Miskitu history as having created a sense of "Anglo affinity"—close, positive relationships with the English and later the North Americans who came to the Coast. Anglo outsiders have been admired and, where possible, made into affinal relatives. Helms (1971: 224) points out that Anglos in general are regarded as distant but benevolent relatives, interested in the welfare of the Miskitu people. To some extent, the war years and the autonomy law of the late 1980s promoted a positive sense of what it means to be Miskitu. The Miskitu were not defeated militarily; and there were some positive practical benefits of autonomy, particularly the bilingual education program and URACCAN, the new university. Nevertheless, the war cut off contact with the Anglo world to a large extent.

A counterpart to the positive relations subsumed under Anglo affinity is a bitter and self-deprecating view that the Miskitu sometimes express. One day as I am riding in a boat with Pancho and several other men, the conversation turns to the oil company that operated for a few years just north of Awastara. Every Saturday the American bosses ordered two cattle killed to feed all the workers, Pancho remembers. Others chime in with similar stories of American largesse. Then another man compares this attitude to the Miskitu character, people always looking out for themselves alone—untrustworthy people, he says. In fact, he claims, "Miskitu" comes from "mistake." "The Miskitu people are a big mistake!" He interprets the name "Miskitu" as a cruel joke on the people themselves. Everyone roars with laughter. I feel depressed rather than happy at being a *miriki* "good guy" in their eyes. Talking with Alvarez one evening, I mention my idea of putting a bank office right on the wharf in Port, where the lobster divers get off the boats with their pay in hand. Many wives gather there to try to get a share of the lobstering money for themselves and their children before the young men can escape to the bars in town. If a bank office were right there, they could deposit their pay immediately. "Ha!" says Alvarez. "The Miskitu are *bad!* They'd get in their canoes and paddle around the wharf to shore, to avoid the bank office and make it straight to the cantinas!" Open and assertive, my Miskitu friends are also well aware of their own shortcomings.

THE MISKITU LANGUAGE

Miskitu ethnicity is defined in part by speaking the language. As I planned my first research on the Miskitu Coast in 1978, I realized I would have to work hard at learning the language. I traveled to Bethlehem, Pennsylvania, to work in the Moravian Archives and to consult with Moravian missionaries who spoke the language. They generously provided a short grammar of the language, a dictionary, tapes, and other materials. I began studying and have continued intermittently since then. At this point, although I can understand and interact quite comfortably in the language, I realize my proficiency is still quite limited.

Miskitu is widely spoken on Nicaragua's Atlantic Coast, as well as in La Mosquitia in Honduras. The number of speakers increases rapidly each year. Although there are minor dialect differences, the language is remarkably similar over the whole area in which it is spoken. This fact probably reflects the relatively recent spread and development of the language, during the last 400 years of Miskitu political ascendancy on the Coast.

Ken Hale (1987) and other linguists have classified Miskitu in the Misumalpan family of languages, along with Mayangna and the now extinct Matagalpa. Hale demonstrates many word correspondences in Miskitu and Mayangna, but the two languages are not mutually intelligible. It is possible that both Miskitu and Mayangna are related to the large family of Chibchan languages to the south, but the relationship remains unclear. The interior, forest-dwelling Mayangna are often bilingual in Miskitu, since they have been in close contact with Miskitu speakers for hundreds of years as trade partners and (during the eighteenth century) as targets of Miskitu slavers.

The Miskitu language has been quite open to borrowing from other groups. In particular, the long period of contact with English-speaking peoples is reflected in the language. Historically, English has been the prestige language on the Coast. The Black Creole population of the Coast continues to speak Jamaican-type English; and some older men, such as Victor, learned the language from Creole friends. Some borrowed words, however, seem to date to the early contact period. The word for "shotgun," for example, is *rukbus,* derived from the English "arquebus," one of the early types of guns that the Miskitu encountered. More recent borrowings include *dur* (door), *windar* (window), *plit* (plate), and *park* (fork). These nouns all describe common items of technology borrowed from English-speaking people. Obviously, the names were borrowed along with the items themselves.

In general, English nouns seem to be replacing the traditional Miskitu ones, which were formed from standard Miskitu verb stems. For example, *dimaika* means a place to enter and is derived from the verb *dimaia*, by adding the *aika* ending. Today, however, *dimaika* has been replaced by *dur*. *Dimaika* and similar expressions are well understood but rarely used. They are said to be the "real Miskitu" from the past. Some curious examples are still in everyday use, however. For instance, cameras are not common on the Coast, and the English and Spanish word "camera" has not yet entered the Miskitu vocabulary. A camera is still referred to as *lilka alkaika* or "image grabber," from *lilka* (image) and *alkaika* (from the verb *alkaia*, to grab or hold onto).

Another sort of loan word is the "combo-verb" (Lemley 1981), which combines an English verb with a Miskitu infinitive to form a new verb. *Wark takaia* thus means "to work," *dril munaia* "to drill," *mix munaia* "to mix," and so on. The combo-verbs seem to express action concepts derived from English, which are not specifically rendered in traditional Miskitu. Some curious examples from Awastara include *kus aisaia* (to cuss or swear) and *divurs munaia* (to divorce). The English verb represents the specific idea or action introduced from outside, and the Miskitu infinitive indicates the notion of action itself. The possibilities for creating new verbs this way seem almost unlimited. Mark Jamieson (1999) discusses the wide variety of combo-verbs (or verbs with auxiliaries as he calls them) that are used frequently and creatively in the community of Kakabila on Pearl Lagoon (map 1), where he did fieldwork. Kakabila neighbors the Creole-speaking communities of Pearl Lagoon, and language borrowing has been extensive. Colorfully expressive Miskitu verb auxiliaries now used in Kakabila include *pil munaia* (to peel), *smak takaia* (to smack), and *stink munaia* (to stink) (Jamieson 1999: 26–29).

At first glance, the Miskitu language seems to contain a high proportion of English-derived vocabulary. To investigate this impression, Lynn Lemley (1981) counted words in five different books of *Dawan Bila* (1974), the earlier version of the Miskito New Testament. She counted the total number of words and then subtracted English-derived proper nouns and numbers. The English-derived words were then computed as a percentage of total words. Perhaps surprisingly, they amounted to only 5–10 percent of the total vocabulary. If this sample is representative, English-derived words may not be as common as first appearances suggest. Of course, the vocabulary in the New Testament is somewhat selective, and everyday spoken Miskitu may contain more English-derived words.

The recent version of the complete Bible, done by native Miskitu speakers (*Dawan Bila Aiska* 1999), may have even fewer borrowed words. Whatever the percentage, English loanwords do occur noticeably and frequently in Miskitu.

Because of the many loanwords, and a phonology that is generally similar to English, Miskitu is relatively easy for English speakers to learn. Ken Hale (1987) outlines some of the difficulties that Miskitu presents for Spanish speakers. For example, there are two forms for every noun, an absolute form and a construct form. The absolute form is used when the noun stands alone in a sentence, but the construct form must be used whenever the noun is modified. Thus the absolute form for the noun meaning descent group is *kiamp,* while the construct form is *kiampka.* Regular nouns simply add *ka* to the absolute form to make the construct. Irregular nouns, however, change in other ways. The noun for "house" is irregular, for example, with the absolute form being *utla* and the construct *watla.* Nouns are also declined to indicate possession (*waitla,* "my house"; *wamptla,* "your house"). A complicated verb system includes at least two present tenses, two past tenses, two future tenses, and various gerunds and imperatives and other verb forms. Word order in sentences is also quite different from word order in English and Spanish, with the verb usually placed last.

Some Miskitu words have clearly been derived from English but have been given very different meanings in Miskitu. One example is *taim,* derived from "time," which is used in such sentences as *Witin bahara wan taim,* "When he went over there." *Taim* seems to indicate the temporal aspect of the verb and can often be translated as "when." It has become an adverb, with a much more restricted meaning than the English "time." Conversely, *la* (and its construct form *laka*), from the English "law," has a much broader meaning. It seems to refer to any regular way of doing things typical of a person or a group of people. *Aisa ba selp raya ban kaia laka brisa* is the Bible phrase for "The Father has his own way of everlasting life." The phrase *kupia laka,* "way of the heart," refers to the conscience. In discussing a dispute, a woman told me: *Witin nani gridi laka brisa,* "They have a selfish way of doing things." *La* is also connected with kings and rulers, as in the phrase *la daukaia,* "to do the law" or "lay down the law." Political authorities attempt to do this in community meetings.

Older people sometimes lament the introduction of so many loan words, pointing out that up in Honduras people still speak more of the "real Miskitu." The Moravian preacher in 1978 made this point frequently, perhaps imitating missionaries who disapproved of so many words being borrowed from English. I suggest that their own investment in learning and working in the local language made the missionaries avid proponents of linguistic purity. In their Miskitu-Spanish dictionary, for instance, G. R. Heath and W. G. Marx (1953: vi) note that recent borrowings from English are indicated with an asterisk and should not be used when an older Miskitu word is available. Jamieson reports a Miskitu friend from Kakabila telling him: "You know, Mark, sometimes we use the word *pants* when we're speaking Miskitu. But that isn't the real word. *Pants* is from English. The real Miskitu word is *trausis* [from "trousers"]" (Jamieson 1999: 25–26; my translation from Spanish). Whatever Miskitu purists may think, the language seems likely to continue borrowing words. In 1999–2000 I noted many loan words from Spanish in Awastara, a new phenomenon. The Spanish word *mochila* (backpack), for example, is now widely used and inflected in Miskitu fashion to indicate possession: *mochiliki* (my backpack), *mochilikam* (your backpack), and *aimochilika* (his or her backpack).

LANGUAGE AND CULTURAL CONCEPTS

The process of trying to learn a language is also the process of learning the cultural concepts embedded within and expressed through the language. *Dawan* and *dukia* provide two interesting examples. *Dawan* means "lord" or "owner" and is applied to the supernatural owners of plants and animals in the natural environment, such as the *swinta*, who is the "owner of the deer." More prosaically, it refers to the owner of a boat, house, shirt, or any other piece of personal property. A polite convention upon approaching an unknown house is to call out *utla dawanka!* (owner of the house!) as a form of salutation. "God" was translated by the missionaries as *Dawan* (with a capital *D*, of course). The corresponding concept is *dukia*, "property" (i.e., what the *dawan* owns). *Dukia* is commonly declined to produce *duki* (my things), *dukiam* (your things), and so on. Almost everything in the Miskitu world seems to have a *dawan*, indicating a pervasive sense of personal property. Interestingly, however, these concepts do not apply to kinship relations. One cannot speak of a wife (or any other relative) as *dukia*.

Body part metaphors pervade the language. *Byara* (stomach) also means "in the middle of," as in the phrase *kabu byarara*, "in the middle of the ocean." *Bila* literally means "mouth" but also refers to what comes out of the mouth or "speech." The voice is referred to as *bila baikra*, "breaking of the mouth." The Bible is called *Dawan Bila*, "God's word."

Mita (hand) refers not only to the hand itself but to the means by which something is accomplished. *Kupia* (heart) appears in such phrases as *kupia baikaia,* "to burst the heart" or get angry, and *kupia kumi,* "a single heart," indicating agreement or consensus. To forget in Miskitu is *auya tiwaia,* "to lose one's liver." An interesting body part metaphor is used to refer to kinship. *Taya* means "skin" but also refers to a person's kindred, to all those people an individual recognizes as kin. Socially, an individual's kin apparently should act as a sort of "skin" surrounding and protecting him or her. Jamieson (2000a: 84) makes the interesting suggestion that Miskitu body-part metaphors indicate that Miskitu speakers do not make a mind-body distinction. Thus the liver may actually be thought of as the physical locus of memory. He reminds us that feelings and emotions sometimes have a body locus in English as well, as in thinking of the heart as the site of contentment or romantic attraction. In English, however, such expressions are considered metaphoric rather than literal. Whether Miskitu speakers think of their own body metaphors in a literal fashion remains to be discovered.

A curious and interesting convention in Miskitu requires that body-part nouns take the first person plural pronoun. Thus "the hand" must be referred to as *wan mita,* "our hand." Friends corrected my usage of such pronouns regularly. Perhaps the Miskitu usage reflects some sentiment of shared humanity. At least, it emphasizes that we all have hands (feet, heads, etc.), whatever else may divide us, and that they are collectively "ours" in some general sense. The human body, after all, is what makes us human. It provides the subject matter for physical anthropology and medicine as well as constituting a topic for reflection in the fields of art, philosophy, and literature. The Miskitu language may thus be quite accurate, rather than simply curious, in requiring speakers to say "our head" or "our hand."

Miskitu is the daily language in Awastara and the only one most people know. The voyage from Port to the village is thus an immersion in the language as well as in a way of life.

CHAPTER THREE

The Village of Awastara

Traveling to Awastara has never been easy. It is forty-five kilometers north of Puerto Cabezas by sea, and the standard way for Miskitu people to travel is in thirty-five-foot sailing dories called catboats, usually packed full of passengers and cargo. One of the worst nights of my life was August 8, 1978. At this point I knew very few people in Awastara. I had made my first brief visit there and completed arrangements to rent a house. Now I was in Port looking for a ride back to the community. I made the mistake of eating a heavy supper in a Chinese restaurant and then going down to the wharf to catch the boat. The normal time to leave is around midnight, when the northeast trade wind usually stops and a gentle land breeze, called the *diwas*, blows out to sea for a few hours. If the *diwas* can be caught, it makes an easy six- or eight-hour trip up the Coast to the Awastara bar. If the strong northeast trade wind is blowing, however, it will be a hard trip, tacking back and forth against the wind the whole way or "beating up." Spending ten to fifteen hours in the boat is not uncommon. Passengers are crowded onto the wooden thwarts of the boat, trying to rest as best they can, ducking the heavy boom each time the boat comes about. Women and children (and strangers like me) are often seasick in rough weather.

I had made arrangements to travel with a captain I didn't know—and neither did I know any of the other passengers. I was simply a stranger in the boat. We left in the middle of the night and were soon caught in a violent storm, with sheets of rain and howling winds and very heavy seas. The passengers crawled down under large sheets of plastic to stay as dry as they could, while the captain steered the boat and the two sailors worked the sheets and sails in the violent sea. I became miserably seasick and quickly vomited my heavy Chinese dinner over the side. But there was no stopping. My dry heaves continued, on and on. I began to shiver uncontrollably, but I could not crawl under the plastic because the boat's motion was unbearable. The sea felt curiously warm as it splashed over us in the boat, compared to the cold, driving rain. Worst of all, the young Miskitu sailors laughed at me, finding my predicament very funny. I quite literally wanted to die, right then and there. The dozens of sailboat trips I have made to and from Awastara since then have often been hard, but not compared to that very first trip. Or perhaps I have gotten used to them. Why pick someplace easy to get to? My own arrival story (Pratt 1986: 31–32) remains as vivid in my own mind as when I experienced it, and a quick review of my fieldnotes from the day after that awful night brings it all flooding back.

THE COMMUNITY

The settlement of Awastara spreads over a broad area (map 3). Local residents recognize three major sections: the *muna* (western) side, the *lalma* (eastern) side, and the *pingka* (from Spanish *finca*, "farm/property") side, to the south. The village is spread out over a broad distance, with trails connecting the different areas. Major trails lead between the *muna, lalma,* and *pingka* sides, to the boat landing on the river to the east, north toward Dakura and Páhara, south toward Aras Bila, and west toward the Páhara Lagoon. A maze of smaller trails runs between houses within the village. It is easy to get lost among the houses, since the many fruit trees restrict the view. The four different Protestant churches are clustered near the center of town, along with the schoolhouse and playing field and the cemetery. The whole village is green and pleasant, with houses scattered about among the thousands of orange, lime, coconut, and other fruit trees. The enormous mango and breadfruit trees near the town center provide shade even during the hottest months of the year. The community gives an impression of prosperity and tranquillity to the casual·visitor and was described by a visiting anthropologist friend who has traveled widely as "the prettiest village on the Coast." My village! I think proudly.

The population of Awastara has doubled over the last twenty-two years, from 664 people living in 81 households in 1978 to 1,328 people in 146 households in 2000 (figure 2). In spite of the war years of the 1980s and the economic problems of the 1990s, the population contin-

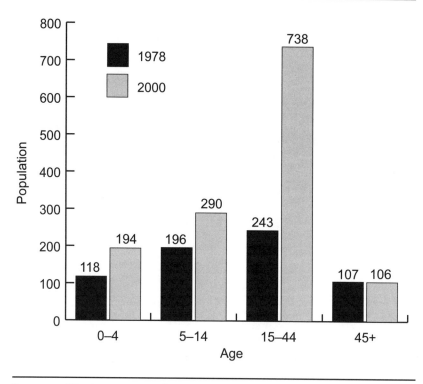

FIGURE 2. *The Awastara population in 1978 and 2000*

ues to increase. The physical growth of the town is striking to me when I return after almost twenty years. The greatest expansion is toward the south; but the village also has grown to the west and north, and the center of town is more densely packed with houses. The average household size continues to be just over eight people. There are many more young children now and almost three times as many young and middle-aged adults. The number of individuals over fifty, however, is just about the same.

I notice many new houses, some of them brightly painted. Almost every house has a metal roof, and I now have to search hard for a house with a traditional-style thatch roof. It takes me quite a while to wander all the trails and locate myself once more in the village. Even after I have been back for several months, I keep relearning, and recognizing once more, houses I had visited twenty years before.

And there is something new on the Awastara trails—bicycles! They are very much a part of community life today but were unknown here in

1978–79. Rodrigo estimates there are about forty bikes in the community, ridden mostly by young men but with a number of daring teenaged women riders as well. In Port the streets are crowded with bicycles—several thousand of them in a city with a population of twenty-five thousand. During the Sandinista years, a bicycle factory in the United States reportedly sent its products to help support the revolution, thus promoting bicycle use. Almost all the bikes are of the new mountain-bike variety. From the city they have also invaded the Miskitu communities. A new bike costs around a thousand cordobas (about $85) in Port, but a used one goes for as little as six or seven hundred. Many younger men in Port peddle with a woman riding astride the bar and a small child in her arms. Three people on a bike is a common sight. Men also peddle their bikes with full, heavy sacks of rice or beans on the bar. A local bicycle culture has thus evolved over the last twenty years. In Awastara bikes are also dangerous not only to their riders but to people walking on the trails. Boys ride silently, at high speed, along the narrow paths, bearing down on unsuspecting people walking on the paths before they have a chance to dodge. Several bad accidents involving injuries have occurred, and I had several close calls myself.

Houses are often some distance from each other, and a complex web of trails weaves around and between them, apart from the major heavily used trails. The major trails connect different parts of the village and continue to other places (map 3). People walking on all the different village trails and those sitting on their porches or working around their houses communicate with each other in an interesting fashion. Questions and replies are shouted back and forth in a special far-carrying tone of voice, at a much greater distance than would be comfortable in English. "Aluuuuuy! Where are you going? Who came in the catboat? Who has fish or turtle meat for sale?" These sorts of questions are asked constantly, and the information is then assimilated. One morning as I sat with Victor on the porch, he called out in a loud, piercing voice to a man passing on the path some fifty feet away: "Did you see my boy Adolpo there in Bluefields? Were they really taking him to jail? Did you see it with your own eyes?" The reply was: "I saw them tie him up and carry him off, but I didn't see what happened after that." Victor then turned to me and commented, in a normal tone of voice: "I guess it's true, then, he saw it with his own eyes." This sort of information exchange seems to lead to a large, constantly updated database of practical information about the community, to which people "log on" by shouting questions at each other over considerable distances. It is hard to keep secrets in Awastara.

A quick exchange of practical information replaces the stock phrases of polite greeting used in English or Spanish. Miskitu speakers get right to the point. My Miskitu friends practiced this style of discourse with me, and I learned to imitate it but never managed it well.

Walking along the trails, one also occasionally hears a voice directed at someone nearby in an angry and high-pitched tone. This style of discourse has a name: *palaia*. The Heath and Marx Miskitu-Spanish dictionary (1953: 79) defines this verb as "to fly" or "to be enraged or furious." A colloquial translation might be "to fly into a rage" (i.e., to talk angrily with someone to get them to do what you want). A common example was Victor talking rapidly in a high pitch at the top of his voice at other family members. One afternoon I listened to him *palaia* at four or five grandchildren, until they finally carried some of Casey's sawdust up to cover muddy parts of the trail. He did not want them just being lazy all the time, he explained later.

People in positions of authority can legitimately *palaia* at those beneath them: for example, parents at children or political leaders at followers. It seems to represent a venting of built-up frustration, a legitimate way of yelling and screaming at others. This sort of verbal behavior would normally be regarded as improper and out of place in the middle-class United States. In Awastara it is frequent and expected, a legitimate tool of authority figures. Interestingly enough, a common response of younger people is simply to ignore the loud, angry diatribe being directed against them by their elders. Being subordinate, they cannot reply in kind; but they can express their own strong will by ignoring the harsh lecture. People say, *Yang palisna kuna walras* (I *palaia*ed at them, but they didn't listen). Personally, I found this style of discourse difficult, since it is so different from my own interpersonal style. It is intended to make subordinates behave correctly, but it is only appropriate from a higher-status person to a lower-status one. Thus it would be regarded as grossly improper for children to *palaia* back at their parents.

LAND IS FREE

When I first started walking around Awastara, people told me that land was "free." This seemed improbable to me, but it turned out to be true. My friends Victor and Bowman out on the *pingka* side told me stories of how they claimed pieces of land by clearing them of trees and brush, planting coconut and mango trees, and building houses. Each wound up with a large spread, where their grown children live today. Victor told me: "It's not good to live too close together. Your neighbors will hear you when you have a fight with your wife, or see you when you have to run to the bushes with diarrhea. That's no way to live!" In fact, one common Miskitu ideal seems to be to stake out a piece of land of your own and plant fruit trees—a sign of ownership—and thus create a homestead for your family. People from Awastara have a right to do this on unoccupied land. In this sense land is indeed free. A man from another community has use rights to land only if he has an Awastara spouse and lives on the land. *Dama* Moreno, in his eighties, married one of Victor's sisters and has lived in Awastara for about fifty years. His homestead belongs to him and his wife, but everyone remembers that he is not really from Awastara.

In April 1999 Rodrigo and I spend three days walking around Awastara and making a large map of all the houses in the community. It is the dry season and we are eaten alive by chiggers or grass lice (*asdura*), a dry-season pest, as we walk from house to house. As with many ethnographic tasks, people seem to appreciate my interest in them and their community, looking at the sketch map and correcting details. I find that Rodrigo can easily identify the owner of each house on the map. It is simply the person who paid to have it constructed. Both men and women are house owners, and in fact we find twenty-six houses belonging to women. When both spouses have contributed jointly to the house's construction, they are co-owners. Hilario and Laurinda, who live near the center of town, are an example. Hilario sent money back to his spouse while he was working in the gold mines, but Laurinda supervised the house's construction and also contributed money of her own. At least three new houses, not including mine, have been built with money sent by relatives who are working in the United States.

If a man leaves his spouse, she normally gets the house. When the couple lives matrilocally, near the woman's parents, she has more security. The man may leave, but she will keep the house, a place near her mother. Individual property rights are strong here. When Gerlinda and Mosely lived together in 1978, they had two houses, with the older one being used as a kitchen. One belonged to Gerlinda and one to Mosely. When they separated, they tore down the two houses; each kept his or her own lumber. Gerlinda was keeping her lumber at her mother's place, planning to rebuild her house there. By 1999 Gerlinda was living in the United States but had sent money to her family to have a new house built close to her mother. Gerlinda's brightly painted new house was one of the nicer ones in town.

On the map, one can easily see a sort of centrifugal force that seems to be pushing Awastara's expansion, particularly on the *pingka* side. There is a powerful desire to be away from all the people in the center, to have more land for the family to grow bigger, to have a place to plant fruit trees and to raise animals. There is also a conflicting desire to be closer to the churches in the center of town, to be closer to the school for the children, and to be close to relatives who live near the center. During her elderly mother's illness, for example, Plora (overweight and suffering from diabetes) made the long walk into town every day to visit. This corresponding centripetal force brings some people back to the pieces of land owned by their relatives near the center. Women, in particular, want to live near their mothers, thus reconstituting a matrilocal settlement pattern, in which groups of closely related women live together.

Helms (1968, 1971: 23–27) provides interesting discussions of the advantages that matrilocal residence has had for the Miskitu over centuries of outside contact. With men away fighting or working, groups of related women constituted the core of Miskitu communities. They preserved Miskitu language and culture and maintained functioning households to which the men could return. The arrangement freed men in a practical way to take advantage of economic opportunities away from home. Nevertheless, Helms (1971: 76) found that in Asang matrilocality was no longer the norm, reflecting more recent adaptations. Current work by Miskitu anthropologist Melesio Peter Espinoza (2002) in the villages of Santa Marta and Auyhapihni, however, found that more than 90 percent of couples did reside matrilocally in both communities. Laura Herlihy (2002) found a similar percentage of matrilocal marriages in the Miskitu community of Kuri in Honduras. Evidently matrilocal residence is deeply rooted in Miskitu culture.

In Awastara grown children usually build their own houses on the family property, close to their living parents' house, even in the case of patrilocal residence. Victor's sons Rodrigo and Hector already have built large houses close to their father. His younger son Adolpo and his daughter Pamela have not yet saved the money to build houses, but they intend to do so.

Property boundaries within the village are well known, although they are not readily apparent to a visitor. The large open areas between houses are filled with mango, coconut, and orange trees, and there are none of the usual boundary markers that outsiders would recognize—no rocks or fence lines. People do often plant coconut trees at the corners of their property, however. These boundary marker trees, called *dusamara,* are well known.

Planting fruit trees is a crucial sign of ownership, and having more room to plant fruit trees is a major reason for moving farther away from the town center. People say proudly, "My grandfather planted those coconuts, those mangos." Victor patiently explains to me how he was the first person to move out to the *pingka* side. Many people were afraid to move so far away, where the *swinta* and the *wahwin* and other dangerous spiritual creatures might molest them. Victor's *rapika* (his father's brother) Sembrano tried moving out to the *pingka* side, but his wife was deathly afraid of the *wahwin* and refused to sleep out there. One night Sembrano was sleeping alone in the house when a horse stuck its nose in the door and snorted. Sembrano thought it really was the *wahwin* and ran off screaming. Victor laughs uproariously as he tells me the story but also adds that in those days there really were a lot of *wahwin*. You could see their lights as they wandered about on the savannah. When Victor himself moved out to the *pingka* side, he cleared off a large area and planted mangos, coconuts, cashews, oranges, and lime trees and then built his own house to raise a family. He never wanted anyone else to be his boss, he said. Eventually, other people began moving out to the *pingka* side near Victor, but a large area still belongs to him because he originally cleared it and planted fruit trees there.

Even as an old man, Victor still fantasizes about moving farther away. One day we climb the low hill called Cigarnaka behind the *pingka* side and stop to rest on the top, where there are no houses anywhere close. "This would be a better place to live!" rhapsodizes Victor. "You could raise chickens up here and make money." But, he says, Plora would never come up here with him. It's too far away, and she would be afraid of the *swinta*. It is a dream that will never be realized, but Victor's voice is animated as he talks of "homesteading" once more before he dies. And of course the very first thing he would do on Cigarnaka would be to plant fruit trees.

While fruit trees are young, they must be protected from the pigs and cattle, which roam freely in the village and will eat the young trees if given a chance. One way of protecting them is by painting the tender young leaves with cow manure. Marcos Hoppington remembers his father making him and his brother get up early each morning to do the nasty job of mixing cow manure with water in a bucket and painting the young coconut leaves with it. Marcos tells me how much he hated this task. But today the Hoppingtons have hundreds of coconut trees from which they derive a good income. Coconuts produce continuously and can always be sold at the market in Port. Once a tree is tall enough to be above the browsing level, it is no longer tended. Unfortunately, in recent years, an unknown disease has killed off many of Awastara's coconut palms. The *cocales* (coconut groves), which Nietschmann (1973: 137–38) describes as lining much of the Atlantic seashore of Nicaragua, may be in some danger, and their loss would be a serious economic blow to the communities.

Although they are one of the sources of life, the tall mango and coconut trees in Awastara are also dangerous. Maura shows me a large indentation on her skull where a coconut, falling from a height of twenty or thirty feet, hit her on the head as a child. It seems a miracle that she was not killed, and she continues to have severe headaches from the injury. Climbing trees to get fruit is also dangerous. My old friend Bowman Hoppington died as a result of a fall from high in one of his mango trees, a few years before I returned in 1997. He broke his hip and leg and eventually died from infection. Casey tells me about falling out of a coconut tree himself as a boy and being badly hurt.

During the dry season, dead leaves from the many fruit trees cover the ground, and women spend many hours raking and burning them. One afternoon in March Eliza and I spend a couple of hours raking up the mango and cashew leaves covering the ground around our houses. We use rakes made of bunches of small branches tied together with string. As the piles accumulate we begin burning them, carrying a smoldering branch from pile to pile. The leaves burn quickly, leaving black patches all over the ground underneath the fruit trees. The burned patches will quickly turn green again, however, once the rains start. Everyone is burning leaves now, and there are black spots everywhere. As Eliza and I work, black and sweaty ourselves, Alvarez passes by and says, "I can see you're helping out the women," making me realize that this is regarded as women's work. I try to pitch in with all sorts of tasks, but for my Miskitu friends most work is clearly gendered.

MISKITU HOUSES

This is a carpentry culture. Large wooden sailing dories or catboats are made locally, and houses in all stages of construction can be seen everywhere in the village. House building and repair is a constant activity in Awastara, with new houses being built, old ones being taken down, and house repairs being made. My neighbors have framed up a new house, a small one, and are putting on sheets of metal roofing to protect the frame from the weather (photo 2). They will finish the walls and floor when

PHOTO 2. *Building a house*

lumber is available. At any moment, from almost any place in town, I can hear hammering and sawing, the sounds of carpentry. Lumber does not last very long (usually only ten to fifteen years) in this wet environment. Two kinds of termites—the *usra* and the *itimur*—eat lumber fairly rapidly. "Those *itimur* are really *saura* [bad]!" Victor comments with ill-humor. It helps to paint the wood; but paint is expensive, and many houses are left unprotected.

Every Miskitu man is a carpenter, capable of building a house for his family. But there are also expert carpenters like Casey and Ernesto in Awastara, and others from neighboring communities, who are always looking for work—someone with the money to hire them to frame up a house. With occasional money from cocaine finds in recent years, there has been more work for carpenters building houses. Buying lumber and paying for carpentry is expensive. My twelve-foot by sixteen-foot house cost about $1,200 in 1999, and an eighteen-foot by twenty-foot house being constructed nearby was said to have cost about $1,500. Houses, therefore, are often built in stages, with posts and foundation beams put

51

up first, the galvanized metal roof later, and the walls framed up only when enough money becomes available.

Modern Miskitu houses are built of sawed lumber, on top of hardwood posts, which don't easily rot, some six to eight feet above the ground. This style was introduced by nineteenth-century Moravian missionaries, and Helms (1971: 51) comments that in Asang it was thought of as the modern or "civilized" way to live. Older people described an earlier-style house, built of pieces of the *waung* tree split lengthwise. The walls were made of thatch, and the floor was a raised platform of hard trodden earth some six inches above ground level. You stepped up into the house from the outside. This arrangement kept some of the water out in the rainy season but was not nearly as effective as building the house on top of tall posts. In the old-style house, the fire was built in the center of the room, on the ground. People slept up above the floor on a sleeping loft called a *tint* and had to come down occasionally to push the logs together as they burned below. Conzemius (1932: 30–31) describes these old-style houses, but I have never seen one.

Although today almost all houses have metal roofs, only a couple of generations back all houses had roofs of thatch. Temporary shelters built of poles used for two- or three-day church conferences, however, continue to have thatch roofs. Thatching a roof is a communal task, and the more hands available the better. It is also gendered, with men and women working in separate groups doing different tasks. One day I help the Adventists roof a shelter for their upcoming conference. I work with the men up underneath the roof, while the women, sitting on the ground some distance away, tie palm thatch together into roofing pieces. Jornel shows me how to take a piece of thatch, pass it up through the roof poles and lay it flat, then take the two tie-down pieces and pull them tight around the roof poles. He is a patient teacher. As we run out of thatch pieces, the men call out, "*Papta* [thatch]!" and children come running to bring us prepared stacks from the women's area. We work on top of makeshift scaffolds of boards, inside the house, reaching up to the roof poles above. After about two hours I am exhausted. Such communal work projects were promoted by early Moravian missionaries. Older people say that clearing of fields in the dry season had always been done with communal labor and that the missionaries used this practice as a model to get people to thatch each other's roofs as well. Communal roof thatching readily became a part of Miskitu culture. Traditionally, the house owner has to provide food and drink for all who help thatch his or her house.

All houses are of standard sizes (for example, twelve feet by sixteen feet or eighteen feet by twenty feet). Today most sawed lumber is bought from the sawmill in Puerto Cabezas and brought to the village in cat-boats. It is then carried up from the Awastara landing on the backs of horses or carried by men with tumplines around their foreheads. Many houses have stacks of sawed lumber underneath them, waiting to be used in the next house-building project. A young married couple (like Casey and Pamela) may be waiting to build their own house, or the house own-er simply may be planning to build a new one. Since houses last only about fifteen years, people are continually building or planning to build. Houses are not a once-in-a-lifetime expense, but an ongoing one, like clothes—something to be replaced in the foreseeable future.

Houses are very rarely bought or sold within the community. People normally don't have large sums of money at one time unless they hap-pen to have found cocaine, a windfall that happened three times during 1999–2000. So there are few potential buyers for a house. The ideal is rather to build your own house, either on your parents' land or on "free" land that you have cleared yourself. Children normally inherit their par-ents' land and houses, and there seem to be few disputes between siblings over the property.

Twenty years ago a great deal of lumber was sawed out of local pine trees from the nearby savannah. A tree was felled, and two sides of the log were squared off with an axe. One-inch or two-inch "chalk" lines, usually made from the black insides of a flashlight battery, were popped on one flat side of the log with a taut string. Then it was pulled up an incline to rest on two log posts firmly planted in the ground. Finally it was laid horizontally across a four-pole log platform called a *tapesco*, with the chalk lines facing toward the ground. Two men could then begin sawing planks out of the elevated log with a long ripping saw. This was very hard work, especially for the man on top, who had to pull the heavy saw up against gravity. The other man, meanwhile, stood below the log, guiding the saw down the chalk lines as it sliced out the planks. I spent a whole day sawing lumber with Casey in 1978, with me working mostly on the bottom. By 2000 the ripping saws had disappeared entirely, re-placed by noisy chainsaws. Although sawing lumber is of course much faster with chainsaws, they are expensive, break down frequently, and use costly gas and oil. They are also dangerous. In 1998 the Church of God preacher cut off part of his hand in a chainsaw accident.

The large, one-room Miskitu houses are used mainly for storage of be-longings, for shelter from the sun and the torrential rains, and for sleep-ing. If two or more couples live in the house, it may be partitioned into rooms. Many people sleep directly on the board floors, covered with a sheet. Some wealthier couples sleep on beds with mattresses, with their children on the floor around them, although others say mattresses are uncomfortably hot. I learned to sleep on board floors when visiting other communities, but I was never comfortable on the hard board floors like my Miskitu friends and family.

Every house has a porch or *beranda* in front, covered by an overhanging roof. This is where family and visitors socialize, sitting on chairs or stools or on the steps leading up from the ground. There is always a hammock hanging from the roof beams inside the house or from the porch. Hammocks are not used as much for sleeping as for relaxing during the heat of the day or after a meal. Visitors are always invited up on the porch to sit and talk but rarely go inside the house.

House floors are occasionally scrubbed hard with soap and water, a procedure called *utla yauhbaia*. One day my neighbor Maura, concerned about my housekeeping, tells me she will scrub my floor. She shows up with buckets and soap and a plastic scrubber. I pick everything up off the floor, and we start to work. I fill the buckets from the well and ladle out water on the floor while Maura scrubs, mostly by using one foot on top of the soapy scrubber. For tough places she gets down on her hands and knees and scrubs with her hands. A surprising amount of dirt comes out of my new floorboards. I follow behind, ladling out more water and sweeping the dirty water out the door and down through the cracks in the board floor. We move from the back of the house to the door, doing the porch and steps last, and using many buckets of water. In houses with small children, floors get dirty quickly. Maura is an unusually good housekeeper. She says she hates dirt; and if my house were hers, she would be scrubbing the walls too. A floor should be scrubbed once a week, according to Maura, but I don't think even she does it that frequently. Victor's opinion, however, is that overzealous housewives cause floor rot with too much washing. Along with the sawed lumber houses themselves, the practice of floor scrubbing every week must have been introduced by Moravian missionaries and incorporated as part of Miskitu "house culture."

Posts to support houses are cut from *níspero* or *mihmi*, two very hard woods. *Mihmi* is said to be the best wood for posts (since it lasts the longest) and is plentiful; but it grows in the swamp, and you have to fight the insects and the mud to get it. Not everyone is willing to make the effort to cut *mihmi*. Posts made of *iban* are sold in Port, but it rots much more quickly. A very recent technique is to use house posts made of cement. The cement is expensive, but people say the *itimur* termites do not crawl up cement posts to begin destroying the house, so it is well worth the cost. Only a few new houses have cement posts, however.

Underneath the house is an open space some six to eight feet high. People often sit here during the heat of the day, with the house itself serving as a kind of giant sunscreen. It seems to be primarily a male space: men sit there and chat, while women are constantly busy with household chores in the house above. I sit at Jaime's house and talk with him and other men, while his wife, Marta, makes coffee for all of us in the house above and then brings it "downstairs" to us. Sitting down there, of course, you have to be careful to stay away from the kitchen window, where dishwater and vegetable peelings and scraps are being dumped out. This "basement" area is thus space well utilized for socializing and is another reason for houses to be set on top of tall posts.

Fire is a constant danger to houses made of wood, and occasionally someone's house burns down. In particular, as people burn the leaves in the dry season, they must keep a close watch on their fires. Sometimes one gets out of control. In spring 2000 a leaf fire at Alvarez's place spread and burned down the small thatched house out back, where his mother-in-law was living. She and the baby got out safely, however. I watched very carefully as we burned leaves close to my own new house in spring 2000.

Interestingly enough, Miskitu houses are portable. Since they are simply nailed together, they can be dismantled and reconstructed somewhere else on one's piece of property. This is very common. I find it a bit disconcerting to go looking for a friend's house and find it moved a hundred feet away, across the trail, or across a small creek. People try to stake out large pieces of property through clearing and then planting fruit trees, thus giving themselves multiple house locations for the future.

In May 2000 Victor begins dismantling his house, built in 1986, to erect a new one. The house has been completely eaten up by *itimur* termites. We work together, climbing up on the roof to tear off the rusted metal sheets and pulling the rotten boards apart with hammers. Victor wants to salvage the usable pieces of lumber and roofing, but there is little left that is worth keeping. As he saves a little extra money, Victor is buying new lumber from Port and also asking Casey to cut lumber across the lagoon in Trakis (map 2) to use for the new house. The plan is for Victor and Plora to live in the kitchen of the old house, where I have eaten so many times, until the new house can be finished. I buy nails and hinges for the new house but have to leave Awastara when only the floor posts have been put in the ground for it.

TRAKIS AND AWAS MAIA

Most people like to live close to their relatives in the village. Awastara's lands are extensive, however, stretching south to the boundary with Krukira, north to the boundary with Dakura, and across the Páhara Lagoon to the boundaries with Sisin and Tuara. Awastara owns a large section of mostly uninhabited land across the lagoon, called Trakis. One day I get a chance to travel over there in a small sailing *duri* with Casey and Pancho and three other men. It is a wild ride with a hard northeast wind blowing whitecaps on the lagoon, the *duri* careening through the water, and the others shouting, "Hang on if we capsize!" I worry most about my camera and my field notebook.

Trakis turns out to be an area of beautiful, rolling hills, covered with pine trees, with a small clear river flowing through it. We walk for several miles, looking for the Awastara boundary markers, and then spend the night at the small settlement of Awas Maia, which has only seven houses. It is legally a distant municipality of Awastara, but it has no school, a problem emphasized by the man who invites us to sleep in his kitchen. As we huddle on the floor, cold and tired, his wife appears in the doorway with a welcome pot of hot lemongrass tea and plates of warm food. One plate is fried armadillo (*tahira*), which none of my companions are able to eat because of the food taboos common among Miskitu people. I fall on it with gusto, explaining that armadillo is our favorite sort of meat in Texas!

Everyone agrees that the large expanse of land at Trakis is beautiful country, unoccupied except for the tiny community of Awas Maia. Here you could build a house, plant fruit trees, raise animals, and hunt the abundant deer and other game. In the evening the men begin rhapsodizing about homesteading in this rich location. Their discussion makes me realize that the ancestral founders of Awastara must have come upon it in similar fashion, exploring it and enthusiastically discussing its potential. They would have noted the elevated location where the cool northeast trade winds blow continuously, the rich strip of river bottomland to be farmed, and all the wild resources of ocean and river and lagoon close at hand to be exploited. The enthusiasm of a new, ideal place to live is being re-created around me tonight. It would indeed be delightful to live in Awas Maia.

In fact, Casey actually built a small shelter here some years ago, but his wife, Pamela, wouldn't live so far from her family and with so many dangerous spiritual creatures roaming about. I become aware once more of the pull of family and of the perceived dangers of creatures such as the *swinta* and the *wahwin,* the centripetal forces that keep settlements together. They restrain the centrifugal pull of wanting to homestead in rich and distant lands, which is a powerful motivation for many Miskitu men. Miskitu women, in contrast, want to live close to their relatives, not in a faraway and dangerous place.

FOUNDING ANCESTORS AND *KIAMP* GROUPS

Within Awastara itself, clusters of houses in different areas represent the descendants of important male founding ancestors, their "seed" or off-spring, called *kiamp.* Helms (1971: 72–76) gives a good description of these groups in Asang, noting that the *kiamp* have never been mentioned in any of the rich ethnohistorical literature on the Miskitu people.

Awastara's *kiamp* are interesting to compare with those in Asang. Helms says that each Asang *kiamp* is traced to a founding couple and that membership is basically patrilineal, with the *kiamp* identified by the founder's surname. Asang has three large *kiamp,* named Bobb, Joseph, and Sanders. The descendants of each continue to live in the general vicinity of the founder's house, and each *kiamp* therefore occupies a well-defined area of the village, as indicated on Helms's map (1971: 74). There were twenty-seven *kiamp* subgroups represented in Asang at the time of Helms's fieldwork, but residents viewed them all as related to one of the two major divisions in town, Bobb-Joseph or Sanders-Herrera. This parallels what seems to be a kind of underlying dual organization in Awastara and other coastal villages, where *lalma* and *muna* sides (east and west) are often recognized.

In Awastara the *kiamp* are generalized descent groupings, focused on important male founding ancestors. The literal meaning of the word *ki-amp* provides a clue to its significance. *Kiamp* means "rootstock" and is used in referring to a stump that continues to send out shoots. In terms of kinship, it also refers to the offspring of a particular important man, also a sort of "rootstock." The usage seems patrilineal and rather biblical. In defining *kiamp* membership, however, genealogical links may be through either males or females, and a person can have ties to more than one *kiamp.* The important thing seems to be the relationship to the founding ancestor himself.

Helms notes that the *kiamp* are not really corporate and serve mainly as reference groups that unite people across village lines. Members of the Bobb *kiamp,* for example, are found in other villages, where they moved from Asang. Helms suggests that *kiamp* serve as patrilineal reference groups uniting nonlocal kin, within the generally matrilocal Miskitu society. Because groups of related women often live close to each other, the *kiamp* provide a bond between nonlocalized male relatives. *Kiamp* members may recognize some general obligation to provide food and lodging to each other away from their home villages.

In Awastara, as in Asang, the *kiamp* are important primarily in terms of settlement. The founder is credited with clearing a large area and planting coconuts and other fruit trees to indicate possession. His descendants continue living in the same area, so that the *kiamp* history is really the history of the important members of the community and the founding of the different settled parts of the widespread village. There is no group ownership of land, however, so the *kiamp* is not a corporate landowning group. As we have seen, land is said to be "free" for anyone who clears it and plants fruit trees or builds a house, and it belongs to that individual as long as he or she continues to use it.

The three Awastara *kiamp* represent the three sides of the village (map 3). This essential fact eluded me when I first lived in Awastara. Gerlinda, who cooked for me, finally answered my perplexed questions about the *kiamp* in town by saying, "Look! The *kiamp* I know are three. Mory Davis is the *muna* side, Dama Hoppington is the *lalma* side, and Obediah Kingsman is the *pingka* side."

Although each *kiamp* has a "home base" in the village where the founding ancestor lived, members are constantly moving away to other places. In 1978 the radio reported one day that a Miskitu man named Kingsman had been wounded while serving with the National Guard near Managua. Awastara people began figuring out who he was. They finally decided he must be a distant relative, since "a Kingsman has to be from Awastara." Today many of Mory Davis's *kiamp* live in Tuapí, and they are regarded as kin that one can call on for help, as Helms reports for Asang.

Each *kiamp* also has its own reputation, and in these terms even other animals are said to have *kiamp*. One woman tells me, for example, that *wangki bip kiampka rugkira takan,* "those Río Coco cattle have turned out to be trouble-makers." The idea seems to be that their bad behavior was inherited through their *kiamp*. The Awastara *kiamp* reputations have to do with the personalities of their founding ancestors, who are regarded as men of remarkable abilities. *Dama* Hoppington, for example, was said to have planted and cared for hundreds of coconut trees, from which his descendants are still gathering and selling coconuts. "Other *kiampka,*" said one of the Hoppingtons, "don't think of those to come; they just eat off the old people." In other words, they are too lazy to go out and plant coconut trees for future generations and just use those planted by their ancestors. *Dama* Hoppington, however, not only planted hundreds of trees himself but encouraged his offspring to be just as industrious. The modern Hoppingtons pride themselves on being good gardeners and making things grow, like their famous ancestor.

Dama Mory Davis is said to have been a black man from Belize who was shipwrecked near Dakura. He came walking down the beach, where he was found by the Awastara people. They brought him back to the village and took care of him. He did not speak Miskitu at first, but gradually he learned; and eventually he became a major figure in the community. He married three sisters and founded a large *kiamp*. He also preached the gospel after the missionaries arrived, apparently as a spirit person who received a special calling to help convert his brethren. The Mory Davis story illustrates just how receptive the Miskitu have been to outsiders. Mory Davis was accepted—in fact greatly admired—as a strong and successful man, and his offspring are just as much "real Miskitu" as anyone else. In Asang the spouses of several of the original *kiamp* founders were also outsiders (Helms 1971: 57–59).

The historical incident involving the 1641 wreck of a slave ship near Awastara must have produced new *kiamp,* as the survivors were absorbed in the local villages. This happened too long ago to be part of the oral tradition, although it is important to note that the sense of time involved in *kiamp* oral histories is mythical rather than literal or historical. For example, elderly Telemaco told me that he was not old enough to have seen Mory Davis; he thought Mory must have been in Awastara about the time Christopher Columbus discovered America. People find comparisons with their own *kiamp,* as well as other aspects of their culture, in the Bible. I heard a sermon, for instance, in which the Miskitu *sasmalkra* spoke of Abraham as founding a large *kiamp*. Abraham was compared to a man from Cape Gracias a Dios who, very much like Mory Davis, arrived in a Miskitu village by accident and founded a new *kiamp,* bringing with him new ideas and new techniques of farming. The moral the pastor drew from the Abraham *kiamp* story was that the Awastara people could plant pine trees on the savannah to replace those being cut down and thus improve their land in the same way that Abraham's *kiamp* had improved Egypt.

In the 1920s a black man from Pennsylvania named Robert Linton arrived in Port on a ship. There he met a woman named Cecilia Hoppington from Awastara. They moved to Awastara together and had six children, one of them my friend Erlita Linton. Bob Linton never returned to Pennsylvania. "He come and he stayed and he dead," Erlita told me in Creole English. Erlita's father liked Awastara, raised cattle and did carpentry work, and taught all six of his children to speak English. He lived the last thirty-seven years of his life in the community.

OBEDIAH KINGSMAN

The most famous *kiamp* founder in Awastara was a Scotsman named Obediah Kingsman. Many people had told me that Obediah was their grandfather or great-grandfather and that he was an Englishman. I had never heard a firsthand account, however, until Parson Elrey Kingsman came to visit Awastara. Elrey remembers his grandfather Obediah well and has preserved a picture of him, which he loaned me to copy (photo 3). Elrey tells me that Obediah came from Kingston, Jamaica, in the late nineteenth century. His father was said to have been a pirate. Obediah arrived on the Miskitu Coast to build a new life for himself and apparently brought considerable money with him. His original name was McDonald and he was Scots; but because he came from Kingston, the name "Kingsman" was tagged on and stuck. That is how he has come to be known. Two other brothers also came to the Coast but wound up farther south.

Obediah married a Miskitu woman from Dakura named Leiticia Brown. He killed four cattle for his wedding and invited a great crowd of people to the celebration. Obediah and Leiticia lived together in Awastara for many years and had ten children, seven sons and three daughters. Obediah didn't speak Miskitu when he arrived, but over the years he learned from his wife and neighbors. He made a Miskitu dictionary of his own. He had a good education and faithfully read his English Bible, from which he taught his children and grandchildren. Elrey remembers his grandfather teaching him the alphabet. He also remembers the large English cookbook in the kitchen, from which the girls learned to cook.

Together Elrey and I walk around the *pingka* side where Obediah cleared the land and built his house (map 3). A piece of the cement floor of the original house is still left at the site where Obediah's grandson Chesley now lives. Obediah had a big house, with a workshop outside where he kept all kinds of tools. He had a foot treadle for a whetstone, a machine for hulling rice, and an electric generating plant made in Germany—"not one of those that breaks down all the time like the ones we have now," Elrey comments. Down at the landing Obediah built a big shed for his four large sailboats, the *duri tara* that were in use before the catboat style was imported from the Cayman Islands. He made sure

60

that all the landing area was kept clean, and he built a large *kral* (fenced enclosure) in the river to keep turtles alive until they could be butchered. Out on the *pingka*-side savannah he pastured many cattle, and he built the first wire fence in town to keep them away from his house and yard. Among his other skills, Obediah was a fine carpenter. Chesley showed me a table of good craftsmanship that his grandfather Obediah had built, using pegs instead of nails.

Obediah is regarded as a genuine culture hero. He had a medicine chest with all kinds of medicines to treat people, and he also gave injections. He had the first house with a cement foundation in Awastara, the first organ, and the first Victrola. Obediah planted all sorts of trees and other plants that people don't cultivate anymore, including coffee, avocados, *pejibaye* palm fruit, and pineapple. They all grew well, according to Elrey, who remembers picking his grandfather's coffee berries. Obediah is said to have kept forty men employed on his farm and in his various enterprises. He also raised various poor children who didn't have families. Any visitors who came to Awastara stayed at Obediah's house, including the Moravian parsons, who were all foreigners in those days. Although Obediah wasn't strictly religious, said Elrey, he was a good Christian, an

PHOTO 3. *Obediah Kingsman*

upright man respected by everyone. He died in 1920 and is buried in the Awastara cemetery, where a rusted iron fence surrounds his grave.

Various "landmark houses" on the *pingka* side that I have frequently visited all belong to Obediah's grandchildren and great-grandchildren. As Elrey and I walk from house to house, I can see it all for the first time: a large part of the modern village, in fact, had been Obediah's property. A legendary figure in Awastara, he seems to be remembered fondly by everyone. I had imagined him as people described him—a big, tall man with red or yellow hair and a beard down his chest, a man of almost epic proportions. His picture, however, shows him as a very ordinary looking older man, of average height, seated, with the serious look on his face favored by convention in older photographs—a dose of reality!

I find it somewhat ironic that people in Awastara have followed through very little on the wonderful innovations that Obediah is said to have introduced. For instance, no one has continued planting coffee or avocados or *pejibaye* or pineapples. Some of Obediah's fabled hardworking, innovative spirit seems to have died with him. I wonder: can the village perhaps be waiting for another Obediah to come along? Obediah's grandson Hilario tells me that his own dream would be to visit England some day and find his own "Kingsman" relatives there.

There are general parallels to the Obediah Kingsman story in other villages. Joel Mercado from Asang tells me a brief story about his ancestor Señor Mercado in that Río Coco community, who also founded a *kiamp*. Helms (1971: 74) mentions the Mercados as one of the twenty-seven *kiamp* in 1964–65, when she was doing fieldwork in Asang. Nolan Webster in Páhara tells me the story of his own grandfather, Captain Nixon Webster, a white man from Jamaica. Captain Webster claimed a large area of unoccupied land, like Obediah Kingsman, and planted fruit trees and raised cattle. Nolan proudly shows me the area where Captain Webster lived in Páhara.

It is interesting that founding-ancestor, culture-hero male figures in Miskitu culture so often come from outside the community. They find local women and leave offspring and a rich cultural legacy behind them. This seems to be a powerful historical myth of how important *kiamp* arise in Miskitu communities. It fits well with matrilocality, phrased in Miskitu as "he came here for the woman" (*mairin mita nara balan*) and with the concept of "capture" of a groom by the male relatives of an eligible woman. A general idea seems to be that white men or black men—outsiders—have come to the community from elsewhere and left it a better place than they found it. This seems to be exactly the opposite of what is reported from the Mayangna communities, which are said to be closed to outsiders moving in, learning their language or culture, or marrying their women. Miskitu ethnicity, in contrast, seems to be defined by kinship relations with powerful, intelligent, successful foreigners, who come to Miskitu communities and found families and *kiamp*. Ethnic success is defined through intermarriage and "improving the race."

"Improving the race" is in fact a local idea. Walking across the seemingly endless savannah one day, Victor comments to me that he would like to bring all those poor black men he has heard about who are suffering in Africa to settle the savannahs and make the land productive. Black men obviously rate highly in his system of "racial values." Victor's friendships with Cayman Islanders undoubtedly have shaped his thinking.

For some people, however, dark skin color is negatively valued. Miss Porla points out one of her light-skinned granddaughters as a *miriki lupia,* an "American" offspring. When you cross a Miskitu with a *miriki,* she said, the baby always comes out looking *miriki.* Some people seem to regard light skin as superior and somehow dominant in individuals of mixed background. Charles Hale (1994: 157–59) found the same sort of preference for Anglo phenotypes in Sandy Bay Sirpi. He refers to the general idea that Anglos are superior as "internalized racism."

"BAMBOO WHITES"

In fact, for centuries, Europeans and North Americans of various sorts have escaped their own backgrounds and origins to come to the Miskitu Coast, where they married local women, raised families, and often prospered. David Brooks (1997: 150–53, 172–73) refers to these "bamboo whites" as crucial economic and political figures along the Río Coco in the 1920s and 1930s. Both Augusto Sandino and the U.S. Marines tried to win their favor and support in the war they fought against each other in that area. Brooks (1989: 321) attributes the term "bamboo whites" to U.S. Marine captain Mike Edson, in charge of the Río Coco patrol in the 1920s. Edson was probably quoting Anglo company officials of the period, among whom the term must have been commonly used to refer to the foreigners living in Indian communities throughout the region. The term indicates a disparaging view of these individuals, who seem to have been seen as renegades from respectable Anglo society. The local perception, however, was probably quite different. These expatriate foreigners often seem to have been highly respected by local Miskitu people. In fact, they appear to define the proper sort of relationship a foreigner might have with the Miskitu—bringing wealth and expertise, employing local people, leaving a large *kiamp*, and "improving the region." Miskitu identity seems to have been defined in part by such mixture with outsiders.

TRAVELING WITH MISKITU COMPANIONS

Like the foreigners who have come to the Coast, the Awastara people themselves are great travelers. In fact, they seem to be traveling constantly, usually to Puerto Cabezas but also to other surrounding villages. When Victor comes by my house at 4:00 in the morning to go to Páhara, it is still pitch black. He calls loudly and I pull on my clothes and get ready, by the light of the lantern. Our neighbors Rubisu and Nolan are also ready to go. We walk in single file, using our flashlights. As we pass other people's houses, Victor and Rubi call out and hit the sides of the houses resoundingly. "Wake up everybody! Come on to Páhara! Going to a picnic! Free food for everyone!" Not unexpectedly, there is no response from any of the sleepy people inside. As we walk out on the savannah, it finally begins to get light and turns into a beautiful morning. There is a constant stream of conversation and banter. Victor has found a new audience for expounding his plan to populate these open savannahs by bringing African men to marry local women and have lots of children. When we get to the creek outside of Páhara, a three-hour walk, everyone stops to bathe. The men strip down to their underwear, which is as far as modesty allows, and splash in the water. Then everyone puts on a clean shirt for the short walk into Páhara. Bathing outside of a neighboring town, in order to make a "clean entrance" as a visitor, seems to be standard Miskitu etiquette. Writing in 1827, Orlando Roberts (1965: 139–40) noted, "In traveling, they only wear the *pulpera* [Indian costume], but they carry with them, and put on, a suit of their best clothes, at a short distance from the house of the person they mean to visit."

Wearing presentable clothes for visiting is an important value. I run into Victor in the Port market one day. I didn't know he had come to town. He is wearing a clean new pair of pants and a white shirt and new baseball cap, and for a second I don't recognize him. I remember paddling through the lagoon with Bowman, who stepped behind a tree to change into his clean city clothes in Krukira (photo 4). Going to another community is like going to church—one must dress in one's best. William Dampier (1968: 17) mentions the Miskitu concern with clothes in the 1600s: "While they are among the English they wear good Cloaths, and take delight to go neat and tight; but when they return again to their own

PHOTO 4. *Changing into city clothes*

Country they put by all their Cloaths, and go after their own Country fashion. . . ." Thus for many centuries fine clothes have been appreciated by the Miskitu.

THE MISKITU WORLD SERIES

A special opportunity for visiting other communities comes each dry season, when the Miskitu World Series takes place in one of the Coast communities. Baseball is in fact the national sport of Nicaragua. It was introduced to the country in the early twentieth century by the U.S. Marines and rapidly became popular throughout the country. An early commentator (Ham 1916) described the early "baseball craze" in Nicaragua and argued that it promoted goodwill toward the marines and toward relations with the United States in general. Clifford Ham (1916: 188) wrote optimistically: "People who will play baseball and turn out by the

65

thousands to see the match games, are too busy to participate in revolutions. Three cheers for the American marine who is teaching baseball and real sportsmanship!" Baseball today is as popular on the Atlantic Coast as it is in the Hispanic part of the country to the west. Men and boys play it avidly in all the Miskitu communities north of Puerto Cabezas.

During the dry season, from January to May, the long Awastara afternoons are filled with baseball games and practice on the diamond just to the south of the school (map 3). It is a male sport, unlike soccer, more recently introduced, which is also played by groups of teenaged girls, kicking the ball barefooted while wearing their long skirts. Soccer was not played in Awastara in the 1970s but was brought back from Honduras by Miskitu refugees after the war years of the 1980s. It is played on the same field by separate groups of girls and boys during the rainy season when baseball is not being played, in the "off season."

During the baseball months, small boys can also be seen playing baseball around their houses, imitating the men and older boys on the ball field. Boys cut their own bats from tree limbs and play with any sort of ball available, including tennis balls and more or less round pieces of native rubber. Squealing with delight, they hit the ball high up into the mango trees and run around the bases. Commercially made baseball bats, and real baseballs and baseball gloves, are in short supply but are highly prized. Nevertheless, the spirit of the game continues, perhaps somewhat Miskitu-ized, and enthusiastic baseball games can be seen everywhere, as in the rest of Nicaragua.

Toward the middle of the dry season, the adult baseball teams from all the villages on the north Coast—Awastara, Páhara, Sandy Bay, Dakura, Krukira, and Puerto Cabezas—compete in a championship series, which rotates among the different communities.

In 2000 it is held in Awastara, and I am able to see the final games. For days, catboats loaded with flour, rice, soft drinks, beer, fruit, and other food have been traveling to Awastara from Port. Business will be good, preparing and selling food to all the visitors. When I finish my business in Port, I try to get on a boat Monday evening, but it is packed with passengers and I can't get passage. When I finally make it to Awastara, I find the village crowded with visitors, all staying in the churches or at other people's homes. At our house, Divor comes by to visit and angrily tells us he has kicked out the two Dakura boys who were staying at his house, because they were drinking and cussing and fighting all night long.

Casey is sewing frantically on his old manual Singer sewing machine. He has been hired at the last minute to make new team uniforms out of blue material for the Awastara team and is trying to finish them in time for the finals. The series is now narrowed down to the semifinals, with both Awastara and Sandy Bay in the running. But Casey can't finish them in time, and the Awastara team is forced to turn up in a shabby array of uniforms, of all different colors and styles. They seem to symbolize Awastara's inability to work together these days. The Sandy Bay men, in contrast, look elegant in their brand-new red and white uniforms, with nifty caps that say "SANDY BAY" above the bill. They seem to be a prosperous, self-confident team, accustomed to working together.

The championship matches up Awastara against Sandy Bay. I am there with my camera, ready to take pictures of the event. Sandy Bay comes out playing hard, relaxed and confident. The Awastara players, however, are nervous and unsure of themselves. Their behavior matches their ragtag uniforms. We make two errors in the first inning, one committed by my friend Alberto from the Church of God at second base. I walk over to the palm thatched "dugout" between innings and try to get him to shake it off. He is disgusted with himself and simply mutters in reply. Victor's son Lobrito lasts only two innings as the starting pitcher.

As things get worse, the crowd gets more and more disgruntled. Rubisu and others begin yelling, "No good! No good [*use apu*]!" Drunks wander here and there. *Dama* Hilario, normally very polite and restrained, buys me a beer and tries to talk to me in Spanish, but he is so drunk I can't understand a word. Almendáriz is also drunk and wanders over into a crowd of players. The current headman, Marcelo, grabs him by the collar and hauls him back. Cornelio, the old headman, is also drunk and stumbles along close to the left field line. As the game ends, several women and children, frustrated, begin throwing coconut husks and beer cans at the Sandy Bay players, who laugh it off good-naturedly.

To go to the baseball games, the women dress up almost as if going to church. Pamela and Barbara and Eliza all bathe and wash their long black hair and put on their best dresses. It seems to be a major outing. Women don't get away from their houses very often and like to take advantage of the opportunity when it is available. Their normal schedule involves hard work all day long, cooking and washing and taking care of children. Men's attire at the games, however, varies from careful dress, pants and clean shirts worn by older men like Victor and Cornelio, to shorts and ragged T-shirts on others, some of whom are very drunk. Women tend to sit all together, whereas men wander back and forth around the field. As a high-status visitor, I am given a special seat on one of the benches that Victor has borrowed from the new clinic.

We can't hit at all in the championship game, and the final score is a dismal 10–0 in favor of Sandy Bay. Back home, I find that Victor has returned and is very upset about the game. "No use at all! They couldn't do anything right! Just drunks everywhere!" he is shouting. I wander back toward my own house. Then I notice Victor's granddaughter Barbara playing "baseball" with Melvin and Lucas and Nena, and the smaller children, in the front yard. They have a tennis ball and a stick and have marked out home plate and the three bases. I join the game, and we hit the ball and go running, shouting and happy, around and around the bases. We tag each other out, screaming with glee. Barbara, an eighteen-year-old mother, is still young enough to have fun running and squealing with the kids. Then Nachalie (one and a half) comes toddling over, anxious to be held. I pick her up between innings, but that isn't enough. I try fielding with her in my arms, but it's hard to play baseball while holding a tiny girl. Finally it gets too dark to see, and we are forced to quit for the night.

Comments afterward about Awastara's sad performance in the series are interesting. One general observation is that the Awastara boys were all drinking heavily during the series. And how can you expect a drunk team to beat a sober one? It is hard to disagree with this point of view. An accusation also surfaces, however, that the Sandy Bay team buried medicine (*sika bikan*) at the ball field and thus won unfairly. A woman who lives near the field is said to have seen the Sandy Bay players digging a hole underneath the pitcher's mound, very early on the morning of the final game, and burying "something blue," which looked like a small cross. The concept is interesting to me, especially since a Miskitu curer in Port has recently shown me sorcery paraphernalia that she dug up from the patio of one of her patients. Here "poison," an important part of Miskitu health beliefs, even turns up in a baseball game.

THE VILLAGE AND THE CITY

For people from Awastara, Sandy Bay, and neighboring communities, the most common travel destination is Puerto Cabezas. Port is what Gonzalo Aguirre Beltrán (1967) has called a *ciudad real* or *ciudad señorial* (urban power center), from which regional elites dominate a large surrounding hinterland of indigenous villages. In the context in which village people deal with city elites, they are treated very much as an underclass. One day I go to the bank in Port with Victor, to figure out a way to send him money from my account in the United States. The bank director receives me graciously enough but is openly contemptuous of my older Miskitu companion, who does not speak Spanish. We quickly decide not to use the bank for sending money.

In spite of such experiences, Miskitu villagers must travel regularly to the city to sell their products, to buy food and clothes and other commodities, to deal with government offices, to go to school, and to seek health care. The city also reaches out into the countryside, as government officials, health workers, traveling merchants, and others visit the communities to promote their own interests. City elites go most frequently to those communities that have easy access, such as Krukira and Tuapí. The roads to these communities are very poor, but the expensive four-wheel-drive vehicles purchased by international organizations can usually make the trip. Awastara, however, with its problems of access, is visited infrequently.

Difficult as the journey can be, many catboats travel back and forth from Awastara to Port each week. They are usually crowded with passengers. The recognized system is for the boat captain to keep a list of passengers for a day or two before the trip, as people ask for passage. Higher-status passengers, such as pastors from the churches, expect preferential treatment. In spite of the list system, additional passengers usually crowd in, and boats are sometimes dangerously overloaded. In May 1998 a boatload of cargo was lost when a catboat overturned, trying to cross the Awastara bar in the dark. One small storeowner told me that he lost 3,100 cordobas' worth of goods (beans, rice, flour, sugar, nails, batteries)—a heavy loss. Fortunately, no one was drowned.

There are a series of factors that pull people from the villages to the city, as regular visitors and sometimes as permanent residents. For example, after years of serious medical problems, Victor finally decides to go to Port for a prostate operation. He trusts only the one Miskitu surgeon in Port, an unusually capable and skilled physician, to do the operation. As it turns out, Victor has to wait about two weeks for an opening in the operating room and then spends another month recuperating from the surgery. He and his wife and several of their children stay in Victor's sister's half-completed house in Port. This sister lives in Miami but has sent money to build a large house. She and her Florida husband intend to live in it when they retire. Quite luxurious by local standards, it has two stories and a big protective wall in front, but as yet no furniture. Nonetheless, village people like Victor and Plora can sleep on the floor, rest in their hammocks, and cook on a makeshift *kubus* or kitchen stove. Plora and her daughter-in-law Josepina faithfully cook for Victor during his stay. After his operation, Victor rests on a bed in a small building outside the house, with his catheter tube running down into a plastic Chlorex jug. The sister's house, spartan by my standards, provides a very useful place for Victor to stay after his operation, with a door that can be locked and a roof to keep off the rain.

Quite a number of older people from Awastara have moved to Port, to be nearer to their grown children and to have access to emergency medical care. Plora's brother Nolan had a stroke in Awastara while I was living there and had to be carried down to the landing in a hammock, to catch the next boat to Port. Several people are said to have died en route in recent years.

Educational opportunities for children also draw people to the city. The Awastara school only goes to the sixth grade, and relatively few children manage to graduate from it. Those who do must go to Port if they are to continue their educations. Parents must have relatives in Port with whom the children can stay, and they must also pay for food and school uniforms and matriculation fees and other expenses. Schooling for children is thus very expensive for village families. The expectation, of course, is that a child may succeed in school and eventually get a job and help support the parents in return. It is difficult for most families to keep a child in school, but for a few the road to social advancement has led straight to Port.

For young women, the pressure of life in the community can make Port seem especially desirable, with its dancehalls and restaurants and bars and other places to escape from watching eyes. "Too many people can see you around here," comments one young woman friend. Families provide security, but they also restrict young people's behavior, especially that of young women. Mothers try to watch carefully over their daughters' behavior in the village, but that is impossible in Port.

In the early morning hours villagers from up and down the Coast meet at the central marketplace in Port, where they buy basic foodstuffs, clothes, and other necessities. The market is always crowded with Miskitu people in the morning, and this is the time and place to look for a person from your own or neighboring communities. Important messages can be given and received here. At various times friends have given me messages to pass on to other people from Awastara or from Krukira or Dakura. They tell me to simply go look for the person at the market at 7:00 in the morning. The market is also the place to hear news and gossip, as knots of people chat here and there around the market area. Victor always goes to the market in the morning when he is in Port, whether or not he is expecting a specific message. It is the place to be, the Miskitu heart of the city.

There is no Miskitu-language newspaper in Port, but in some ways two local radio stations that broadcast in Miskitu serve the same purpose. They play popular music and also broadcast church services and hymn singing. Most important, for a small fee they will broadcast a message to anyone in the region. From 3 to 4 P.M. most families in Awastara have their radios tuned to the announcements being broadcast on Radio Atlántica. Common notices have to do with the condition of hospitalized family members, deaths in the family, happy birthday wishes, and even instructions on how to meet someone at a given place. If you don't happen to hear an announcement having to do with your family, someone who was listening in will dispatch a child with the news. A late Tuesday afternoon program on women's issues is especially interesting to me, and I try to remember to listen to it each week with Plora and Pamela and Eliza. In general, the Miskitu-language radio stations tie together the whole north Coast in a communication network. They define the Miskitu-speaking region within broadcast distance of Port, since Spanish and Creole English speakers obviously don't listen to broadcasts in Miskitu.

Puerto Cabezas is also a financial center. The one small bank does a booming business, but a great deal of the money coming into the region does not pass through the bank. Victor introduces me to an interesting man he has known for many years, who can cash checks and money orders. This man, in his sixties, is from Waspam, on the Río Coco. He is perfectly trilingual in Miskitu, Spanish, and English, although his elderly mother speaks only Miskitu. A devout member of the Assembly of God, he is well known as being honest and reliable. He also has a very useful connection with the bank, where his oldest daughter is the head cashier. One day over coffee this man explains his business to me. He works with four different companies that specialize in remitting funds from other countries: Servicentro, MoneyGram, Inversiones Mercurio, and Rápido Giros. He makes a 1 percent commission on each transaction. Every month he pays out about sixty to seventy thousand dollars to people in the region. Most of the money is sent from the United States, but money also arrives from *costeños* working in Mexico, Costa Rica, and Guatemala. A meticulous, conscientious man, he shows me the neat, organized notebooks in which he keeps records. There are four other men in town who have similar businesses. I ask how much money he estimates comes into Port each month from family members working elsewhere. He thinks for a while and then estimates perhaps two hundred and fifty thousand dollars in total. This seems like a very large sum to me, for a city of only twenty-five thousand people and its surrounding hinterland. He reminds me that a great deal more may come in through the drug trade, although no one knows how much. But it is clear that these *remesas familiares* (family remittances) are a major contribution to the local economy. Port is thus the financial capital of the north Coast.

In spite of Port's regional importance, for many Miskitu friends Awastara is more attractive as a place to live. There you can have your own house and can plant fruit trees and have animals and not worry about what your neighbors think. *Pri laka,* "you can do what you want." You can enjoy the trade winds blowing in the evening and not be bothered by the clouds of mosquitoes in Port, which breed in the latrines and other standing water sources. There is a rhythm of life in Awastara, built around trips out to the Miskitu Keys to catch turtles, then into Port to sell the turtles and buy supplies, and finally back to Awastara with foodstuffs and other supplies. Family members living in Port provide lodging for the frequent visitors from Awastara. Victor and I, for example, often stay with Plora's sister in Port, since she lives conveniently close to the wharf. In the city as well as in the villages, life centers around kinsfolk.

CHAPTER FOUR

Life in Victor and Plora's Family

The first year I lived in Awastara, I rented a house and lived as a resident investigator, a temporary visitor to the community. When I returned in the 1990s, I came to continue my research but also to live as a community member in the way Miskitu people normally do, as a member of a family. In 1978–79 I watched family life from a distance; now I am right in the middle of it. The pressures, obligations, and joys of being in a family surround me.

Family relations—the web of kinship—can be so all-encompassing in traditional societies that some anthropologists have argued that personhood here is not conceived in terms of individuals, the units that have figured so prominently in Western thinking. McKim Marriott (1976: 111) suggests that people in South Asia are thought of as "dividuals," constantly giving to and taking from others within a social network. Not only food and material items are exchanged but also words and ideas. Rights and responsibilities to others, and the flow of constant interaction expressing them, define what it means to be human. Based on fieldwork in South Africa, Isak Niehaus (2002: 190) adds that such a dividual person can never be expressed as a whole number. Rather, each is constantly being added to and subtracted from through the process of gift-giving. Reciprocity is thus more than a form of economic connection between individuals. It actually defines the composition of each dividual at any given moment, providing a sort of accounting or balance sheet of the current state of social transactions.

This concept seems to explain a great deal about social life in Awastara, particularly relations between kin in a large family such as Victor's. Edward LiPuma (1998: 56–57), however, warns that pushing the concept of the dividual too far causes problems. Individuals do exist as discrete biological entities, and the individual body serves as the referent and signifier for varying concepts of personhood in all societies. I would add that in Awastara each individual, in addition to being immersed in a web of social exchanges with others, is also recognized as having his or her own powerful individual wants and desires, in a very Freudian sort of way. Each individual, even a small baby, has a strong libidinal energy of his or her own, which motivates much behavior, especially that which goes against rules of proper behavior. This libidinal energy is clearly expressed by Tibang the wily rabbit, a major figure in Miskitu folklore. Tibang is always on the lookout for his own personal advantage—social, monetary, and sexual. His exploits are regarded as antisocial but natural—a part of human nature. Tibang's improper, selfish behavior is in fact very funny. Everyone laughs at his exploits, presumably identifying with his individual impulses, not his dividual relations with others. I agree with LiPuma that the concept of personhood, in Awastara as elsewhere, must derive from the tension between dividual and individual aspects of each human being.

As I live in Awastara, I share my dividual self with Victor and Plora's large family (figure 3). Four young couples all live nearby and have recently begun families of their own: Rodrigo and Gladys, Casey and Pamela, Adolpo and Eliza, and Hector and Maura. Plora's brother Nelson lives just down the trail toward Aras Bila, and Victor's brother Pancho lives the other way up the trail toward the village center.

KINSHIP TERMS, NAMES, AND NICKNAMES

One of the first things I have to do is understand the terms by which people call each other and refer to each other in the third person. Victor and Plora call each other *maia* (spouse). The term for siblings of the same sex is *moihka* inflected to *moihki* for *my* same-sex sibling. Thus Victor and Pancho refer to each other as *moihki*, but so do Plora and Sanita (figure 4). The term for opposite-sex siblings (for example, Plora and Nelson) is *lakra*. Victor and Plora call all their children *lupia* (child), regardless of sex. In a similar way, they call all their many grandchildren *mula*. Children refer to their mother as *yaptika* or *mamika* and to their father as *aisika* or *papika*. Grandfather is *dama* (also used respectfully for any older man), and grandmother is *kuka*. Adolpo and his siblings refer to Nelson, their mother's brother, as *tahti*, and he refers to his sister's sons as *tubani* or *tuba* and to his sister's daughters as *yamsika*. Adolpo calls Pancho, his father's brother, *rapika*, and he refers to all of Victor's chil-

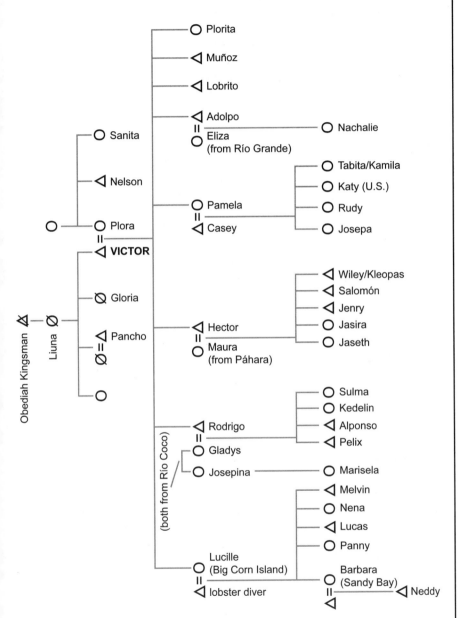

FIGURE 3. *Victor and Plora's family*

Victor	< .... >	Plora = *maia*
Victor	< .... >	Pancho = *moihka*
Plora	< .... >	Sanita = *moihka*
Plora	< .... >	Nelson = *lakra*
Victor and Plora	.... >	child = *lupia*
Victor and Plora	.... >	grandchild = *mula*
child	.... >	mother = *yaptika* or *mamika*
child	.... >	father = *aisika* or *papika*
grandchild	.... >	grandfather = *dama*
grandchild	.... >	grandmother = *kuka*
Adolpo and siblings	.... >	mother's brother (Nelson) = *tahtika* or *tahti*
mother's brother (Nelson)	.... >	sister's son (Adolpo) = *tubani* or *tuba*
mother's brother (Nelson)	.... >	sister's daughter (Pamela) = *yamsika*
Adolpo and siblings	.... >	father's brother (Pancho) = *rapika*
father's brother (Pancho)	...... >	brother's children = *lupia diura*
father's sister (Gloria)	.... >	brother's children = *saiura*
Adolpo	.... >	mother's sister (Sanita) = *antika*
Adolpo	.... >	father's sister (Gloria) = *taihka*
Hector	< .... >	Casey = *waikat*
Pamela	< .... >	Maura = *lamlat*
Maura	< .... >	Eliza = *maisaiya*
Plora and Victor	< .... >	Maura, Gladys, Eliza = *mula yaptika*
Maura, Gladys, Eliza	< ...... >	Plora = *mula yaptika*
Maura, Gladys, Eliza	< ...... >	Victor = *dapna*

This diagram reads as follows: Victor and Plora call each other *maia*. The double-headed arrow indicates a reciprocal term. Victor and Plora call any child of theirs *lupia*, and any child calls his or her mother *yaptika*. These are not reciprocal terms. Rather, the person on the left uses the term indicated to refer to the person on the right, as shown by a single-headed arrow. Farther down, Hector calls Casey, his sister's husband, *waikat*, and Casey uses the same term reciprocally, again indicated by a double-headed arrow. Thus we see Miskitu kinship terms as they are actually used within Victor and Plora's family.

FIGURE 4. *Miskitu kinship terms*

---

dren as *lupia diura*. Gloria referred to Victor's children as *saiura*. They in turn call Sanita, their mother's sister, *antika*, and she refers to them as *lupia diura*. Adolpo and his siblings called Gloria, their father's sister, *taihka* during her lifetime.

Hector and Casey refer to each other as *waikat,* sometimes shortened to *waik. Waikat* translates as brother-in-law (male speaking). Women refer to a sister-in-law as *lamlat.* This is what Pamela and Maura call each other. When two marriage ties are involved, for example, when Maura is speaking of Eliza (two unrelated women married to brothers), they use the term *maisaiya.* Two men married to sisters would also call each other *maisaiya.* Victor and Plora refer to their daughters-in-law, Maura, Gladys, and Eliza, as *mula yaptika* or "grandchildren's mother." They in turn refer to Plora by the same term, *mula yaptika,* but they refer to Victor as *dapna.* Helms (1971: 63–108) provides a detailed description of Miskitu kinship terminology and kinship roles in Asang. The terms are fairly simple, once you understand them and hear them used within a family setting.

Bell (1989: 87–88) reports that the nineteenth-century Miskitu preferred not to use personal names. It is still so today. In Victor and Plora's house only little children are called by name. Even there, the youngest is *plaisni* (youngest child), which also means "my darling" or "my sweetheart." A number of other terms can also be extended beyond their literal meanings. For example, Victor and Plora call each other *kuka* and *dama* (grandmother and grandfather). Victor calls any younger man *tuba* (sister's son) when he wants to emphasize seniority. He and I now call each other *moihka.* Although kinship terms are the preferred way of addressing others, *saiura* and *lupia diura* seem to be infrequently used this way. Names are still regarded as quite personal and not to be told to just anybody. The proper, respectful, yet close way of addressing someone or referring to him or her is with a kinship term. In fact, it is common *not* to know the names of casual acquaintances. Everyone, however, knows the names of powerful or important men in the community, such as Victor, Cornelio, Jaime, and Hilario. In speech, though, they are often referred to indirectly or by nicknames instead of by personal names. Anyone who can trace a kinship tie to them will prefer to use a kinship term.

A name is given to a newborn baby soon after birth. In general, no one wants to have the same name as anyone else, although sometimes people are named after respected senior relatives. People are always searching for interesting names from other places. Ideally, names should be unique—another reflection of the strong Miskitu sense of individuality. In Awastara there is only one Casey, one Cornelio, one Almendáriz. Conzemius (1932: 106) reports foreigners being asked to give names for children in the early twentieth century. In Victor's household, Pamela, who is pregnant, asks me for a list of girls' and boys' names. We sit together one afternoon and I make her a long list of all the names I can think of in English and Spanish. She doesn't really like any of the ones on my list, though, and names the baby Tabita after her husband's sister, who lives in the United States. Names also change frequently as a person grows. Someone coins a nickname or simply begins calling the child by a name he or she likes better. Plora calls little Nachalie (one and a half) Clarita; but nobody else likes this name, and all of us except Plora continue to call her Nachalie.

To a visitor, the fact that a particular person is referred to by multiple names can be very confusing. When I first met him, for example, Maura's small son was called Kleopas, after his dead grandfather. A year later he had become Wiley. Adults, too, are known by multiple names. Maura's husband is called Azo by almost everyone, even though he prefers Hector. Everyone calls the elderly storekeeper (*Dama* Hilario) Carlos Fonseca, the name of a Sandinista revolutionary hero. Hilario wears rimless glasses and vaguely resembles the pictures of Fonseca. I ask myself if the constantly changing names represent a continually changing concept of identity or if they simply indicate playing with identities over time. Casey's sister Tabita tells me, "Whatever you say or do, that is what people will call you." Of course, the playfulness involved in this practice may not be appreciated by the person concerned. In introducing themselves, people always say their formal names, not their nicknames. Others sometimes laugh on hearing firsthand the formal name of someone they only knew by a nickname.

Names apparently have greater significance than in Western culture. They indicate some sort of unique personal identity, and knowing a person's name is the key to having some control over him or her. For example, one curer told me that he had only to know a young woman's name in order to concoct medicine to make her fall in love with a man. One of the techniques of witchcraft is to write the person's name on a piece of paper and bury it where the person walks. And during the *grisi siknis* epidemic in Awastara, the young women affected would call each other's names as a way of causing them to come down with the condition. These uses of personal names indicate some of the reasons why people are cautious about using them and prefer instead the emotionally positive practice of using kinship terms.

Although kinship terms are the preferred form of address, they can be confusing to the visitor as well, requiring quick mental algebra. When a man refers to "my brother" (*yang moihki*) or "my brother-in-law" (*yang waikatki*), I have to think quickly of which brother or which man lives with this man's sister. Teknonymy—referring to someone by his or her relationship to another person—is also thought to be much more polite than using personal names, at least for adults. Helms (1971: 61–63) noted the same phenomenon in Asang. Thus, "Nachalie *aisika*" (Nachalie's father) is more polite than simply "Adolpo."

Kinship relations constitute a huge mental database shared by everyone in the community. In doing a complete household census in 1978, I found that the two young women helping me knew the names, kinship relations, and whereabouts of all the people in the 81 households in town at that time. They didn't know the names of young children, but they knew everyone else, from teenagers to adults. In 1999 as Rodrigo and I work on the village map, I find that he also knows the names of all the adults in each of Awastara's 146 households, even though the community has now doubled in size. He says he also knows the names of almost all the adults in Dakura. When I comment on the tremendous amount of information involved, he laughs and says, "Yes, but I don't know the names of the children." Knowing the large kinship calculus that defines the village seems to be part of what it means to be a community member.

MEN AND WOMEN

The preferred, traditional way of arranging unions is called *maia baikaia*. Mary Kingsman, Casey's sister, tells me how this is supposed to work. When a young man finds a woman about whom he is serious, he asks his parents to go and talk to her parents and ask for their daughter. The couple asking for the young woman should bring gifts. A woman can also request that her parents talk to a man's parents, however. If both sets of parents are in agreement about the match, they talk to the young couple, preaching in the traditional *smalkaia* fashion. They tell the man not to hit his spouse and to provide her with money for food, clothes, bedding, and kitchen utensils—everything she will need. They also tell him not to leave her for another woman. They tell the young woman to obey her husband, to fix the food, and to take care of the house. They tell them to live together until one of them dies. If the man was raised as a Christian and leaves his wife, his parents and in-laws may be able to catch him and lecture him about his mistake, Mary adds. This idealized description of the *maia baikaia* procedure rarely corresponds to reality, however, and probably a minority of unions actually take place this way.

In the case of Victor's large family, other factors intervened. Victor and Plora have lived together for a long time, about thirty years, and they are prosperous and well respected by village standards. They have been able to arrange unions for most of their grown children, although in all cases it has been in a somewhat modified form. Their oldest daughter, Lucile, simply ran away from home when Victor turned down a number of suitors and their parents. After losing his oldest daughter, Victor has worked hard to *maia baikaia* for his other children.

Their son Rodrigo met a girl named Gladys from the Río Coco, whose only close relative was her elderly grandmother. Victor and Plora asked the grandmother for Gladys, on Rodrigo's behalf. Eliza, their son Adolpo's spouse, is from a village far away on the Río Grande. She was living in Awastara with her uncle, who was the preacher at the Church of God, which Victor and Plora attend. They asked their friend the preacher to give away his niece to their son Adolpo. Since both Gladys and Eliza were poor and had few close relatives to support them, it was easy to convince them to come live with Victor's sons near his house. This sort of patrilocal residence is not the pattern that Miskitu women prefer, since mothers and their grown daughters like to live together. But the precarious economic situation of these young women allowed Victor to bring them to his large household. He also actively recruited Casey, the best carpenter and all-round mechanical genius in the village, to come live with his daughter Pamela. Casey had separated from his first spouse and agreed to come live matrilocally. He is a close friend of mine and also built my house near Victor's, with the agreement that he and Pamela could live in it when I am not there.

Maura's union with Victor's oldest son Hector came closest to the ideal pattern described by Mary Kingsman. Maura tells me about it in the late afternoons as we sit on her porch playing with her kids. Maura is from Páhara, some ten miles away. Her parents were very strict and made sure Maura was never alone with boys. In Miskitu, "talking together" is a euphemism for sex. "A girl who 'talks' with a boy and gets pregnant will never find a husband," Maura's parents said. Her father also told her, "When you see a boy you want, tell me and we will *maia baikaia* for you. That way people will have respect for you." But Maura said she really was not interested in any of the boys from Páhara. Her sister would sneak off to the Christmas dances without permission, but Maura would only go to the church services. One Christmas, however, she came to her aunt's house in Awastara for a visit. Her aunt told her that a boy named Hector had seen her at church and was interested in her. He tried to talk with Maura near the church and bought her a plate of food, but she refused it. "I was afraid and ashamed," Maura said. Hector told her he would ask his family to go to Páhara to *maia baikaia* for her.

When Maura returned to Páhara, her mother was absent, staying in Port for a few days. When her mother returned, somehow she had already heard out about Hector' interest in her daughter. "Did you talk with Hector in Awastara?" her mother asked. "No!" lied Maura. "Of course," she tells me, "we really had talked, but not '*talked.*'" Maura didn't believe Hector's parents would actually come to Páhara to ask for her.

But Victor and Plora and Hector did in fact go to Páhara, taking sacks of beans and rice and salted turtle meat, a dress for Maura, and other presents. They asked that Maura come live in Awastara with their son, where he would build her a house. This went against traditional practice, in which many young couples live near the girl's parents' home. Matrilocal residence keeps groups of related women living close together, teaching their children Miskitu language and culture. It is also comforting for women to be close to their mothers and sisters. Maura's mother warned her about one of the practical consequences of not living matrilocally: "If you live in Awastara and have to leave him, you know it will be him that gets the house." To this day Maura's parents are not happy that she lives so far away from them. But, like his father, Hector is a very good turtle fisherman, and his financial success made it possible for him to bring his wife to his own community to live. He has built a large house for Maura and his five children near his father's house. I mentioned to Maura one day that her house was so big that all her children could come live there with her when they grew up and got married. Her sister-in-law Gladys corrected me: "You mean all her married *daughters* will come live with her." Matrilocality is clearly the desirable arrangement for women, although prosperous men would also like to keep their sons at home when they begin families.

Matrilocal residence brings together an older man and his son-in-law as work partners. Early sources (Pim and Seeman 1869: 306–7) report a kind of bride service in which a young man provided for his future in-laws for some time before his marriage. In general terms, young men still provide help for their in-laws during the early stages of a relationship with a woman. A man often expects to live with his in-laws and to help his father-in-law at work. In fact, father-in-law/son-in-law work teams are quite common, and there is a general expectation that such relatives will get along well. They call each other by the reciprocal term *dapna*. A good man, it is said, will help his son-in-law get started on his own after some years. Conversely, a good son-in-law does not forget his wife's father. One young man from Páhara who prospered and bought an outboard motor, for instance, employed his father-in-law as a boatman to carry passengers back and forth to Puerto Cabezas. The strong authority relationship in father-son relationships is replaced by a kind of easy familiarity and an expectation of cooperation between two *dapna*.

Before Casey came to live with Pamela, I listened to a conversation between Victor and several other men about young men who might make good *dapna*. Among the young men mentioned, Casey was especially praised, because he was so hard-working and successful as a carpenter and boat builder. Victor was later able to bring him to his own household as Pamela's spouse, thus "winning the competition" for this desirable young *dapna*.

CASEY KINGSMAN

I am especially close to Casey, whom I have known well since 1978. We both see Victor's family as outsiders to some extent: as a visitor from the United States and as a son-in-law married to Victor's daughter. Casey is quite literally a genius: a master carpenter, a mechanic, a tailor, a man of enormous mechanical and practical talent. He is widely respected for his abilities. He commented on my ragged blue jeans in 1978 and asked me to get him some blue jean cloth in Port. When I brought it back to him, he sewed me a new pair, the exact size and style of my old ones. He regularly builds catboats and houses for clients, fixes chainsaws and outboard motors, and makes ingenious children's toys out of wood. I give him my portable typewriter in 2000, and he practices typing out English lessons from the class he is taking from me. Once, paddling together across the Páhara Lagoon, we watch a satellite tracking across the night sky. Casey asks me how they really work, and I explain what little I know about satellites, but my Miskitu splutters and fails. Casey listens carefully, his inquisitive mind obviously unsatisfied. I realize that had he had the opportunity, Casey could have been a space engineer himself, designing the satellites we are watching.

A quiet man, Casey explains things in a few, simple sentences. He does not tell stories like his father-in-law, but our trips together hunting ducks and deer, and working together in the plantations, give us plenty of time to talk. I come to realize that in spite of his obvious practical genius, Casey has little common sense about saving money and getting ahead in life. After years of building catboats and houses for other people, he does not currently have either a house or a catboat of his own. The money he makes seems to disappear without a trace. Casey doesn't drink or take cocaine and works steadily but has nothing to show for it. His spouse, Pamela, also spends every cordoba she gets. I give her twenty cordobas every day or two for washing my clothes, but she quickly spends it on penicillin injections and other immediate needs. Pamela and Casey seem to have a good relationship, though, spending time together with their three small children and rarely arguing. It hurts my sensibilities to see a man so talented in one area of his life but so improvident in another. His crafty old father-in-law Victor, a man who has prospered by Miskitu standards, just snorts when I mention Casey's problem. Victor wanted Casey as a son-in-law, but he now has to reconcile his financial impracticality with his technical genius.

Victor was unable to bring a son-in-law to live near him for his oldest daughter, Lucile, however. Several young men came to ask for her, but Victor didn't think any of them would amount to much and refused all of them. Finally Lucile fell in love with a lobster diver from Honduras, who came to Awastara to talk with Victor and Plora about marrying her. Victor told him that first he had to build Lucile a house near Victor's. That way, if they did not stay together, she would at least have a house of her own. But the young man wasn't willing or didn't have the resources to do that, so Lucile ran away with him to the Corn Islands, where there was work diving for lobsters. Twenty years later, Lucile is still living with the same man, and they have had eight children together, five of whom she has sent back to Awastara for Victor and Plora to raise. They complain bitterly about the fact that she never sends money to help with child-raising expenses. Victor's early attempts to be strict with his daughter, and make sure she had a responsible man, clearly backfired. In effect, Victor lost his daughter as well as a future son-in-law to help support the family. In the case of his second daughter, Pamela, however, Victor seems to have overcompensated, going out of his way to win his son-in-law Casey's cooperation and support.

In striking contrast to the relaxed, cooperative attitude that is supposed to characterize the father-in-law/son-in-law relationship, the young man's relationship with his mother-in-law is formal and tense. Casey does not address his mother-in-law Plora directly, and it is his wife, Pamela, Plora's daughter, who serves him his food. Conzemius (1932: 147–48) reports a strict mother-in-law taboo among Mayangna people, and a less formal taboo still exists among the Miskitu people of Awastara. A classic explanation of such behavior (Radcliffe-Brown 1952: 92–93) is that a new son-in-law and the kinship unit into which he marries necessarily have opposed interests—a "social disjunction" in Radcliffe-Brown's terms. The potential conflict is prevented by a rule of avoidance that keeps the son-in-law and mother-in-law from speaking to each other. Such avoidance is to be taken as a sign of respect, not open hostility. It serves as a sort of social insulation that prevents "sparks" from starting an open conflict. In this family, Victor himself harbors resentment toward his mother-in-law, illustrating the potentially explosive nature of such a relationship.

Mark Jamieson (2000b) provides another perspective from his own fieldwork in Kakabila. He describes the concepts of "respect" and "shame" that govern certain difficult relationships. For instance, *swira* (shame) can be understood as careful concern about inappropriate behavior—banter or sexual joking—in relationships that should be respectful, especially the relationship between mother-in-law and son-in-law. To avoid giving offense, or what Jamieson (2000b: 314) calls "making a performance 'error,' " a son-in-law simply uses avoidance behavior; he does not speak to his mother-in-law. Thus the Miskitu continue to practice an interesting form of mother-in-law avoidance.

GROOM CAPTURE

From the point of view of adult men, finding good sons-in-law is an important family task. Jamieson (1998) argues persuasively that for several hundred years Miskitu men and families have regarded English-speaking foreigners, in particular, as desirable in-laws and have in fact practiced "groom capture" to secure them as in-laws. "Trade thereby transformed the Miskitus' relations with English-speaking visitors into one of affinity, as the exogamously inclined Miskitu men attempted to secure partners by offering these traders their sisters and daughters, thereby developing institutionalized forms of 'groom capture' through which trading alliances could be secured" (Jamieson 1998: 716).

The ethnohistorical evidence (Roberts 1965: 110) in fact suggests that early English traders, pirates, and others also found such unions desirable, since as in-laws they obtained exclusive trading rights in Miskitu communities. Most were probably occasional visitors, but some undoubtedly settled permanently, to become local patriarchs as Obediah Kingsman was later to do in Awastara. From a modern point of view, it is tempting to interpret relationships between Anglo visitors to the coast and local women as sexual exploitation, but the matter may have seemed different to local people. Using sexual relationships to form ongoing practical ties may have been seen simply as wise strategy: cementing useful relationships by creating kinsfolk. These alliances eventually affected ethnicity. Writing in 1699, M. W. (1732: 288) noted cases of intermarriage, commenting: "indeed they are extremely courteous to all Englishmen, esteeming themselves to be such." If they were not actually Englishmen, they were at least kin to them.

I had a very personal experience with groom capture. When I returned to Awastara in 1998, divorced and without a woman in evidence, Victor suggested that if I were lonely he could find a mate for me. Later, walking back from the landing, Maura and Gladys began teasing me about marrying their father-in-law's youngest daughter, Plorita, then fifteen. It was best, they said, for an older man like me to marry a very young woman and raise a family. Victor himself had done this, bringing Plora to his household when she was quite young. I mentioned that my oldest son had married a woman older than himself, who already had three children of her own. Maura and Gladys said that was a very bad idea, because "no man likes to raise children who aren't his own." I had the clear impression that the family had talked about the possibility of marrying me to Plorita, perhaps without consulting her. I realized that in spite of the teasing they were quite serious. This put me in the perplexing situation of being groom captured myself! I quickly backed away from the situation, although I realized that my close relationship with Victor's family in fact lent itself to groom capture in Jamieson's terms.

Women who go to live with a man early in life may never experience the freedom of being young and single. Maura tells me somewhat wistfully, "I never got to *kirbaia* as a young woman. I went straight from my mother's house to my husband's house and started having babies." *Kirbaia* refers to strolling around having a good time and enjoying oneself. The period of being unattached can be a time to *kirbaia* for a young woman, because, once she has a man, she has responsibilities and must stay near the house, under the watchful eye of relatives. In fact, there is little opportunity to *kirbaia* within the village. Church services and trips to Port offer the only opportunities for escape from the house, to dress up and at least flirt with young men. There are few other opportunities. Elsie tells me:

> If you go *kirbaia* in Bilwi, meet a Spaniard or an American, done! Bilwi has its own secrets. If you have bad luck, maybe you will get pregnant. But when you come here to Awastara, you can't *kirbaia*. The townspeople look down on it, and your mother is here, too. When a young woman is here, she must act like a *señorita!* Paula and I, for example, we can't *kirbaia* here. Well, maybe a little bit at Christmas time. But you could never bring a man home with you, because your mother is there.

Women with spouses usually stay close to their homes, cooking, washing clothes, and taking care of children. At Victor's house, Plora is in charge, *palaia*ing at the children and making sure that the meals are cooked, the firewood is brought, the water is drawn. Her daughter Pamela and daughter-in-law Eliza live in the same house, but I like to think of Plora as the head bosswoman. She is the pillar of the household. Victor is bright but tends to be scatter-brained. He very much depends on his household manager, Plora. The small children all go to her for comfort as well. They call her *mama tara* (big mama), quite an appropriate name. She goes to visit her daughters-in-law Gladys and Maura, who live close by, almost every day. With so much work to do, women just don't have the time to *kirbaia*. A mother trains her older daughters from the time they are small (six or seven years old) to help with their younger siblings. Jaseth, age ten, carries her ten-month-old brother Wiley everywhere, entertaining him, wiping his bottom, and taking major responsibility for him. Women must have a specific reason to go somewhere in the village, and they usually take full advantage of church activities, school meetings, or other public events to escape from household chores for a while. I was quite surprised to find that the young women in my household did not know where various people in town lived, because they had never been to those people's houses. Helms (1971: 67) noted the same phenomenon: women in Asang were sometimes uncomfortable walking in parts of the village where they had never been, but which she herself knew well. Men's activities, by contrast, take them to all corners of a village, and Awastara men are quite familiar with every household's location.

Washing clothes, in particular, is a very time-consuming chore. Any woman with small children spends several hours a day washing. Victor pointed out to me that this is a fairly recent development. When he was a boy, he said, people had a lot fewer clothes, just a set of work clothes and another set of good clothes for church. Children didn't wear diapers then either. Women spent more time working in the fields in earlier days and less time washing clothes than they do today.

SEXUAL RELATIONSHIPS IN AWASTARA

Unions rarely last a lifetime, in spite of the Christian church ideal for marriage. Ongoing unions, whether or not a *maia baikaia* procedure has taken place, are referred to in Miskitu simply as "having a man" or "having a woman" (*waitna briaia* or *mairin briaia*). The understanding is that a couple will live together, have reciprocal economic obligations, have children together, and constitute a new social unit. All adults expect to live this way. Church marriage or legal civil marriage is regarded as a higher level of commitment, since it costs money and involves paperwork as well as potential economic loss when relationships end. Relatively few people in Awastara are actually "church married." Victor tells me he and Plora were only "government married" after their first child was born. I was surprised to learn this fact about these devout churchgoers. After having five children, Victor's son Hector and his wife, Maura, are still not church married either. Church marriage seems to represent the highest possible level of commitment; as in Asang (Helms 1971: 92), it carries considerable prestige. Although most adults live with partners, legally constituted marriage seems to be rare. A few older people, like *Dama* Moreno, proudly refer to being church married and use the term *maridki* (my wife or husband) to refer to their spouse. The common term *maia* simply means mate or domestic companion or partner. Thus most adults have a *maia*, but few people have a *maridka*.

Kissing, holding hands, and other physical signs of affection are not common in Awastara. Young couples talk together as they walk, but they rarely touch each other. Kissing with the lips Western style is not a traditional practice. Rather, the Miskitu practice is called *kia walaia*. This involves putting one's nose next to the other person's cheek and breathing in deeply, thus, as the Miskitu phrase poetically describes it, "listening to your smell." On their birthdays, people of all ages stand up in church on Sunday, so that the congregation may file by and "kiss" them in this fashion, smelling their cheek. Babies and children are "kissed" this way, and adults of both sexes and all ages who haven't seen each other for some time also greet each other in the same fashion. It seems to be thought of as very close and affectionate, but not erotic.

Bell (1989: 86–87) noted that husbands and wives were not expected to be openly affectionate with each other, and this is also true today. A friend of mine, a North American nun who worked as a nurse among the Miskitu of the Río Coco, described the classes that she gave to groups of young married people. She found that the couples were brusque with each other and were embarrassed to talk about the emotional quality of their relationships. My friend lamented what she regarded as a lack of tenderness in marriage, perhaps not taking into account that adult male-female relationships are constructed very differently among the Miskitu.

For one thing, love and affection are expressed in very practical terms, by giving food or clothes or other necessities. These gifts, practical expressions of affection, are carefully remembered. Gladys's four-year-old son Alponso says to me without prompting, "*You* gave me these pants," referring to a ragged secondhand pair of shorts I had bought for him, along with the secondhand clothes I bought for all the other kids. The number and cost of gifts seem to be taken as direct reflections of the degree of feeling involved. Nine-year-old Nena came to me furious one day. "Marisela [her ten-year-old cousin] got three dresses!" she said. It was true. Marisela had gotten two used dresses from the sack of clothes I brought, and I had also bought her a new one, out of gratefulness for her help around the house. Marisela had promptly worn the new dress to church. Nena, who had slept on my floor so many times, had been passed over in favor of Marisela. "Are you going to take Marisela to the States with you?" Nena then asked me, quite seriously. Naively, I hadn't realized how powerful a nine-year-old's jealousy could be. After receiving her three dresses, Marisela brought me a big bunch of mangos, gathered up in her skirt, in *pana pana laka,* the rule of reciprocity.

It is sad, people tell me, for a single adult to have to live without a partner. A woman living alone would have no source of support, and men would have little respect for her. A woman often tolerates a difficult relationship rather than have to live as a single person. Mary Kingsman says:

> A girl by herself with a baby has a very hard time. She can only make a little money by washing clothes for people or cooking for them. When she goes home, her father will remind her how hard it was to raise her. With good luck, maybe a boy from another place will come and like her and want her to live with him. But he may want her to leave the baby with her mother.

Most adults have lived with several partners during their lifetimes. In practical terms, if a husband leaves his *maia* for another woman, the former spouse usually gets the house. Occasionally a woman runs away, leaving the man with the house and children. This happened to Jornel in 1998. A year later, however, his *maia* returned, asking forgiveness and bringing with her another child by the man with whom she had run away. Easy-going Jornel accepted her back.

Victor himself has lived with a number of different women. For twelve years he lived with Rudila, who is now married to Koldero. Uniquely among Awastara women, Rudila put on pants and went to the Keys with Victor to fish for turtles. They got along well, Victor said; but when he found out she was sleeping with other men while he was away, he left her. He then had several other women before meeting Plora, his current wife. Plora was just a young girl at the time, fourteen or fifteen years old. They have now been together for almost thirty years; but Victor says openly that if she leaves him or dies, he will quickly find another woman. When his brother Pancho's wife died, Victor told Pancho to quit feeling sorry for himself and go find another woman. He also tells me about having a daughter with his neighbor Rubisu's wife ("a small mistake"). Overall, Victor has had a colorful sexual/romantic life here in Awastara, and he is not shy about discussing it. He says regarding his nephew, Pancho's son, "How is he ever going to get a woman, just playing on his guitar all the time? A woman wants a house, clothes, and food to eat. She wants a man who will provide that, not someone wandering around all the time plinking on a guitar."

Victor's own marriage to Plora is conflictive, in a way I don't understand until 2000. I go to Plora's sister's house in Port one day in February and to my surprise find Plora there, by herself. She smells my cheek and then says, "Look at what your brother did to me." She raises her shirt to show me the heavy bruises across her breasts. In an angry tirade, she tells me she is going to the police to have him put in jail and to make him pay her medical expenses. I am shocked. I am obviously deep in the middle of a serious marital dispute, one I don't understand. Victor, hitting his wife? I leave Plora some money and return to the village. At the house, I ask Victor what happened. Angrily, he says: "She has never treated me with respect. She is always arguing and causing trouble." His daughter Pamela tells me that her mother cut down one of his favorite fruit trees in the yard, a *pastara* tree that was always dropping fruit and making a mess. When Victor saw the tree stump, he lost his temper and grabbed a stick and hit her. His grown son Adolpo then knocked the branch out of his father's hand and saved his mother from a worse beating.

My own instinct is to try to act as a peacemaker, since I care about both of them and they both call me brother. Victor expects Plora to come back. "Where else can she go?" he says bitterly. About two weeks later I return to Port and go to Plora's sister's house. I give her more money and ask if she wants to return to the village with me. She says yes. When we arrive in Awastara, I walk up the path to the house first. All the children come streaming out, down to the landing, to see their mother and grandmother, the emotional center of our household, our head bosswoman. I sit with Victor on a bench, awaiting Plora's arrival. When she comes up the path, she marches straight past Victor without saying a word, into the house. Things are obviously very tense.

As the days wear on, I notice that the old couple speak to each other very little, except to bicker loudly from time to time. Victor begins sleeping at Maura's and Gladys's houses instead of in his own house. Maura asks me, "If she has my father-in-law put in jail, who will take care of things around here?" I wonder the same thing myself.

Interestingly, the details of the quarrel are known by everyone in town. At his store, *Dama* Hilario asks me, "Well, is Victor still hitting his *maia?*" Cornelio, a bitter enemy of Victor's, tells me that this is no way for a man to treat his woman. I agree but don't want to give Cornelio any more ammunition to use against my own Miskitu brother. The Church of God, to which Victor and Plora belong, is temporarily without a preacher. Unfortunately Eliza's uncle has been transferred to Port. A good preacher, Hector tells me, would come to *smalkaia* at his father and teach the old couple to live together peacefully. No one else has the age or authority to do so.

Over the next several months the quarrel subsides, but the tension remains just underneath the surface. I sit with Victor and Alvarez in the yard, talking, with Plora a short distance away. Something touches off another tirade from Plora, who says she still has the paper to put Victor in jail. Victor just laughs sarcastically. I try to make a joke, saying, "If you put him in jail, you'll just have to go cook for him and take his food to the jail." "I won't take him anything to eat!" she says loudly. Turning to Victor, she says, "My brother Pelipe is the only one who helped me when you hit me. You never sent me a penny." Victor laughs again, nervously this time.

By the time I leave in June, the quarrel is still simmering. No resolution has been reached. I realize that my own friendship with Victor has cooled after the incident. I am caught in the middle, very fond of both Victor and Plora but unable to help them resolve their situation. Victor shows no repentance for what he has done, and Plora remains bitter and angry. The children watch cautiously but do not try to advise or counsel their parents. It is not regarded as their place to do so, even though they are now adults. I am proud of Adolpo for knocking the stick out of his father's hand and protecting his mother. I find the incident similar to many other kinds of Miskitu disputes, in which issues seem to simmer beneath the surface for a very long time, with no resolution or reconciliation occurring. But it is also deeply disturbing on a personal level.

Men and women to some extent live in different worlds, and there is a sort of institutionalized sex antagonism between them. Elsie tells me:

> The Miskitu way is, men are just bad, they're always looking for a younger woman. After a woman has a baby, it's over, her man won't want her anymore. "Drop the old lady, grab a young one" [*kuka swiaia, tiara alkaia*] we say in Miskitu. When a spouse dies, a man always finds another woman, but it's hard for a woman to find a man who will help with the children.

Women fear that men will spend all their money on liquor or drugs or other women and not support them and the family. It is a fear that is well founded. Men, for their part, say that women are never satisfied with what they have and always want more. They are always tempted by a man who can offer more to them in the way of security. "If you're poor," Alvarez told me, "your wife will leave you for someone else if she gets a chance. You can only trust your mother. She's the one you should respect the most." The same sentiment applies to women and helps explain their desire to live matrilocally, close to their mothers. Young men, correspondingly, prefer to find a spouse within their own community, so they can be close to their own mothers. Often this does not happen; and since the man should go where the woman lives, he is forced to live far away from his own mother, an unhappy situation. "Our mother truly loves us," says Roquis, "while our woman just scolds us and is jealous."

Living near the margin, the question of economic security is more important here than romantic love, even though young men compose and sing romantic love songs like "Sirpi Ki Mairin." The game of sex between Miskitu men and women seems to be played around this fact: men get sex from women, and women in return expect support for themselves and their children. Young women can bargain with their attractiveness, but older ones come saddled with children and aging bodies.

A few men in Awastara have an unconventional sexual life: they are flagrantly open homosexuals. The term in Miskitu for such individuals is man/woman, *waitna/mairin*. Renny is one of them. He wears earrings and women's clothing and speaks with effeminate mannerisms. When he stands to recite in church, people in the congregation titter and laugh at his way of speaking. When all the townspeople pull Tito's new catboat down to the landing to be launched, Renny pulls with the women. "Yes, and he squats to pee just like a woman!" says Victor. When the schoolgirl dance team performs for independence day on September 14, Renny demonstrates even fancier dance steps for them, in front of the whole town. Renny takes part in all aspects of community life, parading his own gender choice in the process. And although he may be ridiculed, he is also accepted. On his birthday he stands in the front of the church, following the local Moravian custom, as the congregation sings "Happy Birthday" to him. Each of us then passes by to congratulate Renny and smell his cheek. He has his hair done up in a woman's braids, and he cries from emotion at the congregation's care and concern for him.

Two of the other homosexual men in town brew *chicha* and sell it every week in Awastara. Their neighbors say they use the *chicha* as a way to entice young men to drink with them and then provide them with sexual services in return for money—a sort of male prostitution. Many people, both male and female, express strong antihomosexual sentiment. *Dama* Rubisu says: "They should be whipped and driven out of town! They ruin the town, and they bring bad luck!" But in spite of these sentiments, the men in this same small group have been open about their homosexuality over the twenty years I have known the community. In fact, they seem to take delight in being outrageous and getting away with it. Flaunting sexual norms, these men provide one example of the strong sense of individuality so prized in Miskitu culture.

LOVE SONGS

An interesting aspect of courting behavior is composing and singing love songs. Young men write and sing them, usually accompanied by a lilting merengue-type beat on the guitar. They are often heard nowadays on the radio. Christian hymns, which are universally known and sung, have not replaced this traditional musical form. For example:

Sirpi Ki Mairin	(Little Darling Girl)
Sirpi lupia mairin,	Little darling girl,
absulki mairin,	beautiful woman,
Mani kumi dukiamra, nara na balri	Yours alone, I came here.
Man mamikamra mamkabi walri	I asked your mother for you,
Mamikam bui man tamwan	But she, for love of you,
wisi laui ai munan.	quarreled with me.
Sarki na tilara kli taui wari	Amidst my sorrow I went back again
Pyu kum na yuara, awalkam bilara,	One day, up the river where
kaubi ni wari	you live, I went paddling [in my canoe]
Ukata mairin kan, mamkabi walri	I asked the woman of the spray
Sirpikam aihka, nahwala kata ba	Where is your little one that was here yesterday?
Nak bal win.	She came this way, it was said.

This song is sung throughout the Miskitu country and is the most widely known of all the Miskitu love songs. It has many, many verses, with new ones continuously being invented, as the merengue rhythm repeats itself on the guitar. The theme is a rejected young suitor, sad over the loss of the young woman with whom he is in love. It is interesting that the person who rejects him is his girlfriend's mother and not her father. It is the mother who figures prominently in Miskitu sentiment and who must be consulted on the most important decisions in the household. Curiously, the expected exclamation when one is hurt or wounded or in trouble is "Ay, Mother!"

Other students of Miskitu life (for example, Young 1847: 77; and Helms 1971: 86–87) have also published love songs. Bell (1989: 88–91, 312), with his characteristically acute observational skill, actually recorded texts of love songs in Miskitu and published them with commentary and English translation. Bell comments that Miskitu love songs are plaintive and sad, which is true, although there are other kinds of songs about other subjects, including the natural world. Many love songs are notable for the delicacy and imagination of their lyrics. Thomas Young (1847: 77–78), an early visitor to the Coast, introduces a song by saying, "The following are the words of a song, emanating from the wild, rude, and uncultivated heart of a savage." He then translates the song as follows:

> Dear girl, I am going far from thee. When shall we meet again to wander together on the sea side? I feel the sweet sea breeze blow its welcome on my cheek. I hear the distant rolling of the mournful thunder. I see the lightning flashing on the mountain's top, and illuminating all things below, but thou are not near me. My heart is sad and sorrowful; farewell! dear girl, without thee I am desolate.

This beautiful song hardly indicates "the wild . . . uncultivated heart of a savage"!

These popular songs that speak of romantic love and draw poetic images of the natural world are a traditional genre of literature, like the bawdy fables called kisi. Both are considered profane by some pious Christian Miskitu. To them, hymns are the proper form of singing. When I first started collecting songs from the young men in the evenings, one older man told me they were "bad" songs and then strode angrily away. My friend Ramsley, the health leader in Dakura, told me wistfully that he had enjoyed playing the guitar and composing such songs when he was young, but since he had occupied the position of Helper in the Moravian church, he only sings religious songs. To my sensibilities, however, the "profane" popular songs involve more artistry and are more pleasing than the loud and often off-key hymns sung in the churches.

YOUNG CHILDREN

Most babies in Awastara are born at home, with one of the eight local midwives in attendance. Of these, Miss Porla has the most experience, having delivered hundreds of babies over a lifetime of work. She proudly says she delivers not only human babies but calves, colts, any kind of baby. After giving birth, women must be especially careful. They are vulnerable to "cold" and should stay in bed, underneath a mosquito net, for nine days, with a cloth wrapped around their head. In Miskitu thought, "cold" is a major cause of disease. Women should always wear a cloth on their heads in the early morning as they go to the plantations and should be careful about washing clothes in the cold creek water. According to Porla, for example, Gladys did not obey the rule about nine days in bed and would not stay inside her mosquito net. Porla says that's why "cold" got to her and later caused her bad breast infection. Gladys is from the Wangki or Río Coco region, and "those Wangki women are like that, right down there in the creek washing clothes, soon after giving birth. What kind of way is that to behave?" says Porla. "But then those women die young, too," she adds.

Another condition affects newborn babies and often kills them. It is called *wasakia munaia,* and I didn't understand it until 1999. When Eliza's baby Nachalie was born in 1998, I visited mother and child soon after the birth and took pictures for them. Neither Gladys or Pamela, however, would go into the room where Eliza was resting under her mosquito netting, with a cloth tied around her head. I thought this strange at the time; but I learned the following year that it was because either or both of them might have been pregnant and thus might have given *wasakia* to little Nachalie.

A baby with *wasakia* may vomit, bleeds from the umbilicus after birth, won't nurse at the breast, and stiffens and contorts his or her back. The symptoms sound very much like those of neonatal tetanus (Werner 1985: 182–84). By the time the baby's umbilicus has healed, however, in two or three weeks, there is no further danger of *wasakia.* It is during the first month of life, when the umbilicus has not yet healed, that the baby is in danger. One main cause of *wasakia* is believed to be a pregnant woman visiting the newborn baby. During the first two months, a woman may not realize that she is pregnant and may go to see a relative or friend with a new baby. Thus she may give *wasakia* to the child inadvertently. To be safe, some women hide their babies and won't show them to visitors. A woman may also tie a piece of cloth around her waist as a prophylactic, to prevent harm to the baby. "Our eyes are hot" (*wan nakra lapta takisa*) when a woman is pregnant, Eliza tells me. In Miskitu thought, this seems to be the mechanism that causes *wasakia*.

I ask Miss Porla, with her midwife's training, what she thinks is the cause of neonatal tetanus, a major killer of newborns in poor countries (Bastien 1994). "Putting dirty cloth on the wound after cutting the umbilicus," she answers promptly. I ask her, "Might not some women think that tetanus is *wasakia munaia*?" "Of course they do," she replies, "but they're wrong!" Porla is never hesitant about expressing her own strong opinions. It becomes clear to me that a good intercultural public health program might be able to help Western health professionals and Miskitu women better understand each other's concepts and thus provide improved health care for newborn infants.

Nursing seems to go on well past one year. I ask the young women in our household how long they nurse babies. About six months, they all reply. But I can see that Nachalie is still being nursed at seventeen months, Kamila at fourteen months, Sulma at about thirteen months, and Leonel at twelve months. The "six months" figure seems to be something that local women have been told by health-care workers in Port. The reality is quite different and could only be discovered through fieldwork. It probably works to the babies' benefit by providing nutritious breast milk for a longer period.

In Awastara children are nursed quite openly, without embarrassment. There seems to be little erotic importance attached to the breasts, as opposed to the thighs and the genital area. Both men and women are extremely modest about exposing the genital region. Men swimming together in the ocean or bathing together in creeks always wear shorts and keep their genitals carefully hidden. Older sources report the same sort of modesty in the pre-Christian past (Bell 1989: 261). Older people say that a man who saw another man's wife's thighs had to pay the husband a fine, thus stressing how strongly modesty was defended. In all my time among the Miskitu, I have never seen either an adult man or an adult woman naked. The missionaries must have been very gratified by this sense of modesty in a "savage" people. But it does not apply to the breasts.

Many young mothers also buy powdered milk for their babies and begin to bottle feed along with the breast feeding, even though powdered milk is expensive. Children are given soft adult foods (for example, mashed-up beans and rice) by the time they are able to sit up. At one year old, little Nachalie loves sitting beside me so that she can share my scrambled eggs in the morning. She has her own small bowl by this time and greedily eats my greasy scrambled eggs with her fingers, as I spoon them into her bowl of beans and rice. "Numm! Numm!" she tells me loudly.

I sit with Maura on her porch one day, as she is nursing her baby, Wiley. Her son Jenry (one and a half) is standing nearby watching his baby brother nurse from the breast that so recently belonged to him. He is really upset; his face is contorted with rage. Maura and the older children simply laugh at him. Maura comments that Jenry is being jealous, *snikwaia* in Miskitu. It happens all the time, Maura says, and in fact sometimes people know the mother is pregnant again when the youngest child begins to show signs of jealousy. Even though the mother is not yet visibly pregnant, the jealousy of an older sibling is a sure sign of her condition. Children who are acting jealous are not consoled in any way; they are just left to work out the problem by themselves.

Toilet training, such a major event in the middle-class United States, happens almost unnoticed in Miskitu households. Small babies wear diapers, contributing to the huge wash loads women do, but mistakes by older toddlers are easily and quickly cleaned off the board floors. As I sit in the kitchen talking to Pamela and Eliza, little Nachalie, one, is toddling across the floor. Suddenly she pees through her little dress onto the floor. Eliza wipes it up and changes her dress. I ask Pamela if children are taken out to the bushes to learn toilet habits. She and Eliza laugh. "No, they just learn by themselves, watching older children. We don't do anything." Pamela adds wryly, "We just wash clothes all the time." Months later, I notice Nachalie, now one and a half, at the bottom of the front steps. She has managed to get her underwear down, has successfully pooped, and is struggling to get her underwear back up. Plora notices her and yells loudly, "Nachalie is pooping!" Eliza comes running and grabs Nachalie to take her to the bathhouse and clean her bottom. Meanwhile, the chickens are greedily devouring the poop. Nachalie has learned all on her own about going outside, pulling down her underwear, squatting, and pooping. Pretty good for her age! I remember my own children's struggles to get to the toilet.

CHILDREN GROWING UP

Miskitu child-raising emphasizes the independence and resilience that characterize adult Miskitu personalities. When a child howls and cries, he or she is left to work it out. There is little coddling or show of sympathy; nor are there attempts to divert or hush up the child. When an iguana bites Gerlinda's six-year-old son Roy on the finger, he comes running to his mother with his bleeding finger, sobbing and crying. "I told you the iguana would bite, but you didn't listen to me. He can just bite you again!" his mother says. On another occasion, Aaron, Roy's brother, cuts his finger badly while carving a wooden boat. Rather than showing sympathy, his mother says, "Hush up while we put some iodine on it!" Howling children, miserable over not getting their way, are simply left to their own devices. The independence so remarkable in the Miskitu character is thus inculcated early.

I watch little Neddy (just over a year old) playing in Plora's kitchen with his small cousins. Neddy's mother Barbara is Victor's granddaughter and is visiting from Sandy Bay. Tabita (one and a half) hits little Neddy hard on the head, and he starts screaming and crying at the top of his lungs. "Who hit you?" his mother asks. He points at Tabita. "Then hit her back!" Barbara commands. So he totters over and tries to hit Tabita. Everyone laughs hard in appreciation. Individualism here means defending yourself aggressively.

This theme of individualism seems to run contrary to reciprocity, the *pana pana laka,* which requires Miskitu people to share whatever food they produce with others and to work cooperatively. Both principles coexist—individualism and reciprocity. Everyone seems to think the old *pana pana laka* is the right way to behave, but it contends with a fierce individualism and a willingness to defend one's own interests as vigorously as possible. Adults are notoriously independent. A common response to a question about how Miskitu people do something is: "Half do it this way, and half do it another way. Each person has his or her own way of thinking [*selp lukanka brisa*]." The Miskitu themselves make fun of their own propensity to squabble. The members of Victor's family grab wildly for the pile of clothes I bring as Christmas presents, each of the five women in the family snatching clothes for her own children in a sort of free-for-all. Rodrigo comments later: "We Miskitu are like the *sumpiki,* the man-of-war birds, who scream and fight with each other over a single piece of fish." People laugh at themselves over their habit of arguing so much, but they keep right on arguing.

Children are often scolded to be quiet or to behave. They expect adults to *palaia* at them; and although they must listen, they often disregard what the angry adult says. Children thus find themselves in power struggles with their parents. They learn passive resistance in the face of scolding, because this strategy is more likely to be successful than disrespect toward an angry adult. In 1978 Gerlinda, Roy, and I walked past her mother's house, on the way to cut firewood. Little Germán (three years old) wanted to come with us, but Gerlinda had told him he couldn't. He came running down the path naked, ran past us twenty feet, stopped, and took up a defensive position with a stick, waving it angrily. Several older children came running down the path, fought with Germán and subdued him, and dragged him back to the house. His mother just commented casually, "It was too far for him to walk." Sometimes children's independence results in them following their mother across the village, even though the mother has told them they can't come. As I am talking on my porch to Elania one day, her small children come straggling up behind. She apologizes but says there is nothing she can do about it. "They just came on their own," she adds.

Occasionally children are whipped for misbehavior. I watch as my neighbor Rubisu whips his six-year-old granddaughter Melcie with a piece of plastic, raising it high above his head and bringing it down with full force. Melcie screams in pain, and the sound of her screams carries through all the neighboring yards and houses. Rubisu shouts angrily as he whips her, although I can't make out the words. I am sitting with Maura and her children, who all become very quiet and serious. Whipping is a traditional sort of punishment for children and is regarded as appropriate for creating well-behaved adults. Teachers at school whip children with small green sticks, stripped of leaves. No one considers it child abuse. But there are people who don't believe in whipping. Nine-year-old Jaseth, Maura's daughter, tells me she doesn't get whipped and she won't whip her own children either. I sympathize with Jaseth, my little friend. As with much of Miskitu culture, one possible source of whipping may have been Anglo patterns introduced by pirates, traders, and Anglo residents over the years. It was, after all, only in the twentieth century that whipping came to be regarded as improper in the Anglo world.

The other side of rough independence training is special concern for children when they are sick. One day little Jenry (four) is bitten on the hand by something in the grass as he plays. It swells up badly, and Jenry runs a high fever. His father, Hector, does not go to the Keys that night as planned, in order to sit up with Jenry. I cut Ibuprofen tablets in two to give the little boy, to help with the pain. Victor also stays home from deer hunting to be with his grandson. The two grown men, father and son, sit huddled together over the small boy all night, worried and trying to think of some other way to help. Hector, in particular, is a very conscientious father who is always concerned about his children.

Around my house, children play all day in small groups, which include both boys and girls of various ages. As I sit on my porch writing in my notebook, eight small children come by to watch me do the wonderful things I do (writing and reading). Marisela has little one-year-old Sulma

PHOTO 5. *Kids playing in front of my house*

on her hip, and Josepa (seven) has ten-month-old Kamila. Girls of this age are completely entrusted with the care of their small siblings. Little boys go entirely naked up until the age of six or seven, but little girls always wear their underwear, even before they begin to walk. This has to do in part with the modesty expected of females and in part with the theories of illnesses that females are believed to suffer when foreign substances enter the vagina. Before the children come by my porch, they have been sitting on a log some distance away, singing church hymns for a long time. When mangos or cashew fruit or oranges are on the trees, the children spend hours climbing into the trees or shaking the fruit down. In photo 5 Nena (in the colorful shirt) holds onto Rudy, while Marisela, as usual, carries Sulma on her hip. Jenry and Salomón don't put on pants unless they're forced to. Behind them stand Kedelin and Alponso, both wearing underpants. Older groups of boys are often busy chasing animals, usually horses or pigs. They carry coils of rope and practice their roping skills. A common sight is a group of three or four ten-year-old boys madly chasing after the dogs as they corner a pig, with one or more of the boys twirling his loop around his head and roping the pig. The pigs are released later, but many wind up with cauliflower ears from the dog bites.

I watch Nachalie (one and a half), Tabita (one), and Josepa (seven) playing outside my house with a ball. Suddenly Nachalie screams and cries. They haven't hurt her. They have just taken her ball away from her. She screams and screams then gets up and toddles over to try to get it back. Josepa giggles and runs away with the ball. The play is rough—rolling and tumbling and hitting each other. The children cry in frustration as much as they do in pain at being hurt. When Josepa takes a puppy away from Nachalie, she screams. Victor yells, "Give it back to her!" But nobody pays any attention. One learns very early to defend oneself from others.

Adults enjoy watching small children and take delight in their behavior and also in their independence and toughness. On one occasion I sit with my family watching as a small child comes sneaking up on a sleeping dog. When the dog jumps, it is uproariously funny, and everyone laughs for minutes, including me. The Miskitu not only like to argue but also like to laugh, and their sense of humor is infectious. Almost anything—people, animals, children's behavior—is fair game. When there is a moment to sit and relax, someone will often begin to tell a *kisi* about the hilarious exploits of Tibang, the trickster rabbit. And even though they argue frequently, the Miskitu also laugh at themselves for their own habit of arguing so much.

Older children do most of the household errands, going to one of the twelve small stores in town to buy food, matches, kerosene, and other daily necessities and carrying messages to other households. Older girls work constantly, taking care of younger children and washing clothes with their mothers. Older boys are quite independent, entertaining themselves by catching animals, fishing, and playing baseball. Lucas (ten) also goes to school in the afternoons; but he is unusual, since school attendance in general drops off after the first two grades.

There are limits to boys' independence. One evening Lucas doesn't come back. It is an hour after sunset, and still no sign of Lucas. The whole household is worried. What can have happened to him? I hear lots of loud, worried talk by Victor and Plora and Eliza and others. Eliza borrows my flashlight to go with the others to look for him. Apparently Lucas has gone to the beach with two other boys and someone's uncle. I become worried about Lucas too. He has always been very helpful with my own errands, and we have become close friends. I even bought him a new pair of blue jeans at Christmas. I finally go to bed but ask Victor about him the next morning. Victor laughs. Lucas came back from the beach a couple of hours later. There was no problem, just some boys having a good time and forgetting about the hour. "I should have whipped him," Victor says, "but I just lectured him [*smalkaia*] and let it go at that." Apart from physical dangers, creatures like the *wahwin* are abroad at night and may hurt someone far from home. Boys are at risk of playing far away and getting lost, but girls are not. Girls are required to stay close to home and have to ask permission to go farther away. When *Dama* Rubisu angrily whipped his granddaughter Melcie, it was apparently for having gone all the way to the landing without permission.

RAISING GRANDCHILDREN

Many young women in town have jobs in Port or are living elsewhere with a *maia*. Increasingly, grandparents are raising their children. I knew Victor and Plora's oldest daughter Lucile in 1978–79 but have not seen her since she ran away to the Corn Islands with a lobster diver. I ask about her in 1997 when I return and learn that four of the children in the household are Lucile's. Her daughter Barbara (eighteen) is now living with her spouse in Sandy Bay. None of her children remember their mother very well, since she has never come back to visit. She does send a large suitcase of clothes while I am in Awastara. When I plan a visit to the Corn Islands, Victor asks me to look for her and give her a message: "Tell her to come home. It's been too many years that she's been on Corn Island. We have raised five of her kids. She hasn't sent any help [money] at all for raising them. Tell her that her father says to come home. Now!"

I find Lucile's house on Big Corn Island, but she is not home. On the second visit she is waiting for me. I have imagined Lucile as being reasonably well off; because she has a lobster-diver spouse and has stayed away from home for years, I have assumed she must be doing well. Nothing could be further from the truth. She lives in an old, run-down, rented company house with her three youngest children. Her spouse drinks up everything he makes diving, she says. There isn't much money left for the family. She hasn't sent anything to help raise her other children simply because there isn't anything to send. We sit watching the rain drip through the leaky old roof onto the floor. I pass along her father's emphatic message. To my surprise, she says that she will in fact come home in May. She gives me a backpack and 200 cordobas to take to her oldest daughter, who is studying in Port. When I finally get back to Awastara, Victor asks, "That backpack, was it empty or full of clothes?" "It was empty," I answer. The question is a telling one. I relay the message about Lucile coming home in May, but her sister Pamela snorts and said "*Kunin!* [a lie], she won't come." And by June when I leave Awastara, Lucile still has not come home.

LETTERS HOME

I often serve as letter carrier for people in Awastara and occasionally write letters for older people who can't write. An elderly neighbor now deceased dictated the following letter to his daughter in Managua in 1978:

> Everyone here is doing all right, and I thank you for the money you sent. Twice you sent money. I received it. I hear there is some trouble over on that side, the war business. I want you to spend Christmas here with me. You said you will spend Christmas there, but I don't want you to. I want you to be here in Awastara. I can't write, so I can't be sending you letters all the time. I can't even get to Port. I tell you one thing, all my clothes are old and torn, so you can be thinking about that. Everyone says, Hello! Hello! Mother and Dad and all the children send you kisses. Your sister is still sick, you know. She also wants to see you, she says. Your brother sends greetings and also wants to see you. An American friend is writing this, his name is Pelipe. The king play is also being done. Try to bring some king clothes or decorations. That's all.

The letter was very emphatic about wanting this man's daughter to come home, using the same tone Victor used toward Lucile. Nevertheless, neither daughter actually came. Later the letter writer told me that he should have said that her mother was sick. Then she would have been sure to come home. He was willing to trick her a little bit to get her to come. He also asked her pointedly for new clothes. At this juncture he was ready to stop dictating, but others in the family chimed in, all wanting to send greetings. The Miskitu letters I write and read are not intended to communicate subtleties of thought or feeling but rather crucial practical messages: Come home! Send money! I am very familiar with such letters from my own working-class relatives in the United States.

THE END OF LIFE

I sit with *Dama* Moreno, now eighty-six, and talk with him for a couple of hours. I knew him well in 1978–79. I ask how he and his wife are getting along. "It's very hard," he says. His grandchildren and great-grandchildren don't come around much. "Our relatives just throw us away," in his own phrase. One son sometimes brings kerosene and sugar and other necessities, but the other son who lives nearby rarely visits. Moreno was out gathering firewood in the brush yesterday and fell down. He shows me his scrapes and cuts. Relatives and self-reliance are the only ways to get by as one gets older. Victor himself is retired from turtle fishing now; but his two grown sons, Hector and Adolpo, have inherited his boats, and they give him a share of each catch. Victor's daughter-in-law Maura tells me that Victor helped his own mother and father when they were elderly. Therefore, she says, his own children will also help him. But Victor's brother Pancho didn't help his parents, says Maura, and so his own children—knowing that—won't help him either. Here love between relatives translates directly into financial support. Kinship is the way that people survive.

One day I watch Eliza going through her father-in-law's hair with her fingers. I assume that she is looking for lice. She laughs and tells me no, she is actually looking for white hairs (*pihwan*) and pulling them out of Victor's head one by one. Victor says his daughters-in-law love him. This is an affectionate thing to do. White hairs are thought to be unattractive, and people also insist that they itch, so pulling them out of elderly relatives' hair is a welcome favor.

Plora's mother is in her eighties and has been very sick. She has not eaten much for fifteen days. I go over to see her with Plora and take a picture of her for the family. She is lying on a cot in the center of the room, with several of her middle-aged daughters gathered around her. The skin on the old woman's arms and hands is paper thin, with brown blotches on it. Her eyes are clear, but she is very weak. She smiles a little when I speak to her. I sit on a chair beside her for a while, holding her hand. She seems very peaceful and resigned to dying. She is apparently in no pain. I think of my own mother and grandmother, who had the same brittle skin and thin old arms in advanced age. Plora's mother seems to be dying a good death. Plora says she is a Christian and knows she will rise from the dead when Jesus returns. The pictures turn out well and are much appreciated. Amazingly enough, two months later the old woman has recovered, is eating well, and is apparently back to normal.

Victor tells me a sardonic story about this mother-in-law of his, explaining how the old woman can be so tough. "She's a devil woman!" he says. When she was young she met a young man from Port, who had a good job working for a company, wearing a uniform and doing "pencil work." But when he met up with the devil woman, she took him back to Awastara and put him to work in the plantation with her there. She would make him get up at 4:00 A.M. to go to the fields.

That woman was like a machine! She must have cleared fifteen different fields, all on her own, with her husband helping her. They would work hard all morning, then she would give him a fifteen-minute break, and then—back to work! She never gave the poor man any rest. Work, work, work. Sometimes they would sleep out there, in a little hut they built at the plantation. In the dry season, she would make him dig in the mud for *mas mas*, until he was covered in mud up to his eyes. She worked the poor man so hard he died young. He didn't realize he had met up with a devil woman!

According to Victor, this all explains how she could seem to be dying but then recover from her recent illness. "That poor man died a long time ago," he says, "but the old woman is still going strong." I reflect again that toughness has to be one of the essential traits of the Miskitu.

Victor himself has always seemed indestructible to me: the tough, friendly senior man, a master seaman. He is getting older too, though. Coming back to Awastara from Port one night, Victor sits up all night steering the catboat while everyone else sleeps. In the morning his oldest son, Hector, takes over the tiller while his father rests. I comment that we haven't made much progress up the coastline. In a quiet voice Hector tells me that his father got mixed up during the rain squalls in the night and wound up steering us back toward Port. Later, at the house, Victor admits that a cross-wind confused him and turned him around. At sixty-eight, Victor has retired from going to the Keys, and his eyesight is failing. He is well aware that he may not have many years left to live himself.

Rodrigo takes me to visit a family on the *lalma* side whose young baby has just died. Many people have gathered. Inside the house, the young mother is singing her lament for her dead child, her *iningka*. I go inside to pay my respects and leave a small amount of money. The family is desperately poor, and I will later give the husband a small job chopping weeds around my house with his machete. The mother is sitting beside the dead infant, which is covered with a sheet. One of the relatives asks me to take a picture of the dead child for the family and lifts the sheet so I can take the photograph. The mother does not stop her lament. I listen carefully and can understand most of the words, which she is improvising as she sings, about her sadness at the child's death. This is the second infant she has lost in this way. In 1979 I watched as a mother jumped into the grave dug for her teenaged daughter who had just died and had to be pulled out so the burial could take place. These laments or dirges are expected of women at the death of a relative. Many visitors to the Coast have commented on them, including Bell (1989: 90):

> If the death is sudden, or the deceased a person very dear to them, the mothers and sisters make persistent attempts to injure themselves by throwing themselves into the fire, banging themselves against the house-posts, hanging or drowning themselves; but they are always watched and prevented. Having been frustrated in this heroic sort of mourning, they settle down to the regular form of it for two weeks . . . they seat themselves on the ground, throw a cloth over the head, and, moving the body, begin a sort of crying song or dirge. After this period, mourning is continued for about a year whenever the bereaved woman is sad or is reminded of the dead. In every large village, no sooner has the sun set than one is sure to hear, amid the laughter and play going on, at least one woman take up the wail for the dead.

It is interesting that expression of grief in these stylized but nevertheless heartfelt ways is so strongly gendered among the Miskitu. It would be unseemly for a man to mourn in this way, but it is expected of women, particularly mothers. Since a mother's love is regarded as the strongest of all possible emotional attachments, it is appropriate that one's mother sing at one's death.

Jamieson (2000a: 91), in a very interesting analysis, calls the death lament "a poetic tour de force," densely packed with images of separation and bereavement and with preoccupation about the danger from the dead person's soul or *isingni*. He points out the connection between body images in the Miskitu language (heart, face, mouth) and emotional closeness. Both are expressed linguistically in a particular inflection of all the nouns referring to the dead person. Jamieson also notes the social function of the lament in reintegrating the community after someone's death. He mentions that death laments seem to have changed very little in the 150 years since Bell (1989: 91, 312) recorded one, and, in fact, M. W. (1732: 295) mentioned them in 1699.

People in Awastara described to me the older custom of taking the dead person's soul or *isingni* from the house where death occurred to the graveyard, to prevent the *isingni* from molesting the remaining family members. This was formerly the responsibility of the *sukia* or shaman. Conzemius (1932: 158), Ana Rosa Fagoth (1999), and others give quite detailed descriptions. I never observed the practice in Awastara, however, and I think it must occur very infrequently these days.

105

The Awastara cemetery is near the ballfield (map 3), roughly divided into *lalma* and *muna* sections. When I visited it in 1978–79, people were buried in wooden coffins in simple graves dug in the ground, with a cross erected over each grave. Graves seemed to be tended for a short time after the death and then gradually abandoned. There were no cement tombs. But by 1999 everyone who can afford it buries relatives in a cement tomb above ground. The cost is 3,000–4,000 cordobas ($250–$335)—expensive but not out of reach for wealthier members of the community. In the new system, the coffin is nailed shut and placed inside the cement tomb, which is then closed with a cement seal. Victor had one made for his sister Gloria, a close friend of mine. He asks if I didn't have a cement tomb built for my mother when she died in 1991. He assumes that cement tombs would be preferred by people in the United States who can afford them. In Awastara they make it easy to locate the burial places of the people I have known. Many earlier graves, even of well-known people in local history such as Obediah Kingsman, are now abandoned and difficult to find.

Victor's brother Pancho explains the appeal of tombs to me in a very moving way. His wife of many years died not long before I arrived in 1999. I took a picture of her and Pancho together in 1998, which Pancho displays prominently in his house. Pancho's wife told him that she didn't want a tomb. It would be too hot, she thought. But Pancho kept thinking of her body in the ground, with the heavy rains and the coffin disintegrating and her body decaying. It made him feel terrible to think of her that way, he tells me. So he had a tomb built for her and still owes most of the money for it. As I loan him money toward his debt for the tomb, he tells me, "Now I can go and see my wife's tomb and know she's in there, and not lost in the cemetery, her body gone forever." The feeling in the wiry old man's voice is apparent. It is important to him to know his wife's body is right there inside the tomb and not lost in the ground. Pancho thus explains to me one reason why people are willing to build these expensive tombs, which seem a luxury, given that daily subsistence is such a constant concern.

CHAPTER FIVE

Food and the Search for *Upan*

Traditionally, many Miskitu subsistence needs were met by hunting and fishing and by raising crops such as cassava and plantains in small swidden plots, called "plantations" in Creole English. Today fishing and hunting are still prized arts, which men pursue whenever they have time away from other work. Deer are hunted in the forest and on the savannah, and *paca* or gibnut (large rodents the size of a beaver) are shot with .22 rifles as they raid the plantations. Fish are seined along the beach and caught in the creeks and rivers. Turtle meat from the Keys is the major source of protein. Nevertheless, most of the calories consumed today come from food bought at stores in Port. Rice, beans, flour, sugar, and lard have become staples of the diet.

PLORA'S KITCHEN

Nietschmann (1973: 104) comments that for a visitor "it may be hard to imagine the intensity and primacy that food resources have in the everyday life of the Miskito"—and this is certainly true in Awastara. In 1999–2000 I eat all my meals in Plora's kitchen. Kitchens are often older houses converted into cooking and eating areas. Houses only last ten to fifteen years; and when the roof starts leaking and the house begins to rot, a new house is often built next door, so that the old house can be turned into a kitchen and used for a while longer. This is the case with Plora's kitchen, where I eat. It is a twelve-foot by sixteen-foot building that used to be the family house; but now (connected by a board walkway to the main house) it serves as kitchen and dining room. Helms (1971: 51–52) noted that bamboo houses in Asang tended to combine the kitchen and sleeping areas under one roof, whereas wooden houses tended to have separate kitchens with walkways. This was probably true in Awastara as well at an earlier point in history. With the newer-style wooden houses now universal, however, an older house, leaky or not, makes a very useful kitchen.

Plora's kitchen has a dining area with a long table and bench down the south wall, where men and children are fed. As a work area, the kitchen/dining room is constantly busy. There are large plastic buckets with tight-fitting lids along the wall, for storing rice and beans and flour and sugar. A separate water bucket is filled continuously throughout the day, from the well some fifty feet away. Along the north wall are two long shelves where plates and glasses and utensils are stacked after being washed.

On the west side of Plora's kitchen is a separate add-on, about six feet by eight feet. It has a large open window with a washboard inclining outward and a small roof to keep out the rain. As dishes are washed here, the dishwater and scraps run out the window to the ground below, where the pigs and chickens devour them. The other main feature of the kitchen is the raised stove or *kubus*. The *kubus* is made of baked clay in the form of a horseshoe and sits on top of a sturdy wooden table. It burns firewood, which must be gathered regularly. Short, stunted *krabu* trees, which grow everywhere, are the principal kind of firewood. They are often cut green and left to dry. Of the easily available woods, *krabu* is said to burn the hottest and last the longest, although many other kinds of wood are also used. In our household, Casey often takes his chainsaw and canoe deep into the lagoon area, to cut *usupam* and *mihmih* and other harder, hotter-burning woods. Gathering firewood is a task that every household must do every second or third day. Firewood is usually cut in pieces two or three feet long, tied into a bundle with coarse rope, and carried home on the back, supported by a tumpline around the forehead. Men and women both go regularly to cut firewood, in between other chores. So far Awastara's surroundings seem to provide enough firewood for the village, although people in the center of this spread-out community have to go much farther than people who live out on the edge. Bottled gas stoves have not yet appeared in Awastara but are common in the richer community of Sandy Bay, up the coast.

Adult men are fed first. They usually eat silently and then move away from the long table, so the older children can eat. Women generally eat from bowls, standing up as they continue to work. Small children eat sitting on the floor, with their bowls of food in front of them. Little Nachalie (one and a half) began by using her fingers to fish the beans and rice and turtle meat out of her bowl. But within a few months she was able to use her spoon. She turned out to be left-handed! As in Bell's day (1989: 82), conversation follows the meal instead of taking place while eating. "Eat first, talk later" seems to be the rule. In fact, it is not considered good manners to try to talk to someone who is eating. This was sometimes hard for me to remember as a visitor in other homes, since in the United States eating and talking at the same time are expected. Just as Bell describes, the hour after everyone has eaten is the time for conversation and storytelling. The day has its own structure, rather different from that in the urban United States.

Many adults rise long before dawn to go to the plantations and work for several hours or to seine fish at the beach. They do not eat breakfast at the house but usually do return around mid-day for the main meal. Breakfast, for those who remain in the house, is not ready until about 7:00–7:30, even though everyone has been up since first light. It takes an hour or more to get the fire going and food prepared. Breakfast consists of black coffee sweetened with plenty of sugar, along with fried eggs, home-baked bread, and perhaps something left over from the previous evening's meal. Schoolchildren must be dressed in clean clothes and gotten off to class before 8:00. The kitchen fire is usually left going after breakfast, for cooking the mid-day meal. After the main meal, however, it is put out until evening, when it will be relit to warm up leftovers. If possible, the main meal should include fish or meat of some kind, most frequently green turtle meat. The starchy food that accompanies the meat is usually boiled cassava or plantains or rice. Rice with beans, Nicaraguan-style, is also a staple. Bread is often baked outside in a cutoff metal barrel, piling coals atop a piece of sheet metal on top of the "oven." Grated coconut is frequently mixed with the dough to provide a delicious texture to this homemade bread. In the evening a simple meal of coffee and leftovers is served, often including a piece of fish or turtle meat and the inevitable beans and rice. After supper is the time for talking and telling stories, until everyone gets sleepy and goes to bed sometime around 9:00 P.M.

The kitchen and the porch are shared by the family and the animals, at least the dogs and chickens. The dogs continually sneak into the house, where they are swatted with a broom and go off yelping, soon to sneak back up again. *Yul ba pruks!* (Hit that dog!) Plora shouts to a child, who runs to hit the dog and drive him away. The chickens are often underfoot, gobbling up the bits of food the children drop. Children, chickens, dogs—no wonder the floors have to be cleaned all the time!

Food sharing is a basic Miskitu value, part of the definition of being a good person. Food should be taken to invalids or the needy, and visitors should be fed along with the family at mealtimes. We frequently have visitors from Port or elsewhere eating with us in Plora's kitchen.

TAMA AND UPAN

All Miskitu meals, including the ones Plora feeds me, are thought to have two necessary components, *tama* and *upan*. *Tama* is called *bastimento* in Spanish or "breadkind" in Creole English—starchy vegetables that have been staples of the Miskitu diet since precontact times. They include cocoyam (*duswa*) and sweet potatoes (*tawa*), but the most important is cassava (*yauhra*). It is raised by almost everyone in the village. Farms along the Awastara River bottom near Aras Bila are planted mostly with cassava, although some rice and plantains and other crops are also grown. Cassava is also grown in smaller, fenced gardens close to the house, where it can be easily cared for and harvested. Most of the calories from a meal normally come from *tama*, particularly cassava and boiled plantains. Rice is also consumed every day and serves as a common starchy substitute for *tama* at most meals today.

Tama represents the starchy component of meals, but it is never the sole ingredient. It must be combined with *upan* (meat or fish), the protein component. Sidney Mintz (1985: 9–13) points out that until very recent times the diets of all agricultural peoples have been built around a complex-carbohydrate core, combined with a "fringe" food that has a contrasting taste and texture. The fringe normally provides some protein and necessary vitamins and minerals but is valued most for its taste. It helps one eat the bland carbohydrate, the main source of calories. The fringe food is the interesting, delicious, and necessary part of the meal. Familiar examples include the maize-based diet in Mesoamerica, with a fringe including hot chiles and tomatoes; the rice-based diet in China and Southeast Asia combined with a fringe of fish and soy sauce; and black-bread diets in peasant Europe, combined with a fringe of vegetables and meat cooked together as a soup. Such food habits seem self-evident to those concerned, since, as Mintz (1985: 3) notes, for most peoples "food preferences are close to the center of their self-definition."

Mintz (1992) describes many fringe foods as being protein-rich legumes. The Miskitu, however, hunt and fish as well as cultivate their fields, and the food they want to accompany their carbohydrate core must be meat or fish. It may be cooked with the carbohydrate core or separately. Such meat or fish is called *upan*, and in Awastara it is most commonly green sea turtle meat. Deer, gibnut, freshwater hicatee turtles (*kuswa*), and other wild animals are also eaten, however, along with beef and chicken.

In Tasbapauni, after painstaking observations over an entire year, Nietschmann (1973: 165) reports that 70 percent of the animal protein consumed was green turtle meat. The figure in Awastara is probably similar. A turtle is butchered every few days by one of the turtle fishermen, and people gather around his house to buy the meat at three or four cordobas a pound, about half the price in Port. Meat is supposed to be given away to close relatives, as Nietschmann (1974: 37) reports, but it is sold to nonrelatives. The Moravian pastor and other high-status visitors have traditionally been given meat, although one Awastara pastor complained to me that he rarely received it. Not sharing food with him was clearly an indication of his unpopularity. The conflict that Nietschmann describes between obligations to give meat to relatives and the need to earn cash by selling it is certainly present in Awastara. In my own case, I try to resolve this problem by helping to pay for the food we consume in Plora's kitchen.

Prices in Port for a large green sea turtle ready to butcher ranged from about 450 cordobas ($65) in 1977 to 300 ($25) or less in 1999. The price has dropped because so many turtles are now being brought to market. The captain of a turtle boat normally brings a couple of turtles back to Awastara out of the catch, to butcher and sell at home. Nietschmann (1973: 197–99) provides a vivid description of a turtle butchering in Tasbapauni, with crowds of relatives and neighbors clamoring to buy turtle meat, while the successful turtle fishermen with stolid faces chop up the meat. In Awastara hungry dogs also circle the crowd, quickly gobbling up all drops of blood and small scraps of meat.

At a turtle butchering, invalids and the elderly are remembered. For example, for almost forty years an Awastara man named Isiring has suffered from hydrocephaly (an abnormally enlarged head). He cannot move and must lie on the floor of his Aunt Erlita's house, with his huge head resting on a blanket. Erlita feeds and cleans up after him each day. She faces this very difficult situation with dignity and kindness. Many people in town help out by bringing Erlita plastic sacks of turtle meat and other food supplies. Erlita is a widow and has little means of support, except for such donations.

Beef is also consumed occasionally, when someone who owns cattle slaughters an animal. The small local herd of cattle wanders about in the village and on the surrounding savannah, grazing freely, with little care being taken of them. Animal husbandry here seems to follow hunting and gathering patterns. Animals are simply left to fend for themselves, rather than being fed or cared for. When needed, they are "hunted" and brought back to their owners to be sold or killed. Cattle owners seem to know the general area where their animals are at any given moment; but when the cattle wander too far away, they may disappear. In 1999–2000 a number of Dakura cattle were simply butchered by cattle thieves in Awastara, and the meat was sold. Three men went to jail briefly for their complicity in the robberies. There were many more cattle in the village before the war years. They were all killed during the conflict, either by the Sandinista soldiers or by local thieves, depending on who tells the story. Buying and raising cattle is one way of investing available money, since cattle can always be sold for a good price, 2,000–4,000 cordobas ($165–$335) each in 2000. Occasionally someone butchers a cow in town for a special occasion such as a church conference. Beef is thought of as a special luxury food and is much prized as a kind of *upan*. Disappointment was high at one conference when people had to make do with turtle meat, because beef was too expensive. Personally, I like turtle meat much more than the tough, strong-tasting local beef.

Many people in town also have small ponies used for riding and carrying loads. Like the cattle, horses normally wander freely through the village grazing. Boys become very adept at roping them and bringing them home when they are wanted. Sometimes they wander all the way to Dakura or farther, but Casey tells me some interesting magic to keep them close. You take a small piece of the horse's hoof and eyelashes from both the top and bottom of the eye and tie them together with a piece of black thread. You then bury this under the steps, and the horse will always stay near the house. I am skeptical; but having seen other Miskitu magic at work, I am not as incredulous as I might be.

Although most households also keep pigs, pork is eaten by very few people. Pigs are omnipresent in Awastara, rooting around in the bushes and continually being chased by small boys and dogs. After his prostate operation in Port, Victor has to spend a couple of months recuperating at home. He quickly becomes bored and makes himself a slingshot with thick rubber straps. Complaining that the pigs are rooting up everything in the yard, he begins stalking them with his slingshot and a handful of pebbles. It is a curious sight to see the tall, powerful old man, the best turtle fisherman in town, bent over, sneaking through the *krabu* and lime trees, trying to get a shot at a wandering pig. He seems to find this as entertaining as do the six- or eight-year-old boys who do it regularly.

In fact, pigs play a crucial role in village hygiene, a role not appreciated by development experts. People normally go into the bushes to defecate, and the pigs appear almost instantly to eat the feces. On one visit to Dakura, I wander off in the bushes very early in the day to conduct my morning necessities. But I forget to arm myself with a stout stick! As I squat, the heads of three large pigs appear in the bushes, grunting with anticipation. They apparently aren't willing to wait until I am through. I shout at them and manage a standoff, then jump out of their way. But I am impressed by their efficiency at cleaning up the steaming treasure—as fast as flushing a toilet. I think how understandable the Miskitu disgust at eating pork is. They classify animals as clean or dirty on the basis of their food habits. Animals that eat "clean food" are also believed to be clean to eat. Sea turtles, for example, are regarded as very clean because they feed on the banks of sea grass off the Miskitu Keys. "You never see worms in their flesh," one man told me. Deer and cattle are also thought to be "clean," because of their food habits. But pigs are at the opposite end of the spectrum, because they eat filth. They are sold to visiting mestizo merchants from Port and provide additional cash income for a household. Miskitu people are not surprised that mestizos eat pigs, since, they say disdainfully, "Spaniards will eat anything."

Food taboos also apply when taking herbal medicine, as we will see. In fact, a favorite topic of conversation is which animals are good to eat and which "nations" of people eat them. Toads and frogs (*sukling*) are regarded as the ugliest, most repulsive of animals. No Miskitu person can imagine eating them. Occasionally I have been asked if it is true that North Americans and Europeans eat frogs. "Yes," I replied once, "and I have too, once or twice." I also mentioned that some Americans eat snakes, that the French eat horses, and that some North American Indians ate dogs. A Miskitu boy chimed in that he had eaten monkey while living in the Mayangna country. Most people in the boat, however, maintained an embarrassed silence at this discussion of unbelievably gross food habits.

When *upan* is not available for two or three days, everyone is unhappy. *Upan* hunger, or protein hunger, is vividly described by Bell (1989: 246) and by anthropologists studying other indigenous lowland cultures in the Americas. Janet Siskind (1973: 105) reports Sharanahua women in eastern Peru as saying, after several days without meat, "There's no meat—let's eat penises!" Upon hearing this comment, the men promptly prepared to go hunting. In Awastara a meal without *upan* is said to be a sad meal. Once Kedelin (about two years old) spends several days sick with a fever. Her mother and aunt say she is crying for *upan* and send someone to look all over town for a piece of fish. In fact, one major rhythm of life in Awastara is the daily search for *upan*. Part of the web of conversation that stretches across the community is information about who may have a piece of fish for sale, or who has killed a deer, or who will be butchering a turtle. A child is then sent out to confirm any rumor of *upan* and buy a piece for the day. There is no refrigeration, so any sort of *upan* must be consumed the same day.

Learning to eat what local people eat is an important part of most anthropologists' experience. There seem to be "ethnic boundary marker foods," the consumption of which plays an important part in defining ethnicity. One of the first times I ate turtle meat was after a very long walk, when I was completely exhausted. Victor took me to his house, where Plora served me a big bowl of indistinguishable turtle pieces, including liver and other internal parts, all swimming in the turtle grease in which they had been cooked. I didn't feel hungry, but I knew that I had better get it down. At some point you realize that your body is a furnace in need of fuel. If you don't feed it there will be a breakdown. You are tempted to be squeamish, but I think to myself: if I don't eat what these people eat, I am depriving myself of the nutrients I need to keep on going. I put the small black pieces of turtle insides and fat in my mouth and chew them up. Not bad! Then I finish off half a plate of rice and all the rest of the turtle meat that Plora serves me. With time, I will learn to love turtle meat almost as much as my Miskitu friends do.

SEINING AT THE BEACH

The next most common *upan* after turtle meat is fish. Awastara's coastal location lends itself to beach fishing with seines. The large seines commonly used are not made locally but are obtained secondhand from fishing boats and then repaired continually. This sort of seine fishing is thus fairly recent, from the last forty or fifty years. In earlier times, people say, they fished with small, homemade seines. Seines are either bought from fishing boats or traded for pigs or other local products. Seine fishing takes place throughout the year, but it is especially productive during August and September, when the shrimp come in close to shore. The land breeze (*diwas*) seems to blow more frequently during the day in those months, and shrimp are plentiful. Many large snook follow the shrimp, and seine fishing can be quite productive. "The snook play with the shrimp," people say in Miskitu. Smaller varieties of fish are caught throughout the year. Shrimp are also caught in the seines and, like fish, are both eaten locally and taken in ice chests to be sold in Port.

Alvarez comes by about 4:00 one morning to take me seine fishing at the beach. He and another man are carrying a heavy, bulky black seine.

They carry it bundled up on a long pole, with two strong men on each end. This seine is forty feet long and about six feet in width. I estimate the seine weighs sixty or seventy pounds when it is dry. Seines have floats on the top side and lead weights on the bottom side and are attached to stout eight-foot poles at each end. Seines are valuable, prized possessions. Victor traded a pig for his, and there are only about ten in all of Awastara. We walk to the landing and find a boat to go down the river, arriving on the beach in the first morning light.

At the beach Alvarez and I take the long line attached to the front pole and begin to wade out through the surf, pulling the seine behind us. It billows out into the waves, with the weighted side sinking and the top side floating. We wade as far as we can, until the water is up to our shoulders. Then we turn 90 degrees and begin to pull the seine parallel to the beach. Behind us, two other men are also wading out, holding the line attached to the back end of the seine. It helps to have additional people to pull a seine, especially with the longer, heavier ones. Women often participate, wading into the ocean in their dresses up to their waists. It is hard work pulling the heavy seine through the surf, and the ocean feels cold in the early morning. Alvarez yells, and we turn back toward the shore. This is the crucial part of the process. The people on the back end also turn toward shore, and we all pull both ends of the seine in the form of a horseshoe toward the shallower water, dragging the heavy seine behind us back to the beach. As we reach the shallow water, we begin to haul in the seine as fast as we can. Twenty feet away the people on the other end are also pulling, and the seine comes closer. We can see the fish trapped inside, splashing wildly. We pull it all the way up on the beach, and everyone scrambles to see what we have caught. This time we catch a few mullet, one or two snook, some small catfish, one small shark about two feet long, and ten or twelve shrimp.

Everyone who helps pull the seine gets a share of the fish. When I ask Alvarez about giving shares, he says that poor people without seines come to the beach and help with the seining, in return for a share of the catch. "The poor people don't have seines, but they have to eat too," he comments—a poignant reminder of the primacy of food sharing among Miskitu values. This time I am given all the shrimp, a special treat for me. Seining goes on for a few more hours, until the sun is hot and everyone is tired. Then we carry the wet, heavy seine back up the river in the boat, where it can be safely stored at the house, so that it will not be stolen at the beach.

People attribute smaller catches from seining along the beach to the increasing numbers of fishing boats. These boats are always visible from

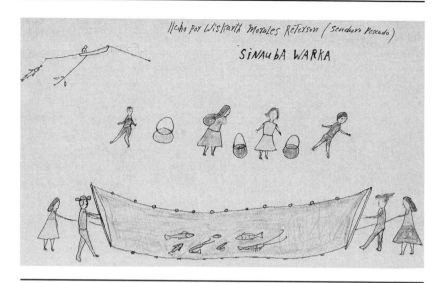

FIGURE 5. *Seining at the beach, by Wiskat Morales*

shore, continually working up and down along the Coast. They are said to seine up everything in the water and kill it, including all the little fish. In fact, the beach is often littered with dead fish tossed overboard by the fishing boats. There is little control of commercial fishing off the Atlantic Coast, and it seems very likely that the fish populations are indeed being decimated, as the Awastara people claim.

A visual representation of the process of seine fishing is provided in figure 5. This picture was done by Wiskat Morales, a young Awastara man (in his twenties). I knew that Wiskat liked to draw, so I bought him paper and colored pencils and asked him to make me pictures of daily life in the village. He himself chose the particular subjects to draw and eventually gave me a stack of twelve to fifteen drawings, each with a title at the top. Wiskat uses a ruler to create straight lines and makes a direct, almost schematic representation of factual details and technical processes. Here Wiskat depicts two couples pulling a seine near the beach, with various kinds of fish and shrimp already in the seine. On the beach, several women with baskets wait for shares of the catch, a visual reminder of Miskitu reciprocity obligations. Even passersby, who may not help much with the seine, are entitled to a share. At the top left, a man far out in the ocean fishes with two sets of hook and line, his boat at anchor. A shark is about to grab one of the baits.

FISHING FOR *MAS MAS*

During the dry season, from February to May, as the creeks and sloughs along the coast begin to dry up, people fish in them for a type of small, spotted bass called *mas mas*. Children and adults both participate with gusto in this kind of fishing, and it is indeed thoroughly enjoyable. Plora is very proud of Melvin (ten) when he brings back a whole bag of *mas mas* for our meal one March day. Lucas (twelve) invites me to go with him the next day.

Lucas and his aunt Gladys come by at 4:30 A.M., when it is still pitch black. We start off in the darkness down the trail toward Aras Bila, a trail I know very well since I run on it early every morning. Gladys says impatiently that we are late—she heard people on the trail by her house much earlier in the morning. It is a long hour's trek as the stars dim and the east grows light while we walk on the trail. Lucas points out Venus, the *slilma tara* or big star in Miskitu. I point to Scorpius, bright overhead, and talk about the legendary Miskitu figure of the Yapti Misri, the big scorpion in the sky, where all souls went after death in aboriginal times (Fagoth et al. 1998: 16). The story arouses no comment from Lucas or Gladys.

Eventually we turn off the main trail, to go to the east, through the swamps right along the coast itself. Pantera, one of Victor's dogs, runs friskily alongside us. We take off our sandals and go slogging along barefoot through the oozy black mud, slipping and sliding. Suddenly I slip and go down in the muddy water! I struggle to hold my small backpack with my camera in it high up out of the water. I laugh, as my Miskitu companions do in similar situations, and manage to get to my feet and keep going.

As we walk along, we hear whooping and hollering on the trail behind us. Lucas grumbles that the noise will scare off all the fish. After a while a small band of high-spirited ten- or twelve-year-old boys catches up with us, running with fishing gear in hand, and plunges on ahead.

Finally, we come to a large freshwater bay, fifty or sixty feet across, with water lilies floating on the surface and thick vegetation along the banks. It is about waist deep in the dry season. On the other side, through some thick bush, is the ocean. We can hear the surf beating on the shore and listen as a motorboat goes by farther out. The boisterous boys, now quiet, are already out in the bay, fishing.

Our fishing poles are saplings about three feet long, stripped of leaves, with a piece of monofilament line about six feet long attached to one end and a hook at the other end of the line. Lucas gives me a plastic cup of worms he has dug and a knit plastic bag for the fish I hope to catch. The idea is to wade slowly through the brown water, along the edge of the bay, where there are lots of water lilies and other vegetation. We flip our worm-baited hooks into the water among the weeds and strike quickly as the small *mas mas* hit the bait. The little boys are very good at it, much better than I am.

Finally, I manage to catch one fish, a *mas mas* about six inches long—a big one for these waters! My hook is too big to snag the smaller ones, and I keep losing my bait. After a while I wade slowly back to the bank, get my camera, and then wade back out to take pictures. Gladys is an enthusiastic angler. She is the only female present, and I never see little girls fishing for *mas mas*. Gladys says she has a hard time hooking them too, but she has already managed to catch four or five. I put up my camera and continue to fish.

The morning is beautiful as we wade slowly through the water, flipping our lines. The boys are fishing with great intensity. I also love fishing and am enjoying myself as well. I might be as dedicated as the boys are, if only I could catch the little rascals. I have to watch my step and move slowly, in order not to fall in the slippery mud. The *mas mas* strike fast, as soon as the bait hits the water. You see a flash in the water, a quick tug—and your bait is gone. I try reacting faster, but I still can't hook them. I vow to myself to buy some smaller hooks in Port. The bay seems to be full of *mas mas,* and they are the only kind of fish we catch here. By the middle of May all these swamps and sloughs are completely dry, but the *mas mas* somehow survive until the following year.

By 7:30 I have used up all my worms. I start wading back, ready to quit. Two of the small boys ask me how many I have caught. When I say, "Only one," they respond by coming over and all giving me two or three of their own fish, out of their full bags. I know that Miskitu reciprocity, giving someone else food you have gathered or caught or harvested out of your garden, is obligatory and traditional. Nevertheless, their generosity still moves me. In all my days of fishing in the United States, no other anglers ever gave me fish out of their bags. U.S. anglers usually hold onto their fish proudly as proof of their own achievement, instead of sharing it, *pana pana laka,* the way the Miskitu do.

It is a long walk back, and I dread telling people I caught only one fish. Once at the bathhouse, it takes me a while scrubbing my legs and feet to get all the sticky black mud off. Eliza makes me feel better as I give her my fish to cook for dinner. "I can't ever hook them either," she tells me.

The *mas mas* are boiled whole with coconut milk, Caribbean style. The flesh is delicate and as delicious as the soup in which it is cooked. As we eat, Victor comments that this is "real Miskitu food." It is a dish as traditional as *wabul* (bananas mashed into a thick milkshake) or *bunia* (fermented cassava). I reply that I think the Miskitu diet would be much better if we ate mostly this kind of food. Victor agrees completely. There is nostalgia among older people about the old-time Miskitu food, which has been largely replaced by food bought in stores. Miss Porla, the midwife, says people were healthier and had fewer illnesses like diabetes and high blood pressure in her childhood and attributes this to a better diet.

Thus there is a fairly constant supply of fish to eat in town. Fish is often fried or boiled to make a delicious fish soup, but it is also cooked, like today's meal, in coconut milk. Coconut milk is made by grating dried coconut, wrapping it in a cloth, pouring water slowly through the cloth, then squeezing the milk out.

CRABS

Crabs are caught year round but especially after the first rains in May. Crabs of a large species called *kaisni* begin to come out of the swampy areas, crawling out onto the savannah in the open. For a few days, dozens of people can be seen with heavy burlap bags, catching crabs. The lucky ones have a glove on one hand to avoid the crabs' pincers. They pull the legs off and fill their sacks with crabs. Then they stagger back up the trail to their homes, carrying the heavy, squirming sacks of live crabs on their backs. Crabs are also taken to market in Port in these burlap bags, as recorded in the following song, composed by my friend Alvarez.

Ay, Cangrejo	(Ay, Crab)

Ay cangrejito, ya me voy,
    cangrejo, para acá
	Ay, little crab, I'm going now,
	    crab, over here,

Laulutara dawanka, kuhma tamaira	Lord of the mangroves, legs covered with hair,
Nakra buhunira, batanka tahplira	Cloudy-looking eyes, bitter fat.

Ai ninara wauwaupra,
    si taura wauwaupra
Cangrejo, para acá.
	On both sides you walk
	    backward and forward.
	Crab, over here.

Krukira wina mairka kum bui,	A woman from Krukira took you,
markitkamra	to market

baku mai briwan	thus she took you.
Saiwan tara takan kan,	In the late evening,
nashun nani mawanra	in front of
bara swiram tara takan kan.	everyone, there she left you.
Bara ispail mairin saura kum bui	And a bad Spanish woman
Wahawi baku alkram taim,	swinging in the air, you grabbed
¿qué es ese	her
animal? mai win kan,	What is that animal? she said
	to you.
Ay, cangrejo	Ay, crab.
Lalmara tani kaikram taim	When you looked to the east
Waking baman atki kan	you saw the (Chinese man) Waking selling
Munamra tani kaikram taim,	When you looked to the west,
Guy baman sipi kan	you saw the tailor Guy sewing.
Yulu wina mairka kum bui,	A woman from Yulu,
markitra baku	to market
mai briwan	she carried you.
Ay, cangrejo.	Ay, crab.

I find this song notable for its originality and the humor of its lyrics. Several characteristics of Miskitu discourse are also evident. For example, the home village of each Miskitu person is carefully specified. This is an important identifying feature, always mentioned when speaking about someone from another place. It is a Krukira woman who first takes the crab to market, but by the end of the song it has become a Yulu woman carrying the crab. The mestiza woman who picks up the crab at the market is, naturally enough, a "bad Spanish woman," given Miskitu prejudices against Spanish-speaking Nicaraguans. She is pinched by the crab and cries out, "What animal is that?" From the marketplace in Puerto Cabezas the crab looks first to the east then to the west. The four cardinal directions *lalma* (east), *muna* (west), *yahabra* (north), and *waupasa* (south) are used constantly in Miskitu speech to refer to physical location, in this case to the crab's eye movements. As he looks around, he sees a Chinese merchant selling in one of the stores and a well-known tailor sewing in his shop. These are lively and accurate descriptions of the Port marketplace, familiar to any coastal Miskitu.

Miskitu fascination with all aspects of the natural world, but especially with animals and their behavior, is expressed in such songs as "Ay, Cangrejo." The *kisi* or fables often deal with personified animals such as Jaguar and Rabbit (see chapter 12), and ordinary conversation is full of references to different sorts of animals. Visitors to my house took great interest in the field guide to birds lying on my table and disagreed with some of the species distinctions among birds made by the ornithologist author. Elderly *Dama* Mulares enjoyed looking at the book so much that I gave it to him when I left.

Miskitu interest in animals is often factual and taxonomic, focusing on characteristics and behavior. Once when I went to Páhara, I was detained by heavy rainstorms and spent an extra day there. In the morning I noticed an egret stalking small fish in the flooded stream nearby and asked several small boys if it was a *yami*. They were delighted that I knew the word for egret in Miskitu and invited me with them to explore the nearby area. In the stream shallows they pointed out five different kinds of small fish: *popo* (the ones the egret was hunting); *bukuwaia* (a two-inch-long, pencil-thin fish); *akaka* (with black stripes on his sides); *krahana*; and *bilam*. Later, I learned to fish for *krahana* with the boys. Patient teachers, they eagerly taught me about the natural world around us. First of all, though, they insisted that I master taxonomy. When I asked another young friend about turtle fishing, he began: "There are four kinds of sea turtles and they are . . ." Fables and songs also reflect careful observation of particular characteristics, such as "walking backward and forward at the same time."

FRUIT EATING

Vegetables such as tomatoes, cabbage, and cucumbers (important parts of the diet in Hispanic Nicaragua) are not normally eaten in Awastara. Fruit is eaten every day but not as part of a meal. Rather, it is eaten between meals as a delicious snack. The verb for consuming fruit is not *piaia* (to eat) but *dabaia* (to suck), thus appropriately describing the act of fruit eating. Alternatively, the juice may be squeezed, sweetened with sugar, and made into *prisku* (fruit drink), which is consumed both with meals and between meals.

All fruit is, of course, seasonal. Awastara has hundreds of huge mango trees, some of them almost a century old. From March through August they are covered with mangos, with different varieties ripening at different times. Men, women, and children can be found on their porches eating the juicy, sticky, yellow and orange mangos. Children forage for them underneath the trees and throw rocks to bring them down from high above. People give each other bags of ripe mangos and sometimes make them into *prisku*. Cashew fruits (*kasau*) are also eaten from March to May, and oranges and grapefruit ripen in November and December. *Krabu* or *nancite* berries, with their incredible mawkish sourness, are gathered from July through September and usually drunk as *prisku*. It took me a very long time to be able to like *krabu prisku*. In fact, *krabu* is another kind of ethnic boundary marker food, universally enjoyed by mestizo, Creole, and Miskitu Nicaraguans but disliked by all the North Americans I have ever known. When I returned to Awastara in 1997, after years of being away, I was given a huge glass of *krabu prisku* to drink in one of the first houses I visited. I decided it was "now or never," held my nose surreptitiously, and managed to get the whole glass down. By 1999 I was proud that I had actually learned to like *krabu prisku*.

People also pick wild fruit as they travel. Two common kinds are *tawa* (beach plums), purple fruits with a puckery white flesh, and *ujum*, a sort of wild grape. People often carry a small bag tied to the waist, which they can fill with fruit and eat as they walk along a trail or ride in a boat. Casual fruit eating is a great pleasure for everyone. Children climb agilely into trees to pick the fruit before it falls. In photo 6 two boys are sitting in a *kasau* or cashew tree, eating its fruit. Each fruit produces only one nut, which grows from the distal end of the bright yellow or orange fruit. The pungent, mouth-puckering taste of the *kasau* is not pleasing to those unfamiliar with it but is relished by everyone in Awastara. The dry nuts from the *kasau* must be roasted over a fire and then cracked with a hammer to extract the cashew nuts familiar in the United States. Other wild fruits include *si* or *sihinak,* a purplish, acorn-sized fruit that grows on a palmlike tree with sharp thorns on the trunk, and *biuhu,* another small, purplish fruit, very sour, which grows on bushes out on the savannah.

With no green vegetables, fruit probably provides the necessary vitamins in the diet. A nutritionist with whom I worked in 1978 thought the Miskitu diet was vitamin deficient. Vitamin deficiency diseases do not seem to be a major health problem, however. The nutritionist's conclusions probably came from considering only Miskitu meals—large servings of *upan* and *tama*—and not noticing all the fruit eating that occurs between meals.

The nutritional importance of fruit in Awastara became apparent in April and May 2000, when the early mango harvest failed. Heavy rains in December turned the mango flowers black, and no early fruit was produced. In April the school director told me that several small children had fainted in class, after coming to school without eating breakfast. Usually there are early mangos by this time, and children forage for them on the way to school. If they have not been fed at home, at least they

PHOTO 6. *Kids eating cashew fruit*

have eaten mangos. This year the trees flowered again after the December rains, however. By the end of May the trees were filled with mangos, and children were eating them constantly. The experience highlighted the nutritional importance of mangos in Awastara.

An occasional treat is wild honey. Bell (1989: 232–35) describes nine different kinds of bees on the Coast, but there are only two or three varieties near Awastara. Once, while I was traveling with Andrew Kingsman, we came across a dead tree with a hole into which bees were flying. Andrew immediately chopped the tree down. Together we pulled out the sticky, dark-brown combs, while small, stingless bees swarmed around us, getting into our eyes and ears. Only one comb had honey, however: a thin, rather acrid-tasting variety that was quite delicious. We drank it on the spot.

Although honey is a rare treat, the common sweetener for coffee, fruit drink, and cakes is refined sugar, brought up in large quantities from Port. In Miskitu, as in English, the idea of sweetness has strong positive connotations. For example, going to heaven after death is expressed as *damni iwaia*, "resting in sweetness." Unfortunately, refined sugar also causes serious health problems, including tooth decay. Many people in Awastara have missing teeth, even individuals in their twenties. Local dentists blame a diet so high in sugar. In Awastara no one currently pulls teeth, so someone with a painful cavity or an abscess must go to Port to have it treated. Filling and repairing teeth is expensive, and most people simply have the offending tooth extracted. Pulling front teeth changes the structure of the face and makes young people look much older. In Victor's family, Rodrigo and Pamela (both in their late twenties) are missing most of their front teeth.

As I finish a year in the village in 2000, hard economic realities begin to sink in. Food is precious. The skinniest puppy in the recent litter at Victor's house starves to death, too weak to fight for its share of the single plate of rice and beans given to the puppies each day. Having sacks of provisions in the house is security. I used to feel irritated by having to buy provisions in Port before each trip back to the village—heavy sacks of flour, rice, beans, and sugar that must be wrestled down to the wharf and into the catboat and then brought from the landing up to the house. I realize how crucial that purchased food is to life here in Awastara. Everyone yearns for *upan*, but it is the bought provisions that now sustain life. And there is the constant threat and frequent occurrence of men drinking up the money that should have gone to buy food.

As was the case last summer, I am the major source of daily cash flow in the house. Each morning I gladly give Plora twenty cordobas (about $1.65) to buy *upan* for the day and for other daily expenses. One morning Eliza comes running to ask for another ten cordobas for a bundle of cassava, which someone has come through selling. Another day I buy fifteen cordobas' worth of beans and a packet of coffee. We all eat the same things, and I realize that I am basically feeding everyone in the house for three to five dollars a day. I like to be generous and share food, Miskitu style. The turtle fishermen in the family buy sacks of provisions when they sell their turtles, but they bring very little home in the way of spending money. I am the daily cash box. Victor's strategy of making friends with strangers is again paying off. I have to remember to bring a stack of ten- and twenty-cordoba bills from Port each trip, since larger-denomination bills are very hard to cash at the small village stores.

Living for weeks at a time in the village, I find it hard at first to eat a big plate of plain rice, or rice and beans, or beans and bread. Accustomed to a variety of fruits and vegetables and salads, I feel as if I will gag if I have to eat another plate of such bland food. I get in the habit of squeezing a lime over my beans and rice, which makes Plora and Eliza laugh. Then a friend brings me several bottles of spices and condiments, and I get in the habit of taking one bottle or another with me to the kitchen every day. When I come back from Port one day in December, I find that Plora herself has bought a selection of food enhancers, the best she can find in Port—ketchup, hot sauce, and vinegar. She hands me the bottle of hot sauce to see if I will like it. I am embarrassed that Plora has been carefully observing my surreptitious strategy of spicing up the bland food and has spent her own money trying to please me.

After one seemingly interminable fifteen-hour boat ride from Port, I help row the boat all the way up the river. By the time I reach the house, I am famished. I fall on my large plate of rice and beans with gusto, voraciously devouring the whole thing, feeling the life seep back into my tired body. For the first time I feel what I imagine Miskitu men feel faced with a big plate of very bland food—aching hunger! My body demands nutritious, filling food, the opposite of no food at all, to satisfy my gnawing hunger. Miskitu men go without food for hours and hours, fishing on the Keys, walking across the savannahs, and working in the plantations. They miss many meals, and the availability of any food at all is a real blessing. Instead of spices for their food, what Miskitu men want is *upan*, the satisfying meat or fish taste that makes a meal a meal. Unlike peasant farmers, the coastal Miskitu have always had an abundant marine protein supply, and eating fish or animal flesh is a traditional food habit. Nietschmann (1973: 217) reports that his Tasbapauni Miskitu friends say they feel strong and full only after eating animal protein. After sharing an oar with me on that trip up the river, Hector also eats with me in his mother's kitchen. But he is not able to eat as much as I can, because there is no *upan* that day. He says he can't swallow the *tama* without *upan* to accompany it.

Having enough food is a preoccupation in Awastara, and providing food is a basic obligation of a husband and father. The importance of plentiful food is made clear to me one night by the fantasies of little Nena, age nine. She begins telling me of the church conference she attended up in Sandy Bay, naming all the good things they had to eat—chicken and turtle meat, rice and beans, cakes of different sorts, bread—a list of all the local foods. It cost twenty cordobas to eat all day, on and on. Nena tells me her child's fantasy about unimaginable quantities of food, more than you could possibly eat. You could keep refilling your plate as often as you wanted. It occurs to me that Nena has probably never had more food than she could eat before. The most wonderful thing imaginable to her was food, food, food!

The reciprocity obligations described by Nietschmann (1973: 183–88) and Helms (1971: 105–6) can be understood in this light, as a social mechanism helping guarantee survival. My neighbor Jinora stops on her way back from the plantation to talk for a moment and, from the large bundle she is carrying with a tumpline across her forehead, pulls out several large cassava tubers to give me. Not only meat but gathered or harvested food in general is readily shared, because there is a strong moral obligation to do so. The verb for feeding someone else is *dakakaia,* and it carries the strong positive implication of nurturance. In fact, the prime symbol of nurturance here is giving food. Ten-year-old Jaseth tells me *yauka kasau ma mai dakakamna,* "tomorrow I will feed you cashew nuts" (which must be gathered and roasted). She is making the kindest and most caring of statements, for food is the master symbol of love and relationships. When I help the neighbors clear the trail out to the *pingka* side, I buy sugar and make a large bucket of limeade for all the workers, and I know it is appreciated beyond the simple pleasure of having a cool drink. When I receive a pound of turtle meat from someone at the other end of the village, brought dangling on a string by a child, I remember the things I have shared with that person in the past and our ongoing friendship. Food defines and reinforces relationships and has strong moral significance. So, for many reasons, turtle meat is always welcome at our house.

CHAPTER SIX

Turtle Fishermen and Others

The turtles sought by Awastara fishermen are *Chelonia mydas,* or green sea turtles. Around the world, in most tropical and subtropical oceans, five different genera of sea turtles are found: loggerheads, leatherbacks, ridleys, hawksbills, and green sea turtles (Parsons 1962: 6). All but ridleys occur off the Miskitu Coast. Only green turtles are found in great abundance, however, and they are the only sea turtles whose meat is regarded as palatable by the Miskitu. Hawksbills are occasionally caught by Miskitu fishermen and are highly prized, since the "tortoiseshell" from the carapace is used to make expensive jewelry and brings a good price. The beautiful mottled shell, once heated and softened, can be easily worked and pressed or formed into almost any desired shape (Parsons 1972: 45–46). The major hawksbill fishing ground is off the south Coast, at a place called Greytown Banks. Starting in the seventeenth century, Miskitu turtlemen made annual trips there to catch hawksbills, which they sold to British agents on the Coast (Parsons 1972: 58). Today the hawksbill turtle is endangered and is protected by the Convention on International Trade in Endangered Species of Wild Fauna and Flora (King 1995: 187). Nevertheless, there continues to be a lucrative black market trade in tortoiseshell in Puerto Cabezas.

Through the work of Archie Carr (1956, 1967), James J. Parsons (1962), and more recent scholars such as Cynthia Lagueux (1998), we have learned a great deal about these fascinating sea reptiles. Carr (1967) describes the life history of green sea turtles, based on many years of field research. For a number of years he tagged female green sea turtles at their nesting site at Tortuguero beach, Costa Rica, about two hundred miles south of the Miskitu Keys. Male green turtles never return to land as adults, but the females return every few years to particular nesting beaches. They have retained a reptilian form of reproduction: although they live in the water, they must lay their eggs on land. Each female digs a shallow hole and lays about one hundred eggs, which hatch sixty days later. When they hatch, the baby turtles head toward the surf with an uncanny accuracy; but before they reach the water they are preyed upon by buzzards, coyotes, dogs, and many other animals. Other kinds of predators are also waiting in the water; nevertheless, sizable numbers survive. The tag of one turtle that nested at Tortuguero was returned fourteen months later from Coche Island in the far eastern Caribbean, some 1,400 miles away (Carr 1967: 36). Turtles born at Tortuguero not only feed on the banks of sea grass near the Miskitu Keys but travel as far away as Florida, Mexico, Cuba, and Venezuela.

Green turtles were once very common throughout the Caribbean. European explorers and colonists quickly learned to appreciate their tender, delicious meat and the fact that they could be kept alive for long periods in turtle pens (crawls) or even out of the water, on their backs, as long as they were kept cool and in the shade. Parsons (1962: 30) suggests that Miskitu men may have taught the early English explorers the art of turtle hunting, quoting the buccaneer Dampier, who wrote that each English ship liked to have one or two Miskitu men on board to keep the ship provisioned with fresh turtle meat.

The Cayman Islands seem to have had the richest turtle grounds in the Caribbean. English settlement there began in the mid-1600s and was built around exploiting the turtle fishery. Soon huge numbers were being captured and exported. Parsons (1962: 27) notes a certain Captain James who loaded 50,603 pounds of turtle in the Caymans in 1657. With such wholesale slaughter, it took only about a hundred years for the Caymans turtle population to be completely destroyed (King 1995: 184). Such destruction of turtle populations has also occurred in Florida, Bermuda, Malaysia, and elsewhere, and King (1995: 187) notes that there is no evidence that any population of green or hawksbill sea turtles has ever returned to abundance after being depleted through overfishing. In the Caymans, after the local turtles were gone, the turtle fishing schooners quickly moved out to other parts of the Caribbean and to the Miskitu Coast. Through the 1940s there were twelve to seventeen Caymans boats fishing for turtles on the Miskitu Keys each year (King 1995: 184). These men brought net fishing technology and boat building skills to the coastal Miskitu people.

Today Awastara is one of the two major turtle-fishing villages on the Atlantic Coast. Only Tasbapauni on the south Coast catches as many turtles. Sandy Bay, to the north, was also a major turtling community in 1979; but by 1999 most Sandy Bay boats were fishing for lobsters instead. Awastara's heavy dependence on turtling developed in mid-twentieth century and seems likely to change in the near future. But as of 2000 turtling was still the major economic activity in the community, the most important way of making a living.

In 1978 some turtles were being caught for consumption just offshore from the village. One day I went with Bowman in his small boat to check his turtle net. It was anchored near the beach and then stretched straight out a hundred feet or more into the ocean, at a right angle to the beach. Bowman and his son fished the beach regularly. When they had caught a turtle, they would simply drag the net, turtle and all, back up onto the beach behind the boat. This particular day we did not catch a turtle, but we did catch a large ray or *yakata,* which Bowman killed and butchered, sharing the meat with me and with many other people. My first experience with turtle fishing was thus close to shore; and my understanding of the process, and of the history of commercial turtling in Awastara, developed rather slowly.

By 1999 all turtling was done on the Miskitu Keys, some twenty to thirty miles offshore. These small sand keys, barely above sea level, support only low, shrubby vegetation and have no source of drinking water. Nearby in the shallow ocean waters, however, are extensive beds of sea grass, the feeding grounds of thousands of green turtles that hatched at Tortuguero. To get to the Keys, the Awastara men must cross the deepwater channel near the coast and miles of open ocean. The turtle fishermen today use their large sailing dories or catboats, built in Awastara, to travel to and from the Keys.

CATBOATS

In 1979 there were fifteen catboats, but by 1999 there are thirty. Brightly painted, they make a splendid sight when all are in the Awastara harbor at Christmas time. Boats are thirty to thirty-five feet long and are made from wood planking, either mahogany or Santa María, with heavy pine keels. They are constructed in the village with simple carpenters' tools: a hammer and T-square, a saw (nowadays a chainsaw), and the ever-present machete. Local carpenters show considerable skill in building them, and at any given time several boats are normally under construction somewhere in the village. The kind of wood used for the planking is crucial. Boats made of pine or Santa María sink quickly if they turn over, but boats made of mahogany stay afloat. Many stories are told in

Awastara of boats overturning in high winds or storms, with cargo lost and occasional drownings. Mahogany is the preferred construction material; but it is hard to obtain these days, since it comes from the mountain country to the west and is no longer sold in Port. Mahogany also has a defect, however: as the boat gets older, the nail holes tend to rot out, something that does not happen with Santa María wood. A newly built catboat should last about five years, before having to be constantly repaired and repainted.

These large wooden catboats (made with a keel and ribs and plank sides) are typical of the Coast north of Port. Such boats are not built on the south Coast, where big dugouts with a mast and a sail are constructed instead. The catboats found south of Puerto Cabezas were all built on the north Coast and brought south. An earlier type of large wooden sailboat on the north Coast was called *duri tara,* a style borrowed from the Cayman Islanders. The Caymans turtlemen used large schooners, but on board they carried smaller boats for work around the Keys. Miskitu men from Sandy Bay borrowed the design to make similar craft of their own (Nietschmann 1979a: 65).

The catboat style is more recent, however, and Victor played a major role in bringing it to Awastara. The older *duri tara* had very thick planking and a jib that was tied tightly to the mast, making it difficult to loosen quickly in a high wind. In the mid-twentieth century a Caymans man named Mr. Peter moved to Sandy Bay, where he lived with a local woman and had a family, and there he built the first modern-style catboat. Its planks were thinner, and the mast was twice as high. The jib sheet was held in the hand by a sailor, so that the jib could be lowered instantly in a gust of wind. Nietschmann (1979a: 65) reports about thirty of these catboats in Sandy Bay in the 1960s, most of them built by Mr. Peter. Victor learned the craft from him and built the first catboat in Awastara. Today these are the only sort of large boats built in the community.

DURI RASKAIA

Since catboats are built next to the owners' houses in Awastara, getting them all the way down to the landing (a kilometer or more away) involves a major community effort. The task is called *duri raskaia* (pulling the boat). I had missed a similar event in 1998, when Rodrigo invited me to *duri raskaia.* I didn't understand the word *raskaia* (to pull) and thought he said *paskaia* (to build), which sounds similar. I had watched many catboats being made and was not interested. Thus I didn't go and missed the big event because of my own misunderstanding of the word. I wasn't going to miss another one. In September of 1999 I finally manage to participate. Maestro Tito's new boat, thirty-seven feet long, is glistening in its new blue and white paint, sitting on rollers in his front yard near the Adventist church with the name *The River Nile* painted on the prow.

When I arrive at Tito's house about noon, a big crowd has gathered, perhaps two hundred people. The Church of God minister is standing dramatically in the prow, praying over the boat, holding a Bible in one hand. Two men with guitars sit on the thwarts behind the preacher, playing and singing hymns in between the prayers. The crowd is gathered respectfully around the boat, with bystanders and children farther away, and several women cooking and serving food close by. Important people in town are being offered plates of food, but there is not going to be enough to feed everybody. Nevertheless, the basic principle is that people who help pull the heavy boat should be fed. Feeding as many people as possible represents a major expense for the new boat owner.

As I hastily finish my plate of food, people line up along the two ropes (each about a hundred feet long) tied to the boat's prow. The Church of God minister disappears after praying and eating and then reappears in old work clothes to help us pull. With lots of yelling (*waitna! kaisa!*) and a "one, two, three!" we all begin pulling. The women and children are closest to the end of the rope and the men closest to the boat. Renny, one of the "men/women" in town, pulls alongside the women, dressed in a natty hat and wearing an earring. A long, stout pole has also been placed cross-wise through the rope oar straps, amidships. The men pushing on this horizontal pole provide a lot of extra leverage and some sideways control of the boat. The crowd seems huge, pushing and pulling the heavy boat through yards and past houses out to the savannah. The heavy vessel goes slowly at first, slipping and sliding down the trail toward the landing (photo 7). Once it moves off its original rollers, no one makes an effort to put other rollers under the keel, which now slides directly on the ground as the heavy boat gains momentum. Out on the savannah the catboat slips along through the mud and the grass, with lots of yelling and loud orders, and no one responding to most of them. No one person is in charge, so many people shout orders.

At various points, when the boat gets stuck in the grass and bushes, we take long rests. Orlando walks alongside the boat with a bullhorn, keeping up an entertaining stream of banter and dialogue, delighting the crowd. He notes with approval that the Church of God preacher is there helping us and that "Mr. Pelipe, from I don't know where, is also here." I

PHOTO 7. Duri raskaia *(pulling the boat)*

shout, "From Awastara!" to roars of approval. When we get close to the water, I jump off the rope and run to one of the anchored boats, to climb up and get a picture of the climactic moment when the big boat finally enters the water. It is a happy moment when *The River Nile* floats free for the first time, with children laughing and splashing alongside in the river. The crowd slowly disperses and wanders back up to the village. Later Victor, who did not participate, quizzes me about the event, particularly about how much food was provided. He says that in earlier years there were many more people to *duri raskaia,* including more strong men to pull. New *duri* owners made sure to prepare enough food for everyone in those days! he claims.

All boats must be dragged up on shore at the landing and re-puttied and painted every few months. A sort of clear sea worm is said to eat the wood very quickly. At Christmas most of the boats are in the Awastara harbor by the landing, and many are being caulked and painted, crowded together in "dry dock" in Awastara's small harbor. I go down to help with Hector's boat. All the men around the landing are called to help

132

push the boat up on shore, with one man deftly moving the rollers under-neath the boat as another man jumps on the stern to raise the prow for the next roller. Up above the high tide line we all halt and let the heavy boat come to a rest. The plug in the stern is knocked out to drain the water in the bottom. No matter how well caulked, wooden boats always seem to leak a bit. A complete caulking and paint job takes several days to finish, in the warm, dry Christmas weather. Common termite nests, called *usra watla,* are burned in a fire and mixed with paint to make a traditional boat putty that is very sticky and durable. Cement is also used nowadays to putty large cracks and holes, which are first stuffed with rags. Oil paint is expensive by local standards (about 150 cordobas a gallon), and it takes at least five gallons to paint a boat. Both the inside and outside must be painted. Boats are usually painted in two colors: one color up to the water line, and another color above that. The Miskitu men comment on how handsome all the boats look in their bright new paint, and I agree with them.

TO THE KEYS WITH VICTOR

Victor insists that I go turtling with him, out to the Keys, just as he insists that I get up at 3:00 A.M. to go work in the rice plantations. He takes seriously the job of training his anthropologist. I dread the trip, since it means about a week in a catboat on the open sea, enduring sunburn, seasickness, and little to eat. But I really do want to see turtle fishing first-hand and learn how it is done. A North American friend named Barbara from Puerto Cabezas also wants to go. She begs me to take her along on this seagoing adventure. Victor is opposed, though. "Women in boats are just trouble," he says. "First they vomit, then they complain about everything—it's too hot, it rains, there isn't enough to eat. Then they have to pull their pants down and hold their butt over the side of the boat. They really don't like that! Everyone is embarrassed. So women in a boat aren't a good idea at all." The only Awastara woman who has ever been to the Keys turtling is Rudila, one of Victor's former spouses. She wore pants and helped row the boat and did all the work a man would do, people say. Later I get to know Rudila (who is now Koldero's spouse) and find her, indeed, a tough, self-confident, and remarkable woman. She has quite a reputation of her own, since she is the only Awastara woman who has worked at sea like a man.

I talk with Victor, arguing that an American woman might be different, and he grudgingly agrees. So Barbara and I wind up going to the Keys with Victor and the two young sailors he hires for the trip. With plenty of time together in the boat, Victor explains turtling to me in detail.

Each trip to the Keys is a separate expedition, with a boat captain and two or three sailors. Some boat owners serve as captains of their own boats; but most owners hire a captain, who is responsible for the boat and the catch. Good captains are said to be hard to find. Many good seamen have drinking problems and can't be trusted with the money from selling the turtles in Port, and therefore make poor captains in spite of their abilities at sea. To solve this problem, some interesting arrangements are made. Except for his drinking, Limston was a good captain for Maidili's boat. So Maidili named one of the older sailors to be in charge of the money from the turtle sales. This arrangement created a win-win situation for all involved, especially for the wives waiting anxiously at home for money and provisions.

Turtling money is always divided in shares, an Anglo system said to have been borrowed from the Cayman Islanders. Nietschmann (1973: 153) also describes a share system in Tasbapauni, in which the owner of a loaned *duri* or shotgun or shrimp net always gets a share of the meat obtained. In Awastara one share goes to the boat owner, one to the owner of the turtle nets, and then a share each to the captain and the sailors. With three sailors, there are then six shares from every turtling trip. Dividing by six is an important local skill in arithmetic. If a boat owner also owns the nets, as well as serving as captain, he gets three shares (half the total proceeds). For many of his turtling years, Victor was able to do this, since he was both owner and captain of his own boat. Thus he brought home very good money from turtling for quite a long time. I am curious as to why any captain would assume more responsibility than the other men, for just a single share. Rodrigo tells me that captains always take a little extra from the turtling proceeds, on the side. It is apparently expected behavior. If a captain takes too much, too often, however, the owner will fire him. Some boat owners have a reputation of being difficult to work for and change captains regularly.

The captain is usually an older man with experience at sea and skill in finding turtles. He has to know where to set the nets and where the turtles are likely to be during any combination of weather and current. In 1979 Victor was generally acknowledged as the best turtleman in Awastara. Victor's brother Pancho was also a captain but apparently lacked the necessary skill his brother had and rarely returned with as many turtles. Pancho served as captain for Victor's second boat for a number of years. Besides knowing where the turtles are, a good captain should take good care of his boat, being careful not to let high winds and bad weather tear the sails, and to anchor prudently with a cable's length of room in each direction so the boat is not blown up on the rocks. Thus a good captain must possess considerable seafaring skills. A boy begins as a sailor, serves some years of apprenticeship, and builds a good reputation as a sailor and as a reliable person. Then a boat owner may trust him to captain his boat. Good captains must also be careful about crossing the shallow Awastara bar, especially in the dry season. In April or May the bar can be crossed only at full high tide. Even at other times of the year, if the captain does not time his crossing exactly right, a few bumps are inevitable. And of course heavy cargo makes the bumping worse. Most of the Awastara boats leak from the constant punishment of crossing the bar. A Sandy Bay man told me with a grin: "You can always tell an Awastara boat because the bottom leaks!"

At the Keys the captain searches for turtle rocks, where the turtles sleep during the day, and also for channels in the shallow waters likely to be traversed by the turtles. As the nets are being set, the captain stands in the bow looking for such places and gives directions to the sailors, who row the boat slowly over the turtle grounds. The sails have been lowered at this point, and the heavy boat is simply rowed with long sweeps, one man on a sweep. When the captain decides on a good place, the sailors drop their sweeps and help him pay out the long nets into the water. Obviously, a large part of the success of the trip depends on the captain's skill in finding the best places to set his nets.

Each trip to the Keys lasts from a few days to a week or more. A couple of days out, our own trip settles into an easy routine: up early in the morning to get in the catboat and go check the nets at first light, to see if we have caught turtles. The turtles come to graze in the huge beds of sea grass in the shallow waters near the Keys, and the turtlemen hope to set their nets in the right places. Each crew sets from four to ten nets and tries to check each one as early as possible in the morning. Victor fears that another crew will find our unattended nets full of turtles and steal the catch.

When we catch turtles, we load them under the thwarts in the boat and then go back to one of the small shelters the turtlemen have built, on posts set in the water near the Keys. We cook and sleep in these shelters, taking refuge from the hot midday sun and from occasional rain showers at night. We eat at most two meals a day, from provisions we have brought and fish we have caught with a handline. One night we have a special treat: a fish stew made from a freshly caught jack. Camping out in these shelters is very pleasant, compared to trying to sleep in the boat as it rides at anchor in the open sea. As it turns out, Barbara and I have to spend only one night out in the boat, rocking uncomfortably as we try to catch a little sleep, cramped in between the thwarts. Food on these turtling expeditions consists of fry bread, oatmeal, boiled cassava, sweetened coffee, and fresh fish. Firewood has to be brought along, with one crewman cooking on top of a piece of metal in the bottom of the boat.

At the Keys we spend our spare time fishing with handlines, swimming, playing cards, and telling *kisi*. Victor and the crew worry constantly about whether one of the other crews will steal their turtles. At night we stretch out on the board floor in one of shelters. Victor and the crewmen tell one *kisi* after another, as I try to translate into Miskitu for Barbara. Then it is our turn. We try to think of jokes in English. Barbara knows more than I do, but they are hard to translate into Miskitu and don't come out sounding as funny as they should. It is actually very pleasant in the warm tropical night, telling stories back and forth, watching the stars, listening to the ocean, and finally drifting off to sleep. Barbara turns out to be a fine companion, never complaining about sleeping in the boat, the quality of our food, or anything else. Victor is duly impressed.

The older style of turtling, before nets were used, was quite different. Nietschmann (1973: 158–59) describes old-style turtling as he actually observed it in Tasbapauni in the 1960s. The traditional technique was to strike the turtle with a harpoon from a dugout canoe. In this kind of turtling, two men in a canoe paddle quietly, looking for turtles resting on the surface. When they spot a turtle, the bowman harpoons it, lofting the weapon high up into the air so that it falls directly onto the turtle's back and the harpoon point embeds itself in the shell. The bowman then retrieves the turtle by hauling in the line attached to the harpoon point. This technique requires considerable skill: stealth in approaching the turtle and amazing accuracy in harpooning. It was being practiced by Miskitu men as early as the late 1600s and was described, for example, by William Dampier, who visited the Miskitu with English buccaneers in 1681 (Dampier 1968: 33–35).

Today in Awastara there is no one left who strikes turtles with harpoons. Some old men remember it, as they do the technique of shooting fish (visible just under the surface of the water) with bow and arrow. Since the mid-twentieth century, however, Awastara men have all been catching turtles in twine nets, of the kind used by the Cayman Islanders. These nets are made by the turtlemen themselves, from twine purchased in Port. The twine is lightweight and is tied into squares about a foot across. Each net is about twenty to thirty feet long and six feet wide and is anchored on one end by a rope attached to a heavy rock called a *keilik*. The other end has a free-floating buoy attached, so the turtlemen can see its location. The net hangs in the water, floating freely in the direction of the current. From the bow of our catboat, Victor anchors one end of the net and pays it out as the boat drifts with the current. The turtle net floats because it has Styrofoam floats attached along the top side, and rocks tied along the bottom side to keep it hanging vertically in the water. When a turtle is taken out of a net, a horrible snarl results; it takes a turtleman with some skill to untangle it. I spend hours trying to untangle turtle nets in Victor's yard and never manage to do it well. In general, much less skill is required to catch turtles with nets than by harpooning, however, and many more turtles are caught.

On our trip to the Keys, we catch seventeen turtles—a very good trip! Victor is especially happy about catching one hawksbill turtle, which are not common in these waters. Each hawksbill has thirteen large plates on its back, providing the tortoiseshell from which jewelry is made. The local market for them continues to be good, in spite of the international agreement prohibiting their capture. Jewelry makers in Port make very pretty earrings and necklaces to sell to tourists at the airport. Back at the house, Victor shows me how he pours boiling water over the hawksbill shell to loosen the plates and then pries them off with a knife blade.

Our trip has gone very well, with generally good weather and a good catch. Often, however, the turtlemen have to deal with high wind, which tangles their nets, and with the driving rain of tropical storms as well as a blistering sun beating down on the open boat, hour after hour. Food is sometimes in short supply, and the men may be able to eat only one meal a day. Many times they are not so lucky in catching turtles. On our way back to Awastara we get a taste of the weather with which the turtlemen often have to contend. The wind picks up and begins to howl in the rigging, and our small boat crests over the huge waves that come rolling across the ocean. We have now left the Keys and are completely out of sight of land. Everything in the boat gets completely drenched with seawater. Barbara and the sailors and I bail frantically, trying to stay ahead of the rising water, which sloshes around the bottom of the boat. Victor sits stoically in the stern steering the boat up and over the waves, with his jacket buttoned up around his neck. We are all exhausted when we finally reach the Awastara bar and cross it successfully with our heavy load of turtles and then row on up the river to the landing.

Several men have turtle crawls along the Awastara River. These are made of long stakes driven into the riverbed in the dry season, which form a small pen or corral in the water. Turtles can be kept alive in a turtle crawl for several weeks if necessary, until the price for them goes up in Puerto Cabezas. Victor has had a turtle crawl for many years. He used to ask his sister in Port to go to the wharf where the turtle butchers work each day, to monitor the supply and price of turtles. When the price was high and few turtle boats were expected in, she would put a notice on the local radio for Victor, in an agreed-upon code, which only she and Victor knew. It could be as simple as "Don't forget your nephew's birthday." Victor's household radio is always on, and someone would run to tell him his sister's message. He would go promptly to the boat landing, load his turtles, and make it to Port while prices were still good.

Back in Awastara, the news spreads fast that Barbara and I have gone to the Keys turtling. Everyone begins asking me about it. A few days later, after Barbara has returned to Port, Victor comments in front of the whole family: "I'm going to get rid of Plora and marry an American woman. They're a lot better! That Barbara spent the whole week with us out on the Keys and never complained once." Plora takes the barbs in silence, but Barbara is very flattered when I see her again in Port and report Victor's compliment.

Wiskat drew a picture of turtle fishing for me (figure 6). Three boats, each with the name of a real Awastara catboat, are in various stages of fishing. On the left, the *Gina Carina* sails under a jib only, apparently looking toward the turtle caught in a net. This boat is probably named after the owner's young daughter. To the right, the *Río Lindo* is under full sail, with the captain (in a baseball cap) at the tiller; the two small sailors don't seem to be doing much at the moment. At the top, two sailors row a catboat, while the captain pulls in a turtle net with a grappling hook and line. This boat has evidently set two nets, and both are shown with a grappling hook rather than a *keilik* holding the net on the bottom. A turtle has been caught in the net to the left. A large shark seems to menace the captain in the prow of the boat, which is named, appropriately enough, *Tiburón* (Shark). Four different turtle nets are shown in the drawing, with turtles entangled in two of them. A smaller shark in the upper left may be advancing toward the turtle in the net directly above him. Sharks do occasionally attack the turtles entangled in the nets.

BOATS, OWNERS, AND CAPTAINS

I am interested in learning exactly how many catboats there are in Awastara as well as something about their histories. Victor's son Rodrigo turns out to be an excellent consultant for this kind of work. He is a former schoolteacher and also gathered turtle fishing data for biologist Cynthia Lagueux. Rodrigo seems to have an encyclopedic knowledge of his own

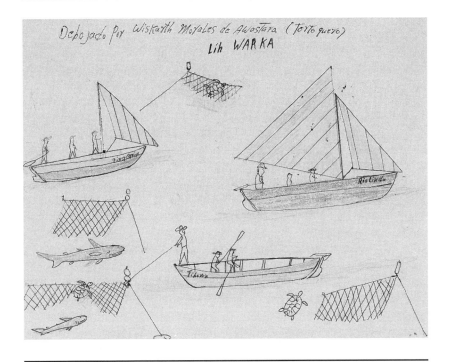

Figure 6. *Turtle fishing at the Keys, by Wiskat Morales*

community and a keen interest in how it functions. He and I enjoy working together to do a household census, a list of stores in town, and a list
of boats and their owners. His own estimates, before doing the empirical
research, turn out to be close to the actual figures in all cases.

Rodrigo had estimated thirty boats in town. There turn out to be
twenty-seven, with three others broken down and unseaworthy. Two of
those are under repair, and one is unrepairable. Three other catboats
are currently being built, one of them by Casey. Building or buying a
catboat seems to require a substantial capital outlay, from a local stand-
point. Of the working boats, only eight are captained by their owners.
For an owner who is not a captain, the strategy appears to be to find a
trustworthy captain and then keep the boat at sea as steadily as possible,
bringing in income. The most trustworthy men to serve as captains are
usually relatives. Three boats are captained by the owner's brother or
first cousin (*moihka*), four by a brother-in-law (*waikatka*), and one each
by a son, a nephew (*tubani*), and a son-in-law (*dapna*). Seven are captained by nonrelatives. Among them are two boats owned by women,

who must depend on hired male captains to manage their turtling investment. Rodrigo comments that in all seven cases the owners have selected responsible, sober men, usually devout Christians. Finally, two boat owners are said to be difficult bosses who change captains so frequently that no steady captain could be identified.

Interestingly enough, only three of the catboats were bought with cocaine money, in spite of the excitement surrounding the occasional cocaine finds on the beach. Apparently these large caches of money have rarely been put to productive use in Awastara. It takes planning ahead to build a catboat: buying or sawing the lumber and many days of painstaking carpentry. Acquiring a catboat is a major investment in a means of production, one that should generate income for many years. Both building and operating one require good money management—something rarely applied in cocaine finds in our community.

To become a captain requires a period of youthful apprenticeship. A young captain usually spends a number of years turtle fishing before he can hope to own his own boat. He looks forward to owning a boat of his own; but once he does so, he often hires a younger man to serve as captain. Victor, for instance, loved being at sea fishing for turtles and managed to build two boats of his own. For years he captained one himself and hired his brother Pancho to captain the other. Meanwhile he took his two oldest sons along as sailors and trained them in the art of turtle fishing, as he had perfected it. In his mid-sixties, he gave each of his boats to these sons and retired. The boys continue to defer to his commands, however, and also give him a share of each turtle catch. The oldest turned out to be extremely responsible, as good a turtleman as his father. The other, however, began taking cocaine and coming home with nothing to show for a week at the Keys. This situation was causing great chagrin and frustration to his father in 1999–2000.

Names of boats are fascinating. Nine of the twenty-seven catboats are named after the owner's young daughters. Thus we have *Miss Jaseth*, *Miss Chayanne*, and *Miss Ivania*, among others. Only two boats were named after wives. The names indicate an especially warm and caring relationship between men and their young daughters and suggest a more sentimental relationship than that between husbands and wives.

LOBSTER FISHING

One night while we are turtle fishing with Victor at the Keys, a lobster boat full of divers pulls up to spend the night at anchor. About fifteen divers are crowded on deck, and the boat is towing a number of metal *cayucos,* or canoes, behind it. The system, I learn from a friend in Port, is to drop off each *cayuco* over the lobstering ground, one at a time, 100–200 meters apart. The *cayucos* should always stay in sight of each other so they don't get lost. Two boys work out of each *cayuco,* one paddling and the other diving for lobsters. In 1978 most divers simply free dove, down to thirty feet or so; but by 1999 most were using scuba gear. The lobster population is overfished in shallow water, and deeper diving is necessary to obtain a good catch. Each diver carries a short staff with a hook on one end, with which he hooks a lobster and pulls it out of the rocks. The divers work all day and are picked up by the lobster boat late in the afternoon, as it makes its circle back around the diving area. The lobster tails are cut off at the boat and packed in ice, and each man's daily catch is recorded. Lobstering trips last about two weeks, with each diver paid in cash for the lobsters he has caught at the end of the two-week period.

The water is cold down deep, and the boys often dive for eight hours at a time. Many take cocaine before diving because it helps "kill the cold" and makes them able to work longer. They often snort a line of cocaine before plunging into the water, a practice that increases the danger inherent in diving. The drug runners peddle the drug all around the lobster fleet, using small, fast boats. They reportedly trade cocaine for money or for lobsters or occasionally for prostitutes, who sometimes accompany the boats to sea. There is thus a sort of seagoing retail cocaine trade. Antidrug laws are very hard to enforce at sea, and there is little effective regulation.

Young men from a number of coastal villages, including Awastara, sign on with lobster fishing boats regularly for trips to the Keys. The divers are paid by the pound for the lobsters they harvest and earn very high wages by local standards, up to several hundred dollars per trip. Thus they have plenty of money for cocaine. Lobstering is the most glamorous, high-paying job now available on the Coast. Lobsters are a luxury food in the United States and elsewhere, and the product is worth a great deal. By 2000 lobster fishing had become one of the mainstays of the coastal economy; and a new international airport building had been constructed in Puerto Cabezas, especially to export lobsters by air. Unfortunately the lobsters are being harvested as rapidly as possible, with no concern for conservation. Boats have to go farther out on the Keys, and divers have to work in deeper and deeper water.

The divers tend to spend most of their money on cocaine, liquor, and prostitutes as soon as they arrive back in Port. At the wharf one day, I watch a lobster boat tie up as a large crowd of women gather around to greet their husbands and sons. By meeting the boat at the wharf, they hope to obtain at least some of the money the divers have earned, before the young men disappear into the city. The binges of the "lobster boys" are notorious in Puerto Cabezas. One taxi driver told me of driving several of them from bar to bar all night long and collecting thousands of cordobas in taxi fare alone.

The lobster-diving business not only leads to alcohol and drug binges but is also dangerous. A World Bank report (1999: 46–50) details some of the factors that contribute to the high accident rate among Miskitu divers. Few have depth gauges or diving tables, and thus they cannot judge their depth or ascent rate properly; diving equipment is old and in poor repair; many divers use alcohol or drugs while diving, impairing their judgment; and most divers have received inadequate training or none at all.

The major health risk is decompression sickness, or the bends, a condition caused by the rapid expansion of nitrogen bubbles when ascending too rapidly from the depths, resulting in severe pain in the leg and arm joints, neurological impairment, and even paraplegia (*Merck Manual* 1999: 2465–68). Decompression sickness results from breathing compressed air, in which nitrogen is the major component, and then rising from the depths to the surface too rapidly. A slow, carefully timed ascent is necessary, to prevent nitrogen bubbles from forming and expanding in the bloodstream as the atmospheric pressure decreases. Such training is a part of all diver certification programs, but it is rarely explained clearly to local lobster divers or practiced by them. The bends occasionally kills but more frequently leaves the victim paralyzed to some degree.

Disabled divers on the Coast certainly number in the hundreds; and one estimate, by the Association for the Integration of the Disabled in Puerto Cabezas, is 1,500 such cases (World Bank 1999: 46). All these young men, disabled in the prime of their lives, face a very tragic future.

I talk to several former divers who live in Puerto Cabezas. One is almost completely paralyzed and cannot move or speak; his face is twisted in agony. Another younger boy in Awastara is recovering slowly from the bends. Both attribute their problems to the *liwa mairin,* the female creature who lives deep in the ocean as well as in fresh water. The *liwa* tries to seduce men and then injures or drowns them. These attacks are a punishment by the *liwa* for taking too many of her lobsters. Divers know that the industry is decimating lobster populations and believe the *liwa,* owner of all the sea creatures, is very angry about the situation. She thus inflicts paralysis and death on the divers.

Some report having seen the *liwa* soon before they begin suffering an attack of the bends. The World Bank report (1999: 43) suggests that such visions may be a result of nitrogen-induced hallucinations, from breathing compressed air at depth. Miskitu people often report seeing the *liwa* in some form, however, while swimming in the rivers or ocean. The spiritual reality of the *liwa* is not to be explained so matter-of-factly.

A cultural materialist explanation (Harris 1979) might rather interpret the *liwa* as an ideological mechanism for preventing overexploitation of marine resources. To the extent that the *liwa* did serve as a sort of "environmental policewoman," the introduction of Christianity (which impugned such beliefs) may have counteracted an important cultural brake on environmental destruction. Cultural materialists might further suggest that the paralysis and death of young divers is a logical consequence of the greed of the current world economic system. Commercial business enterprises, having exploited the forests and the gold mines, now turn to what is left: the ocean resources. The current system is obviously willing to sacrifice both lobsters and divers for quick profits.

The regional hospital in Puerto Cabezas now owns a hyperbaric recompression chamber for treating decompression sickness victims. It usually takes several days for the divers to reach the hospital from the scene of an accident out at sea, however, and the bends has often taken its toll by this time. In spite of the dangers involved, the high wages and glamour of lobster diving continue to attract and seduce many innocent young Miskitu men.

ACCIDENTS IN BOATS

All seafaring occupations have their share of danger. Like other sailors, the Awastara men are well aware of the dangers of the sea and tell many stories of boat accidents. The extremely strong northeasterly winds that occur periodically from November to January, the *yaslam*, cause many accidents. Bundled up inside the house, away from a cold *yaslam* wind one day, Casey tells a story about being out on the Keys turtle fishing at night when such a wind came up. He and his three sailors had found a sack of marijuana and were smoking it and were not paying attention to the changing weather. When the hard *yaslam* began to blow, a huge wave overturned the boat. Casey and the sailors held on and climbed up on the keel of the overturned boat. Luckily it was made of mahogany and floated upright in the water. Some of the personal belongings inside the boat came floating up. Casey, who is extremely strong, jumped off the keel and swam some distance away from the boat to retrieve his own plastic sack of belongings, but the others were afraid to jump off the keel. They lost everything. When the sea calmed down a bit, Casey swam underneath the boat and tied a line onto one of the thwarts. Then he and the sailors braced themselves against the line, standing on the keel, and began to pull with all their strength. They finally managed to right the boat and began to bail it out. If they hadn't been able to right it, Casey pointed out, they would most likely have died at sea. Their only hope would have been another boat passing close enough to hail, which might have come to their aid. This time the *yaslam* was blowing so hard that it carried them all the way to the Río Grande bar, on the south Coast, where they waited out the northeaster for several days. Only then could they sail back up the Coast to Awastara. It was a close call indeed.

In 1998 Octavio's boat overturned at the Awastara bar. The catboat was attempting to cross the dangerous bar in the dark when a wave caught her amidships and overturned her. No one was drowned in the shallow water, but all the boat's cargo was lost. *Dama* Hilario says he lost more than three thousand cordobas' worth of supplies for his store, including sacks of beans, sugar, flour, and rice as well as nails and batteries. Octavio tells me that many people walking the beach that night and in the morning found remains of the cargo, stowed in plastic bags, but they did not return any of it. It was a heavy financial loss.

TREASURES FROM THE SEA

Scavenging useful items from the sea is probably a mainstay of seacoast communities around the world. Nietschmann (1979a: 112–13) describes Tasbapauni people walking the beach systematically to find plastic fishing floats, sheets of plywood, metal drums, and anything else that might be useful. Some good stories are told in Awastara of unusual material items from the outside world that have washed up on the beach. In March 2000 Victor's son Adolpo found a good fifteen-foot boat out on one of the Keys, with a powerful 115-horsepower motor, now rusted, still attached to the transom. He towed it back to the village behind his catboat. It was said to be the kind of boat Jamaican fishermen use, rather than drug runners, but even so it had what appeared to be bullet holes in the motor cover. Victor hid the boat and motor in the bush until he managed to sell it for a few thousand cordobas.

Victor himself tells a story of finding a strange object floating in the ocean many years ago. He had gone to Bihmuna, north of Sandy Bay, and was coming down to Port in an eighteen-foot dory with a load of oranges to sell in the market. But right behind him was an older man, also with a boatload of oranges. Victor realized that whoever got to market first would get the best price on his oranges. Suddenly, off the Coast near Awastara, Victor noticed a strange contraption floating in the water. He steered over to it and found that it had a big "clock" on the outside and a long aluminum antenna and was well sealed. It looked like a big radio of some sort. Victor did not really know what it was, but it looked like it might be worth a lot of money. He threw a line around it and started towing it behind the boat. It was heavy, however, and caused a lot of drag in the water, slowing down the boat considerably. He looked back and could see the old man gaining on him, getting closer and closer. So he cast off the contraption and went on down to Port to sell his oranges. "What a mistake I made!" he says.

The device washed up on the beach near Bowman's house, and he cut it open with an axe. It was full of colored wire and had nine big batteries that Bowman took to Port and sold. Perhaps it had something to do with early space shots or with weather research. Bowman also noticed a metal plate on the outside with an address and asked someone write a letter to that address. Then, according to Victor, a man came all the way from England and flew up to Awastara from Port in a light plane, landing at the airstrip outside town that is no longer in use. When he looked at the device, cut open with an axe and stripped down, he became very angry. "What fools you are!" he said. "There would have been a big reward for recovering it whole." "Just think!" says Victor. "I could have had anything I wanted. A trip to England. I could have had an English woman! But it was ruined and there was no reward." Bowman's widow, to this day, has the big round metal case from the device, in which she washes the family clothes.

THE WIND

The wind is all important to men who make a living sailing. The direction of the wind is instantly apparent to them. Even after a second year on the coast, however, to my chagrin I often was not aware of exactly the quarter from which the wind was blowing. When a north wind (ya-habra pasa) is blowing, it tangles and fouls the turtle nets out on the Keys and causes major problems for the fishermen. The extremely hard north and northeast winds from November through January, the yaslam, bring many normal activities to a halt, as people huddle inside their houses to escape the cold. These storms only hit two or three times in a normal year, but they are dangerous and make life miserable for several days in a row. When the land breeze (*diwas*) blows, however, life is quite delightful. This breeze is common in the early morning hours and is used for coasting up northward along the shore from Port. When it occasionally blows all day, in August and September, the shrimp move in close to shore. People catch them in large numbers with their seines, especially at the river mouth. As soon as the wind shifts back to its normal northeast quadrant, however, the shrimp quickly move offshore. During most of the year, the northeast trades blow steadily. Some houses, like mine, are built facing the east or northeast, to enjoy the constant, cooling breeze, even in the hottest days of March and April.

THE TRIANGULAR TRADE

When Victor pioneered commercial turtle fishing on the Miskitu Keys, he introduced a kind of triangular trade, in which turtles caught on the Keys are taken to Port for sale in the market, and the money is used to buy provisions. The boats then make the trip back to Awastara with food supplies, to re-outfit and return to the Keys. During the mid-twentieth century, work at the mines and at the oil company near Dakura also provided cash wages. Such work, however, did not allow the regular weekly trips to Port with money to buy purchased foods that are common today. Captains with boats full of turtles arrive in Port, sell the catch, and then return to the village heavily loaded with sacks of provisions. Of course, they also bring one to three turtles home, to butcher in the village.

Nietschmann (1979b) notes that as the Miskitu people began working for wages and purchasing most of their food, earlier practices of fishing and gathering wild animal products declined. In Awastara subsistence farming also has declined over the twenty years I have known the community. Perhaps most important, sharing within villages also has been threatened. There is a contradiction between the need to sell turtles for cash, to buy foodstuffs and other necessities, and the obligation to share food with relatives and the needy. Miskitu people, caught up in producing for a broader market, are faced with a difficult dilemma: to sell local resources or share them. Nietschmann (1973, 1974, 1979b) describes this dilemma quite eloquently. Once involved in the broader economy with its market pressures, people find it almost impossible to extract themselves. Nutritionally, the result has been "greater participation in securing protein for export (turtles, shrimp, lobster, fish) in exchange for money to buy imported and increasingly expensive carbohydrates" (Nietschmann 1979b: 18). This certainly has been the case in Awastara, where the major part of the diet now consists of rice, beans, flour, sugar, and cooking oil. Turtle fishing provides the money for the weekly purchases of these imported foodstuffs. The triangular trade has made possible Awastara's dependence on purchased foodstuffs.

Intensified turtle fishing has been accompanied by a decline in turtle populations. Cynthia Lagueux has carefully documented turtle fishing off Nicaragua's Atlantic Coast in recent years. She estimates (1998: 96) that in the early 1990s between 6,000 and 11,000 green sea turtles were harvested each year. Lagueux carefully refrains from stating that her data prove that turtles are being overharvested, although it seems extremely likely that this is the case. She suggests enforcing limits on turtles harvested and protecting females from being taken, among other conservation measures.

Nietschmann's widely read article (1974) and the accompanying film (Weiss 1973) portray the situation in the mid-1970s, when two foreign turtle companies began to buy turtles for export from local fishermen. The article and film make the case for turtle conservation very pointedly, and they contributed to enactment of a prohibition on purchase of green sea turtles by foreign companies in the late 1970s. The article and film also seem to imply, however, that all Miskitu people live by turtle fishing. In fact, by 1999 only Awastara and Tasbapauni, where Nietschmann worked, continue to be major turtling communities. Traditionally, most coastal communities also practiced other sorts of fishing as well as agriculture. The economy of the interior Miskitu villages, and of the many villages lining the Río Coco, depended heavily on agriculture. Men from most Miskitu communities have also worked at wage labor, when available, for centuries. Thus not all Miskitu men are turtle fishermen.

During the 1990s, the Awastara turtlemen found their turtle fishing practices increasingly criticized from various quarters. For instance, a Nicaraguan mestizo construction foreman who rode up to Awastara with me in a catboat kept up a constant stream of criticism about hunting these large, defenseless creatures, pointing angrily to the two turtles lying underneath the thwarts. Cynthia Lagueux also gave a public talk in Awastara, presenting her data in an effort to promote turtle conservation. The World Bank, under pressure from conservation interests, has come up with a perfunctory plan to promote long-line fishing rather than turtling. But for the Awastara men, the question remains: how can they make a weekly income to support their families, if not by the turtling practices at which they have become proficient?

Coastal Miskitu people have always caught turtles for subsistence. In Awastara, however, it was not really a commercial enterprise until Victor and Pancho developed it as such by borrowing a new technology, catboats and turtle nets, from the Cayman Islanders. Fifty years ago, the Awastara men say that there were plenty of turtles on the nearby Keys; but now those turtles are all gone. The turtlemen must go farther and farther, and the turtles are harder and harder to catch. Everyone in Awastara agrees that the long-term prospects for turtle fishing are not good.

Pressure to regulate turtling has increased sharply. For a number of years the Nicaraguan government has instituted a closed period for turtle fishing, from April to June. There are many conflicting stories in Awastara about exactly what the regulations are. In 1999 and 2000 it was clear that the prohibition was not being enforced, and the Awastara men were continuing to sell their turtles in Port.

They had also saturated the market. When three or four boats arrive at the same time, all carrying turtles, the price in the Port market goes down. A large female turtle that should bring 350–450 cordobas sells for only 50–100. When even more turtles arrive to be sold, the butchers stop buying them, because they can't sell all the turtle meat. The men are then forced to try to sell their catch in Bluefields or the Corn Islands or Sandy Bay. Victor's son Adolpo once took a whole boatload of turtles to Bluefields but could not sell them there either, and eventually they all died in the boat. The small markets in these other towns provide an alternative for turtle sales, but they are farther away and involve more time at sea and the danger of losing all the turtles.

A general opinion in Awastara is that the local economy must change. Dakura and Sandy Bay both used to be turtle fishing villages, but only a few boats from each community now catch turtles. Awastara has been left as the only major turtle fishing village on the north Coast, and change is imminent. One day in May I counted thirty-two turtles at the Awastara landing, resting in the shade on their backs. Their owners had not been able to sell them in Port and were trying to figure out what to do with them.

If turtle fishing in fact diminishes in the near future, and Awastara men find some other way to make a living, the turtle fishing boom will have been a blip of fifty years or so in the community's economic history. With a market for turtles in Port, and the catboat/net fishing technology, Awastara men took advantage of a new economic opportunity. Unfortunately, like other booms on the Coast, it may represent rapid exploitation of some natural resource until it is threatened or depleted and then closure of the industry. The end of a boom usually means hard times and economic stagnation. Any sort of sustainable development has yet to be implemented on the Coast.

OTHER WAYS TO MAKE A LIVING?

In Awastara the local economy is highly monetized, and most goods and services are exchanged for money. Owning a catboat for turtle fishing or working as a sailor on one is the most important way of making a living. Finding cocaine on the beaches is a random occurrence, rather like hitting the lottery. What are the alternatives within the village?

People use the Spanish word *camarón* (shrimp) for any little job to make the money that people constantly require. Working as a porter is one of them. Each time a catboat arrives at the landing, a small crowd is waiting there to carry the cargo a kilometer or more up to the village. Several older men whose backs are still strong, *Dama* Julio and *Dama* Cristo among them, seem to spend part of each day at the landing waiting for boats to arrive. Heavy sacks of provisions, lumber, personal possessions of all kinds—porters are ready to carry whatever cargo has arrived. The standard price is fifteen cordobas for as much as a man can carry. When Casey and Hector bring back 1,000 board feet of lumber from across the lagoon, a large crowd of men gathers. Victor watches carefully as all the lumber is unloaded from the catboat, to make sure none is stolen at the landing. Hector supervises the task of carrying it up to his house. He pays 300 cordobas for labor that afternoon and comes to ask me for change for his three 100-cordoba bills. He tells me that in building a house you have to figure in portage costs as well as the cost of the lumber, nails, and hinges. Individuals with horses make good wages, carrying heavy sacks of building materials and food up from the landing on horseback.

Daily expenses add up for local people. Passage to Port in a catboat is twenty cordobas for a man, twenty-five for a woman. Men travel at a discount because they are expected to help with the work in the boat. In almost every household women raise chickens, both to eat and to sell. Chicken eggs are sold for one or one and a half cordobas each. Juan Padilla, the local baker, makes bread and peddles it from house to house two or three times a week. He says that he can make a good profit when he manages to buy flour in bulk in Port. He is not from Awastara but has a local spouse and children and is able to earn a reasonable living in the village making bread for sale. At my house one day another, very small entrepreneur arrives: a boy seven or eight years old, selling watermelon slices for one cordoba each. I buy ten slices for the whole family, thus confusing the little boy. Until then he has sold only a slice at a time, and he has a hard time figuring out the price for ten slices.

LOCAL STORES

Small stores have existed for many years in Awastara. I am interested in the operation of these stores, partly because my grandfather ran a small grocery store in the town of Miles, Texas (population 900), for over forty years. By 1999 there are fourteen small stores in Awastara. All of them sell local necessities, particularly food supplies: rice and beans, flour, sugar, and cooking oil. They also sell matches, kerosene for lanterns, candy and crackers, school notebooks and pencils, patent medicines, and assorted other goods.

Rodrigo once had a store of his own but eventually went broke. He estimates that it costs about two thousand cordobas to stock a store at the outset. One should be able to clear five hundred or six hundred cordobas a month—a small but constant profit and an important source of income for a family. Many people would like to own a store, if they could only amass the capital to start one. Our neighbor Victoria has the closest small store to our household, and we patronize it daily for necessities. Like everyone else, we normally send children to buy goods at the store and to check on prices. I notice that the kids are more enthusiastic about going across the field to the store if I give them an extra cordoba to buy a cookie. If any store in town is even slightly cheaper than another, the news will soon spread. Normally, we go to the closest store; but if there is a price difference, people will walk all the way across town to get the cheapest price. Children are often quizzed when they return about exactly how much each item cost and how much change they received. They carry a used plastic sack to bring back food provisions, since storekeepers have only a small stock of sacks. "Bring your own sack" is the rule.

Friends and relatives frequently ask storekeepers for credit, called by the English loanword *trust*. This creates a dilemma for the storekeeper. It is hard to refuse a favor to a relative, but some people are known not to repay their debts. Rodrigo said he tried never to give out more than 20 percent of his sales on credit at his store and to give credit only to people who had paid their debts in the past. Credit sales are usually written down in a school notebook by the storekeeper. Sometimes it is possible to get someone to work in your fields, or to do some other sort of labor, to repay a debt at your store. Taking bad credit debts to the *alcalde* to be settled rarely seems to work, although storekeepers occasionally try it. When turtling has not been successful, or when times are otherwise difficult, the pressure for credit by local people goes up.

The profit margin at the local stores is really quite small; and the risk of going broke, as Rodrigo did, is high. My grandfather reportedly went broke in Miles for exactly the same reason. *Dama* Hilario describes his store operation in Awastara, giving a complete list of prices. A hundred-pound sack of sugar costs 310 cordobas in Port. But you must pay portage from the supplier down to the wharf in Port, passage up to the village in a catboat, and portage costs up from the landing. He has been selling sugar for 4 cordobas a pound in the village, leaving a very small profit margin. When sugar goes up to 325 cordobas a sack, he decides he will have to start charging 5 cordobas a pound, even though he knows most of his customers will object strongly. "They don't understand I'm just passing on the increase in prices," he complains. "They think I'm trying to gouge them!"

Starting a store is recognized as one of several profitable investments that a person can make in Awastara. The others are building a new house, building a catboat, buying an outboard motor, or buying cattle to raise. All require a substantial cash investment. The only way to obtain such cash is to find cocaine or to save money from lobster diving. Both Jesse and Julián, for instance, have been lobster divers and saved some money from their work. Jesse bought cattle with part of his earnings. Twelve men from Awastara have been lobster divers, I am told—a small number compared to Dakura or Sandy Bay, where a substantial number of younger men are engaged in this work. One day as I pass in front of *Dama* Hilario's house, several young men are eagerly signing on for a three-week lobstering trip with a visiting captain. Unfortunately, many of the divers spend their earnings on cocaine and liquor and prostitutes in Port, before they ever get back to their home communities. A few boat captains actually drop the men off at the Awastara river mouth on the return voyage, close to the village, instead of in Port. This practice increases the chances of their actually bringing money home to their families.

It seems to be very difficult to earn enough money to invest from turtle fishing alone. Turtle fishing provides cash for daily subsistence (for food, provisions, and clothes) but not enough to invest for the future.

151

PEDDLERS

Itinerant peddlers pass through Awastara every week, selling used clothing, household utensils, and other needed items. These items are quite a bit cheaper in Port, but it is convenient and tempting to buy at your own house in the village. In the weeks preceding Christmas, peddlers show up in even greater numbers. The peddlers all seem to work in pairs, for safety and to help carry the merchandise from place to place. Most of the ones I encounter are mestizos, but the hired helper is frequently Miskitu and can thus serve as a salesman with local people. Peddling is regarded as risky business these days, given the high level of cocaine-related violence. I have heard various stories of peddlers being assaulted and robbed.

I talk at length with one mestizo peddler selling clothes in Awastara. He brings them from Managua, he says, and travels all over the country selling them, even to the isolated Atlantic Coast. In Awastara he trades clothes for coconuts as well as for money and rents a house from Maestro Opresiano to store the coconuts until he accumulates four or five thousand to take back to Port. People complain of his high prices, but he comes back several times during the year and seems to be doing well. He says he sells more stylish clothes to the Creole people in Port, but he also notes patronizingly that he likes to bring new styles to the villages so the Miskitu people can become accustomed to them. Although transportation to and from the villages is difficult, and there is a language barrier and the threat of robbery, these problems don't seem to stop the small but constant stream of peddlers from reaching Awastara.

I give away photographs regularly to friends in the village, and one day I learn why they are so much appreciated. I meet an itinerant photographer wandering through Awastara, who is charging 180 cordobas per picture!

CHAPTER SEVEN

Working in the Plantations

Early in my first year in Awastara, Victor asks me to go with him to help work in his fields. In addition to the more dramatic activities of turtling and seine fishing, people continue to plant and harvest subsistence crops. Agriculture has declined in importance over the twenty years I have known the community, but it still provides an important share of the food people consume. The most important crop is cassava.

PLANTING AND HARVESTING CASSAVA

Also referred to as "manioc" in English, cassava is called *yauhra* in Miskitu. It is a plant, originally domesticated by Native Americans, that is now a major subsistence crop in Africa and in other parts of the tropical world as well. The white, fleshy tubers are edible from the time they are very small but get bigger and bigger the longer they are left in the ground. They are a rich source of calories and contain compounds called cyanogens that may provide some protection against malaria (McElroy and Townsend 1996: 91). In Awastara we plant sweet cassava, which does not have to be processed to remove cyanic acid, a lethal poison found in the bitter variety of manioc grown in some parts of South America.

It is about 5:00 A.M., still pitch black outside. Pamela and Josepina have just come by my house and called out to me. Time to go to the plantation with them to harvest *yauhra*. We start along the path up over the hill and down onto the savannah, walking due south parallel to the coast. It is easier to walk barefoot on the mud path, so I take off my sandals.

It is about an hour's walk down the path to the bridge across the swamp at the north end of Aras Bila. The bridge is a long one, made of palm logs tied together with cord. It was built by communal labor when a man named Kilbon Coe was headman in Awastara and represented a major community improvement. Victor says that in earlier times people had to wade or even swim through the deep water to get to their fields. Last year the bridge was in good condition, but this year it has fallen down in many places; and we have to crawl gingerly over them, sometimes descending into the dark, chest-deep water below. Reaching the beach on the other side, we turn south again and then turn back into the bush on a trail that is very hard to see. This is what Nietschmann (1973: 136–40) calls "beach ridge agriculture," in which alternating ridges and wet bottomlands just behind the beach provide small but fertile strips for planting. As we go through the brush, Josepina cautions me not to touch the *tubal,* a plant with sharp leaves that cuts like a knife. We pass through someone else's cassava field and then get to Pamela and Casey's field. It is about a hundred and fifty feet long by fifty feet wide. The cassava plants are approximately the height of our heads, but the tubers are still small, five to eight inches long. It is late October. By February or March, when the last cassava is harvested, the tubers will be larger. This field was planted the previous March, after being burned over.

We work by grabbing the cassava stalk and shaking it hard to loosen it in the soil. Pamela shows me how to wiggle it so as not to break off any tubers in the ground. We break the small, edible tubers off the stalks and put them in a sack. Then we chop the ends of the plants off clean to stick them back in the ground. With luck they will grow again. We put a large armful of cut stalks together in one hole, sticking them in as far as possible. When I ask Pamela about this, she says that it is so she will know these were the plants she pulled and not the young drug addicts. When they steal cassava, they just throw the plants on the ground.

It takes about an hour to fill our three sacks. Plenty of cassava is still left in the field. These three sacks should last for several days at the house, *tama* to go with our turtle meat. As we walk back out to the beach, two older women appear, also carrying sacks of cassava. One of them comments bitterly that the men don't care about fixing the bridge at Aras Bila, because it is mostly women who come daily to harvest the cassava. I remember that vaginal penetration is an important cause of women's illness in Miskitu belief; walking through the dark, swampy water is therefore dangerous for women. We take a different way back to avoid the worst part of the fallen bridge. On the path back to the village, we stop at a clear puddle and wash all the mud off the cassava tubers, which float in the water. When we get back to Awastara, I take off my mud-encrusted jeans and shirt and bathe and put on clean clothes.

A trip to the plantations often involves this sort of slogging through the mud and walking through water up to your waist. People thus wear their oldest, "going to plantation" clothes, which may be little more than rags. Standard plantation attire also includes a machete, a net bag hung on the shoulder to carry things, a piece of rope or bark line to use as a strap or tumpline for carrying loads, and a headcloth for women, "to keep out the cold." People often go barefoot and save their shoes to wear after bathing and putting on fresh clothes back at the house.

Cassava, the main plantation crop, is planted anytime between March and May. It is planted by chopping the cassava stalks into short pieces about twelve to fifteen inches long and sticking them in hillocks of earth, two or three sticks to the hillock. From this simple planting technique, large towering cassava plants grow, with sizable tubers in the ground. Awastara people begin digging up the tubers in October and harvest it little by little until it is all gone by February or March. This use pattern requires going to the plantations every few days to harvest more cassava and cut a few plantains or bananas. Richard Lee (1968) and other anthropologists have described the encyclopedic knowledge that hunters and gatherers, or foraging peoples, have of their local environment. Given such knowledge, the environment effectively serves as a warehouse. Here, however, the garden is also the warehouse, and the constant trips to the plantations are really "shopping trips" to gather enough breadkind for the next few days' meals. This is a traditional Miskitu pattern.

The locally produced cassava lasts longer if you "mix" it with breadkind bought in the market in Port or from Sisin or Tuara or one of the inland villages. Most trade with these inland villages is now through the marketplace in Port, but in 1978–79 there were still boatloads of cassava being brought to Awastara for sale in August and September, months when the local crop is not yet ripe. Cortés Kingsman made good money with his catboat, carrying heavy sacks of cassava to Awastara from Sisin across the lagoon. Helms (1971: 22) describes in some detail the pattern of trade from the interior Miskitu and Mayangna villages to the Coast. The coastal Miskitu communities had access to foreign traders and thus served as middlemen for imported items and also supplied the interior with coastal products. In modified form, this trade is still going on. Turtles and salted fish and coconuts are still sold to the interior, with agricultural produce coming back in return, especially cassava from Sisin and Tuara and beans from the Río Coco. Large canoes cut out of single hardwood logs are still handmade in the interior and paddled down the rivers for sale in Port. Although direct trade with the interior still takes place, it seems to have declined since 1978, whereas trade through the

Puerto Cabezas marketplace has increased in importance.

The fertile land in the interior villages is said to be "cold" and good for growing crops, unlike the sandy "hot" soil of Awastara. Miskitu people in Sisin are reported to have big cassava tubers even in September, which they can dig and sell to the Coast people. By September last year's cassava crop in Awastara has long been dug up and eaten, and people are still waiting for the current crop to get big enough to dig up and eat. The strategy used to be to leave the cassava in the ground as long as possible, to let the tubers get bigger. But stealing by young drug addicts has complicated matters.

Beans are a major product of the Río Coco region, where the soil is also said to be "cold" and good for crops. Almost every meal in Awastara includes beans, but they are all bought from the interior, usually through the marketplace. Occasionally, however, someone makes a special trip to the Río Coco to trade salted sea turtle meat for a hundred-pound sack of beans, during April or May, when beans are being harvested.

Agricultural work is clearly tied to the phases of the moon. Nietschmann (1973: 113) and Helms (1971: 188) both comment on beliefs about the power of the moon as it relates to agriculture and to the rhythms of living things in general. In Tasbapauni, says Nietschmann, "the moon controls all." In Awastara cassava or coconut trees (or anything else) should be planted at the full moon rather than the new moon. Anything planted at the new moon won't do well, people say. Posts and lumber for a house should also be cut at the full moon or at least when the moon is high in the sky. Otherwise the lumber will rot quickly. You can't even get a woman pregnant at new moon, one man told me—it has to be at the full moon! The full moon is regarded as life-giving or procreative, while the new moon is dangerous to life.

The long strip of land east of the village called Aras Bila, south along the Awastara River bottom and beyond (map 2), is the main agricultural area for the village. The river changes course constantly, and each year the river bar shifts slightly, moving farther toward the south. Over thousands of years the river has deposited miles of alluvial soil, leaving a long, narrow stretch of rich black bottomland, ideal for agriculture. I believe that this is the main reason Awastara was founded in its present location. The original inhabitants did not pick just any strip of coast. They chose a living place that was slightly above the savannah and covered with pine trees and that had fertile agricultural land along the river bottom. A different problem is occurring now, however, as the ocean encroaches on the strip of fertile land, eating it away and reclaiming it for the sea. Victor says the grove of tall coconut palms at Iskri, near Awastara's boundary with Krukira, used to be far inland. Now they are right at the edge of the sea and will soon be washed away. The coastline seems to be receding, threatening Awastara's agricultural land.

The plots of farmed land along the river bottom are all private property and pass down through families from generation to generation. Occasionally a plot is sold; but with plenty of unused land available, there is little incentive to buy land rather than clear a piece yourself. Victor says that in his father's time there was still tall forest (*insla disang*) in places along this strip. When felled and burned, it made especially rich farmland. Nowadays people just let a plot rest for a few years then chop down the scrub forest again and burn it to plant. "The land is old," as one man put it. Cassava and plantains and bananas, with some rice and maize, have always been planted here.

In late May we go back to another of Casey's plantations, very close to where we were harvesting cassava in October. He has already felled the small trees growing on this plot and burned them, so our job today is simply to clear away the burned logs for planting. Casey and his wife, Pamela, and Eliza and Melvin and I are the work crew. We leave at 5:00 A.M., in the morning coolness. This is the height of the dry season, and by midday it will be sizzling hot. It is almost a picnic atmosphere, with ten-year-old Melvin in his Chinese-looking rain hat and Casey with his chainsaw and tools loaded onto his bike, which he pushes all the way to the plantation, using it as a sort of mechanical packhorse. The trail is completely dry. At the plantation, our work consists of pulling apart the burned branches and small logs and carrying them off to the side of the field, so that Casey can plant cassava. It is dirty work. All of us get black from head to toe within minutes. Casey saws up the larger pieces with his chain saw. But most of the burned branches or *klangni* we just man-handle and woman-handle off into the brush. Melvin turns out to be a good worker, and he and I and the two women work steadily. Casey builds a fire to windward to keep off the insects, which swarm around our sweaty bodies. It is humid and dank in the small field, which is about a hundred feet by thirty feet. Inside the low scrub jungle there is little light, and I know my pictures won't turn out well.

After three hours' hard work, we have cleared the whole field. Casey says he didn't think we would finish it today. We "knock off," as Casey says in Creole, and drink some water and joke about how dirty we have gotten. The only thing left here is to plant the cassava shoots. Good timing. The rains should start at any moment. Casey stays on to work in another plot of his; and the rest of us start back, carrying bunches of cassava shoots from a nearby field back to the village, to plant in a much

FIGURE 7. *Plantation work, by Wiskat Morales*

smaller, fenced garden near the house. Along the way we find *biuhu* berries, small and purple and sour, which we pick and eat with our blackened fingers.

Wiskat's picture (figure 7) illustrates plantation work. A man and woman are walking from their house to a cassava field, along a path. The field is surrounded by a fence and has green cassava growing inside. The woman carries a net bag and a machete and has an old cloth around her head as protection from the cold early-morning air (*kauhla*), which causes sickness. The raggedness of the clothes usually saved for plantation work is not really apparent in Wiskat's picture. A man and his dog, inseparable companions, follow along behind the woman on the path. Meanwhile, a younger woman, probably a daughter, feeds chickens, a dog, and a pig near the house. This last activity is described as animal-raising work (*daiwan sahwaia*) by Wiskat. The picture portrays this constant if not overly arduous daily activity, which is as typical of Miskitu life as is going to church.

COCONUTS

Awastara people plant coconut trees around their houses as soon as they begin clearing a lot and building a house. The young coconut trees must be protected from foraging cattle and pigs until their branches are tall enough to be out of reach. Wire fences around the trees are expensive, so some people paint the coconut leaves regularly with wet cow dung, a disagreeable chore. A coconut tree will begin to bear after four or five years; and when it is fully grown, ten to twenty nuts will ripen each month. Along Awastara's strip of fertile agricultural land, several individuals have large plantations of coconuts. Often they are harvested every three months or so, when there should be one bunch on the ground, one bunch on the tree ready to fall, and another bunch on the tree that are green but can still be cut. A gathering team includes several men: one to climb the tree and cut the coconuts, another to gather them in big piles, and a third to husk them. The husker uses a *macana,* a three- or four-foot-long stick planted in the ground with a sharp triangular piece of metal pointing upward. With a few quick motions, the husker impales the coconut on the *macana,* twists it, and takes off the husk (photo 8). A good husker can

PHOTO 8. *Husking coconuts*

159

do several nuts a minute. The nuts are then loaded in catboats and taken to Port for sale. Coconut trees provide another small but steady source of cash income as well as daily coconuts to drink. A green coconut provides a cool, refreshing drink of coconut water when it is cut open, and soft white flesh to eat with a "spoon" cut from a piece of the hull. Dried coconut meat is grated and put in a cloth, and water is squeezed through it to produce "coconut milk," an ingredient in many local dishes. Rice and fish are cooked with coconut milk, for example. A family that does not have coconut trees will have to buy coconuts from someone else—a situation regarded as shameful, since people should plant their own trees as soon as they establish residence.

RICE

Miskitu people in general started growing rice only in the late nineteenth century (Offen 1999: 242–43), encouraged by Moravian missionaries. In Awastara a Swedish missionary named David Hagland tried to promote rice cultivation early in the twentieth century. He supposedly offered a free dinner to the man who produced the most rice. He gave out a new six-month rice, called *wilibi*, which takes longer to mature than the three-month variety. It also has a spine that prevents the birds from eating it and causing as much damage as they do to the three-month variety. Like many of the early missionaries, Hagland left a legend behind. One story is that an old man came to the Reverend Hagland, very proud of having produced one hundred and fifty bunches of rice. Hagland asked, "How many are in the family?" There were thirteen. "How much rice do you eat a day?" Four bunches, or two bunches when there is other food. So Hagland said, "Well, for two bunches a day, that rice would last you for seventy-five days. For almost three hundred days of the year you wouldn't have rice of your own. Why is it that a big family of thirteen people can only produce one hundred and fifty bunches of rice?" The cryptic story indicates the attitudes of missionaries from farming backgrounds, as opposed to the Miskitu practice of including agriculture as just one part of a multiple-resource subsistence base. People try many different strategies to obtain food, among them subsistence agriculture. The constantly increasing Miskitu population seems to indicate that the multiple-strategies approach has succeeded.

One morning in September Victor and I leave at 3:00 A.M. for the rice plantation that he needs to harvest down in Aras Bila. When we get to the field, we rest for a few minutes and let it get lighter so we can see to work

Photo 9. *Harvesting rice with Victor*

and also avoid any snakes that may be in the rice field. Victor planted this field in April, and the heads of rice are full on the tall clumps of green rice, planted every few feet throughout the small field. He has not been back since then to weed, but a neighbor who works the next field over has told him the rice is ready to be harvested. With two other people Victor has hired, we work cutting off the stalks of ripe grain (photo 9) and carrying them to an old cloth spread in the center of the field. We finish cutting the rice in about three hours, stuff it in large burlap sacks, and carry it back to the house. We have three sacks full, perhaps fifty pounds of rice once it is hulled. At the house, we spread the rice sheaves on the hot metal roof to dry. Later it will be pounded in a wooden mortar called an *unu,* to remove the hulls. This homegrown rice is unpolished and presumably quite nutritious. It tastes delicious.

As we walk back up the path to the house, a neighbor calls out, "How much did you get?" On hearing the answer, only three bags full, she retorts, "What did you expect, Victor, you lazy thing, you never even went back to weed the field since planting it in April." Victor doesn't like agri-

161

cultural work and makes no secret of it. He would rather spend weeks at a time out on the Keys turtle fishing.

Some individuals and families are enthusiastic farmers, however. In 1978 an older man named Juan Esteban proudly showed me his house full of sacks of rice that he had harvested. "I am one of the few people here who really like to work!" he said. Juan Esteban claimed that instead of selling turtles in Port and buying food, it was better to raise your own. Although the agricultural land in Awastara is not as good as farther inland around Tuara and Sisin, Juan Esteban simply regarded this as a challenge. "Most people are just too lazy to work at burning a new plantation every year!" he told me. He was proud of never having to buy rice at the market. Other people laughed and admitted he was a good farmer, but few tried to imitate him. Juan Esteban exemplified the strong sense of individualism, of doing what one wants to do, that permeates Miskitu culture.

By 2000 Victor points out to me that we rarely hear the "thump, thump" sound that used to be a constant in daily life, the rhythm of women hulling home-grown rice in their large wooden mortars or *unuh*. The *unuh*, carved out of a tree trunk, has a large opening in one end that serves as the mortar bowl and an attractive hourglass shape. It looks very much like similar wooden mortars used in West Africa. Plora's *unuh* is now hanging from a tree in the yard, unused. In 1978–79 women hulled rice almost every day, but the rice now bought from stores in Port comes already hulled.

AGRICULTURAL WORK AND MISKITU LIFE

After being planted, cassava and rice fields have to be weeded several times before the harvest. But agricultural work is not really intensive or year-round, and in Awastara it rarely requires the long daily toil that so many of the world's agricultural people experience. Working in the plantations in the morning usually involves a few hours' work, gathering some food for the next day, and if possible finding some wild food along the way—perhaps gathering *biuhu* berries or catching crabs or a freshwater turtle. These habits remind one more of the food forager's use of resources than of the farmer's daily work in the fields. Juan Esteban and the Reverend Hagland may have thought of Awastara people as lazy farmers, but their farming practices must be seen in terms of a broader subsistence strategy.

Nietschmann (1973: 142–44) calculated that one acre of agricultural land in Tasbapauni required only about 602 hours of labor per year. One-quarter of those hours was spent simply walking to and from the fields, an activity that also yields wild food products. Such agriculture is in fact quite productive, compared to other regions of the world in which swidden agriculture seems to require considerably more labor. With the relatively low labor input, one might assume that agricultural inputs would have intensified over the last twenty years, given the increase in population in Awastara.

This is not the case, however. Rather, there has been a general decline in agricultural efforts. Fewer fields are planted, and fewer people work at subsistence agriculture. One reason is cocaine. The young men with drug habits steal the cassava out of the fields and sell it to buy crack cocaine, which is made locally. Pamela and Casey have tried to hide their cassava field this year, and so far the "drug boys" haven't found it. But another man tells me that he planted cassava fields three years in a row and never got to harvest any of it. He became discouraged and is not planting any this year.

One evening after dark I am sitting talking with Victor when a young man comes to the house with a sack of cassava tubers for sale. Victor buys a large handful of tubers for ten cordobas and tells me later that they must have been stolen. "Why else would a man come at night to sell cassava?" he asks. Nevertheless, Victor buys cassava from him. It's too good an opportunity to pass up. Ten cordobas is also the price of one rock of crack cocaine. The young man goes on from our place to others living nearby and presumably sells his whole sack under cover of the darkness. I begin to understand why it is difficult to stop thievery within the village. The next day for lunch we have stolen cassava as our *tama*.

Thinking toward the future, what is likely to happen to subsistence activities in Awastara? Turtle fishing, if practiced simply for subsistence needs, would continue to provide ample protein in the diet, a fortunate situation among the world's people. It is ironic from a nutritional point of view that large quantities of such high-quality protein are currently sold in the market for money, which is then used, in part, to buy low-quality carbohydrates, refined sugar, and white flour. Meanwhile, village agriculture continues to decline, as turtle fishing has intensified. Nietschmann's careful work (1973: 228) has shown that agriculture of the type practiced in Awastara has much higher calorie productivity than other subsistence strategies. The problem is that locally grown food does not produce enough income to buy other commodities in Port. Tools, lumber, clothing, kerosene, and other manufactured products have become necessities. Hooked into the market economy, the Miskitu people of Awastara continue to overexploit their natural resources to obtain the cash they need. It is difficult to criticize their current economic strategy too severely, however, while the rest of the world continues to pump oil reserves at a furious rate, cut the remaining forests, and pollute the atmosphere and the oceans. It might be comforting to be able to think of my Miskitu friends as native environmentalists, but for better or worse they too joined the world economy several centuries ago.

CHAPTER EIGHT

School Days

Making a living is a basic concern of families in any community, but so is preparing the next generation for new and perhaps different adult lives. From my first days in Awastara, the rhythm of children going to and from classes has been a part of the weekly routine. I sit in on classes and talk with teachers (first in 1978 and then for longer periods in 1999–2000), trying to understand what role the school plays in children's lives and in the community.

The school dates from the mid-twentieth century and has changed considerably over the years. In 1978 there was a one-room schoolhouse where Maestro Opresiano, himself from Awastara, had been the sole teacher for many years. The original schoolhouse had been close to the Moravian Church, but it was moved to its present location at the recommendation of a regional school inspector, who said the children would study better if the schoolhouse were farther back from the main path to the lagoon (map 3). Maestro Opresiano himself organized the children and parents to clear the area that became a playing field and to plant fruit trees along the side of the school.

In 1978 Maestro Opresiano had strong opinions about how children should be educated. His own classes were conducted entirely in Spanish, which he speaks well. His theory, also the one promoted by the school system in the 1970s, was that children should learn strictly by immersion. Although none of the students spoke any Spanish on their first day of school, presumably by listening to the teacher and copying sentences into their notebooks they would begin to learn the national language. Classes seemed to consist mostly of having the children laboriously copy out words and sentences in Spanish. Maestro Opresiano moved from group to group, punishing a child every once in a while in the small, noisy classroom by bringing him or her to the front of the room for a scolding. But he also laughed and smiled with the children and seemed good-natured. My impression at the time was that the children learned little, and certainly very few of them went on to secondary school. School attendance, then as now, dropped off rapidly after the first grade, with only a handful of children reaching the sixth grade. Promotion rates in 1999 are also low. Only 55 percent of first-graders pass on to the next grade, and 58 percent of second-graders. Three of the four sixth-graders do manage to pass, however, indicating very serious motivation on the part of the few students who make it this far. Many of the standard subjects covered in classes seem curiously divorced from the realities of village life, I think, with no clear indication of the final benefit to be obtained.

BILINGUAL EDUCATION

The Spanish immersion program of the 1970s had changed to a bilingual program by 1998. In the late 1990s two of the few remaining achievements of the 1980s Sandinista government were the new *costeño* university (the URACCAN) and the Intercultural Bilingual Education Program (PEBI). After the Autonomy Law of 1987, CIDCA contracted with Terra Nuova (an Italian development organization) to create the PEBI, a new, intercultural bilingual program for Miskitu schoolchildren. Work groups of Miskitu educators and foreign linguists labored to produce a series of elementary school textbooks through the fourth grade. First-grade students now learn to read and write in Miskitu, their mother tongue, and then begin learning Spanish. By the third and fourth grades, most lessons are in Spanish. The school texts are interesting and well done, and the program seems very progressive. It recognizes the existing language skills of the first-graders and attempts to use those skills as building blocks for further education. Conservative central governments in Nicaragua in the 1990s, however, have not supported the program financially or in principle. Unfortunately for the children, support from international groups continues to dwindle as the idealistic Nicaraguan Revolution recedes into the past.

By 1998 the PEBI had been implemented in many of the Miskitu communities in northeast Nicaragua. Riddled with problems, it nevertheless represents a major effort to use the indigenous language in formal education and thus give it recognition and prestige in the region.

Paola Venezia (1996) outlines some of the problems confronting the PEBI. They include poorly prepared teachers who are not bilingual themselves, high turnover of teachers because of poor pay, children who stay in school for only one or two years, and lack of community support. A survey of communities in the Región Autónoma del Atlántico Norte (RAAN) showed that 124 had no school at all and in 94 schools education went through only the second grade (Venezia 1996: 6). Awastara is unusual, then, in having a school with classes continuing through the sixth grade, even though very few children reach the higher grades.

ATTENDING SCHOOL

I go to school with the children from my family a number of times during 1999–2000. It's a long walk through the village, and we arrive about 7:30. The teachers and the school director or principal, Moisés, have a short faculty meeting outside the building before classes begin. Maestra Juliana's first-grade class begins about 7:45. She calls roll and reminds the kids, "You have to be in school every day, unless you're sick." Juliana then checks the children's fingernails and hands before class starts. "We have to be clean to come to school," she tells them. She also carries a small branch with the leaves stripped off, to pop the kids on the hand when they misbehave. "Your mother loves you and that's why she whips you," she explains. Morality lessons delivered *smalkaia* fashion occur repeatedly. People who don't listen to their mothers and fathers, who steal and take cocaine, will die young. But people who live properly will live on into old age.

Maestra Juliana begins with reading, in Miskitu. "There are three vowels in Miskitu, *a, i,* and *u—la, li, lu—ka, ki, ku—ma, mi, mu.*" As the children review the Miskitu vowels, there is a deafening roar of response from the kids to Juliana's questions. She tells them in Miskitu, "I will be very happy when you learn to read, and to know that you learned it from me." Juliana uses a double-edged Gillette razor blade to sharpen the children's pencils. Ouch! I think to myself. I'm relieved the children aren't using the Gillette themselves. Each child seems to need his or her pencil sharpened. Some early readings in the first-grade book, *Wan Ing-wanka—Our Dawning,* include:

Limi bip kum alki pisa.	The jaguar is grabbing and eating the cow.
Lukas bui ikaia lukisa.	Lucas is trying to kill it.
Bip nani ba main kaiki kaia sa limi pibia apia mata.	The cattle must be guarded so the jaguar won't eat them.

167

Kukiki ai kukuka kaiki ki.

FIGURE 8. *Sample page from first-grade reader in Miskitu:* Wan Ingwanka 1: Aisi-kaikaia wauhkataya mani ulanka pas *(Bilwi, Nicaragua: Programa Educativo Bilingüe Intercultural, Ministerio de Educación, 1993)*

Page 14 from *Wan Ingwanka 1* (figure 8) deals with how the *k* sound in Miskitu is written. It provides a tongue-twister sentence with lots of *k*s: *Kukiki ai kukuka kaiki ki.* This is one of my favorite pages, and it also makes the children giggle when they read it. It translates: "My grand-mother is looking at her coconuts."

In her class next door, Maestra Juana tries to use both Miskitu and Spanish. "Spanish is not our language," she says, "but a language we take from others. *Yawan bila apia kuna upla bila implikaia."* "You won't spend all your lives here," she continues. "You will have to learn Spanish. Even though we speak it badly, we must learn it." As far as I can tell, very few of the students understand the Spanish part of the lesson. But as they did twenty years ago, the children work at writing, slowly and laboriously, in their notebooks. Juana walks around the room looking at each child's work and putting a check mark on it. She doesn't make any corrections on the work or show them how to improve it.

About half the students have brought their copies of *Wan Ingwanka*. What has happened to all the other copies of the expensive textbook given out to them? There are very few in evidence, and most are ragged and tattered. Several thousand copies of the elementary bilingual education texts were distributed to schoolchildren in the region, but many of them seem to have disappeared. Taking care of books is difficult in Miskitu households, with few shelves and many children and adults living together. Books and papers don't last very long in this climate anyway. And there is little tradition of caring for books, except for Bibles, which are treasured and handled with respect. I know that my own house is unusual, since Casey has built long shelves for all my books and papers. "You have a lot of Bibles," Nena comments one day, as she looks at my shelves.

The bilingual program is controversial. Many Miskitu parents oppose it, arguing that their children already speak Miskitu and don't need to improve their skills in their own language. The pressing need, they say, is for children to learn Spanish and be able to read and write it and thus function well in Nicaraguan society. Maestro Opresiano expresses his opinions in no uncertain terms. He speaks for many parents when he says: "Why do they need to learn Miskitu in school? They already speak Miskitu at home! It is just foolishness to spend time in school learning a language they already know. What they need to learn is Spanish! You have to speak Spanish or English to get along anywhere else in the world."

The sixth-grade teacher, Maestro Jali, and I visit with Maestro Opresiano and try to explain the bilingual program's philosophy to him. In the first grade, children will be taught about 75 percent of the time in Miskitu and 25 percent in Spanish. In the second grade it will be 50/50. And by the sixth grade, school will be mostly in Spanish. The children will learn to read and write first in their native language, while they also learn Spanish in school. Then they can begin to write in Spanish as well as Miskitu. Opresiano just snorts and repeats that it is all foolishness. I point out that many different kinds of texts are now being written in Miskitu. He replies that if people want reading material in Miskitu they can go to the Moravian church and read the Moravian prayer book or hymnal. He is obviously not going to change his mind about the PEBI. The teachers tell me that many parents have similar criticisms, but their comments may not so much reflect negative attitudes toward their own language, as recognition of the practical need to learn Spanish these days.

Maestra Zulaina, a thoughtful bilingual teacher, has worked in the PEBI since it began in 1987. Before that education was all in Spanish. "Both programs work," she says, "although with the PEBI, at first it is difficult for the children to try to learn to read in both languages. But by the third grade they catch on." The small number who continue on to the fourth and fifth grades can translate from Spanish to Miskitu, but it is much more difficult for them to translate from Miskitu into Spanish. Even the few sixth-grade students can't really converse in Spanish. It is a language they hear only on the radio or when they go to Port. No one speaks Spanish as a daily language in the village. "Up on the Río Coco," Zulaina says, "more people are bilingual in both languages, but here along the Coast we only speak Miskitu." One of the problems is that in Awastara most of the teachers speak very little Spanish. It is hard for them to teach effectively when they themselves don't know Spanish, Zulaina points out.

One of the controversial proposals of the neoliberal government of President Arnoldo Alemán is to bring hundreds of monolingual mestizo schoolteachers from the Pacific side of Nicaragua to teach Spanish in the Miskitu-speaking region. Such a program is directly contrary to the principles of the PEBI and has been vigorously opposed by educators and *costeño* leaders. At any rate, the Ministry of Education has so few resources that the president's plan is not financially feasible. There is no housing for teachers in the communities, and teachers' salaries are so meager that they cannot afford to rent or buy houses. Salaries are in the range of $50–100 a month and must be supplemented by other economic activities. Local teachers from the village all have subsistence plantations nearby, fruit trees and animals, and male relatives who are turtle fishermen. They could not survive on their teachers' salaries alone. Mestizo teachers wouldn't be able to live in a "foreign" community like Awastara.

A FUTURE FOR THE MISKITU LANGUAGE?

The PEBI clearly functions in a situation of diglossia, in which one language is accorded high social status and is used in a context different from that of another language of lower social status (Saville-Troike 2003: 45–46). The high-status language is usually employed in formal situations related to education or government, and the lower-status language is used in the home and in other informal contexts. It may have a connotation of warmth or intimacy. Miskitu is the daily language for tens of thousands of villagers in Nicaragua, but Spanish is the prestige language in broader Nicaraguan society, necessary to find a good job or pursue any kind of career. In earlier centuries English was the prestige language on the coast, and for some older people in Awastara it continues to be so. They point to relatives in the United States and contacts with different sorts of English-speaking visitors. Nevertheless, it is apparent to many Miskitu parents that their children must now learn the language of their traditional enemies, the "Spaniards" or mestizo Nicaraguans.

Various Miskitu leaders and intellectuals have promoted efforts to raise the relative prestige of their language. Nineteenth-century visitor Captain Bedford Pim of the British Navy reported that King George Augustus Frederick wrote poetry in Miskitu (Pim and Seeman 1869: 304), and various contemporary authors continue to write and publish stories and poetry in their own language as well (Silva Mercado and Korten 1997). Moravian missionaries, who worked hard at learning the language and translating religious texts into it, were one set of prestigious outsiders with a deep appreciation of the Miskitu language. The PEBI organizers represent a more recent group that also values language preservation.

During the Sandinista years (1980–90), significant linguistic work on the Miskitu language was accomplished. Danilo Salamanca (1988) provides a very detailed grammar of the language. He states (1988: 33–34) that he hopes his work might stimulate secondary school courses in Miskitu and a more respected role for the language in public affairs generally. The work has never been published, however, and thus is not readily available. The Centro de Investigaciones y Documentación de la Costa Atlántica published a useful grammar of Miskitu (CIDCA 1985b), intended primarily for Spanish-speaking Nicaraguans who wanted to study the Miskitu language. Unfortunately, no modern Spanish-Miskitu dictionary is available, making it necessary to rely on the older Heath and Marx (1953) dictionary. A trilingual Spanish-English-Miskitu dictionary has been published by Catholic missionaries on the Coast (Vaughan Warman 1962), but I was never able to obtain a copy. Jorge Matamoros's small sociocultural dictionary of the language (1996) is interesting and helpful. It explains the cultural context of many words in both Spanish and Miskitu, for the benefit of teachers and students in the PEBI. It does not pretend to be a complete dictionary. Nevertheless, its small line drawings and careful bilingual explanations of words, by a native speaker who is himself a scholar, indicate the quality of work that might be accomplished in the future.

In the near future, however, mestizo Nicaraguan society seems likely to exert stronger and stronger pressures for language conformity. An influx of Spanish speakers from the west is already occurring, and "economic development" in the region is conducted primarily in Spanish. Ties with the Moravian Church and other churches based in the United States have declined. Emigration to the United States, however, has created many ties between people on the Coast and their relatives in various U.S. cities. A few years ago my telephone rang, and the caller spoke to me first in Miskitu then in fluent American English. It was Tabita, who cooked for me when she was about sixteen and at that time did not know a word of either English or Spanish. She came to the United States during the war years, is happily married to a U.S. citizen, and now lives in Berkeley, California.

It is clear that for the immediate future Miskitu will continue to be the daily language in dozens and dozens of *costeño* communities. Whether it will remain a low-prestige, village-based language, or—through the efforts of Miskitu leaders and intellectuals—manage to become a respected language for use in business and education on the Coast, remains to be seen.

LITERACY AND TEACHING ENGLISH

Parents recognize that school is helpful in at least one specific way: it provides literacy, a very useful skill. Young people usually write letters in Miskitu for older ones. When I visit Elsie on Little Corn Island, for instance, she wants to send a letter back to her mother in Awastara. She asks her teenaged daughter to write the letter. Back in Awastara, her mother gives the letter to a granddaughter to read aloud. Victor, who doesn't write, asks me to write a letter in Spanish to his brother-in-law in Miami. Victor does not know his address but sends the letter in care of the Moravian pastor in Port, who will send it on to the Moravian Church in Miami. I myself am asked to write various letters about the development projects of the local women's organization, the World Bank fishing project, and other matters. It is clear that older people like Elsie and Victor have very limited reading and writing skills and depend to some extent on younger people who have been to school. This is one reason some young, inexperienced people have been chosen for important village offices, such as *síndico* (land magistrate). With only four students graduating from the sixth grade in Awastara this year, it seems that literacy will continue to be a limited skill in the community.

In 1978 I taught a short course in conversational English by popular request. I am asked to do so again in 1999. I am a bit reluctant, since I remember my earlier effort as being pretty much a failure. But the experience turns out to be enjoyable for everyone involved. I have eighteen students, from young teenagers to people in their forties. Casey, the master craftsman, is one of them, as is Juan Padilla, the local baker. Most of them can read and write in Miskitu, unlike most of the young adults in Victor's household. My students are reasonably serious, as we go around the class asking, "What is your name? How old are you? What color is his shirt?" and so on. I rummage for whatever English language materials I can find locally to use in class and write lessons and songs on the blackboard for the students to learn. I find that I really enjoy being back in my role as a teacher, waiting for Maestra Zulaina to finish her own class in the afternoon, so that I can begin mine in the same schoolroom, writing on the board and leading discussions. With encouragement, most of the students participate and some of them, at least, struggle with their homework. At first, everyone in town seems interested in attending, but I manage to limit enrollment. Given the widespread attitude of Anglo affinity, or identification with English language and culture, the language itself has high prestige, and the value of learning it seems self-evident. In several public situations people mention that I am giving an English class, as a contribution to life in the community. At my last class, Maestra Juliana, one of the teachers who also has been taking the class, gives a moving speech, thanking me on behalf of all the students for taking the time to teach them English. It makes me feel very good about the effort.

EDUCATION: THE ROAD TO THE FUTURE?

One day I sit in the back of the sixth-grade class, listening to Maestro Jali talk about how things were in the old days. He is teaching his class mostly in Spanish, as suggested by the school authorities, but lapsing frequently into Miskitu to make sure the children understand. His textbook is in Spanish, since the new bilingual education program only goes through the fourth grade so far. He is a masterful teacher, talking in both languages with the kids, maintaining their attention, pausing to let one girl tell a *kisi*. I quickly get lost in the intricacies of the *kisi* and miss the punch line.

173

Maestro Jali uses both languages very effectively. In the social science period he talks about *wan natka, wan kulturika, wan iwanka*—our culture, our way of life. "When I was little," he says, "we only had houses made of palm thatch, *papta watla*. Only Margarita and Maestro Opresiano had zinc roofs. The *papta watla* is much cooler when it's hot. We also used to use a *kahmi* gourd to drink water, and in a *kahmi* the water is cool and pleasant, better than from a glass." I have never heard anyone in the village describe Miskitu culture in these terms. I am very impressed. In fact, I feel like cheering him on, since these general ideas parallel the anthropological concept of culture as the defining characteristic of a group, the practices that give meaning to our social lives.

Maestro Jali's presentation is clearly derived from the PEBI materials and workshops of recent years. He explains that each group of people has its culture and that each is different. "We Miskitu people are Indians, and when the Europeans came they stole our wealth for themselves. We also have our own culture," he says, "but we are losing it. *Wan kulturika tiki auya.*" Then he describes earlier Christmases, when different families would make *saman laya* (old-style fermented beer) in their houses, and people would wander from house to house drinking it. At the old schoolhouse someone would play the *tungban* (drum) and the guitar, while the young people danced. Someone else would also play the horse's jawbone, the *kmakmaya*, with a nail. "Nowadays," Jali says, "people just bring their jamboxes and play Jim Reeves and Charlie Pride." He continues in Spanish: "To lose our culture is to lose our rights. We should preserve our culture and be proud of it." He speaks slowly in Spanish, translating frequently into Miskitu. At one point he asks for someone to tell another *kisi*, as a kind of entertainment break in the class. Jali laughs with the students and seems to enjoy his class thoroughly. I recognize Jali and Juana, Juliana and Zulaina, as colleagues, fellow teachers who truly enjoy working with students.

In 1999 there are 286 children enrolled in the Awastara school, about a third of the school-aged children in the community. Each year there are fewer children attending, according to Maestro Jali. Only four children graduate from the sixth grade in 1999. One of them is Jali's daughter, who goes on to the secondary school in Port. Interest in school is clearly declining. After school one day, I ask Zulaina and Jali why there is so little interest in school in Awastara and why the parents are apathetic about repairing the broken school chairs and the deteriorating school building. Jali replies that it's because the parents never saw any benefit to school themselves. It does not seem to them to lead anywhere. It's just a place to send their kids for the day. Literacy is recognized as useful, but career opportunities don't seem to develop naturally from success in school.

One day in the civics part of Maestro Jali's class, he lectures the students. "Why don't your fathers help take care of the school?" he asks rhetorically. Indicating one girl, he says that her father is one of the men who play cards in the schoolhouse after hours and break the children's chairs. He shows the class a picture in the textbook of a father making a chair with a hammer and saw. "Take the book home," he urges, "and get your own fathers to make us new chairs. They can make chairs too." He concludes: "We're also at fault, since the teachers and the students should take care of the school, whether or not the parents do."

Some children really like school, of course. Maura's daughter Jaseth, age ten, is an excellent student. Almost every moment that she is not taking care of her infant brother she spends studying. I try to work with her for a few minutes each afternoon. Jaseth knows numbers and body parts in Spanish, and we work on more questions and answers and useful phrases in Spanish. In turn, she teaches me words that I don't know from the Miskitu textbook. Jaseth writes diligently and neatly in her notebook and tries to guard it from her four siblings and others in her house. We both look forward to these study sessions in the afternoon, especially since I think of school as a good thing to do and like to encourage Jaseth. But I wonder what it means in terms of most of these children's chances in life. Everyone knows that schoolteachers themselves earn very low salaries. Is there any clear career path for motivated children to follow? It is very difficult to see one.

All the teachers complain about their miserably low salaries. Nevertheless, a salary is still a kind of safety belt, a guarantee against being penniless and hungry in this new, neoliberal Nicaragua. I mention the low teachers' salaries to my fisherman friend Alvarez. "Yes," he says, "but at least they have a salary! I am forty-four and I have never had a salary. I don't know where or when I'll get a little money next. The teachers at least have a payday. I don't." Social programs in the country, including education, are vastly reduced, and salaries are very low. But if you've got one, at least, you don't want to lose it. Social protest is therefore blunted. Teachers with whom I work at the university in Puerto Cabezas point out that they haven't been more vocal as a group in defending the PEBI, under attack by the central government, for fear of losing their jobs.

Jali himself went to the Colón School in Port and says that he was a very good student. During the Sandinista years, he was offered a scholarship to go to school in Bulgaria for six years. He wanted to go, but his mother was opposed, and he lost the opportunity. A friend of his did go, married a Bulgarian girl, and is still living there. Jali is bitter toward his mother, who prevented him from taking advantage of the one big opportunity in his life. He has applied for a transfer to one of the schools in Port, so that he can take night classes at the URACCAN.

Moisés was school director in Sandy Bay before he came to Awastara. He has been here ten years now as director and has two children with the Awastara woman with whom he lives. After small yearly raises, he now makes just over one hundred dollars a month. He works hard at his job, but he is frustrated with the situation. The parents' organization doesn't function, he says, either in Awastara or in other Miskitu communities where he has worked. A few parents take an interest in school activities, but they are a small minority. The money given by international organizations to support the PEBI passes through the Ministry of Education in Managua, and by the time it reaches the villages very little is left. The representatives of the international organizations come to the communities to observe the program and are disappointed in what they see, having imagined something much more far-reaching and effective. Parents find it hard to buy school uniforms, pencils, and notebooks for their children. And the boys drop out of school and go off to the Keys turtle fishing and making money, as soon as they're old enough. It is difficult to be optimistic after listening to Moisés describe the problems he faces.

Back in 1978 I listened to Mr. Fredley Bushey, a regional leader married to a woman from Awastara, as he enthusiastically expounded his ideas about education. Earlier generations didn't believe in schools, he said, and thought it was better to have young men off fishing or working in the plantations. But now, he argued, they were seeing the advantages of having an education. Mr. Fredley himself had lived on Corn Island as a boy and learned English, and he spoke fluent Spanish as well. I enjoyed listening to him talk to mixed audiences, code-switching back and forth between all three languages. He could charm, delight, and persuade an audience equally effectively in each language. Bible stories, funny anecdotes from his own experience, and folk analysis of how Miskitu vs. mestizo vs. Creole people think and behave were all combined in his discourse. Through it ran astute analysis as well as an obvious enjoyment of different people's personalities and behavior. His pithy lectures were a good example of the activity called *smalkaia,* and they were a most entertaining form of teaching. I found his language ability, his eloquence, and his progressive ideas very impressive, as did Cornelio, Pancho, Victor, and other leaders in Awastara. Well educated himself, Mr. Fredley always emphasized the value of education as one of his themes.

Nevertheless, the current situation makes Mr. Fredley's enthusiasm for education seem a bit naive. One factor that detracts from more positive local attitudes toward schooling is that some individuals who received a good education are felt to have done little for their community. In all fairness to them, Marcos, Ráfaga, and other local graduates have tried to help their community in difficult times, as best they could. Through Marcos's efforts, Awastara was able to get a new school building in the 1980s; and Ráfaga has spearheaded the recent effort to develop deepwater hook and line fishing as a substitute for turtling. Nevertheless, the tangible benefits seem few, and many with an education are seen as mainly concerned with their own personal advantage.

BILINGUAL EDUCATION, MULTILINGUALISM, AND LANGUAGE LEARNING

Bilingual education programs make intuitive sense to Miskitu people, given the multilingual social milieu in which they have lived for hundreds of years. To be successful in any social arena outside the village, one has to speak a language other than Miskitu. In the past this was often English, but in recent years it has come to be Spanish. The personal histories of several Awastara friends are interesting in terms of their language abilities. Maestro Opresiano, who served as the Awastara schoolteacher for thirty years, was sent as a boy to the Corn Islands. His father arranged for him to go and live with a Creole family there and learn English, but he was unhappy and came home. So his father put him in Bible school in Port, where he lived with a Spanish-speaking family. The Bible school was very hard and strict, he said, but he did learn to speak Spanish and also to read and write in that language. When he finished school, he got a series of office-boy jobs with different companies and government agencies. His ability to do paperwork was the crucial factor in getting these jobs. One day the school inspector asked him if he would like a teaching job. He said yes and was sent back to Awastara as the local schoolteacher. In turn, he taught his two sons Spanish, and both have gone on to careers in the broader Spanish-speaking world of Nicaragua.

Another of my friends, Bowman Hoppington, was also sent to the Corn Islands as a boy, where he lived with a Creole English–speaking family. He cried and cried to go home, but his father insisted that he stay and learn, and he obeyed. His Creole host father lectured Bowman about not smoking and drinking and wasting his earnings carousing with the other boys and also sent him to school, and after three years he could speak Creole English well. This skill was highly useful, as he went on to get a series of good jobs with U.S. oil companies later in life. An "apprenticeship" away from home, with a chance to learn another language, seems to be highly esteemed among Miskitu people. It opens up new life opportunities, not within the grasp of monolingual individuals.

My brother Victor was also sent to Port as a boy, but he was homesick and cried and begged his father to take him back to Awastara. His father finally did bring him back. Today Victor remarks regretfully that if he had been able to withstand the homesickness, he might be as well off as the old schoolteacher. As a young man, he made friends with the Cayman Islanders who came to the Coast to fish for turtles and learned Creole English from them. His English has served him well in interacting with various North Americans who have come to the Coast, including me. His patience in teaching me Miskitu has been remarkable, and in part it reflects his own struggle to learn English.

Language learning is thus regarded as one key to success. A person who is bright and quick to learn is said to have a *lal swapni* (soft head), as opposed to a person who can't learn, who has a *lal karna* (hard head). To "have a woman," that is, establish an ongoing sexual relationship with her, you have to know her language. Juan Downs, the Awastara healer, had learned some Carib and proudly told me that as a very young man he had lived with a Carib woman in Orinoco. A few Miskitu have also learned some Mayangna, from living in Mayangna communities, but this is rare, since most Mayangna are said to be fluent in Miskitu as well as their own language. Several Miskitu friends argued with me, much to my delight, that the Mayangna and Chinese languages are mutually intelligible. The Mayangna even *look* Chinese, they said, and the languages sound similar. Of course they must be able to understand each other!

Helms (1979: 135) reports that language skills are one kind of esoteric knowledge that is highly valued among the Cuna of Panama. Chiefs, as part of their leadership role, are expected to have esoteric knowledge and make great efforts to acquire it. Young men go off to study with distant shamans and travel widely in the outside world, returning to the San Blas Islands with impressive kinds of knowledge, including new language skills. In general, such experiences are also valued among the Miskitu, although in terms of language it is the practical advantages of bilingualism that they emphasize.

Individuals who are completely bilingual earn a great deal of respect. Moravian *sasmalkra*, schoolteachers, and local political leaders must all be bilingual and often trilingual (Miskitu, Spanish, and English). Eloquence in public speaking is a requirement for success in local-level politics, and church meetings and community meetings provide a forum in which the art of verbal persuasion in Miskitu can be used. I am always impressed with the clarity and oratorical skill of Miskitu people in public gatherings, arguing opinions with force and vigor. Fluency in Spanish, on the other hand, is necessary to deal with outside authority figures of all kinds, from health personnel to government officials to international development visitors. Villagers have to be able to speak Spanish to go into offices in Port and argue effectively for local causes.

Traditionally, foreigners were expected to learn the language to get along with Miskitu people in the villages. The foreign missionaries who came to the Coast in fact devoted great efforts to learning Miskitu. Many of these parsons are well remembered for their fluency in the language, and they remain the role models for achieving language competence. During the Sandinista years, however, few if any Sandinista political workers learned the local language, thus providing another topic for criticism and an opportunity for Miskitu to be used as a secret language in meetings with Sandinista leaders present (Jenkins Molieri 1986: 274). Frustrated by Miskitu use of their own language during the war years, one Sandinista leader actually stated that "the Miskito language is very limited and does not allow for the intellectual and cultural development of people, and within this, there is still the matter under debate whether it be treated as a language or a dialect" (Luis Carrión, quoted in Ohland and Schneider 1983: 202). Unfortunately, this ethnocentric point of view about Miskitu as a "backward" language probably still persists in Hispanic Nicaragua. Publication of scholarly articles in Miskitu, as well as the Bible itself, should be a more than sufficient rejoinder.

In my experience, the Miskitu have been extremely encouraging to an outsider struggling to learn their language. But there is also a sort of "baby Miskitu," with a simple vocabulary and simple sentences, spoken very slowly, which is used with newcomers. It is easy to flatter oneself about "really understanding the language," until a moment when Miskitu companions don't care if you understand or not, and switch into a rapid-fire and complex version of the language that is very difficult to follow. An early missionary (Moravian Church, Periodical Accounts 1879: 200, "from Br. Sieborger") wrote:

> As regards the language, I still feel far from perfect. Br. Blair, who lives in such close proximity with the Indians, that he can almost hear it in his house, when a native at the end of the village turns round in his hammock, has for more than nine years been preaching in the Moskito-Indian language. Yet he recently told me that he cannot understand anything, when

women carry on a conversation together. These Indians are very clever at expressing themselves as simply as possible, when speaking with strangers, making use of a very small stock of words, and one can easily indulge in the idea that one has mastered the language, until you hear two natives conversing together in such a way that you can understand scarcely anything of what is said.

I sympathize with Brother Sieborger, because I had exactly the same experience.

From the viewpoint of most Creole and Spanish speakers, Miskitu continues to be a low-status language associated with and spoken by the poorest part of the population. Because of the huge influx of poor Miskitu people from the countryside, Miskitu is today the language most commonly heard on the streets of Puerto Cabezas. But a disdainful attitude toward these poor people from the countryside is common. It is partly to counter such prejudice that Miskitu people from the villages dress in their finest clothes to come to town. In the city, disdain for the ragged Miskitu is accompanied by other stereotypes about them as possessors of powerful witchcraft and love magic and participants in heathen curing rites. I found that Miskitu shopkeepers and market sellers themselves, however, were delighted to find that I spoke their language. My own slow but steady progress in learning the language has always been greeted with warm encouragement by Miskitu speakers. Speaking Miskitu in fact begins to open up whole new realms of interaction for visitors to the Coast, including attending church services with Miskitu friends.

CHAPTER NINE

Miskitu Christianity

Early on Sunday morning in Awastara, the Moravian church bell can be heard ringing, all the way out to the *pingka* side where Victor's family lives. Many people are devoutly religious, but not all are Moravian. Newer churches, the competing Church of God and Assembly of God, also ring bells, alternating with the Moravian one. By 9:00 A.M. a stream of people, adults and children, can be seen winding along the paths toward church. People dress up, men in clean shirts and slacks, women in bright Sunday dresses. Children and adults alike seem to enjoy dressing in their best clothes and visiting with friends from other parts of the community. Sunday services are clearly a high point of the weekly routine. The Moravian church still draws the largest crowd, but smaller groups attend the other churches, with the Adventists meeting on Saturday instead of Sunday.

Sunday school begins at 9:00 with a Bible reading and lesson for the day. Then the Sunday school teachers take the children outside for their classes, while the adults remain inside discussing the Bible lesson. Those who have Bibles or hymnbooks, in either Spanish or Miskitu, bring them to Sunday school. At about 10:30 church services begin, with adults and children reconvened. Services include hymns, prayers, announcements, financial reports, collection of offerings, and, of course, a sermon. The organization of the service is identical with similar services in the United States, except that everything is conducted in Miskitu. In the Church of God, however, there is as yet no printed material in Miskitu, so the Bible readings and hymns are all in Spanish, in which few church members are proficient. Miskitu editions of the Moravian hymnbook and Bible have been available for many years.

THE GREAT AWAKENING

In the mid-nineteenth century the Moravians' first converts were Creole people; they had little real success among the Miskitu people until 1881, when large numbers of people up and down the Coast began to be converted in a mass phenomenon that the missionaries called "The Great Awakening." It is said to have begun on February 13, 1881, when Mary Downs, a young Creole woman helping with a burial, fell to the ground unconscious, which the missionaries interpreted as being "seized by an overpowering sense of her sinfulness" (Mueller 1932: 88). After three days the cataleptic condition of her body disappeared, and she could eat again. Following this experience, hundreds of Miskitu people up and down the Coast began to have similar experiences.

The Great Awakening represented sudden success for the missionaries after thirty years of work. Some Miskitu appeared, reporting visions that required them to be baptized immediately, although the missionaries usually refused to baptize them until they had received Christian instruction. Some shamans (*sukia*) and other influential individuals also came to the missionaries asking to be baptized, although soon some of their behavior became difficult for the missionaries to tolerate: "Others still imagine that they receive direct and wonderful revelations from the Lord. One man, since his awakening, is said to have spoken occasionally in a strange and unintelligible tongue. Others are at times overcome with a sort of paroxysm, when their whole frame is convulsed, and they seem to lose entire control over themselves" (Moravian Church, Periodical Accounts 1883: 546).

Talking directly to God or Jesus was not acceptable to the missionaries, although the new converts insisted on the veracity of their experiences. They were obviously integrating earlier, pre-Christian ideas of spirituality into their new faith. From the Miskitu point of view, this must have been a creative, self-affirming strategy, a logical combination of spiritual concepts and practices. To the closed-minded missionaries, however, it seemed heretical, a clear demonstration of the low level of understanding of the Christian faith so far achieved and the long distance yet to be traveled toward acceptable Christianity. The Great Awakening was a major event in "the making of the Miskitu people," to use Claudia García's (1996) phrase. Charles Hale (1987: 42) notes that an adequate historical explanation for the Great Awakening has yet to be given.

García (1996: 71–72) describes a new social role that emerged during the Great Awakening. Individuals called *spirit-uplika* (spirit people) received direct revelations from God and, like the traditional shamans (*sukia*), worked through spiritual means to prevent natural catastrophes such as hurricanes and floods. They also preached the gospel as they understood it, although they were not literate and could not read the Bible or other missionary texts. García credits the *spirit-uplika* with a large share of the missionary success in converting the Miskitu people. She says most of them were women, although the ones remembered in Awastara were all men.

Helms (1971: 214–16) provides one key to understanding the success of the Moravian missionaries. She notes that there was an underlying compatibility between the Moravian emphasis on the unity of Christian kin and the kinship-based nature of traditional Miskitu society. The Moravians felicitously extended the Miskitu terms for siblings to include all members of the congregation. Thus *moihki* (my same-sex sibling) and *laikra* (my opposite-sex sibling), instead of referring just to particular siblings, came to refer to all brothers and sisters in Christ. Furthermore, the Moravian faith reinforced the traditional Miskitu obligation of brothers and sisters to show each other love and respect and to help each other in times of need. Thus in some fundamental way the Moravian Church built upon, extended, and strengthened the existing kinship system.

THE CHURCHES IN AWASTARA

The first Moravian church in Awastara is said to have been built on the *muna* side of town, near the present-day site of Cornelio's house. It was founded by Mory Davis, a Creole man who was shipwrecked off the Coast and eventually found his way to Awastara. He married a local woman and founded a large *kiamp* in the early twentieth century. Mory, the grandfather of the current Moravian *sasmalkra*, was a *spirit-uplika* as well as a major figure in local church history. Before Mory's time, most people were "heathen," according to *Dama* Telemaco. The word "heathen" is used even today to refer to non-Christians. Mory taught God's word from the heart, not from a book, and was inspired to preach to the people even before the missionaries arrived. Telemaco says that he later got along well with the Moravian parson who lived in Dakura, however.

One day Mory found the remains of a wooden sailing ship on the beach. He took it apart and with the lumber built the first church in Awastara, naming it the "Triumphant Church." Before that Awastara people had had to walk all the way to Dakura, where a mission church had been established, to attend services. Telemaco says that when the white parson first walked down to Awastara, he was surprised to find the Triumphant Church building already standing. In 1979 I visited the original mission church in Dakura, a handsome white church building of exactly the same design as Moravian churches in Pennsylvania. On one wall was a plaque from the church's commemoration in 1912. The old Dakura church has since been torn down, and a new, cement-block church constructed. The Moravian community in Awastara grew, once the people had their own church. Telemaco says, "In those days people lived in peace and harmony [*kupia kumi*]. People say they weren't civilized, but they still lived the Christian way."

Mory's partner in preaching the gospel was a man named Vicente, who lived on the *lalma* side. As more *lalma* people joined the church, they said it was too far to go all the way over to the Triumphant Church on the *muna* side. So a compromise was reached, and a new church was eventually built at the present location, right in the middle of the community, where *lalma* and *muna* sides meet (map 3). The first Moravian church in Awastara had a mission house alongside the church, for the pastor and his family, and a fence around the church buildings. Miskitu Moravian churches continue to have mission houses next door, but the fences have disappeared along with the foreign missionaries. The fences apparently represented the foreign missionaries' need for privacy and served social rather than strictly religious purposes. Two new church buildings have since been erected on the same site; the current, cement-block building was constructed during the 1980s.

Moravian local church organization includes not only the pastor or *sasmalkra* but also a committee of older church members and several Helpers, who should be among the oldest and most respected members of the congregation. Part of the Helpers' job is making sure the *sasmalkra* has enough food and firewood. Committee and Helpers serve as lay leaders in the local church, entrusted with resolving problems. As in Asang (Helms 1971: 202–5), however, disputes between church members are frequent and at times acrimonious. And pastors can easily become embroiled in disputes with their congregation, including the Helpers and committee. "Speaking," a sort of public confession of sins before taking communion, is also described by Helms (1971: 203). It is said to be done three times a year in Awastara, but I was never able to observe it.

The Moravian parish record book in Awastara begins in 1922 and lists church membership, births, baptisms, and punishment of members for improper behavior. Most of the familiar Awastara last names (Renales, Hoppington, Kingsman) are present, in notations referring to the parents and grandparents of people I know. The most interesting entries are the punishments, of varying degrees of severity: *contramarcas* (black marks), "discipline," and suspension. Among the reasons listed for punishments were drunkenness, stealing church funds, adultery and fornication, consulting a *sukia,* and becoming an Adventist. Many individuals I know seem to have been disciplined and reinstated at some time in the past. Even Victor was sanctioned for drinking at Christmas, and one woman tells me that this was the reason he originally left the Moravian Church and joined the Church of God. Conflict with the Adventists, the first competing church, was apparent: one entry noted that a member had "fallen into Adventism" (*fracasó adventista*). Early Moravian preachers must have been zealous about disciplining their congregations. But by 1999 there was much criticism that un-Christian behavior such as drunkenness went totally unpunished by the Moravians. *Dama* Moreno, one of the older Moravians and a pillar of the congregation, remarked disgustedly that, when everyone was Moravian, people could readily be disciplined for behaving badly. "Nowadays, if you try, they just go to the Adventists or the Church of God. This town is too small for more than one church!"

For many years only the Moravian Church existed in Awastara. But by the early 1960s there was beginning to be competition, starting with the Adventists. Two prominent men in town, Kilbon Coe and Cortés Kingsman, were the first converts to the new Adventist Church. Each brought with him his large family, who became the core members of the new congregation. Most of these families are still Adventists. In fact, many of the children and grandchildren of the original converts have remained in the same church, which indicates the importance of the two original conversions. In 2000 one of Kilbon's sons was still the local Adventist preacher. When a young couple have attended different churches and begin to live together, there seems to be strong pressure for the woman to join the man's church. For instance, when Pamela and Casey began living together, she switched from the Church of God, her family's church, to Casey's Adventist Church. Casey's sister Mary commented that it can work the opposite way, too: "If the woman is stronger, they will both go to her church."

At Christmas in 1999 Joel Mercado, who had founded the Church of God in Awastara, came back to spend the holiday. He explained to me how he came to be a Church of God pastor and founded the church here. As a young man growing up in Asang, on the Río Coco, he had wanted to become a Moravian *sasmalkra* and go to the Bible Training School in Bilwaskarma. But he was told he was too young. An uncle of his managed to enroll him in the Church of God theological school in El Salvador, however, and he spent three years there learning to become a minister. When he graduated in 1964, he was sent to Awastara as his first post.

The Church of God had already been established in Port and had sent a missionary to visit each of the surrounding communities. When someone in a community showed interest, that individual became the contact person upon whom the missionary could concentrate. The missionary would then devote a great deal of effort to building a strong relationship with the contact person, encouraging him or her to join the church and participate in all its activities. Such a person was identified in Awastara, and Joel stayed in that house when he first came to the village. He began to preach and look for other interested people and planned eventually to build a church.

One of the first new converts was Victor. He helped build a small wooden building that served as the Church of God for many years. The new cement church building has only recently been completed. Joel says he will always be grateful to Victor for helping him so much at the beginning. Young Joel met the daughter of the schoolteacher in Awastara, Maestro Opresiano, and eventually married her. In 1999 they had been married for thirty-two years and had three children. The process he describes of getting a foothold in Awastara is probably typical of alternative church proselytizing in general: identifying a sympathetic person in each community, sending a young missionary to work with the potential convert, using the convert's kinship ties to create a core congregation, and trying to build a church as quickly as possible to serve as a worship and meeting place.

Today the Church of God is the second largest congregation in Awastara. A majority of families in town are at least nominal members of the Moravian Church, but the number active in church affairs is much smaller, perhaps twenty to thirty, roughly the same number active in the Church of God. The Adventists have made few converts in recent years, and only a handful of the original families remain in the congregation. The newest church in town, the Assembly of God, is now in the process of building a church, and its congregation is very small. It had no resident pastor in 1999–2000. The only church actively growing is the Church of God, and some of its members attribute its growth to its strict code of behavior.

Discipline in the Church of God is indeed taken seriously. Individuals who misbehave can be disciplined for a year, until they repent and promise not to sin again. A short list of prohibited behaviors includes drinking liquor, smoking cigarettes, stealing, telling lies, going to movies, having enemies, and being unfaithful to your spouse. Discipline is so strict that few men in Awastara can qualify as members of the congregation. Maestra Juana, a faithful member of the church, tells me that her husband drinks rum and is a heathen and therefore doesn't come to church. In 1999 a scandal occurred when the young Church of God preacher's wife ran away with another man, and the preacher promptly invited a young local woman to come live with him. He was disciplined by the church authorities in Port and removed from his position, leaving the pastor's position in Awastara open for many months.

It would be easy to look at the missionization of the Miskitu people only from the outside and underestimate local people's own interest in their new faith. Mexican anthropologist Guillermo Bonfil Batalla (1996: 136–37) argues, for example, that we have tended to see culture contact situations as ones in which indigenous cultures are forced to change or in which they simply borrow from intruding national cultures. The result is interpreted as "syncretism." This interpretation, however, underestimates the ability of local peoples to search for foreign cultural features they find useful and then integrate them into their own ongoing cultural system. Bonfil Batalla suggests that often local peoples actively appropriate foreign cultural items and make them their own, transforming them in the process. This is certainly the case with the Miskitu. The important things to note, according to Bonfil Batalla, are the usefulness of that which is appropriated, the free agency of those doing the appropriating, and the preservation of the underlying integrity of the appropriating culture. In this case, instead of seeing the adopting culture as under pressure and reluctantly succumbing to outside pressures, one can see the Miskitu people as finding and embracing a religion they liked and found meaningful: Protestant Christianity. The self-perceived integrity of Miskitu culture was thus preserved. From this perspective, the Miskitu have indeed appropriated the message and the style of Protestantism—even its tendency to splinter into different, competing sects.

FINANCIAL SUPPORT FOR THE CHURCHES

The church building itself is a powerful symbol of the presence of a particular church in the community. In 1999 the Church of God members had almost completed their new building near the center of town. It has a cement floor and walls and represents a major investment. Rodrigo estimates that up to this point it has cost the congregation more than fifty thousand cordobas (around $4,200). A long drive to raise the money from the sixty members has taken place, with each turtle fisherman asked to make a substantial contribution after every successful turtling trip. Constructing the building thus involved a heavy "religious tax" on local members. Obviously, it is one they are willing to pay. During a fundraiser, I loan Eliza a hundred cordobas to contribute toward the building fund in her name and Adolpo's. Adolpo will pay me back when he returns from the Keys, but Eliza wants to contribute right now, during the fund drive. Local pressure to contribute is strong.

Church members are also supposed to pay their tithe (*diezmo*) each month. In the Moravian Church the pastor asks the congregation to give their tithes publicly, during the church service. One Sunday when I attend, perhaps fifteen to twenty church members file up to the front of the church to put their contributions, in sealed envelopes, in the plate at the front of the church. People also contribute to the normal collection plate, passed around at each service. In addition, community members living far away often send money. At one service I attend, Agustín, one of the church Helpers, proudly takes four hundred-dollar bills from an envelope and shows them to the congregation. They have been sent to him by a church member living in the United States. Special projects, such as a building fund, are most likely to be supported by distant members. Except for the remittances sent by family members, only the local churches receive financial contributions from abroad. No local civil organization or project is regarded as trustworthy enough to merit such support. Villagers' support for their churches is indeed quite remarkable. Pastors' salaries and living expenses are provided mostly by local congregations and can be a heavy burden and a subject of dispute. Local people are expected to bring the pastor gifts of cassava, turtle meat, and other food when they have it and to provide his firewood.

In the Church of God the preacher and his family subsist on the congregation's contributions, but the preacher is also expected to contribute 10 percent of the tithes collected to the central church in Managua. But, as Victor complains, none of the money sent to Managua comes back to the village. For instance, there was no financial help at all in constructing the new Church of God building in Awastara. Local people did it all themselves. This contrasts with earlier years in both the Moravian Church and the Church of God, when financial contributions of various sorts were forthcoming from "brothers in Christ" in richer places, especially in the United States. Victor interprets this in ethnic terms:

> For hundreds of years the "Spaniards" have tried to keep us Miskitu as prisoners, deny us our rights. Now they're doing it from the churches.

It's time for autonomy for our churches, too! The Adventists have gone on strike. They're only going to deal with the Adventist office in Port now, not the Managua one. They have the right idea. It would be better for us here on the *pingka* side to build our very own church, so that any one of us can hear prayers right here, whenever he wants to.

Although there are occasional accusations of mismanagement, in general church funds seem to be conscientiously managed. This is not true of public money in the political sphere. Pastors are expected to keep careful records and announce publicly in church what contributions and expenses have been. The amount of money contributed to the churches always surprises me. I think that knowing it will be spent conscientiously on church projects is one reason why people are willing to contribute hard-earned money. Church contributions for buildings and other projects represent a kind of "economic development" on the local level that local people strongly support. Economic development schemes in general have failed to take account of community members' willingness and ability to tax themselves and spend the money carefully, within this religious context.

ATTENDING SERVICES

To live in Awastara and be considered a good person, you have to attend church services at least occasionally. I have always tried to be open minded and respectful in going to church with my Miskitu family. It is difficult for me, though, to sit through long fundamentalist services.

In 1999 I go to a special Saturday evening prayer service at Rodrigo's house, close to my own. It lasts more than two hours, with prayers and hymns and a long sermon. It is also a beautiful night, with a sky full of stars, and then an almost full moon that comes up about 8:30. I sit in a wooden chair outside with two children on my lap. The sermon is about the horrors of going to hell. "There are two places to go—which one will you go to?" is a theme to which the preacher returns again and again. His voice and gestures all seem to me modeled on those of fundamentalist preachers from the United States. The central location of the Church of God is in Tennessee, and at least one preacher I met has been trained there. I reflect that I might come to understand the local version of Christianity in some intellectual way, but I will never be able to identify with concepts of hell and sin and salvation that are so important to Miskitu Christians.

189

A week later, however, I sit with Victor in Port. I ask him what he thinks about all this. He is recuperating from his prostate operation and is sitting, gaunt and emaciated, on the edge of his bed, with his catheter coming out of his underwear and running into a plastic Clorox jug. He laughs at my description of the hellfire sermon and gives me a long, detailed talk about a more palatable way of understanding Christianity. He mentions the Jehovah's Witnesses he befriended the year before. They told him that Christ was a compassionate, just man who took pity on one thief on the cross, the one who spoke kindly to him. After death, Victor explains, our souls are transformed into something quite different from our bodily appearance, if we have led a good life and have been baptized. He skips over the hellfire part and winds up telling me how important it is that I be baptized in Awastara. The sly old rascal! He is very reasonable and convincing, my wise older brother, presenting the Christian story in such a sympathetic way. In his own subtle manner, he seems to be telling me: "We are not fundamentalist fanatics. We have a reasonable, kindly vision of spirituality. Come join us!"

Evangelists with microphones are now common in the market in Puerto Cabezas, working the crowds as their strident voices carry over the noise of the marketplace. Their harangues irritate me tremendously at first. But after watching the effects of rum and cocaine in the communities, fundamentalist Christianity starts to seem like a more reasonable option. Compared to drinking up your earnings and fighting and stealing to get money to buy crack, the fundamentalist alternative—dressing neatly, going to church, reading the Bible, saving your money—begins to seem more attractive. There appears to be no obvious middle road, just the possibility of a wasted life or a reasonable one. For someone as intelligent as Victor, the fundamentalist Church of God at first seemed a strange choice to me. But in this local context I think it makes sense. Victor likes the strict behavioral rules. He also laughs at some of the intellectual dead-ends of the preachers—for instance, the claim that the world would end when the year 2000 came along. He reminds me of old Telemaco, whom I knew well in 1978. Telemaco never planted any fruit trees, Victor says, because he took seriously the preachers' claims that the end of the world was at hand. "Anyone who doesn't plant fruit trees is just dumb," Victor commented, "whatever the preachers say." Some of the fundamentalist ideas seem silly to him as well. Nevertheless, the fundamentalist code of behavior offers a better life, a saner and more prosperous life, than drinking and fighting, from Victor's point of view.

I ask Alberto, one of the leaders in the Church of God, about his church's extremely strict behavior rules. I point out that the Awastara congregation is mostly women, because so few men can live up to the strict code of conduct. "These aren't the church's rules, they are God's rules. The Moravians let men like Cornelio take communion after they have been drunk in public. What kind of church is that?" Alberto replies. "The new Moravian *sasmalkra* smokes two packs a day. Why should I pay my *diezmo* there to pay for his cigarettes?" he continues. Alberto gives the same rationale for joining the Church of God that Victor does—they have strict conduct rules that really mean something. Joining the church ten years ago changed his life, he says. Before that he drank and never brought food or money home to his family. As we talk, sitting in a catboat bound for Awastara, he tells me, "I am bringing 350 cordobas' worth of food back to my kids at home. When my children see me coming, they will be happy!" Still, Alberto's fanatic attitude makes me somewhat nervous. "People won't get into heaven by drinking and smoking and using drugs!" he says emphatically, staring hard at me. I think guiltily about the bottle of Flor de Caña, Nicaragua's finest rum, hidden behind the books in my Awastara house.

Alberto's comments suggest that the Church of God members find some of the same attraction in its strict behavior rules that early twentieth century villagers like Mory Davis did in the Moravian Church, which was then new. It offered an alternative to drinking and family disruption and a possibility of saving and getting ahead in life. In the last twenty or thirty years it has fallen on hard times, but the Church of God has in some sense come to replace it, as the new option for serious Christians who want to change their lives.

THE MISKITU BIBLE

In the late nineteenth and early twentieth centuries the Moravian missionaries worked hard at producing religious materials, written in Miskitu, for their congregations. During my fieldwork in 1978–79, the New Testament was available in Miskitu, as well as a selection of stories from the Old Testament and hymnbooks and other materials. Translated by missionaries who had learned Miskitu as a second language, these texts were much appreciated by the local congregation. The dedication of the missionaries to working in the local language and giving it written form unquestionably has been a major contribution toward preserving the language and giving it higher status. Charles Hale (1987: 42) points out, however, that the missionaries' sincere interest in the Miskitu language should not be mistaken for tolerance of cultural differences. Their ef-

forts to combat the *sukia* and stamp out "heathenism," and their intoler-
ance of other aspects of Miskitu culture they didn't like, were historical
influences at least as important as their positive efforts to work in the
language.

The new translation of the complete Bible appeared during my second
stay in Awastara, and I bought a copy, apparently the first one in town.
As a result, the Church of God preacher enjoyed putting me on the spot
during Sunday school, asking me to look up and read Bible verses for
the congregation. This is highly entertaining for my Miskitu friends, as I
struggle first to find the verses and then to read them aloud as fluently as
I can in Miskitu. I don't know the Bible as well as my Miskitu friends do,
I often stumble over unfamiliar words in Bible verses, and I can't always
remember the order of the different books. Thankfully, however, after
having read the verses I can leave most of the subsequent discussion to
the congregation.

As Susan Hawley (1996: 322) points out, the Bible has become a Miskitu text. Even people who are illiterate (like my brother Victor) have heard
Bible stories from the pulpit, and from other people, all their lives. This
ancient text from the Middle East has indeed become a part of Miskitu
culture. At night, as we sit on his porch enjoying the evening, Victor tells
me familiar Bible stories: Moisés leading the Jews out of Egypt, and the
Red Sea opening to let them cross; the time when everyone spoke the
same language and the Tower of Babel; and Solomón settling the dispute
between the two women who both claimed to be an infant's mother.
There is good reason for the Miskitu to have appropriated these Bible
stories as their own. They are stories of inherent human interest, about
miracles and kings, lust and greed and envy, kindness and compassion,
love and honor. Gripping and exciting, they represent the real stuff of human life, the eternal questions all people struggle to understand, as Isaac
Bashevis Singer (1988: 337) has commented. Singer argues that they are
the best stories for children to start reading, for precisely these reasons.

Bringing my own Bible to church effectively moves me across the divide from observer to participant. One Sunday Alberto is preaching, using Luke 12:16–20 as his text. A man spends his life accumulating riches,
earning honors. But God tells him, "This very night you will die, and
then what will become of your riches and honors?" It hits me hard. Here
I am, far from home, from my children and people I love, doing fieldwork
in this isolated village. For whose benefit? Why haven't I chosen a sim-
pler life, closer to home, filled with love and work? Life is short, and we
don't determine the moment when we will die. Alberto said, *Wan moihni
Pelipe aisi kaikbia, wan bila kat.* "Our brother Felipe will read to us in

our own language." Tears came to my eyes as I read the passage. Suddenly I am there in the service with the others, deeply moved by the truth in the text, by the profound truth I had forgotten. I am participating in Miskitu Christianity with all my might.

CONFERENCES

Church conferences at each of the different churches provide an opportunity for eating and socializing, apart from worship services. They are major social events in the community and help raise money for the church. Food is cooked outside on a covered patio and sold by the plate, or participants can pay a single fee to eat meals during the whole conference. The local church must pay for most of the food, but the money collected should leave a sizable profit. Photo 10 shows congregation members working together to make large quantities of bread for a Moravian Church conference. Miskitu artist Wiskat Morales stands next to Miss Porla, the midwife, and smiles out from under a baseball cap. If possible, a cow is butchered so that people can eat beef (the preferred meat); but cows are expensive, so people often have to make do with turtle meat. Each visitor is expected to bring his or her own plate and cup and utensil with which to eat. At mealtimes people line up to eat from the huge

PHOTO 10. *Making bread for the Moravian Church conference*

193

cauldrons of food that have been prepared. They then wander off under the mango trees to sit and eat with groups of friends and relatives. Visiting preachers and other high-status individuals are often asked to eat in the host preacher's house. He and his wife are the official hosts of the conference, and after it is over he will announce to the congregation the amount of money spent and taken in and the net gain for the church. Church conferences are compared to each other and critically evaluated by townspeople. Factors compared include the amount of food provided, the number of people attending, and the quality and enthusiasm of the singing and the preaching. There is an implicit competition between the different communities, and between different churches in the same community, to see who can put on the finest conference.

Prayers and church services go on all day long for two or three days, with visitors and local people wandering in and out of the services. I attend the Moravian conference in May 2000. At the evening service five preachers are present, including the local Moravian *sasmalkra,* the local Assembly of God preacher, and three visiting Moravian clergy. Tomás, the highest-ranking preacher, leads the opening prayer. As he prays out loud in a strong voice, everyone else prays individually from the pews. This produces a jumble of voices in the church. Then a musical group in bright red shirts and black pants comes to the front to sing and play guitars. The long service includes many hymns and a long sermon. *Dama* Rubisu serves as usher, moving up and down the aisle seating people who have been standing outside. Most of the congregation are young people. The girls are wearing their finest dresses; the boys are dressed in slacks or pressed jeans. Alstin is wearing a black T-shirt with two buxom blondes on it and a racy phrase in English underneath. To me it hardly seems appropriate to wear to church, but it is clean and freshly ironed. There are also many adult women in church, but only a handful of adult men.

Such conferences are especially important as a place for young people to gather, providing a chance to dress up and talk and flirt with youth of the opposite sex, including visitors from other communities. They provide one of the major opportunities for young people to meet the single girls or boys from the surrounding communities and to strike up courting relationships with them. Barbara, Victor's pretty eighteen-year-old granddaughter, has come with me and the children. After the service, she finds herself surrounded by three very attentive young men. She seems to enjoy their company very much and keeps me waiting as she flirts with them.

During the service, one group after another comes to the front to sing. Alvarez plays the guitar for two girls to sing a church song. I remember when he and I practiced singing "Silent Night" in Miskitu (*Tihmia na, lamni sa*) and then sang it together in front of the congregation during the Christmas service in 1978. Afterward he asked me quite innocently, "Are there any songs like this one in English?" I still remember the Miskitu words to the carol. A teenaged girl gets up from the back and comes to sing by herself in front of the whole congregation. I think of the small children in Victor's family standing up to sing hymns for me before going to bed. I think of wild political meetings where one impassioned, almost theatrical speech follows another, but in which everyone eventually gets to speak. People seem to like performing in front of others, taking turns being on stage. The Christmas plays will exemplify this even better. People watch each other's performances appreciatively but critically. Is this a performance culture?

Roger Coleman, the Moravian preacher from Páhara, speaks to the congregation in his loud, deep command voice. Then Octavio, the new Awastara *sasmalkra*, introduces me, saying I have lived here who knows how long and speak their language. He asks me to come forward out of the congregation and sit up front with the preachers. I know it is an honor to do so, but I realize I will now have to sit through the whole service and be on exhibit in the front. No yawning or daydreaming now, no sneaking out early with the young people. As Tomás gives his sermon, the choir behind him sings at full voice, making it hard to hear him. I can only catch a few words here and there, during the lulls in the music. But since the themes are familiar, I imagine the congregation follows the sermon well enough.

The electric plant outside provides a steady drone of noise, the back-drop against which the service takes place. Rhythmic music is interspersed with prayers and the sermon. The man playing the horse's jawbone is really good! He uses a ten-inch nail to rattle it, thump on it, and then make a rapid staccato noise inside it. Another man plays on an empty freshwater turtle (*kuswa*) shell, also using a long nail to rap the shell both inside and out. Together these two percussionists get some interesting sounds going, to accompany the guitars. The percussion instruments seem to me shades of the indigenous past, here in the middle of the Protestant Christianity that the Miskitu have made their own. At one point three young people, two men and a woman, dramatically come forward to receive Jesus and declare themselves Christians, as one of the preachers blesses them with his hand on their head and prays over them. Alstin in his blonde babes T-shirt is one of the young people. Finally the service is over, and the congregation disperses rapidly. I shake hands with the preachers and go outside to gather up Barbara and the children and go home.

CHRISTMAS: DIONYSIAN ASPECTS OF A RELIGIOUS HOLIDAY

The religious aspects of Christmas are well celebrated in Awastara: with candlelight church services, carol singing, and church plays based on Bible stories. Christmas also has a pagan side, however, involving heavy drinking, sexual affairs, and fistfights. Drunkenness, as in many other societies, provides a sort of "time out" from the usual social norms (Mac-Andrew and Edgerton 1969), a time when ordinary rules of conduct do not apply.

In fact, since early times European visitors to the Miskitu Coast have commented on a pattern of periodic feasts with drinking, dancing, airing of old grievances, fighting, and sexual license. Tribal societies from elsewhere in lowland Latin America, distant cultural relatives of the Miskitu, are well known ethnographically for their indulgence in such rites. Among the Cubeo, for example, Irving Goldman (1979: 216–17) reports that the periodic drinking parties inevitably end in quarrels, as old grievances are remembered and brought up, and men fistfight while their wives try to prevent serious bloodshed. Mourning ceremonies among the Cubeo involve dramatized sexual play between men and women, climaxing in a scene of actual group sex between normally forbidden partners (1979: 239). These kinds of rites seem to exemplify a sort of "Dionysian excess" among participants.

Among the Miskitu, the best-known festivals were the *sikru* (feasts in honor of the dead), which took place about a year after the death had occurred. Great quantities of *mishla* (cassava beer) were brewed, and it was all consumed in one sitting, until everyone became completely intoxicated and passed out. Fights broke out between men, sexual promiscuity was rampant, and a rollicking time was apparently had by all.

> Young girls hand round the drink in calabashes, which an old woman fills and skims with her fingers at the great earthen jars. The alcohol in the mixture soon takes effect; weak stomachs get sick, as generally happens to European beach-combers, who are often found living with the Indians and married to Indian women. The stronger get furiously drunk; all grievances are raked up, insults resented, payment of ancient debts demanded, long-forgotten jealousies remembered. The women rush to hide all weapons; fights with the fist are going on all round, women are felled to the ground, men pound and abuse each other, children cry, dogs bark, until, overcome with drink, the whole population collapses and lies drunk on the grass. (Bell 1989: 94)

English sailors, European beachcombers, and other casual visitors to the Miskitu seemed to share easily in the spirit of the *sikru*. M. W. (1732: 294), the anonymous buccaneer who visited the Miskitu in about 1699, noted:

> After three or four days [the pineapple *mishla*] becomes clear and fit to drink, and tastes almost like new canary, or hath rather a variety of rich tastes and odours together, no more to be described than that of the fruit itself . . . Tis very strong, and commonly too potent for these Indians to deal largely with; wherefore they drink it the more sparingly, that they may hold out the longer in a good modest drunken trim.

The Moravian missionaries, of course, disapproved heartily. After their arrival in 1849, they seemed to see as one of their main tasks the eradication of the *mishla* festivals. Negative descriptions of the feasts by missionaries (Moravian Church n.d.) are interesting to compare with the earlier buccaneer accounts:

> A drum and little reed flute announce the dance. The drink is served in small calabashes. This is to animate the players. Soon it becomes an awful spectacle. The celebration lasts for days and is sometimes repeated, thus continuing for weeks. With it is combined all kinds of heathen lusts and pleasure . . . About the third day, when the participants have become somewhat crazy, the captain announces *aro baikaia* which means something like the feasting of all different sorts of animals, which they have dressed to imitate. While the captain and his fellows are singing *aro gi,* every imaginable sound of birds and animals is heard; and the players roll and tumble about. After a lengthy performance of this sort, naturally the crowd is so drunken and tired that it falls asleep. The *sukia* are keen enough not to have overdrunken or over-exerted themselves. The play cannot stop until the captain orders so. He arranges this to come at nightfall. The hours of darkness are the time for the darker deeds. When the crowd, drunken and tired, falls asleep, the *sukia* give pent [*sic*] to their pent-up lusts.

Apart from the extreme ethnocentrism in these observations, there must also be a wealth of misinterpreted ethnography. It is tantalizing to speculate about what the *aro baikaia* really was, but the missionaries were so successful in stamping out such ceremonies that they are difficult to reconstruct.

In a different format, however, festivals of excess continue to be a part of the yearly round. The Christmas/New Year break has many of the same elements. Christmas was apparently introduced early among the Miskitu. As early as 1827 Orlando Roberts (1965: 270) could report:

> Christmas is universally observed all over the Mosquito Shore, by both Indians, Samboes, and Kharibees; but for no other reason that I could ever learn, except that it was "English fashion," and happens at a time when it does not interfere with their fishing and other pursuits . . . The principal men send presents of rum, etc. to the King, which enables him to gratify fully their drunken propensities, as they come from the most distant settlements, and none of them appear empty handed, the houses are usually crowded to the door, and there is for several days a constant scene of intoxication.

Christmas apparently took its place alongside the *sikru* feasts as a culturally licensed "time out" from normal social obligations, a time of drinking and rowdy, normally improper behavior. The pervasive kinship ethic in Miskitu society normally requires respect for many categories of people; but during festival times it seems to be relaxed, so that conflict and sexuality are openly expressed and even encouraged. Some tragedies inevitably occur as well: one young man was reportedly killed in a fight in Sandy Bay during Christmas 1978.

Today the *mishla* has been replaced by *chicha* (homemade beer brewed from fermented corn), but some underlying principles remain the same. The Christmas/New Year's season represents two weeks of relaxation. Plantation work is at a standstill; one year's crop has been harvested, and the plantation fields have yet to be cut down and burned for the next year. Everyone looks forward to the leisure of two weeks away from work. Village residents living elsewhere come back to their villages. In particular, the communities are crowded with young people, back from working in Puerto Cabezas, Bluefields, and Managua. They go to the plantations early in the morning with their relatives, and the young men go to the beach to seine for fish with the Awastara boys. Visitors and their local relatives fish diligently in the small streams with hook and line for *krahana* (a type of small fish). Mostly, however, the visitors come to relax, to sit around porches in the afternoons talking with their relatives, and to attend Christmas services in the churches. The young people drink *chicha* in the evening and go to the social dances, keeping an eye out for attractive individuals of the opposite sex.

To deal with Christmas carousing, the Moravian lay preachers seem to try to substitute church activities for the traditional drinking, dancing, and love affairs. Helms (1971: 193–94) reports that during Christmas

1964, when she was doing fieldwork in Asang, there was no drinking or rowdy behavior. She reports that the lay pastor successfully organized footraces and other games and established the Moravian Church as the center of Christmas activities. Evening candlelight services and a church-organized gift exchange were well attended. In 1978 the Moravians did seem to regard Asang as an especially upright and "Christian" community. The lay pastor who had been Helms's host and friend in Asang told me that her description is quite accurate. During the same time, however, he noted that there was heavy drinking in many of the other Río Coco Miskitu villages.

In Awastara in 1978 the lay pastor tried to foster this kind of serious religious atmosphere, but without much success. A group of devout Christians gathered around the church each day during the holidays, planning for services, decorating the church, and acting very disapproving of all the drunks wandering around town. The pastor said the young people could play games around the church, cook food and *kirbaia,* and sing Christmas carols; in other words, they could have clean, wholesome fun instead of going off to dances in the schoolhouse where they might drink and get into fights and where girls might have illicit love affairs. Unsurprisingly, the wholesome entertainment at the church was less appealing than the excitement to be had at the schoolhouse.

The missionaries seem to have been successful at making some Miskitu disapprove of Christmas carousing but not at eliminating it. A double standard prevails as far as the sexes are concerned. Young men are expected to *kirbaia,* to wander around at night drinking and playing the guitar and looking for women. Their mothers may even give them money to enjoy themselves. A young companion of mine got twenty cordobas from his mother to buy *chicha* and have a good time and remarked, "It's our mothers who truly love us!" Young women, in contrast, may want to go to the dances and have boyfriends but find themselves under the strict surveillance of their mothers, brothers, and other relatives, who chaperone them and try to keep them out of trouble. Young women who have been working in Port or elsewhere, however, often refuse to accept these restrictions and go out to *kirbaia* anyway and thereby get into loud arguments with their relatives about their behavior. One mother told me she would not watch her grown daughter's children anymore while the daughter went to dances with men. "She's not a man, but a woman. Who will take care of her children? If a man hits her or mistreats her while she's out, who will protect her? She was looking for it! She was looking for trouble!" At one Christmas dance, a mother actually showed up and forced her daughter to come home, saying, "You're not a man! Get back to the house. Your baby is crying!" The daughter only protested meekly before leaving with her mother. I wondered if this daughter, in turn, would rule strictly over her own daughters when they became young women.

The Moravians thoroughly disapprove of the evening dances. In Awastara in 1978 Maestro Opresiano, the village schoolteacher and an important community leader, shared this opinion and refused to let the young people use the schoolhouse for their dances. They appealed to me, however, and through the efforts of Mr. Fredley Bushey we were allowed to use the schoolhouse. My fieldnotes record the scene:

12/31/78

A flickering diesel lamp is sitting up in the schoolhouse window, three guitars strumming lilting rhythms that make up all Miskitu love songs. Four or five girls from Port, dancing their feet off, lots of drunk young men grabbing them for every dance. Most local mothers won't allow their daughters to come to these dances, although some do show up. Jimmy is playing the drum in a corner and I am standing close to him, scraping the *kmakmaya* [horse's jawbone] with a big nail. The feet of the dancers make a regular thump, thump, thump, on the floor as they really get into the music. In between dances everyone pours out onto the porch to smoke cigarettes and drink *chicha*. A fight almost breaks out at one point. A big, tough trouble-maker, recently back from Honduras, insults another man's mother, and they tumble outside to fight. The whole crowd follows them, and a big, eager group surrounds the brawling men. The dance floor is temporarily deserted. But some other young men pull them apart and the instigator goes off looking for trouble in other directions. Awastara has escaped serious trouble this year although there are rumors of killings in other villages.

THE CHRISTMAS PLAYS IN THE CHURCHES

Less Dionysian entertainment is also available. Each Christmas season the young people put on short plays or skits in the churches, usually reenacting Bible stories. The plays are a highlight of the holiday season, and in 1999 I attend several of them. A few older people are scattered about in the church, but the audience is mostly children and young people. The first play is in the Assembly of God Church and has seven different short pieces. Two curtains are stretched across the altar area in the front of the church. The first can be opened to show a stage area behind, with the second curtain as a backdrop. The first play is about a young man trying to read his Bible. Young women come out one by one and try to induce him to go off and make love with them. He tells each one she has to become a Christian first, and they have to get married, and only then will he be able to go with her. It is interesting to me that the young women play such sexy, lascivious roles, while the young man is prudent and responsible: a stunning sex role reversal. The dialogue is hilarious. Barbara and Eliza and the children and I are giggling and laughing, as is everyone else. Several plays are about kings—favorite topics in Miskitu thought. In one, three kings are celebrating another king's birthday. He sends for Herodias to come and dance for him. Herodias's mother tells her to go, and so she does. Her dance for the king is very provocative, and the audience howls for more. These young women are finally having a chance to cut loose! In return for dancing, Herodias may ask for anything. She finally asks for John the Baptist's head on a platter, which the king's soldiers obligingly provide.

The last piece brings the house down. It is about Satan whipping a sinner. Satan drags the offender in through the door, kicking and screaming. Children scramble frantically out of the way. Little Jasira climbs up on my lap, scared. Once the sinner makes it to the front of the church, God appears and asks him if he wants to repent and be saved from Satan. When he says yes, God calls for Gabriel, who comes out and beats the tar out of Satan, to the screams and cheers of the young audience. The fight is very realistic, with lots of pushing and shoving and smacking the cement floor with a rope end. At the end the excited audience, whipped into a frenzy, pours out the door without waiting for any final words by the preacher.

The following week the Adventist Church, not to be outdone, puts on its own plays. One is about Samson, a strong young man with long hair. In the first scene he is lectured, *smalkaia* fashion, by his father. He listens respectfully as children ought to. Then he begins to live with Delilah, who keeps trying to figure out his weakness. At one point he fights a lion and actually tears the lion's mask apart in the church aisle, much to the delight of the excited, squealing children. But through Delilah's treachery, he is finally subdued and his eyes are put out by the soldiers. In the final skit, pointed references to Miskitu domestic life are evident. A bad woman gets up in the night, leaving her baby at home, while she goes off to *kirbaia* and drink rum. When she comes back home, she finds her baby deathly ill. I think of the definition of a bad woman as someone who goes off to *kirbaia*, usually leaving her baby with her mother. I glance at Eliza, sitting next to me, who in fact has just left her baby Nachalie with her mother-in-law so she can come to the Christmas play with the rest of us. I wonder if she is feeling any guilt pangs as a result of the play.

These Christmas plays all represent a good piece of "performance in front of a group," Miskitu style. Once the teenaged actors get into their performance, they give it their all, with no hesitation or shyness. Early on, the preacher stands up and tries to calm down the audience, saying if they keep on shrieking she will close down the performance. But by the end, with the dramatic fight between Gabriel and Satan, the house goes wild, and pandemonium breaks loose. The preacher has lost control.

As I have watched dramatic political meetings, arguments around the household, sermons and speeches in church, and occasional arguments leading to fistfights, I am always impressed by how much the Miskitu like to act in front of a group. Being on stage in front of others, and having an audience to play to, is a much appreciated opportunity. It provides an occasion to give a stylized but also highly individual dramatic performance. Others have noticed the same phenomenon. For instance, Bell (1989: 278–82) gives a delightful description of the king's *kwatmus* (quartermaster) carrying out a public mock whipping of disobedient youths in Dakura in the mid-nineteenth century. As Bell describes the scene, each youth tries to put on a better performance than his predecessor, thus entertaining the assembled crowd.

The tough, assertive, individualistic Miskitu character seems to flourish in front of an audience, leading to these dramatic and flamboyant performances. They occur not only in the church plays but also in political meetings and other cultural arenas. I think as well of the little girls singing church hymns for me in loud voices before bed, happily performing before a one-person audience.

THE DECLINE OF THE MORAVIAN CHURCH

The Moravian Church, once dominant in the region, now seems to have gone into a decline. Roger, the Awastara *sasmalkra* in 1997, tells me about his own experiences. At a Moravian regional conference that year, some twenty-two Miskitu villages said they could not support having a *sasmalkra* of their own. What had seemed an attractive career had begun to look like a dead-end to this young man, and he was planning on going back to his home community on the Río Coco to farm. Several factors have been involved in the decline of the church. They include the Nicaraguanization of the church, which began in the 1970s. The church hierarchy would no longer include North Americans, thus breaking important ties with the Anglo world, which had been important to Miskitu identity (García 1996: 99–100). This also meant a substantial loss in terms of direct contributions of money from the United States, shipments of clothes and other gifts, and regular visits by U.S. Moravians.

Even more important was the role the Moravian Church played during the war years. Susan Hawley (1996, 1997) eloquently describes how Protestant Christianity came to be the cultural, ideological framework within which military opposition to the Sandinista government was expressed. Some pastors identified the Sandinistas with the anti-Christ, and many served with Miskitu Contra troops in the field, occasionally even participating in the fighting. Every military group included a pastor to offer prayer services for the troops (Hawley 1996: 337). The Sandinista government responded by persecuting Moravian clergy, jailing some eighteen pastors, of whom eight died while being held prisoner.

A close friend of mine, a Moravian bishop in Port, described his own experiences to me. He was only in jail about four months but was then kept under house arrest for a much longer period. In jail he was put in a hole in the ground, as if he were to be killed, and was beaten on the head and neck with a pistol. He became very sick while in prison and began suffering health problems with which he is still struggling. My friend survived, but the church as a whole has never recovered from the war years and their aftermath. The Moravian Bible Center, where the *sasmalkra* were trained, and the Moravian Hospital in Bilwaskarma were burned to the ground by Sandinista troops in the early 1980s.

The Moravian Church in Awastara seems old and tired, mirroring its position on the Coast generally. The services seem to attract mostly the older members of the congregation: Cornelio, Hilario, Rubisu, Sims, Miss Porla. Younger people interested in church work seem to be more attracted to the alternative churches. These churches claim to preach the "real Christianity," to be true to what the Bible actually says, and to promote strict adherence to Protestant rules of behavior—saving money, not drinking, and being a good family member and member of the congregation. The Moravian Church is accused of hypocrisy. Alberto says angrily that it even allows people who have been seen publicly drunk to take communion. A former pastor from Awastara was also accused of allowing a drug purchase to take place in the mission house while he was serving as the Awastara *sasmalkra*. He knew the drug people involved in the deal personally, because they were from another community where he had also served as *sasmalkra*. He was publicly accused of complicity in drug dealing, an accusation that led to a rupture with some people in town and his eventual retirement from church activities.

In 1978–79 the Moravian *sasmalkra* was a central figure in each Miskitu community. When I visited some twenty Miskitu villages with the University of Wisconsin health team, we began each visit by contacting the *sasmalkra*. With his permission, we slept in the church at night, paid his wife to prepare our meals, and sometimes used the church building to hold clinics, give vaccinations, and weigh babies. The support of the local Moravian Church was crucial to these public health efforts. The Wisconsin health program in Port was also based at the Moravian hospital.

During the war years, the structure of the local Moravian Church facilitated mobilization against the Sandinista government (Hawley 1997). Identifying the church as an enemy, the Sandinista military responded not only by persecuting Moravian clergy but by quartering troops in some Moravian churches. After the conflict had ended, such bitter experiences left the Moravian Church much weakened. Thus the war years, the end of close ties with the U.S. Moravian Church, and the success of competing Protestant denominations have all contributed to the debilitated state of the church on the Coast today.

Although the Moravian Church in Awastara certainly seems much less a center of the community than it was previously, it does still play this role in Páhara, where there are no competing churches. When I attended a regional political meeting in Páhara in 2000, it was actually held in the Moravian Church and hosted by Roger Coleman, who had now been transferred to Páhara as *sasmalkra* there. In Awastara meetings of general community interest are no longer held in the Moravian Church but in the school building or on the playing field underneath a large cashew tree. The three competing churches in the community have taken away the "community center" function of the church building. *Dama* Moreno's comment "This town is too small for more than one church" rings true in the sense that the competition between churches makes it very difficult to conduct community-wide activities.

Flying from Port to Managua, a traveler looks out the airplane window and sees a number of Miskitu villages pass underneath the wing. He or she immediately recognizes the large, white Moravian Church in the center of each community. Highly visible from the air, they seem like powerful symbols of a center that exists no more. The original energy of the church seems to have dissipated, filled in to some extent, perhaps, by the competing churches, but with a clear center missing. A strong, centralizing force in the communities in mid-twentieth century, the Moravian Church is now weak and seems unlikely to regain its former position.

CHAPTER TEN

Health and Curing

An integral part of Moravian missionization, since the mid-nineteenth century, has been providing health care. My own interest in the Coast also began through research on health. Health, in general, can be seen as a measure of human adaptation (McElroy and Townsend 1996: 12), and the inquiry into health issues leads logically to all other areas of culture.

The early Moravian health programs were the first organized Western health services ever provided to the Miskitu people. The Moravians, however, set up clinics and treated illness with the express purpose of converting people to Christianity:

> In this sickroom we have Bible pictures hanging on the walls, by means of which we are able to draw the patients' attention to Jesus . . . The sick are expected to attend the services; for our medical work serves as a mean to an end, viz., to win souls for the Lord . . . I am persuaded that there is no better means of opening men's hearts for the reception of the gospel than medical aid, which we render to them, following the example of Jesus. (Moravian Church, Periodical Accounts 1910: 562–63, "from Rev. G. Grossman")

These sorts of values differ from those of modern governments, which tend to regard health services as something valuable in and of themselves. During my fieldwork in the 1970s, the Moravians operated hospitals in Puerto Cabezas and at Bilwaskarma on the Río Coco. A University of Wisconsin health program worked closely with the Moravians, providing outreach health services in the villages. Each community was encouraged to select a rural health leader, a midwife, and a nutrition leader. Training and support for these rural health leaders was provided at the hospitals. Some of the health leaders became highly competent and respected health providers in their communities and continue to be called by the prestige title *daktar* in Miskitu.

THE AWASTARA HEALTH CLINIC

In a more secular context, the 1980s Sandinista government made concerted efforts to improve health services. The ongoing civil war made this difficult, especially because both sides in the conflict targeted the health system. The Sandinista military burned the hospital in Bilwaskarma (after forcing the relocation of the Río Coco Miskitu population), and Miskitu rebel groups attacked government-sponsored health clinics and killed health workers in many places along the Coast. Bruce Barrett (1992, 1994) gives detailed descriptions of the intensive efforts of the Sandinista government in the realm of health, in very difficult circumstances. The Sandinista government built the first health clinic ever established in Awastara. Even villagers who are critical of the Sandinistas are quick to point out the serious efforts the government made in the field of health. After the Sandinistas relinquished power in 1990, however, funding for rural health services declined drastically. The Awastara clinic building was eventually turned into an adjunct schoolroom.

When I returned to the community in 1997, the walls of a new clinic had been erected. The project had not been finished, reportedly because the contractor had absconded with the money. By 1999, however, the building was being finished in quite elegant style, built with United States Agency for International Development (USAID) money, like many other projects in the country. Awastara had been selected as one of six communities in the region to have a new clinic. The decision was apparently made at some high level in Managua. There was no consultation with local people or with the regional health authorities in Port about the project. The construction crew in Awastara was brought from outside, and building materials were delivered from Port by catboat. Predictably enough, because local people had provided no input, problems began immediately. Lumber and floor tiles were stolen from the construction site. The project foreman, a mestizo from Managua, was outraged. "How can people steal materials from a clinic being built for them?" he asked. Imposed on the community without their support, the clinic became a target of thievery. The village authorities, with no personal investment in the project, did nothing to remedy the problem. When the clinic was finally finished—a very handsome new building—there was no inauguration, as had been planned. It simply began functioning. The whole project flagrantly violated basic principles of community development: that local people's own priorities be determined and that local people be involved in planning and carrying out projects, in order to ensure that the local population has a stake in the eventual product.

THE LOCAL HEALTH LEADER

Since the years of the Wisconsin program, Awastara has had a local health leader. This person, selected by the community, continues to receive some health training in Port as well as regular consignments of medicine. Some neighboring communities, such as Dakura and Krukira, have had very effective health leaders. When I first went to Awastara in 1978, the school teacher, Maestro Opresiano, occupied the position, but he continued for only a short time. The position has become more important over the years in Awastara.

In 1999 the health leader was a son of Cornelio, the old political strongman. Unfortunately, this young man was irresponsible and was strongly disliked by many people in town. I heard many stories about his drinking and drug use and his practice of selling medicines he received free from the Ministry of Health (MINSA). I went to talk with the health leader's regional supervisor in Port. She turned out to be from Awastara herself, a granddaughter of my old friend Bowman Hoppington, and also one of my graduate students at the university. She promised to investigate the problem, which she had already heard about. In September two MINSA representatives arrived in Awastara to hold a hearing about the matter. They said that a letter had been received from six town elders, accusing the health leader of sexual harassment of women, taking and selling illegal drugs, not attending sick people, and selling MINSA medicines. At a fiery town meeting, a young woman openly accused him of sexual harassment, and others added their own serious accusations. The leader's relatives quickly spoke up to defend him. The case seemed clear to me. I also wanted a good health leader for our community. The visiting representatives said their policy was not to impose MINSA rules but to follow the town's decision. No action was taken at the meeting; but when the new clinic was completed, the untrustworthy health leader was transferred to Sandy Bay, and a new leader was appointed.

Asterio, the new leader, had good training during the Sandinista years and is very competent and respected by local people. The health leader position has become especially important since many of the traditional healers have died. No one has replaced men such as Asta and Wilfred, older curers I knew in 1978. Asterio spends a large part of his day walking around the community seeing patients. He carries his stethoscope around his neck and a black medicine bag and looks very professional. In the afternoon he attends patients in the clinic, and there is usually a small line waiting for consultations. He also took a careful health census in March 2000 and later shares the findings with me. I find that I myself am listed in the census, as a resident in the over-fifty category!

Many interesting facts about health emerge from Asterio's census. For instance, there are 224 women of child-bearing age (fifteen to thirty-nine), and more than half of them are using birth control. Asterio can provide either pills or injections. A small number of men also receive condoms from him. In addition, Asterio points out, some women get contraceptives in Port. This explains the fact that there are currently only thirteen pregnant women in town, even though there are eight midwives. Only five women have ever given birth by caesarean section. In the whole community, there are only sixty-two children below the age of two, which confirms my impression that the birth rate is dropping. In our household, Maura (age twenty-seven) has five children, but Eliza (age nineteen) has only one and is not planning to have any more in the near future. Asterio shows me the contraceptive injections he has available. One kind lasts for three months, and another kind for one month. Neither shot creates problems for nursing mothers, he tells me, but the contraceptive pills do, causing diarrhea in babies. Men don't seem to object to their wives' using contraceptives, according to Asterio. The large number of women using contraceptives is surprising to me.

Twenty years earlier I learned about an herbal medicine used "to close the womb" and prevent women from ever conceiving again (Dennis 1988: 25–26). Unfortunately, I never managed to have these particular plants identified. The medicine is said to be a combination of a bromeliad that grows on tree trunks and the green fruit of another tree, boiled together. When drunk for two weeks, the medicine "dries up your womb" and causes a heavy vaginal discharge that stiffens clothes like starch. The woman who showed the plants to me had a personal history of six children who had died in early childhood, and she used the medicine to avoid the personal heartache of even more infant deaths. Nevertheless, contraception in general still runs counter to the widespread desire for children and the need to have children to support one in old age.

High blood pressure is a major problem in Awastara, Asterio tells me, with twelve current patients. Plora's brother Nolan, a neighbor of mine, has a stroke in April 2000 and is carried to the landing wrapped in a hammock and taken to Port by catboat. He survives but today has partial paralysis on one side of his body. The word "pressure" itself has passed into Miskitu, but the biomedical explanation is not well understood. I talk to friends about dietary factors that contribute to high blood pressure. Diet also plays an important role in traditional Miskitu medicine. A very useful project would be to phrase biomedical explanations and recommendations about blood pressure in terms that would make sense locally.

Sexually transmitted disease is also a problem. Asterio sees cases of gonorrhea frequently and has also treated several cases of syphilis. Last year he had to deal with a small-scale gonorrhea epidemic, which he traced to a woman from Krukira who visited all the north Coast communities. The URACCAN's Institute for Traditional Medicine and Community Development (IMTRADEC) coordinates a small AIDS program in Port. Little information is available on the prevalence of the disease, however. Large numbers of prostitutes provide sexual services for the lobster and turtle fishermen but themselves have little access to regular healthcare.

Breast infections and breast cancer are prevalent. Two young women neighbors of mine have large lumps in their breasts, probably mastitis, and obviously need medical treatment. By May 2000 one of them, Rodrigo's wife, Gladys, is getting thinner and thinner. She goes to the hospital in Port and is told she must go to Managua for surgery. This would cost money the family doesn't have. The injections prescribed by the doctor don't seem to arrest the course of the disease. Plora says, "If Gladys dies, I will have to raise her four children." I have not really come to grips with this reality until then. No other woman would raise Gladys's children; it really would have to be Plora. She has already raised five of her daughter Lucile's children. Plora is ill herself and had gall bladder surgery two years before. The hard reality of sickness and death hits home. Gladys probably needs intensive antibiotic treatment or surgery, and she won't get them, although I try to help by providing small amounts of money.

Most patients who come to Asterio's clinic are of course seeking relief from common problems such as stomach ailments and respiratory infections. What many of them want is an injection. In fact, people seem to be continually seeking injections, for which Asterio charges twenty cordobas. The most common injection seems to be penicillin, but the specific medicine injected seems to be of less interest to local people than the injection itself. Maura, for example, gets penicillin injections for her migraine headaches, caused by a coconut hitting her on the head as a child. Eliza borrows twenty cordobas from me to get a penicillin injection for little Nachalie's cold and runny nose. Injections are regarded as strong: "they make the blood work hard," as it is phrased in Miskitu. The mildly painful act of inserting the medicine directly into the body with a sharp needle seems to be thought of as efficacious. From the biomedical point of view, however, this generalized use of injections is an abuse. Injections can even be quite dangerous, but local people don't see it that way. I explain my own fears about injections to Maura and Pamela and Eliza, who all get injections regularly for themselves and for their children. They are not impressed. In fact, a large share of the available cash in the household seems to be spent on injections.

TRADITIONAL HEALTH CONCEPTS AND THE WESTERN HEALTH SYSTEM

Like all cultural groups, the Miskitu have their own system for classifying and understanding illness. The early Moravian missionaries argued against Miskitu health concepts as pure superstition and regarded local practitioners, the *sukia,* as agents of the devil. Thus the missionaries set themselves up in direct competition with the local health system: "when a patient is under our care and still retains connection with the *sukia* or drinks any other bush medicines, we dismiss them at once, no matter how ill they may be" (Moravian Church, Periodical Accounts 1903, "from G. Grossman").

The result was not the destruction of the local system but rather its enforced separation from the introduced one and a loss of communication between local and foreign health professionals, whose goal—better health—was the same. In 1978–79 I suggested that Western health professionals might collaborate with indigenous healers, treat them as colleagues with professional expertise of their own, and make herbal medicine a part of therapy. These ideas, however, were regarded as radical and unprofessional by the Wisconsin health team. Herbal medicine is in fact cheaper and more easily available than commercially produced drugs, and the Miskitu believe it to be more effective for certain problems, including ringworm, diarrhea, and snakebite. I suggested that such remedies, in particular, be investigated and made part of health leader training.

In terms of ideology, except for my inquisitive brother Victor, Miskitu people do not seem to ask, "Which medical system is right?" Rather, this question seems to be the one that the biomedical system demands its opponents answer. Instead, local people ask, "Which of the available alternatives will be cheapest and most effective in curing my family member of illness?" Miskitu people in general do not question the reality of their traditionally recognized illnesses. They know that people suffer from them, even if doctors don't accept them as real. The fact that medical personnel don't believe in such illnesses doesn't lessen the reality of people getting sick and dying from them, from the local point of view. In 1999 one of my physician students conducted some research among trained Miskitu nurses at the Puerto Cabezas hospital and found that, without exception, they believed in illnesses caused by the traditional spiritual creatures. Thus there seems to be a deep stratum of traditional health concepts, on top of which the introduced biomedical system operates. Local medical personnel may or may not understand this situation.

By the time of my second period of fieldwork, however, the situation in terms of collaboration had changed dramatically. Although less funding was available for health programs, the new university (the URAC-CAN) was making concerted efforts at including local concepts and practitioners, through its Institute of Traditional Medicine. The institute in fact employs local healers along with physicians and maintains a herbal medicine farm at Krabu Tingni. Many of the young physicians and nurses on the Coast are open minded and anxious to implement the idealistic new model of health (Comisión de Salud 1996) devised by the regional health commission. The class I gave at the URACCAN in 1999–2000, "Anthropology of Health," enrolled thirty-eight graduate students and was intended to broaden understanding of the local system on the part of health personnel.

TRADITIONAL SPIRITUAL CREATURES

The spiritual beings that inhabit the Miskitu world are closely related to health; many of them are dangerous and cause illness or death. A rich complex of traditional beliefs that predate the missionaries has survived and been integrated into the Miskitu worldview. Most of the Miskitu illness concepts have been mentioned only briefly in the ethnographic literature (Helms 1971: 211–13; Nietschmann 1973: 55–56; Pijoan 1944, 1946). More recently, however, Miskitu scholars such as Ana Rosa Fagoth (Fagoth et al. 1998) and Avelino Cox (1998) have themselves given excellent descriptions of traditional health beliefs. The powerful spiritual creatures in the natural world that harm people include the *swinta,* the *liwa mairin,* the *wahwin,* and the *prahaku.*

These supernaturals are all different kinds of *lasa,* the general term for spirit creatures, and they all cause illness when they come in contact with people. Fagoth et al. (1998: 18–19) have suggested that the belief in these *lasa* has served to protect the environment from overexploitation. If a person follows rules that maintain equilibrium in the natural world, he or she will remain healthy. If the rules are broken, the *lasa* will punish the offender with illness. For example, the *swinta* is the owner of the deer. He herds them with his whip and punishes hunters who kill too many deer. Casey tells me he has seen the *swinta*'s light at night in the brush, when he was deer hunting, and then realized he was killing too many deer and should be careful.

The owner of the water-dwelling creatures, who protects them against abuse and overexploitation, is of course the *liwa mairin.* Not only paralyzed lobster divers but also individuals drowned at sea, or in the rivers and lagoons, are victims of the *liwa.* In drownings, it is said that the body may not appear for several days and that the blood coming out of the nose may still be warm. Such signs indicate that the *liwa* is responsible.

There is a psychosexual aspect to the female *liwa mairin:* she seduces men and then eventually drowns them. Men cannot resist her beauty and her sexual charms. In Awastara Gerlinda told me the following story:

> The *liwa mairin* had a man here. Afterward, she drowned him in the creek. He was found with blood coming out of his nose and ears. Every new moon he would go crazy. He would say, I have a woman companion, I don't want any other women! Sometimes at new moon he would go to the river, down by the landing, and go in and bathe—at night! Both he and the *liwa* were bathing, or so he would say. People would go and get him and bring him back to the house. He went on this way for a long time. When he was about thirty-five, the *liwa* killed him one night. [Did he get sick?] No, in just one minute, going into the water, he was lost. He saw the *liwa* clearly, he said, and he was talking with her. But no one else could see her. He was the only one that could see her, in his mind. He had her as a mate, just as you would a person.

The *liwa* was reported in the mid-nineteenth century as Leewire, translated by Young (1847: 73) as "water ghost." Women often get *liwa mairin siknis* from bathing in the creeks or standing in water to wash clothes. The disease causes menstrual problems and vaginal bleeding and may cause skin infections as well. Male *liwa* may also visit women in the night and have sexual relations with them. Sometimes, it is said, a woman will cry or whimper during the night, and in the morning you can see black and blue marks on her skin where the *liwa* has beaten her. *Liwa* sometimes impregnate women, resulting in albino and deformed children. Newborn infant deaths are often attributed to the *liwa* as well. Single individuals without a mate are especially liable to attention from the *liwa*. Juan Downs, the well-known Awastara healer, was rumored to have relations with a *liwa* that lives in a small creek behind his house.

As indicated by the survey of nurses, Miskitu people almost universally believe in these supernaturals. My brother Victor is often cynical about them, saying they are just foolishness—more "Miskitu devil business." As our friendship deepens, however, he himself begins telling me stories about the *liwa* and the *swinta*. For example, he tells me about a woman named Leidina who was being molested by the *swinta*. The *swinta* came to her every night, a short man dressed in boots and black pants, with gold bracelets and chains. He wanted to take her away as his mate. At the time the woman's husband was a drunkard who never brought any money home for his family. With his sardonic sense of humor, Victor told Leidina, "If I were you, I'd go with the *swinta*. He's got to be better than that worthless husband of yours! At least he'd feed you and take care of you."

The *swinta* is said to be a short fellow with a big hat, fine clothing, and a whip with which he herds the deer, his own special creatures. When you shake hands with him, you have to fold your thumb down; otherwise he may pull if off. He has only four fingers himself. He may appear to you and offer to teach you anything you want to learn—for example, knowledge of medicinal plants or skill at playing the guitar. But in return he will ask you for something, perhaps the life of your oldest child. If you accept, you will learn what you want to know, but your child will get sick and die quickly (Jamieson 2002).

The *wahwin* is another creature, something like a pig, with one large brilliant eye in the middle of its forehead. It roams about the savannah at night. Young men out at night carousing sometimes run into it as it wanders through the village. It is said to be the *wahwin*'s odor that causes illness, especially in children. The smell is said to be very disagreeable and to produce fallen fontanelles in children. I listen as the *sasmalkra*'s wife warns women that if they leave their children's clothing out to dry over-

213

night, a *wahwin* may pass by, leaving its odor on the clothing and thereby making the children sick when they put on the clothes. The sense of smell in fact appears quite frequently in Miskitu concepts about health. The *wahwin* is said to be an ugly, nasty sort of animal. It is something like a toad, which is the epitome of ugliness and the symbol of loathsomeness. One woman told me she thought the diet of the *wahwin* is toads or frogs.

Just south of Awastara, along the path to Aras Bila, there is a petrified *wahwin*: a large outcropping of dark rock poking up out of the savannah. This kind of huge rock is very unusual along the flat, sandy Coast. Rodrigo takes me to see the rock, and Victor later tells me a story about it. A long time ago, there was a huge, terrible *wahwin* that ate a lot of people. The shamans, the *sukia*, got together and talked about how to deal with it. They decided to lure it down near this spot and trap it with strong ropes made of native cotton (*wahmuk*). They did trap it; once it was struggling in their *wahmuk* ropes, they beat it to death, and it became the unusual rock that is visible today. Victor, in spite of his cynicism about many traditional ideas, tells me that he thinks this story, at least, is true. Ana Rosa Fagoth (in Silva Mercado and Korten 1997: 34–43) tells a similar story about a huge *wahwin* on the south Coast that also killed and ate many people. A group of Miskitu people, fleeing frantically from the *wahwin* in their canoes, asked for help from God, our Father, who sent a lightning bolt to kill the *wahwin,* thus saving their lives. Wahwin Key, off the south Coast, is said to be the petrified remains of this other primeval *wahwin*.

The *prahaku* is the spirit of the wind and the clouds. Avelino Cox (1998: 65–66) says this is the spirit that sends lightning bolts to strike people. If they recover, they may become a *prapit* or *pasa yapti* (mother of the wind), individuals who have special powers to predict hurricanes and floods and to deal with plagues of grasshoppers and other pests. Like other kinds of curers, these remarkable individuals receive revelations in dreams. In Awastara, however, I heard many more stories about the *liwa mairin* and the *swinta* than about the *prahaku*.

These traditional spiritual creatures have been culturally incorporated into Miskitu Christianity, and Awastara people often find scriptural justification for their existence. Thus, as Hawley (1996: 322) points out, the Bible in translation has become a Miskitu text, not an imposed Western one. Read carefully by local people, it explains the relationship between traditional beliefs and Christian ones. José Diego in Awastara patiently explains to me that when God expelled Satan, one of the angels, from heaven, he descended into different parts of the natural world. He came to inhabit the sea, the forests, and the air, thus taking the form of the different *lasa* that continue to molest people today. The *liwa mairin,* the *swinta,* and the *prahaku* are really different forms of Satan. This interesting interpretation seems to combine the missionary point of view that the indigenous supernaturals were devils, with the real danger represented by these spiritual creatures in traditional Miskitu thought. The biblical story about Satan is thus extended into the Miskitu natural world.

Personally, it has always been difficult for me to come to terms with these dangerous spiritual creatures that inhabit the natural world. Rodrigo, however, offers a sophisticated theory about why some people see them frequently, and others don't. If you believe, he says, you will see them. If you don't believe, you won't. He skirts around the underlying philosophical question of whether these creatures really exist, putting everything into the perspective of the observer: what you believe becomes true for you. Postmodern philosophy thus arrives on the Miskitu Coast. Rodrigo and his father, Victor, say they don't believe in the spiritual creatures—most of the time, at least. They know that Americans, Nicaraguan mestizos, and others don't believe in the Miskitu spiritual creatures, and contact with these people has apparently created doubt in their minds. Miskitu scholar Ana Rosa Fagoth insists, however, that all Miskitu people, including the Moravian pastors, do believe in the Miskitu magical world, whatever they may say. During the war years, she mentions to me, the pastors who fought with the Miskitu forces wore amulets or *kangbaika,* to prevent bullets from hitting them. She tells me of being frightened to death as a child of the dangerous spiritual creatures. But today, as a well-educated Miskitu intellectual, she leaves open the question of her own personal beliefs in her conversations with me.

All these malevolent supernaturals are thought to be capable of carrying a person away, never to be heard from again, if they are encountered. Avelino Cox (1998: 34–35) says that the *swinta,* also called *duhindu,* materializes to carry a particular person away and is only visible to the victim. Many people return having lost their reason, especially hunters who are punished for having killed too many animals. But others, having lived with a supernatural figure, come back with riches and knowledge. Cox presents the *wahwin* and the *swinta* and the *liwa mairin* with complete faith in their ontological reality, as far as I can tell from his text, and with no hint of Victor's skepticism. His book provides an accessible catalogue of these beliefs.

Today the word *lasa* (evil spirit) is often replaced by the English loanword *seitan.* The illness that results from being molested by some kind of *seitan* is then *seitan alkan,* "being captured by the devil." A particular

215

kind of *seitan alkan* condition sometimes affects large numbers of people, in epidemics of what is referred to in Miskitu as *grisi siknis*. Young women are those most likely to be affected. When possessed by particular devils, they run from their houses, strip off their clothing, have sex with the devils, and sometimes threaten those who attempt to restrain them, brandishing knives or other weapons. I first went to Awastara to study such an epidemic, which had affected some sixty-two individuals in the community in the 1960s and 1970s. I witnessed four attacks and took pictures of one of them and interviewed almost a hundred victims of the condition in Awastara and neighboring communities (Dennis 1981b). I could find no simple explanation for the condition, but it is clearly related to many other aspects of Miskitu culture. For example, the "hysterical" behavior exhibited during *grisi siknis* is similar to grief reactions after a death, to frenzied, trancelike behavior during the Great Awakening, and to wild, unrestrained behavior during drinking bouts (Dennis 1985). It also seems closely related to adolescent female anxiety over sexuality and rebellion against parental control. First attacks were all among young women. Women who had previously suffered from the condition, however, were at risk of renewed attacks at crisis points later in their lives. *Grisi siknis* attacks provide a dramatic example of the "hysterical Miskitu" character that foreign observers have noted for many years. For Miskitu people themselves, however, *grisi siknis* attacks, especially in epidemic form, are major social problems that disrupt family and community life and seriously threaten those affected.

In 2000 an epidemic in the Luxembourg Normal School in Puerto Cabezas affected about a dozen young women teachers studying there. Other students began to leave the school out of fear that they too would have attacks. I was a member of the multidisciplinary team that interviewed the victims and gave them complete biomedical exams and investigated the whole context in which the epidemic was taking place. The Institute of Traditional Medicine, which sponsored the research, eventually hired a traditional healer to treat the affected women. I worked as an assistant to the healer, as she prepared and administered the herbal medicines. Her treatment stopped the attacks and demonstrated the effectiveness of traditional medicine in dealing with this particular "culture-bound syndrome." This action-research project (Carrasco et al. 2000) was a remarkable example of collaboration between physicians and a traditional healer, something that would not have happened in the 1970s. Working with such culture-bound syndromes leads directly into the heart of Miskitu concepts of health and the nature of the human body, including its nonsomatic or spiritual components.

216

LILKA AND ISINGNI

The human spirit is spoken of in Miskitu as *wan lilka*. It is something like our shadow, the same size as our body, but it isn't normally visible. *Dama* Telemaco tells me: "Satan wants to take away our *lilka* [pointing to a small girl's shadow]. If he kills our *lilka,* our body will quickly die." The *lilka* is like the body; but instead of being flesh and bones, it is a sort of image of the body. Miskitu scholar Ana Rosa Fagoth (Fagoth et al. 1998: 19) calls the *lilka* "the animating principle of the person himself or herself." During illness, the *lilka* is weakened or taken away; and if it is not recovered, the person may die. A curer is able to see a patient's *lilka* and determine if it has been affected or has suffered some loss. One technique the curer may use is to sleep with a piece of clothing recently worn by a sick person and thus see the *lilka* and understand what is wrong with it. Interestingly enough, the word *lilka* is also used to refer to a photograph.

The *isingni* is a different sort of spirit of the dead, the "phantasmagoric soul," in Fagoth's eloquent translation (Fagoth et al. 1998: 19). It often returns and causes sickness among the living. According to one man, the *isingni* actually represents the dead person's affection for his or her living relatives. It may be jealous of a new spouse or may want to take away a child of which it was especially fond. This does not necessarily represent an evil wish on the part of the *isingni* but rather the love the dead person felt for his or her relatives.

I was present two different times when small children were diagnosed with *isingni siknis.* The first case involved a small girl who had already been diagnosed by a visiting physician as a probable tuberculosis victim, based on her pale color and loss of weight. The second case involved Eliza's daughter Nachalie (one and a half years old), who in 2000 had also been losing weight and running a low-grade fever. Eliza had Nachalie treated twice for *isingni siknis,* but both treatments were unsuccessful. Finally she agreed to take her to the hospital in Port, where she was diagnosed by the pediatrician as having a bad chest infection (but not tuberculosis) and was successfully treated. Unfortunately, the symptoms of *isingni siknis* are very similar to those of tuberculosis: loss of appetite, weight loss, paleness, and a low-grade fever. This makes prompt treatment for tuberculosis less likely, since the *isingni siknis* is usually treated first.

Traditionally, after death, a ceremony was conducted to take the *isingni* from the place where someone died to the cemetery. This ceremony was called *isingni sakaia* and was conducted by a shaman or *sukia*. I have never seen this ceremony in Awastara, but Fagoth (1996: 10–17) describes it in some detail. During the evening ritual, the *sukia* catches a firefly and brings it inside the house. With the help of the firefly, the family can speak with the dead person and sometimes with other deceased relatives. Then the *sukia* takes the *isingni* to the cemetery so it will not continue to stay around the house and cause illness. A variant procedure is to take the *isingni* to the river, put it in a canoe, and let the canoe drift downriver. The eventual home of the *isingni* will be in the sky, with the Yapti Misri, or mother scorpion, identified as the constellation Scorpius. The journey to the Yapti Misri is said to be long and dangerous, passing through the constellation Orion.

The *sikru,* or one-year commemoration of a death, is no longer performed in Awastara. The *sikru* also allowed communication with the *isingni* of the dead person, and for someone of importance it involved a large celebration. Large quantities of *mishla* were consumed, and dancing, merrymaking, and the appearance of masked spiritual creatures were also part of the celebration. Conzemius (1932: 161–63) called the *sikru* "the most important of the bacchanalian orgies" of these people, and he provides a detailed description of two *sikru* that he attended in the early twentieth century. The Moravian missionaries regarded these celebrations as works of the devil and worked as hard as possible to stamp them out, apparently with considerable success.

DREAMS

One of the ways in which healers find remedies, and in which spiritual creatures appear to humans, is through dreams. In general, dreams are believed to predict the future; and people try to pay close attention to them, to find the clues for protecting themselves against misfortune that dreams contain. While I am eating in Plora's kitchen one day in 1999, she confronts me with a recent dream of her own. In the dream, she came into her kitchen and found me lying drunk on the table. She quizzes me carefully to see if I drink (yes) and if I sometimes pass out drunk (no). Defensively, I ask her if dreams always come true. "Sometimes," she hedges. In fact, as far as I can tell, Miskitu people believe that in some sense the information contained in dreams is necessarily true. Interpreting that information correctly, however, may prove to be difficult.

The Moravian *sasmalkra*'s wife in Awastara tells me two of her dreams. In the first dream, a baby in Tuara was very sick. The parents had come to see the *sasmalkra* and his wife about it. It looked as if the baby would die. That night she saw an American, a *waikna pihni*, who pointed up to a cloud. There on top of the cloud was a small figure, the *lilka* of the child. There was a ladder up to the cloud. Climb up! he said. She said she was afraid, but he told her not to be; it wouldn't fall. So she climbed up the ladder and got the child and brought it down. When she went to see the child the next morning it was better, and she knew she had saved its life.

In the second dream, she dreamed that a boy of about twelve she knew was near a creek where she was washing clothes. She saw a ship come right up the creek, above the grass. There were two white men sitting on the ship, in white caps and shorts, but they didn't get up. A black man came off the ship, though, and grabbed the boy by one arm. She saw what was happening and grabbed the boy's other arm. The black man couldn't get him away and started off but said, "You'll see what will happen!" When the *sasmalkra*'s wife woke up, she told the boy's mother to be careful and not take the boy to the creek to wash. But the mother laughed at her and went anyway. When they came back from the creek that evening, the boy had a high fever. They came to ask for pills, but by morning the boy was dead. It was the *liwa mairin*. When she kills a person it doesn't take long. The *sasmalkra*'s wife told the mother not to take the boy, but she took him anyway.

White men are present in both dreams, and in the first one the white man plays a positive role in pointing out the child's *lilka* on the cloud. In the second dream the white men play little role, but the black man is really a *liwa* in disguise. Anything negative having to do with water is usually associated with the *liwa*. In the first dream the cure for the sickness is actually provided in the dream; but in the second the dream merely provides a warning about avoiding danger—a warning that the child's mother disregards. The child dies rapidly, with the pastor's wife indicating that this is the way the *liwa* works—very quickly. Dreams have important information to tell us, Miskitu people say, and we disregard them at our peril.

Helms (1971: 186) also noted that "dreams are taken quite seriously" in Asang. Perhaps the curious thing is that in modern U.S. culture many people pay little attention to their dreams, even though psychologists tell us they are keys to understanding significant and even crucial things about ourselves. Miskitu people interpret their dreams differently; but like psychologists, they regard them as extremely important. It is common for Miskitu people to ask each other their dreams in the morning and then try to figure out what clues for behavior are present in them.

POISON

In many cultures around the world, hostility toward others seems to be conceptualized in terms of witchcraft beliefs. E. E. Evans-Pritchard's work on the Azande (1937) and Clyde Kluckhohn's study of Navaho witchcraft (1967) are among the classic works on this topic in anthropology. In Miskitu thought, sorcery or witchcraft behavior is often subsumed under the category "poison." An enemy kills someone by burying poison in his or her path. This poison affects only the person it is intended for, who walks over it and later becomes ill. Various horrible poisons were described to me, all supposedly practiced by the Wangki Miskitu of the Río Coco, who are believed to be especially prone to this sort of evil. One kind of poison is said to be made by letting the body of an animal putrefy until it is rank and dripping and then sticking a thorn in it and placing the thorn where it will prick the intended victim. More abstract methods include using a scrap of paper with the victim's name written on it or the dirt gathered from a person's footprint and burying it on a path on which the victim frequently walks. It seems that "poison" is really the mechanism by which sorcery is accomplished, since it can be something as apparently harmless as a piece of paper with writing on it. This idea emphasizes the power of the written word and provides an ironic illustration of the multiple uses of literacy. People who know medicine can also prepare a prophylactic against poison (an amulet called a *kangbaika*) to carry on your person and protect you against harm. During the fighting of the 1980s, many Miskitu soldiers, and even some Miskitu *sasmalkra nani* who served as military chaplains, carried *kangbaika* against enemy bullets.

One sorcery case in Awastara involved a young man who had been ill for some time. After visiting several different curers and getting no relief, he visited a well-known specialist in sorcery practices who lives some distance from Port. This man told him, without his having to ask, important facts about his life. For instance, the curer said the man was building a boat, that he had three children, and that he lived a short distance from his father. These facts were all true, and the curer's ability to divine them convinced the man of the truth of the sorcery diagnosis. According to the curer, four men from Awastara with whom this man had quarreled had made him ill. The cure was still proceeding when I left in 1979, and the patient's father had by then spent a large sum on the treatments. The patient himself had not been able to work for several months.

A well-known story involves a man named Charlie Fox who married an Awastara woman and came to live in the village with her. They had a son who began to see frightening monkeylike shapes in the trees and then died quickly. Convinced that Awastara people had bewitched and killed his son, Charlie went to Port and hired "an African man" who returned and stayed at Charlie's house. He buried something under the much used path to Aras Bila, and people began to die. Many died, perhaps twenty or thirty. Finally the Awastara people brought a famous curer from Sandy Bay named Arnold Williams. He did medicine to remove the poison from the Aras Bila path, and no more people died.

An almost mythological person of evil repute in Honduras is named Parson Taylor. He is said to be very adept at killing people magically, for hire. For example, a family may want to take revenge on people who poisoned their son or daughter, as in the Charlie Fox case. Along with the Wangki Miskitu, people from Honduras are said to be especially vengeful and prone to sorcery. Victor told me:

> You can go to Parson Taylor's house in Honduras. He lives there all alone. As you go in, you may see a jaguar, or a snake, or something else instead of the man himself. But he's right there. He shows you a looking glass, and in it you see the image of the person in your family that died, and the image of the person who killed him. How do you want him killed? Parson Taylor asks. The same way your brother was killed? Or he could be made to die through an accident, or in some other way. But Parson Taylor charges a high price, too. He already knows why you're coming to see him before you get there. He's a sort of devil person, like the *sukia*. Whatever way you choose, that's the way the person will die. They call him "parson," but I think God will punish him after he dies.

Poison and other forms of sorcery are thus very much a part of contemporary Miskitu life. Sorcery beliefs are also widespread among the Black Creole population, who do not share the pantheon of Miskitu dangerous supernaturals. Poison, however, is the recognized Miskitu specialty. Helms (1971: 184) may be correct in attributing some poison stories to actual chemical poisons brought back from the gold mines, but the belief in sorcery by poisoning goes back much earlier in Miskitu culture. A missionary report (Moravian Church, Periodical Accounts 1890: 90, "Official Visitation by Br. Romig") describes these beliefs:

> When anyone dies, or is seriously ill for some time, the suspicion is aroused that poison has been buried somewhere in the village. The rumor is cunningly encouraged by the "Sukias." These men are believed to have the power to discover the hidden evil. A Sukia is called for, and as a mat-

221

ter of course, after considerable necromancy and apparent searching, he comes upon some mysterious-looking objects, the skeleton of a toad, fish bones, something else which he himself has previously hidden there. This is at once proclaimed to be the cause of the trouble. The villagers, convinced that their suspicions were correct, forthwith forsake the place for some other locality—for a season, at least.

The poison complex and the various malevolent supernaturals reflect the indigenous past of the Miskitu people. Nevertheless, they are not regarded as being in conflict with Christianity, because in the Bible Jesus himself drives out demons and functions, in part, as a traditional healer. The foreign missionaries regarded Miskitu beliefs as pagan and superstitious, but the Miskitu themselves seem to have found the two systems compatible. They are even able to use the missionaries' form of argument—textual exegesis of the Bible—in their own favor.

Traditional Miskitu beliefs imply a dangerous, hostile world. Aggressive and sexual impulses are personified in the *liwa mairin,* the *prahaku,* and the *wahwin.* Psychologically, they project hostile social relations, involving threatening and dangerous people, out into the natural world. Ideas about poison clearly refer to a world of hostile social relationships as well. The prudent individual response to living in such a world is clear: you have to be careful, and also tough and resilient, to deal with these threats.

YUMUH

A category of illness beliefs that has less to do with hostile social relations involves the concept of *yumuh.* This illness involves severe abdominal pains. The *yumuh* causing them is said to be something hard inside the belly that contracts and pulses with the heartbeat. It can be felt through the skin, and treatment involves vigorous abdominal massage with oil. The stages in diagnosing and treating *yumuh* were described to me by a curer in Port who specializes in treating the condition.

1. Look at the person's abdomen and palpate it [*byara ba kapi kaikaia*]. This is to see what sort of *yumuh* may be causing the problem. Look at the patient's feces and see what color and consistency they are.

2. Give boiled herbal medicine to drink. The particular medicine will depend on the sort of *yumuh* being treated.

3. Rub oil, often *ujum* oil, on the abdomen, working it in until the belly is soft and pliable.

4. While rubbing, chant a secret incantation, or *yabakaia,* for the particular *yumuh*. Nobody else may hear or understand what the curer is chanting.

Nietschmann (1979a: 89–90) describes watching the *yumuh* healer in Tasbapauni at work. He stroked the patient's stomach with oil while whistling a soft melody and gave commands to the animal responsible for the problem (for example, the alligator) to be gone from the patient's body. Nietschmann cautions that such cures are complicated and cannot be reduced to simple explanations such as psychological conditioning.

The one treatment I saw in Awastara was for a young boy. It was unsuccessful, and the curer reported that the treatment should have taken place earlier, at the moment the boy was having the pains. She said secret magical words, with her hand held close over her mouth, while blowing over him, in the process called *yabakaia*. It used to be used in other spheres of life as well: for instance, for charming fish to the surface and making sure an arrow hit its mark. Not many people know how to *yabakaia* nowadays, however, and curing *yumuh* is one of the few problems for which it is commonly used. One elderly woman who used to cure *yumuh* by *yabakaia* no longer practices. "Her mouth has grown cold," it is said.

A common procedure seems to be to try a cure for *yumuh* when someone has abdominal pain, before submitting to surgery. "Doctors always want to cut, and Miskitu people are afraid of that," one man told me. With problems of infection in this humid tropical climate, they probably have good reason to be wary of surgery.

There are several different kinds of *yumuh*: rabbit, alligator, snake, spotted jaguar, and others. Avelino Cox (1998: 63–64) interprets *yumuh* as possession by the spirit of a particular animal, and the cure as a request for the animal to leave the patient's belly. The invocations sung by the curer are a form of poetry, with quite beautiful images. Ana Rosa Fagoth (1999) has collected and published a large collection of *yumuh* invocations. The curer sings the following invocation for snake *yumuhka,* as the patient's stomach is rubbed with *ujum* oil (Fagoth 1999: 39; my translation):

Piuta yumuhka man,	You, snake *yumuhka.*
Kiama lihnira man,	You, who are obedient.
Tatahkukam dakbi	You, *prak!* Broke your vine

prak piram,	and ate it.
Bukan slaunka dakbi	You, *prak!* Broke the tender
prak piram,	grass stem and ate it.
Amyapah takata baku.	And thus you were satisfied.
Kalalukam wahya	Your leaf of *calalú,*
Prak brih piram.	*Prak!* You broke it and ate it.
Saura saura mai daukan,	It made you feel bad, terrible.
Lalalwi waram,	You went slithering away,
wainhkikam sut takan,	and your mate came out,
Lamara prak prauram	And lay down beside you.
Tingnikamra kiup dimwaram.	In your creek, you dove down into the water,
Aikabi waram bara,	You were vomiting as you went
Kupiam kan aimakata baku	And thus you began to feel better.
Kiama lihnira man.	You, you are obedient.

These poetic invocations have yet to be analyzed in depth and understood more clearly within their own cultural context. Fagoth's valuable work in collecting and publishing them lends itself to this sort of analysis. *Yumuh* curing, as Nietschmann (1979a) suggests, is a fascinating cultural puzzle that remains to be understood by outside observers.

TRADITIONAL CURERS

Herbal medicine is used by everyone in Awastara and by Miskitu people in general. In a broad survey on the south Coast, Barrett (1992: 177–79) found that 70–80 percent of respondents in indigenous communities knew some medicinal plants and used them for health care. Some plants, such as *sus tara saika* (*Senna alata*), used for fungal skin infections, and *singsingia* (*Senna occidentalis*), used for pain, are known by practically everyone in Awastara (Dennis 1988). Many plants have an *aimia* or partner, another plant that must be used together with a particular plant for the cure to be successful. The rich, biologically complex environment of the Coast provides a large pharmacopoeia that continues to be utilized. In fact, Barrett found more than four hundred species of plants that are used for medicinal purposes.

Specialized plant knowledge is private property and must be purchased from the person who knows the plant, often for a substantial sum of money. The plant itself also has its price, the *sika mana*. When medicinal plants are picked, a coin or paper money bill is placed near the plant's root, and a short speech is made, thanking the plant. Older people say that in earlier days other sorts of gifts were given; but today the price of a particular herbal medicine always seems to be a small amount of money. After the leaves or some other parts of the plant have been picked, the money may be retrieved by the curer. The Reverend G. R. Heath, an early missionary, described this practice (1947), with his characteristic acuity: "Some think that the effect can only be obtained by 'paying' the plants from which the leaves are taken, either by pouring pork broth over such a plant, or by laying a coin at the root and leaving it there for a little time."

In one of the cures I observed, I accompanied the healer to the house of his young woman patient. He had already picked the plants and had them wrapped up in brown paper packets. At the house he then boiled the packets outside over a fire and brought the pot inside. The patient sat on a stool with the pot of medicine between her legs and a sheet draped over her head, so she could inhale the vapor from the boiling plants through her nose. He "steamed" her in each of the four directions, taking time to reboil the pot of medicine between each steaming. At first I interpreted this sort of procedure as a kind of "steam bath," such as might be used to clear lung congestion during a bad cold. I later realized, however, that the Miskitu concept is quite different. The essence of the plant is believed to enter the body through the nose, in the vapor, and then diffuse through the entire body, thus curing the illness. The medicine remaining in the body continues to act as a prophylactic to prevent the illness from recurring. After taking herbal medicine this way, the Miskitu say *wan lilka pukni takisa,* "our soul becomes hazy." In this condition the sickness-causing agent cannot see the *lilka*.

In Miskitu theory each plant medicine has not only its price but also its counteragents (*waihla*), which can destroy its effectiveness. Three basic counteragents seem to be common to all medicines: seeing or being close to a dead person; being close to a pregnant or menstruating woman; and eating certain kinds of meat or fish, especially hawksbill turtle, tarpon, jack, lobster, or armadillo. The common element in all these things is said to be their strong smell (*kia saura*). The "bad smell" of the fish or menstruating woman counteracts the medicine, entering the body through the nose, as did the steam containing the essence of the plant medicine. Because of their odor, fish may not be cooked upwind of the patient; nor may anyone walk upwind of him or her after medicine has been done. The reasoning is that some casual passerby might be a pregnant or menstruating woman or someone who has recently eaten a prohibited food. A rope may even be stretched across a path to force passersby to detour around a house where someone has taken medicine. As long as its counteragents are carefully avoided, however, herbal medicine should be effective. In Miskitu terms, the malevolent being causing the problem will not be able to see the patient's image, once the essence of the herb has been absorbed.

MENSTRUATION

Menstrual taboos are frequently mentioned in the early literature on the Miskitu. Bell (1862: 254) and Conzemius (1932: 148–49) both describe women as sleeping in a house apart from their families during their menstrual periods. They were unable to cook or prepare food and instead had their own food brought to them by others. In Awastara a woman no longer lives apart during menstruation, but nevertheless she should not cook for her husband during her period. If a man eats food cooked by a menstruating woman, people say he will have no strength to work and will feel weak and unable to draw his breath. He loses all his manly strength. Because they menstruate, women have potential power over men. One man told me, "You have to be careful because you never know if their period is really over."

Being close to a menstruating woman is especially dangerous to anyone taking or providing herbal medicine. A striking example comes from the well-known woman curer with whom I worked in Port. She is past menopause herself and lives with a much younger man. He does all the cooking in the household, while she works full-time in her healing profession. She explains to me that if another woman cooked for her, her medicine would lose its power during the times the cook was menstruating. Living with a young woman who menstruated regularly would represent a constant menace to her medical practice. Her young male companion is the ideal solution to this problem. Although he cooks and does housework for both of them, he makes it clear that he is not to be considered effeminate. He laughs, telling me that he takes time out from housework to play on the Cocal baseball team from Port. He is himself an apprentice curer, learning herbal medicine from his spouse as they live and work together. And most important, since he is male, any menstrual danger is obviated.

From the work of Thomas Buckley and Alma Gottlieb (1988) and more recent anthropologists (Hoskins 2002), it has become clear that the term "menstrual taboo" obscures a wide range of ideas and practices related to menstruation around the world. Women themselves may conceptualize menstruation differently from men and deal with it in interesting ways, even finding in it a potential source of power over men. Research to develop a woman-centered understanding of menstruation among the Miskitu people remains to be done.

THE *SUKIA*

Anthropologists have been particularly interested in shamans and other kinds of traditional practitioners around the world and have even suggested that the specialized role of treating health problems is the most ancient of the professions (Wood 1979: 291–92). Among the Miskitu there are several kinds of traditional curers, including people who specialize in herbal curing (*sika uplika*), snakebite doctors, and midwives. The most famous, however, are the *sukia*. Fagoth says of them (Fagoth et al. 1998: 28–29; my translation from Spanish):

> The prototype of the indigenous shaman is the *sukia*. His power connects with the supernatural, the mythic, the magical. He learns the secrets of life and death through plants. He predicts the future and has the cure for the illnesses of the corporal body (*wina tara*), the astral body (*lilka*), and the supernatural body (*isingni*) of each person.

I have never seen a *sukia* curing, but earlier writers provide descriptions. Ephraim George Squier, for example, writing under the pseudonym "Samuel A. Bard" (1965: 239–40), claimed to have seen a nineteenth-century *sukia* dancing in the center of a hot fire and suffering no harm, while she handled a poisonous snake as she walked in the embers. Michael Olien (1985) has called into question Squier's credibility in general. Nevertheless, there is no doubt that dancing in fire, drinking, sacrificing black chickens, and singing songs in an arcane version of the Miskitu language were all part of traditional *sukia* practice. Throughout Central America, the Miskitu word *sukia* has passed into local Spanish to mean "shaman" or "witchdoctor."

In Awastara an elderly man named Juan Esteban told me of watching a *sukia* cure someone when he was a boy. The *sukia* built a large, hot fire and danced in the middle of it without getting burned, while the sick person rested on a bed to one side, according to *Dama* Juan. The Moravian missionaries conducted all-out war against such shamans, considering them agents of the devil. Today it is difficult to find people who self-identify as *sukia,* although they are remembered well. García

(1996: 85) reports that she could find no one recognized as a *sukia* in Puerto Cabezas in the late 1980s. The role of *sukia* probably had mixed connotations even before the missionary attacks on these practitioners. *Sukia* were recognized traditionally as being able to harm people as well as cure them and were feared as well as respected. Michael Brown (1998) describes the well-founded ambivalence that surrounds the shaman's role in traditional societies, reminding New Age enthusiasts that shamanism is a double-edged weapon.

Mory Davis, the early twentieth century religious leader who built the first church in Awastara, was also a *sukia*. Evidently, before he was inspired to start preaching God's word, he had practiced this traditional role, using the spiritual world to aid in healing. The missionaries often had problems with such individuals, seeing them as blending "heathen" beliefs with Christian ones in an unorthodox manner. Their worries about indigenous preachers paralleled in a curious way the ambivalence local people felt about shamans. On the Coast, the years of conflict between the missionaries and the *sukia* not only diminished their legitimacy but also resulted in the rise of a new social role: that of *prapit* or foreteller of the future (García 1996: 93). This role flourished in the postmissionary period and seemed to have more legitimacy than the stigmatized role of *sukia*.

Nonetheless, there are still *sukia* practicing today. One conducted several days of curing ritual in Awastara in 1997, just before I arrived in the village. Ana Rosa Fagoth, a tireless fieldworker, is currently collecting songs and incantations still in use by *sukia* on the Río Coco. *Dama* Juan Esteban commented to me: "The missionaries said the *sukia* cured by using the devil's power. Maybe so, but he cured people! Now we have only Juan Downs." Everyone laughed, the implication being that the only alternative left was a watered-down version of the real thing. In fact, Juan Downs had provided medical care to Awastara people for many years.

I first met Juan in 1978 and asked him how he learned to cure. He told me that when he was sixteen he was working for a German man in Bluefields. One day he became very sick, started vomiting blood, and was running a high fever. He may well have been suffering from a severe bout of malaria. Juan was taken to a doctor, but the doctor could find nothing wrong. He lost consciousness for a week or more. In his delirium he saw spirit people who told him he had to change his life, stop drinking, and cure other people. Otherwise, he would die. Juan agreed to do this. He was then given a small, perfectly round stone, which he still has and which he showed me after telling his story. Juan told me he puts the stone in water and boils it then "rubs up people with it." The curing stone must be buried with him when he dies, Juan said, and a child should put it in his coffin. In Bluefields, Victor adds, Juan was regarded as a *prapit*, because he could divert hurricanes and make them veer toward some other place. One of Juan's nieces told me that another part of Juan's promise, made when he first became a curer, was never again to wear shoes and never to live with a woman. In fact, every time I saw Juan he was barefoot, and he did not have a spouse or any children. In 1978 he told me he had been curing people for thirty-three years.

Some people ridicule Juan. His shabby clothes, his twisted, callused bare feet, his penetrating gaze, and his quick temper all make him an object of derision, particularly for younger people. One of the stories that circulates is that he has a *liwa mairin* for a mate, one that lives in the small creek near his house. In spite of these aspersions on his character, when someone was sick, Juan was always willing to go and try to help. Personally, I am grateful to Juan, since he cured me of various problems, including the skin infections that are endemic in the region and are almost impossible to cure with commercial pharmaceuticals. I published a photo of Juan curing the bad case of athlete's foot from which a physician friend was suffering (Dennis 1988: 23). The cure was successful and provoked a radical change in the young physician's attitude toward bush medicine.

In figuring out his patients' problems, Juan's basic diagnostic tools are dreams. Once when I was ill, he asked me for an undershirt I had recently worn, for him to sleep with that night. Through the shirt, placed underneath Juan's head as he sleeps, the spirit people come to him in dreams and advise him as to the patient's problems. He cured me of stomach problems as well as skin infections and other minor problems during the first year I lived in Awastara. He has always been at pains to explain carefully to me that he does God's work, not the devil's work. The sort of *sukia* who sings and dances all night is doing the devil's work, he says, but it is God who sends spirits to visit him and helps him cure people. In my experience, Juan never charges people for cures, but he does expect gifts of money or other things in return. He lives a very poor existence, continually walking barefoot, usually in ragged clothes. Making large sums of money from curing is certainly not his goal.

Juan's niece tells me that he had slept with a shirt of hers and then told her all the details of the problems she was having with her current boyfriend. She says that once he broke the promise he had made never to have a woman and did live with a mate for two or three years. The woman was younger than Juan and only wanted his money. She insisted that he charge his patients instead of simply accepting whatever gifts they gave him, so that she could have more money. He began losing his power, and it was not until they separated that he got it back again.

In 1998 when I lived in Awastara for a month, I visited Juan and took a picture of him (photo 11). I wanted to sit with him and record his life history in more detail but did not take the time to do it. It was high on my list of projects when I returned for a year in 1999–2000, but I had waited too late.

When I arrive in Awastara I am told that Juan is extremely sick. I go to see him. His sister's husband, his *waik*, takes me to an empty house where Juan is lying on the floor, wrapped in a blanket. He is extremely thin, his eyes glazed, his gnarled old feet sticking out from under a ragged blanket. His *waik* tells me that he fell the week before, walking back from Sandy Bay, and has been delirious ever since. "He speaks, but you can't understand what he says," says his *waik*. It is true. Juan talks almost nonstop, but his continual stream of words is totally unintelligible to me. I think back to twenty years before when he cured me and wish I could do something for him. I recall the story he told me of learning to cure and remember his dark, deep-set eyes that always seem troubled and pained. I remember that he has no wife or children to take care of him, a terrible

PHOTO 11. *Juan Downs, traditional healer*

230

misfortune in this culture. He has given selflessly of his own knowledge to cure people for so many years, taking only the gifts that people gave him in payment. I feel an enormous sadness to see the old man, those great eyes of his still burning in his head, now lying here dying. I wish I had known him better and had taken advantage of the opportunity to learn more from him. His troubled eyes see deep into another reality that ordinary people can't see. It would have been a fascinating world to learn about.

During the rest of the year, Juan remains in the same condition. I visit him occasionally, but he never regains his lucidity. For his sisters, it becomes a great burden to take care of the infirm old man, feed him, and clean up after him. Bringing small amounts of money is the only way I can help. I wonder if, in fact, his small round curing stone will be put in his coffin by a child when he dies.

CHAPTER ELEVEN

Public Affairs and Community Development

THE MISKITU KINGS

Although the number of practicing *sukia* is greatly reduced, their memory is very much alive in the Miskitu collective consciousness. In a similar way, the Miskitu kings, gone for more than a hundred years, continue to reappear in various ways and also seem firmly entrenched in Miskitu thought. From my first few weeks in Awastara, I began hearing stories about them. In 1979 I was asked to participate in a celebration in which a local teenaged boy was chosen to be "king" and to come back in pomp and circumstance on New Year's Day to visit his people (Dennis 1982). He handed out entertaining punishments (such as kissing a toad) to various "lawbreakers" and gave a speech in a foreign language (Spanish), exhorting his people to be good citizens of the community. A number of coastal communities continue such celebrations today, symbolic reminders of the kings of previous centuries. Kings also figure prominently in the *kisi* or folktales, and they appear as important characters in the Christmas plays.

Historically, from the 1630s until 1860, the most prominent Miskitu political leaders were known as "kings," a loanword from English but also a political concept that became Miskitu-ized. There were also "generals," "admirals," and "governors," who may have competed for authority with the kings (Olien 1998). In 1860 the British signed the Treaty of Managua with Nicaragua, which established a Mosquito Reserve, and the title of king was changed to that of chief (Olien 1983: 230). Nevertheless, local Miskitu people continued to call their leaders kings. The last king was Robert Henry Clarence, who fled to Jamaica when the Nicaraguan army "reincorporated" the Atlantic Coast into the country in 1894. Various twentieth-century visitors to the Coast met descendants of the kings, and Karl Offen (1999: 368–71) even photographed a scepter-cane and a crown, symbols of kingly status that these families still proudly retained.

Exactly what the Miskitu kingship represented politically has been the subject of some interesting scholarly controversy. Michael Olien's careful work (1983, 1998) has provided detailed genealogies and histories of the kings and some of the generals and admirals. A traditional view was that these leaders were simply puppets of the British (Conzemius 1932: 101). Olien and I (Dennis and Olien 1984) have suggested that the kings had more legitimacy than commonly supposed. Their British uniforms and English educations may have served as symbols of esoteric knowledge and important foreign connections, giving them legitimacy in their people's eyes. They seem to have had considerable power to command labor and punish crimes and appeared as powerful leaders in their own time. Mary Helms (1986) has countered that—although the kings may have been personally despotic on occasion—there is little evidence that they held legal authority derived from a formal political office. In her interpretation they were regional Big Men, competitive war leaders whose power waxed and waned, rather than true kings. Wolfgang Gabbert (1990, 2002) adds that the kings seemed to depend on a privileged position in trade networks with powerful outsiders and not on the extraction of wealth from their followers. He argues that in the nineteenth century they became totally dependent on foreign support and alienated from their own culture. Kingship among the Miskitu, like many other topics suggested in this book, remains a fascinating problem for further research.

Some of the stories told in Awastara about the kings are quite delightful. Victor's version of how the Miskitu got their first king is as follows:

The English had been fighting for many years but couldn't win. The Miskitu people in those days were tough. Really tough! They had animal bones through their noses and used bows and arrows. But when they did *yabakaia* [magical incantation] over those arrows, they didn't miss! They heard that the English king couldn't win the war he was fighting, and they wanted to help. They paddled all the way to Jamaica in their big dugout canoe. The Jamaicans were surprised to see them. "Where are you going?" they asked. The Miskitu said, "We're trying to go help the English." But they didn't really understand how far it was. So the Jamaicans put their dugout on a big ship and took them all the way to England. The English king received them and asked them why they had come. "We have come to help you win the war," they replied. The English king thanked them and offered them guns, swords, whatever they needed to fight with. "We don't need them," they replied. "We brought our own weapons." The way it was, you see—there was a flag on a tall flagpole where they were fighting. Whoever's flag was flying on top of it, well, that was who had won. So the Miskitu men waited until it was early morning and completely dark. The watchmen would be asleep. They paddled quietly in their canoe underneath the big wharf and very quietly climbed up on it. They began to shoot those arrows they had *yabakaia* over. They didn't miss! They killed the watchmen, all the foreign soldiers. They pulled down the other flag and ran up the English flag. When dawn came, everyone could see which flag was flying—the English had won! The English king was very happy. He received them again and asked what they wanted in return for the victory. "You can have gold, arms, clothes, anything you want," he offered. The Miskitu replied, "No, what we want is a king of our own, just like the English king. But you will have to provide the crown, the robe, and all the other necessary things." The English king was glad to agree, and so the Miskitu got their first king. You could find that story in England. There they know that the Miskitu people helped them out when things were hard.

Victor told me this story a number of times, adding different details. The long wharf underneath which the Miskitu ran their canoe sounds very much like the long wharf in Puerto Cabezas, under which the Miskitu run their small boats (although not their big catboats). Intriguing elements in the story include the fact that the Miskitu first helped out the English and not the other way around. The Miskitu also used superior skill and craft to win the war, somewhat like the wily Tibang of the *kisi*. They made a long and difficult trip, because they respected and admired the English king. It is interesting to note that in the story the institution of kingship was not imposed on the Miskitu. Rather, they requested it and were conceded the institution by the English, who also provided what the Miskitu needed to implement it—the recognized symbols of royal status. Agency here belongs to the Miskitu, who were better fighters than the English, helped them out of a desperate situation, and were then granted a sumptuous reward. They chose something belonging to the English that they wanted for themselves: the kingship.

HEADMEN

Although there have been no kings since 1894, there are village strong-men whose word carries a good deal of weight. Traditionally, a *wita*, or headman, was recognized in every village as the town political leader. Under the Somoza dictatorship, the *wita* was given the title of *juez de mesta* (local judge). The *juez de mesta* had a regular source of income in Awastara, collecting two cordobas from each catboat that sailed for Port and then stamping the captain's passbook. The captain had to show his passbook upon docking in Port. Thus the *juez de mesta*'s authority was reinforced by his control over catboat travel, which provided a steady source of income.

Since the revolution, two different leadership positions have been in-stituted in each community. One is the *síndico*, an official who is sup-posed to deal with land matters, boundaries, and relations with neigh-boring communities. Collecting revenue from outsiders who may want to cut timber or use other community resources also falls to the *síndico*. The other official is the *alcalde*, who is supposed to settle the frequent disputes within the community over animals damaging others' property, fights between drunken youths, and so on.

Another new organization is the council of elders (*consejo de ancia-nos*), created during the Sandinista years. It includes respected elder men in the village and, like the *síndico* and the *alcalde*, is now a feature of po-litical life in every Miskitu community. Informal councils of elders have always existed, but they were not institutionalized. Some of the ethnohis-torical literature mentions informal village councils of elders: "[the prin-cipal men] never attempt any thing without a council of such old men as have influence among those of their countrymen who live around them. When any thing of importance is to be done, the people of consequence meet, and argue, each as he pleases" (Hodgson 1822: 47, quoted in Olien 1983: 199).

Marcos Hoppington provides his own interesting analysis of local po-litical leadership. In 1978 Marcos was the only university student I knew from Awastara. He went on to become one of the important Miskitu leaders during the war years. He comments that the informal councils of elders had always held a sort of moral or spiritual authority in each community. It was important to consult them because of their years of experience and wisdom, and because of the respect they had earned. But when MISURASATA and later YATAMA institutionalized the councils as legal authorities in the 1980s, Marcos says that they created another source of division. People would then say, "If the headman doesn't agree, then we'll just go to the council of elders."

Marcos comments that the Miskitu leaders criticized the Frente Sandinista for introducing many forms of organization from the Pacific that did not function well on the Miskitu Coast—for example, the Association of Agricultural Workers (ATC), the Luisa Amanda Espinosa Nicaraguan Women's Association (AMNLAE), and many other special groups that functioned underneath the Sandinista umbrella.

> But we ourselves did something very similar. There had been one headman, the *wita*. He was called a *juez de mesta,* but he was the headman, the authority. He took care of everything that happened in the community. Then we began to pick "coordinators," a "coordinator of health," a coordinator of this and that. Instead of supporting the institution that existed, we brought it down. The people began to be divided. Who is in charge here? they said. And then the *síndico* was introduced. Before, the *wita* was a single job, he had an income from the tax on each boat that left for Port . . . All these competing institutions resulted in a kind of anarchy in the communities. That anarchy worries me a lot. I wish there could be someone in control, and not anarchy.

In fact, Miskitu leadership has always seemed to center around ambitious strongmen, who gather circles of relatives and supporters around themselves. They rely on their persuasive skills and eloquence, and their ability to manipulate others, in order to achieve and maintain their status. Helms (1986: 519) prefers to call such leaders Big Men, following the Melanesian model described by Marshall Sahlins (1963). Leaders similar to the Miskitu strongmen are familiar from other parts of the world. F. G. Bailey (1969: 39–42), for example, summarizes the leadership style of the Pakhtun khan in Pakistan. The khan can command loyalty from a group of relatives and neighbors, simply because they expect him to be able to deliver resources. As Bailey points out, such a relationship does not depend on moral authority but rather on practical abilities. Men may follow a successful khan even though they regard him with distaste.

Among the Miskitu, authoritarianism is a valued quality, and a leader is expected to be able to enforce decisions. In 1978 Victor's brother Pancho was *juez de mesta* but was said to be "weak," because in spite of yelling at villagers in meetings and striding up and down in front of them in National Guard fatigues he was rarely able to get them to do what he wanted. *La sip daukras,* "he cannot rule," it was said. He was compared unfavorably with "real headmen," who could make their decisions stick. Some people admired President Anastasio Somoza simply because he was able to enforce decisions. One man commented to me, "You have to have a strong leader to get this town to do anything. Otherwise they just act 'proud' [arrogant] and won't obey. But just let the National Guard show up, and they hang their heads like dogs and do anything they say!" The interesting point is the expectation that rightful authority figures will be able to enforce their decisions.

Miskitu authority relations are expressed in the concepts *ta uplika* and *sulyir* or headman and followers. Many social relationships are thought of as authoritarian, with a headman directing and his "soldiers" presumably following behind. In practice, however, individuals usually assert themselves, and disagreements are stated in no uncertain terms. The proud, outspoken nature of "the Miskitu character" was noted by Bell (1862: 250):

> They are a fine set of men, lively, intelligent, and high spirited; but they have learnt no good from the intercourse of English and American sailors . . . They are a violent, quarrelsome set of Indians, and most terrible drinkers. From the king being of their tribe, and the remembrance of the deeds of former days, they have still a great propensity to plunder and ill-use the surrounding tribes, in spite of all the king can do to prevent them. They are lazy, insolent, and have a most overweening idea of their own consequence and capabilities; yet these questionable propensities show an impulsive nature with some character.

Even though they may admire successful strongmen, Miskitu people are often cynical about the political ambitions of people who are not their own relatives. The various Awastara leaders in recent years have done nothing but steal for themselves, it is said. Leaders themselves, however, are under strong pressure to share any proceeds from their dealings with their own relatives first. Sharing with kin is part of the definition of being a good person. Divisions and factionalism are thus inevitable and occur frequently. There is thus a structural contradiction between the strong obligations of kinship and any institution that requires an impersonal, even-handed political authority.

Cornelio was the headman in Awastara for many years. One of his daughters cooked for me in 1978–79, and I have always worked hard to maintain good relations with him. Shrewd, intelligent, equally eloquent in Miskitu and Creole English, Cornelio was recognized as the man who spoke for Awastara in most matters. Other men occupied the post of *juez de mesta,* but Cornelio was "the man." In 1978–79 Cornelio reminded people of his good relations with the Somoza government at every opportunity. When he wanted to brew corn beer or *chicha* at Christmas time, for instance, he told me he asked the National Guard colonel for a permit. "You are the Somoza people," the colonel replied. "You don't need a permit."

By 1997, however, I found the town deeply divided. During the war years of the 1980s, Cornelio was rumored to have collaborated with the Sandinistas and was said to be implicated in the killing by Sandinista soldiers of the large cattle herds villagers owned at that time. In the 1990s he had also mismanaged funds from the Moravian Church, according to those who opposed him. Cornelio's family and neighbors on the *muna* side still supported him, but most of the *lalma* and *pingka* side expressed extreme distrust. At eighty-three, Cornelio still tried to be involved in all community matters, but many no longer respected his opinions.

From the time of my first visit, I recognized what an influential role Cornelio played in Awastara affairs. It was also apparent that he was controversial, and I tried to be diplomatic with both Cornelio's supporters and his opponents. One evening in 1998 Cornelio came to my house and asked for a loan of a hundred cordobas, which I gave him. To my surprise, he carefully paid me back a few weeks later. I interpreted the loan as a kind of test of my political loyalty—had I believed the stories told by his political opponents, or could I still be relied upon in some basic ways?

In Cornelio's summary of the current situation in Awastara, "They no longer listen to me, so we'll see who they *will* listen to." Although he no longer occupies any formal position, some people still bring personal disputes to him to settle. After one public meeting under the cashew tree near the baseball field, I watch as Cornelio delivers his opinions after he has heard heated arguments in one case of a girl who left her husband and another case involving theft. All the townspeople still listen to him, and some, at least, respect his opinions. Shrewd, crafty, and persuasive, Cornelio still tries to act as the Awastara leader in a community that is now deeply divided.

CONFLICT RESOLUTION

The Miskitu willingness to wrangle over all sorts of issues has been noticed by outsiders for many years. In 1881 a missionary wrote: "We could observe at Kukalaya that Indians are given to quarrelling. The houses stand so close that almost every word spoken in them is audible in the mission-house. On the evening of our arrival two women in the opposite house quarreled about a man. On another evening a man and his wife fought together, and made such a disturbance that we had to interfere" (Moravian Church, Periodical Accounts 1881: 511, "from Br. H. Zrock").

In fact, one duty of a *wita*, or headman, has always been to settle disputes. Theft is the most common problem. It was a problem in 1978–79, as it was in other Miskitu communities. Nietschmann (1973: 203–4), for example, reported theft from plantations in Tasbapauni in the 1960s. By 1999, though, a crisis situation had developed in Awastara. Many fewer plantations were being planted, in part because there was so much theft from them, and theft of personal items seemed to be constant.

Accusations of theft or other infractions are brought to the headman, nowadays the *alcalde*, often in written form on pieces of notebook paper. They usually state the facts of the case and claim that judgment should be rendered in the amount of "x" number of cordobas. If the headman agrees with the accusation, he may stamp it with his official seal and order the defendant to pay, although he really has no way of enforcing his decision. In 1978 I listened to a long dispute between Agustín and Cornelio over the destruction of Cornelio's plantation by Agustín's pig. Cornelio killed the pig, and Agustín demanded payment for it. Cornelio argued, however, that the damage done by the pig was worth far more than the value of the pig.

If arguments can't be settled locally, the next step is to go to the Nicaraguan authorities in Port. This whole procedure is called "going to law" (*laura dingkaia*) and is a fairly frequent occurrence. I was asked a number of times to write up legal accusations or to carry them to relatives in Port. Self-help solutions are also sought at times: for instance, stealing something back from the other person's plantation or catching someone just returned from the Keys with turtles and demanding a share. Gossip about who may have been "thiefing" what from whom is frequent.

Avelino Cox (1998: 84–87), in *Cosmovisión de los pueblos de Tulu Walpa*, a book about his own Miskitu people, describes conflict resolution. Traditionally, he says, a case of murder was settled by the killer's family agreeing to pay a substantial sum, called *tala mana* or "blood money," to the victim's family. The *sukia* and the village authorities mediated the conflict and arranged for payment of the *tala mana*. People in Awastara say this was true for minor disputes but not for a murder. Within living memory, the police have always come to arrest a murderer and try him in Port. In Somoza's time, said Victor, the National Guard would show up right away and handcuff a criminal and take him away. Today, however, the situation has changed. There are many automatic weapons and other firearms in the villages, left over from the war years, and many men with experience in using them. Before the war years, the National Guard did come to the villages to arrest criminals, but Awastara people say the police are now afraid to come because it is dangerous. The police are no longer any better armed or better trained, or more willing to use violence, than the villagers.

POLITICAL MEETINGS

Political meetings allow an opportunity to bring disputes out in the open and provide an open forum for the self-assertive Miskitu. In 2000 I am able to attend a two-day regional meeting of the communities of Awastara, Páhara, and Dakura, run by Rodolfo Spear, a prominent Miskitu politician from the region. The purpose of the meeting, which takes place in the Moravian Church in Páhara, is to demarcate the lands of the three neighboring communities. It opens with a prayer by the host Moravian preacher, Roger Coleman. An international human rights organization is paying expenses for the hundred or more conference attendees, and the organization's two women representatives are introduced. Their picture is taken with the leader of the Páhara women's organization, presumably to show that women are indeed involved in the political process, although no women speak publicly for the remaining two days.

Rodolfo and other leaders explain land titling on the Coast and the fact that communities now have a chance to obtain new communal titles. These meetings are to lay the groundwork for new titles. He then opens the floor for anyone to speak. The Miskitu men, never likely to miss an opportunity to express themselves in public, rise to speak one by one, describing land problems as well as all sorts of other concerns. The eloquence and forcefulness of these speeches always impresses me. As in village meetings, this forum becomes an opportunity to air all sorts of grievances. Rodolfo skillfully keeps steering the matter back to land boundaries, however. At one point an angry argument erupts. Suddenly Roger, the local *sasmalkra,* appears dramatically in the back of the church, like a wrathful angel of God. In his deep, booming voice, he says, "This is the Lord's house. I already told you not to be disrespectful. You can't stay here if you want to argue." Order is restored immediately. I suddenly grasp the authority that the early Moravian missionaries must have had in village affairs. At noon we adjourn to eat.

The food provided is plentiful: huge tubs of rice and beans and turtle meat and cassava. Everyone except me is disappointed that there is no beef, only turtle meat. The turtle meat tastes much better to me than the tough, stringy beef. Luckily, Victor's wife, Plora, has remembered to put an extra plate and cup and spoon for me in Victor's backpack. I forgot that participants are expected to provide their own utensils, just as at church conferences.

On the second day, participants break up into work groups, two communities to a group, and try to come to agreement on their mutual boundaries. There are very few serious disputes. Awastara and Dakura agree that their boundary runs straight from a boundary point called *il pauni* (red hill) in the west to the old Dakura lighthouse. Alvarez gives an animated speech about the far eastern end of the boundary line, saying he knows it well from hunting there so many times over the years. He mentions a huge *usupam* tree, a small creek, a big termite nest. The other Awastara men exclaim, "Yes! Yes! That's right!" in agreement. Alvarez mentions men from the two communities who, like brothers, used to work back and forth in each other's fields across the dividing line, *pana pana*, helping each other out. There isn't much of that anymore, he says. Everyone agrees it is a shame. Sixto Blanco, the bearded, elderly *síndico* from Dakura, writes up a formal agreement between Dakura and Awastara, and all the men sign it. The last afternoon is devoted to reading the agreements reached, with all the various local authorities present. And we all get another free meal. The meeting seems to have achieved its objective, steered very capably by Rodolfo, who has higher political aspirations on the Coast. In my mind, I compare this successful meeting with recent village meetings in Awastara, which have resolved nothing and always seem to end contentiously.

The traditional time for meetings in Awastara is on Sunday afternoon, after church, and the meeting place is underneath the shade of a cashew tree on one side of the baseball field. The local *alcalde* is nominally in charge. Attendance is voluntary and varies widely, from a handful of people to a large crowd. Most participants are men, but some women are always present too.

In April 2000 I attend a long meeting about naming a new *síndico*. I sit on the sideline with notebook and camera, in my customary role of visiting anthropologist and community member. No one pays much attention to me. Cornelio, the old village headman, begins the meeting with a very long speech, saying the community members can name whomever they want as *síndico*. He won't do it by himself. In spite of his eighty-three years, it is clear to everyone that he is still a major authority figure in town, even if he is no longer *wita*. Then other men follow, one by one, each standing up in front of the group and arguing, quite eloquently, it seems to me, for his point of view. I can follow the general points made in all the long speeches, but, as usual, I get lost in particular points that the speakers make. One procedural rule is clear: when someone tries to speak more than once, he is shouted down—the people say, "You've already spoken! Let others have a chance!" No women speak, although Ana, leader of the women's organization, is standing on the sidelines with several other women.

The main candidate for *síndico* is a young man named Lego, who is favored by several of the men who traveled to Páhara with us for the meeting of regional *síndicos*. They have decided to propose Lego, who was also at the Páhara meeting. Cornelio supports Lego. But many other men object. "Just because a bunch of you went to Páhara together and decided to name Lego doesn't mean the town wants him!" says one man. "Only the town can name a *síndico*," says another. It isn't clear who constitutes the town, since there is such divided opinion. One reason for naming Lego, Cornelio says, is that he has been to school and is competent at reading and writing. But Orlando argues, "It's better not to name people who've been to school. We've tried that, and look where it got us. Look at Marcos and Ráfaga [two Awastara men with higher educations]. When we named them they didn't do anything for the community." After Orlando's speech opposing his father's candidate, Cornelio stands up and says of his son, "Don't ever name this guy to any position. He is a regular Satan!" All the other young men, however, speak respectfully of their fathers and the senior men in the community.

Several of the *síndicos* from neighboring communities are in fact older men like Sixto Blanco in Dakura, who have kept the *síndico* job for many years and are obviously skilled at handling important issues and staying in power. People say that without a strongman to follow, people lapse into bickering and nothing gets done. This certainly seems to have happened in Awastara. I wonder how well a very young and inexperienced man like Lego will perform.

The meeting finally divides into different groups of men, circling angrily and talking in loud voices. They edge closer and closer into the center, talking, gesticulating, shaking angry fingers in the air—a slowly revolving core of men all talking at once in raised voices. I snap several pictures of the swirling mass of angry men underneath the cashew tree. The women join in from the sidelines on particular topics. Almost everyone at the meeting is now involved in some side arena of the verbal fray taking place in front of me. I am completely forgotten, sitting on the sidelines scribbling in my notebook. No one is charge by now, and there is no clearly defined end to the meeting.

Later I talk to Maestra Zulaina and Divor about the Sunday meeting. They have strong opinions. "People go crazy at those meetings," Zulaina says. "I might go crazy, too, so I don't go." Divor went to the meeting but stayed in the background and didn't speak. He says: "People in Awastara are like that. They can't agree on anything, and they can't get anything done. Arguing, fighting, stealing—that's the way it's become here. I'm surprised you came back to this town, knowing what has happened to the place." Zulaina says: "Cornelio tries to manage things at those meetings, but he can't do it anymore. But if he weren't there, things would be even worse."

Angry factional disputes erupt in other arenas besides the political one. In 1979 such a dispute was brewing within the Moravian Church in Awastara. Several people from the *lalma* side, all closely related, were very angry with the *sasmalkra*. Two of them were Helpers in the church, and they wrote the parson in Port to try to have the *sasmalkra* removed. They accused him of "proud behavior," of being overbearing and forcing people to do things his way. At the same time, he also accused his opponents of proud behavior, which included forbidding him to use the coconuts from the trees near the church, so his critics could sell the coconuts themselves. Other complaints against the *sasmalkra* included accusations that he had not paid back in full the money that the congregation had loaned him to start a small store and that he had engaged in a sexual affair with a young woman while his wife was away. A letter was written to the parson setting forth these complaints, and the Moravian parson for the region actually came to Awastara personally to straighten out the dispute.

I attended a general meeting of the congregation, at which both opponents and defenders of the *sasmalkra* stood up and expressed their views. As in most Miskitu meetings, there was a vigorous and occasionally angry exchange of opinions. One woman stood up to say they had not wanted a new *sasmalkra* in the first place, since they couldn't afford to pay his salary. Through it all, however, the Miskitu parson remained in full control and shut off the angry debate when it threatened to get out of hand. The parson seemed to have an unquestioned authority that few other figures have. He was very much in the strongman role. He sat as a judge in the case, as people stood up one after another to argue with each other. The leadership role of the Moravian Church was evident. I was told that at an earlier meeting the *sasmalkra*'s opponents had accused him in front of the parson of having sex with the young woman in question, as the *sasmalkra*'s wife sat crying. The parson questioned a number of people, including the young woman concerned, decided the rumors were false, and said he did not want to hear the story again. From reading Moravian Church records, it seems that investigating accusations of "immorality" within congregations has long been a standard part of a parson's job.

The *sasmalkra*'s problems continued as I prepared to leave in May 1979. At one Sunday service Cornelio, who had obviously been drinking, stood up during the announcement period. He accused the *sasmalkra* of not caring about the Awastara church and of pocketing the money the congregation was contributing toward a new church building. The *sasmalkra* finally cut him off and asked him to sit down. In the following weeks the *sasmalkra* prohibited anyone from making an announcement without asking him first, a requirement that one congregation member labeled "communism." In this case Cornelio was apparently voicing the opinions of a significant part of the congregation, those people who strongly disliked the *sasmalkra*.

Many disputes seem to take a typical course. An initial blow-up occurs, as people get angry about some controversial issue. They rant and rave at each other (*palaia*), may hit each other, threaten to call the headman (and sometimes do), and further threaten to take the case to authorities in Port. Relatives on both sides line up to give support to their own people. Threats are made to bring soldiers or the police from Port. Then, interestingly enough, the whole thing seems to fizzle away. The end of most disputes seems to be anticlimactic: nothing much happens. Months later, bitter disputes do not appear to have been forgiven or forgotten. No real resolution has been reached, and reconciliation rarely occurs. Resentment continues to simmer, although the conflict seems to fade into the background and to dissipate in intensity. Years later, some conflicts are still remembered clearly. People who have had serious disputes sometimes stop talking to each other at all for some time, paralleling, in a curious way, the pattern of noncommunication between mother-in-law and son-in-law. In these situations not talking prevents either strained or potentially strained relations from escalating and getting worse.

In the Moravian Church dispute, the congregation's big meeting with the parson turned out to be something of an anticlimax. Accusations were aired, and the parson decided they were false. The *sasmalkra* kept his job, but his accusers remained certain that their accusations were true. There was no reconciliation, and many people remembered him with bitterness when I returned years later.

KINSHIP ETHICS VS. COMMUNITY SPIRIT

Divor and Zulaina's opinions are telling. My visits to Páhara and Sandy Bay in 2000 indicated that at least the bridges and roads and school buildings were being kept in good shape, which was not the case in Awastara. Public affairs do not function very well in our community anymore: the schoolhouse is falling apart, the drug addicts steal people's belongings, the *lalma*-side bridge and the Aras Bila bridge are falling down. The New Year's king play, which I observed and took part in in 1979, has not been put on again in the 1990s. I am disappointed that the king will not return in January 2000, and I tell people so. They just shake their heads. Public projects in town simply don't get done anymore. No recent political authority has been able to do much about it.

The divisions in town are clearly related to the divisions among the various churches. When a new Moravian *sasmalkra* comes to town, I go to visit him. In the evening I mention to Victor and Plora that I hope he will do something to bring the town together, to fix the bridges, to make our community a better place to live. Plora says emphatically, "He's not our preacher. We have our own preacher. Each group [*guinka*] has its own preacher, and there isn't one for the whole town." I mention to Victor that it would be good if all four preachers could work together for the benefit of the community. "Yes," he says, "but they can't. *Asla sip takras.* They cannot work together."

An elderly Moravian preacher, now retired in Awastara, tells me that the community is too small to have four different churches. I interpret his remark as a complaint from the point of view of the dominant church. Later it comes to seem an accurate symbol of the lack of unity in town. Elderly *Dama* Moreno comments, "When you try to discipline them, they just run off to another church." From the authoritarian Miskitu point of view of *la daukaia* (laying down the law), this makes control impossible. How can you *la daukaia* if people just run off to another church? Recently the town has decided to name three different *alcaldes,* one from each side of town (the *muna,* the *lalma,* and the *pingka* sides). Having three different leaders represents the same problem on a political level. In both political and religious spheres the community is very divided, and the division of authority reflects this fact.

Individuals look out for their families first. This was as true in the late 1970s as it is today. In 1978 the Evangelical Committee for Aid to Development (CEPAD), the development organization of the Moravian Church, had loaned several Awastara men money to begin a small cooperative store, which would sell basic consumer items more cheaply than the private stores. *Dama* Kilbon ran it for a while but refused to open on Saturday, since he is Adventist. Non-Adventists were furious and told him he *had* to open on Saturday. He still refused, so the store was moved to the house of Santiago, Victor's brother-in-law. The co-op had started with thirty members; but the number kept dwindling, and the store eventually closed, amid accusations that Santiago had "eaten up" all the remaining capital. Co-ops are very difficult to manage in any case, since they cut across kinship groupings and thus cannot bring into play the strong bonds and obligations of kinship. In sharply divided communities like Awastara, a successful co-op seems almost impossible from the outset.

In 2000, new experiences in the village seem to confirm the priority of kinship obligations over everything else on an almost daily basis. For instance, a student of mine at Texas Tech sends me two large boxes of supplies for the school in Awastara. I bring them up by catboat and carry the heavy boxes up to the house from the landing. Victor's family and others immediately tell me that Moisés, the school director, will sell the school supplies and put the money in his pocket. Victor then asks me for notebooks and pencils for his own grandchildren, which of course I can't refuse. The irony is apparent only to me. As I carry the boxes to the schoolhouse, people beg me for notebooks for their own kids. "Give me! Give me! Give me!" As I explain over and over that the boxes are community property for the school, for the good of all the children, no one seems to listen. I remember the madhouse at clinics in the villages when I worked with the Wisconsin health team. Everyone pushed and shoved to try to get in to see the doctor. At trail cleaning and bridge building projects in the community, the squabbling seemed endless.

A new project develops in 1998. A prominent local man named Jaime Hoppington invites me and several other people in town to his house for coffee. He is establishing the Office for Peace and the Environment (OFPMA) of Awastara and wants us to work with him. The idea seems to be to raise money from foreign companies to protect the sea turtles. Jaime also wants to bring tourism to the Coast and work on various other projects. I am cautiously enthusiastic, although I don't really know what I'm getting into and tell Jaime I can't serve in any official capacity. Jaime says that Cornelio, the old *wita,* is corrupt and people don't trust him.

Therefore, the new organization will have nothing to do with Cornelio or his people. At the Moravian Church service the next Sunday, Jaime appears with a large banner he has made for his organization, and I take pictures of him and his collaborators as they describe the OFPMA to the congregation. I am curious as to how it will work out.

When I return in 1999, Jaime and his OFPMA have indeed been working. According to Victor and others, they are using a motorboat to stop lobster boats and fishing boats off the Coast and then requesting a tax or donation for their organization. They have collected many thousands of cordobas. They have given a small amount to the current *alcalde* for the town's benefit, but according to most people, they are keeping the bulk of the funds collected for themselves. Jaime is now living in Port and rarely comes back to Awastara. He has apparently done little to keep local people advised of what his organization is doing. Hilario, Victor, and various older men say that he is in big trouble as far as the town is concerned. After accusing Cornelio of corruption, Jaime seems to have opened himself to the same accusation.

In terms of almost all community affairs, a weak sense of community responsibility seems to run up against the underlying reality, the ferocious Miskitu kinship ethic. People's first duties are to their kin. Any sort of earnings or benefits received are to be shared first with family members. The Moravians, by organizing villages into congregations in which everyone called each other "brother" and "sister," seemed to capitalize on kinship obligations and create some sort of communal center in each village, but that is breaking down. Ostensibly public organizations like Jaime's OFPMA turn out to be personalistic opportunities for gain. Cynicism among local residents is strong.

THE WORLD BANK SCHEME

In 1999 a delegation from the World Bank visited Awastara and proposed an alternative to turtle fishing. They return in April 2000 to propose training the Awastara men to catch deep sea fish with long lines as a substitute for turtling. The meeting occurs at the traditional meeting place under the big cashew tree near the ball field. The World Bank official speaks through an interpreter, Maestro Jali, the Awastara sixth-grade teacher, who works valiantly trying to translate instantly from Spanish to Miskitu and back again. The World Bank official says that they have finally received $30,000 to provide an alternative to turtle fishing. Half can go for long lines, hooks, and other supplies, and half will go for training in the new technology. The World Bank man's speech seems imperious and insulting to local men and to me. "You have to show that you can learn, that you have the willingness to learn, and to repay the loans," he says. His speech provokes angry responses from the Awastara men. They say that they already know how to fish and don't want to spend half the money on training. This seems to them to be simply a way of channeling half the money to World Bank "friends" in Port, who will do the training. I tend to agree. The man's arrogant attitude irritates me as well. The Awastara men also say they want fish pots, Jamaican style, rather than long lines, because they catch more fish that way. The meeting becomes a swirl of angry voices with no agreement reached—a complete impasse. The visitors finally leave en masse to catch their boat, as quickly as possible, and it seems unlikely that Awastara will actually get any of the World Bank money.

The Awastara women's group, however, decides to submit a separate proposal, a modest one, to ask for help for women in marketing fish and in starting a women's cooperative store in the community. I write a letter for the women's group and take it to the World Bank people in Port, who like the idea.

Victor and Pancho tell me of two other failed fishing projects in recent years. One was promoted by a Chinese man named Jonathan Hong, from Costa Rica. He helped finance sails, hooks, line, and other materials for shark fishing. There is a good market for shark fins, believed to be aphrodisiacs in Asia, and the shark meat can also be sold. Most of the money he gave the Awastara men, however, was drunk up in rum. A U.S. entrepreneur also promoted a fishing scheme and advanced funds, which were drunk up as well. So there is good precedent for the World Bank to be careful with money. The temptation of drink can easily be overwhelming.

A few days after the World Bank visit, Victor asks me to write a letter for him to take to the World Bank people in Port. One of Victor's nephews spoke up strongly at the meeting and convinced Victor and others that they should press for money, in cash, to buy fish pots for themselves. I write the letter in Spanish as they request, but privately I tell Victor that it won't work. For one thing, it is probably against World Bank rules to give out cash. Besides, Awastara has a very poor track record of managing money from outside groups. A week later I go to Port myself and visit the local representatives of the World Bank. They tell me that Victor has already been to see them, pounding on their table and demanding money and other favors. Of course, he is not going to get any. They paint a picture of a petulant, stubborn, angry old man, demanding unreasonable things. It is a strange image of Victor, who has always been so thoughtful and supportive with me. Somehow he couldn't see that this sort of behavior would be self-defeating and would certainly not result in obtaining money from the World Bank. So wise and crafty in dealing with other kinds of visitors, Victor has really acted foolishly this time. His daughter-in-law Maura shakes her head when she hears the story and says, "*Daipna lal pain apia.* My father-in-law's head just isn't right."

OUTSIDE GROUPS "DEVELOP" THE MISKITU

For many years development organizations of different kinds have worked in Awastara and other Coast communities to improve life in terms set by the development groups. Communities constantly play a sort of game with these outside organizations, to get the maximum resources possible from them. I was living in Awastara in both 1979 and 1999 when human rights groups visited the community to find out what the local problems were and presumably help solve them. In 1978 CEPAD, the Moravian Church development organization, sent a traveling team from village to village, with a three-day seminar scheduled in Awastara. The meeting began with a prayer by the pastor and then proceeded with an exercise aimed at "getting to know each other." Small notebooks and pencils were passed out for note-taking. The information exchanged between visitors and the Awastara people included their marital status and whether or not they were Christians. Interestingly enough, the hardest thing for the Miskitu to remember about the visitors was their names.

The workshop seminars began with an attempt to find out what participants wanted to learn in the way of development. Each person was asked to write this down in his or her notebook. The things people wrote down included learning to be a carpenter or tailor, having more coconut trees, and having an outboard motor. A large "wish list" of very practical items was composed from all the responses. Opportunities for public participation were seized upon by prominent men in Awastara. They were not about to miss an opportunity to be heard! The seminar progressed through the three days with discussion sessions, drawing of posters representing better nutritional and agricultural practices, and speeches by the development people. Long lectures and exercises on human rights ended with a list of positive ways to behave, written on the portable blackboard and laboriously copied down by some of the participants, including me. They involved working together, obeying the leaders' orders, willingness to cooperate, love, helping each other out, truthfulness, cleanliness, and respect. My own role in the meeting was to try to be positive about the potential benefits such outsiders might bring, even though I had a great deal of skepticism about the underlying assumptions. After listening to all the things that the people of Awastara had to learn, I suggested to the visitors that they could learn a lot themselves about turtle fishing, which Victor had patiently been teaching me. They brushed off the suggestion, making it clear that they were not here to learn from local people.

Late in the seminar, Pancho stood up dramatically and asked, "What can you provide us to work with? We are poor: what can you do for us?" The parson in charge replied, "First we have to prepare people through these seminars and organize a committee with a president and secretary." He explained that the long workshops were to prepare the groundwork for development, not actually finance it.

People all dressed in their best clothes, as a group of women cooked all day long in a shed outside the church. CEPAD had budgeted funds for rice and beans and flour and lard and had bought a turtle from a local fisherman. Participants ate very well for the three days, with local people providing only the firewood and labor. People seemed very happy that CEPAD had come but hoped there would be some further practical benefit from the visit. Pancho said that CEPAD is a *pundu tara* (big money) group and could easily provide a motor for the village, or tools to work with, or other useful things.

The organization of such development efforts indicates wholesale borrowing from another cultural context. A committee has to be organized with a president, secretary, and treasurer. Notebooks and pencils are distributed even though the audience may be barely literate. In fact, people usually save them and take them home for their children to use in school. A schedule of events is posted, which includes a 10:15 coffee break and so on. Miskitu communities have become used to the Western cultural agenda for such meetings, although they do not necessarily coincide with local cultural realities. Committee organization, for example, rarely works well. Miskitu local political organization is not democratic but is organized around prominent local men, each of whom gathers around him a circle of relatives and supporters. Committee members tend to be marginal villagers who can accomplish little. Alternatively, the positions are monopolized by one of the important men, in which case the committee hardly functions.

In 1999 I am present at another community meeting, this one organized by the Commission for Human Rights in Central America (CEDEHCA). This is only a one-day meeting, held in the schoolhouse. As I

PHOTO 12. *Maestra Zulaina presenting community problems*

sit through the meeting, it is striking to notice how little the format and content of such efforts have changed in twenty years. The participants are given notebooks and pencils and large sheets of paper. They are then asked to caucus and report on the problems facing the community, the resources available, and potential solutions. The list of problems presented by local people includes the making of *chicha* every day and selling it, lack of respect for the parson and the local authorities, use of cocaine, a high level of theft, and the distance to the hospital and difficulty of travel when a serious accident or illness occurs. The resources available include fish and turtles from the ocean and agricultural products from the swidden farmland south along the river. No one lists cocaine as a financial resource.

Maestra Zulaina gives a cogent presentation of Awastara's problems (photo 12). The discussion that follows is also animated and drawn out, with many telling points made. No one can come up with good solutions to local problems, however. The thieves in town are well known, someone says, but nobody does anything about them. Professionals from the community, Marcos and Ráfaga and others, have tried briefly to help with problems but have quickly become disgusted and left. Neither have community leaders done anything to resolve the problems, it is pointed out. There is no political willpower evident to resolve any of the problems, and there seems to be a sort of resignation about them. No real leadership is evident either: no one speaks authoritatively for the community, although Cornelio still tries to do so.

THE WOMEN'S ORGANIZATION

In recent years the concern with women in development has resulted in outside agencies' promoting women's organizations in Miskitu communities. Ana Moody is president of the women's organization in Awastara, which has existed for the last twelve years. She shows me long lists of names of women interested in participating in the organization. But, says Ana angrily, "we don't get any support for our projects." Neighboring towns have gotten help with sewing projects and other activities, but not Awastara. Ana says she has tried to get the local Awastara authorities to set aside even a small amount of money for the women's organization, but they won't do it. One plan was to buy sewing machines for local women and thus provide them with another source of income: making clothes. Another project, requiring seines and ice-chests, was to organize groups of women to catch shrimp at the river mouth. If the women could establish their own small fund of money with which to work, they would take care of it carefully and not spend it on liquor. "Women know how to take care of money and make it grow!" Ana tells me. Women in general do seem more responsible than men in Awastara. Women don't drink or take cocaine, and they give the welfare of their families first priority. But they are also tied closely to their houses, raising children, cooking, and washing clothes. It is hard for most women to participate in any projects that require significant time away from home. Men have always dominated local political affairs, and this situation seems unlikely to change in the near future. Ana says that although many men oppose the women's organization, others (like her husband, Enrique) are supportive. She suggests other activities, such as a workshop on sexually transmitted diseases. Many fishermen visit prostitutes in Port, she points out, and return home with sexually transmitted diseases that they then pass on to their wives.

TOILET-IFICATION

A prime example of development efforts by outside agencies is the recurring campaigns to persuade Miskitu communities to build and use toilets. Control over fecal material and the diseases it spreads has been a major focus of public health efforts in Western countries. There is no question that successful efforts have contributed to much improved levels of health. In rural Miskitu communities, however, human feces are eaten almost immediately by pigs—a fact not recognized or appreciated by development authorities.

In December 1999 two mestizo men show up in Awastara to build ten public toilets, a project of the new regional RAAN government. The toilets are supposed to be of the new, improved type, the so-called composting toilets (*letrinas aboneras*). Instead of a hole in the ground, the toilets are built with two enclosed cement boxes above ground. Steps lead up to a small outhouse building and a raised toilet seat. When one compartment is filled with feces, it is supposed to be opened and cleaned out with a shovel, with the other compartment being used in the meantime. This is a nasty task—one at which the Awastara people recoil in disgust. After the crew has spent about two weeks in the community building these unsolicited toilets, ten have been completed. A month later none of them are being used for the intended purpose, as far as I can tell. The door on one has disappeared, and lumber from several of the others has been scavenged. People seem reconciled to periodic projects to build latrines but regard them as unclean and don't use them. The project seems like a silly, wasted effort to me—an attempt to impose something useless on local people. People dislike latrines because they are foul-smelling and also because in the rainy season the ones built over a deep pit in the ground fill up with water. The accumulated feces then flow out over the surrounding area, creating an unsanitary mess.

Twenty years before in Tuapí, some thirty miles away, I watched another latrine project being completed. Money for these projects inevitably comes from international development agencies. Since these projects are ineffective, they lend themselves especially well to corruption. No one at the local level cares whether they are completed or not. The foreman of the Awastara project tells me that more than half the toilet budget was appropriated by the regional government council, before he even received the building materials. Thus he has been able to build only half the number of toilets programmed for the communities.

Toilet and water supply projects are two basic parts of all rural development programs. But it is difficult to convince development planners that: people regard latrines as filthy and don't like to use them; pigs clean up human feces very effectively; and Miskitu people therefore don't like to eat pigs. Pigs never leave feces on the ground for very long, and the village seems remarkably clean. Nietschmann carefully observed pig behavior in Tasbapauni and noted how effective they were in maintaining village hygiene. Pigs make the major contribution toward keeping the village clean, but turkey vultures, dogs, and chickens also help; consequently, waste materials do not last long on the ground; there are no waste disposal problems. All organic debris is quickly recycled (Nietschmann 1979a: 80).

Miskitu people have strong feelings about hygiene and the contamination represented by feces, but they already have a disposal system. Clean drinking water *is* regarded as a problem, however. Many people have open wells that are subject to contamination, and well improvements are welcomed. Victor's house has a simple hand pump installed over the well by a Dutch graduate student studying in Puerto Cabezas. It works beautifully, pumping water from the now completely covered well beneath. Should development efforts concentrate on more sanitary wells? Awastara people may be right that nasty latrines are worse than pigs running around gobbling up feces. The existing sewage disposal system seems to be better than the new one outside "experts" keep trying to introduce. Ethnocentrism appears to have won out over the realities of public health in this case.

GLOBALIZATION ARRIVES IN AWASTARA

An exciting visit from outsiders occurs in spring 2000. Ráfaga and Jaime, two local men who have become prominent in Coast politics, have arranged a visit by a U.S.-owned seafood company, which is interested in hiring Awastara men to provide fish for the company. A great deal of fanfare goes into the visit. On the morning of the appointed day, the company foreman arrives by boat and speaks at a general meeting in the schoolhouse. The basic idea, he explains, is for the Awastara men to use their catboats to catch deep sea varieties of fish near the Keys and sell them directly to a large company boat that will patrol the area. The company will maintain an icebox at the Keys, sell lines and hooks, and advance money for provisions during the trips. The foreman thinks the plan might work well: sailboats don't use fuel, and rising gasoline prices have made motorboat operation prohibitively expensive farther south on the Coast. The company is especially interested in this area because so many of the local men own their own means of production, the local catboats.

The meeting is marked by many questions and heated discussion in Miskitu. The foreman speaks only Spanish and English, and one of his hosts translates for him. It is clear that the foreman is understanding little of what is being said—specifically, the many concerns of the fishermen and the lack of local leadership that is evident. During the morning break, he speaks with me and mentions forty-five catboats being available in Awastara. In fact there are only twenty-seven operable ones. Their names, owners, and current captains are all carefully written down in my fieldnotes. Evidently his hosts have purposely inflated the real figure. Self-promotion by the two Miskitu organizers has clearly been involved. Forty-five boats sounds more impressive than the twenty-seven that actually exist. The meeting ends with a dramatic confrontation between the current *alcalde,* Marcelo, and several other Awastara men. Marcelo has asked that some of the profits be dedicated to community use. Hamilton, another prominent local citizen, stands up and says, "These village authorities cannot be trusted—it's best for each man just to work for himself and do the best he can." The deep divisions in the community, eloquently expressed in Miskitu by Hamilton and others, are not apparent to the foreman.

In the afternoon a red helicopter circles the sky over the village. Children begin running toward the ball field where it will land. I run along behind them, along with many of the adults in town. Nobody wants to miss this big event! When I arrive at the ball field, the helicopter has landed and a large, excited crowd has gathered. The two guests are the Nicaraguan president of the fish company and his U.S. partner. Both are dressed in casual clothes and are unctuously friendly. The American speaks first to the assembled crowd, in English with a Midwestern accent. The Nicaraguan businessman translates into Spanish, and Jaime then translates into Miskitu: "I come from an immigrant family. My father was a poor carpenter from the old country who came to Cleveland, Ohio. I went to college and then into business and built the largest glass-recycling business in the U.S. I sold it in 1989. I just recently came to Nicaragua and I really like the country! And I am grateful to the Lord for my success."

The irony of this testimonial speech, intended for a U.S. audience, is apparent to me. It must be barely comprehensible to my Miskitu friends, especially since it has been twice translated at incredible speed.

The Nicaraguan business partner then speaks, emphasizing that people should realize that this is a business operation, not a government social service program. People shouldn't expect something for nothing, just a chance to work hard at fair wages. Globalization with its built-in assumptions and buzzwords seems to have arrived in Awastara, via helicopter. The ties between a wealthy U.S. businessman and a Nicaraguan entrepreneur, and their links to minor Miskitu political figures on the Coast like Jaime and Ráfaga, function as connections to the world system. The Miskitu Coast is still perceived as an unexploited business opportunity, just as it was by settlement companies promoting colonization schemes in the early nineteenth century. British historian Bryan Edwards (1819: 208–11) long ago gave an idyllic description of the Miskitu Coast and its inhabitants:

> Every variety of animal and vegetable nature, for use or beauty, for food or luxury, has been most liberally bestowed on this country. It is everywhere plentifully watered; and the soil is almost every where fertile in a very uncommon degree . . . The Musquito Indians . . . were formerly very numerous . . . Their modesty, docility, good faith, disposition to friendship and gratitude, ought to engage equally our regard and protection . . .

Today the friendly, cooperative local population (proud owners of catboats) is still billed as a major advantage of the region, just as it was almost two hundred years ago. In fact, money talks. The Awastara men are very interested in the scheme, although the practical problems involved seem enormous.

The obvious strategy for local people, it appears, is to try to impress the visitors well and thus obtain whatever local benefits might accrue. Unfortunately, the speeches by Awastara elders don't help much. The Moravian *sasmalkra* says that local people have been lied to before and don't want to be lied to again, and Cornelio makes the same point. Nobody really welcomes the visitors. The businessmen, logically enough, respond by saying they aren't lying to anybody or making any promises, just looking for business opportunities. The American businessman calls me over and chats for a few minutes. He comments on all the children gathered around us. He has a special interest in orphanages, he says. I think: "He must assume all the village children are orphans!"

A month later, the Awastara men are scheduled to do a trial fishing operation with the company, to see if they can manage to catch enough deep-water fish—10,000 pounds in one week—to make it worth the company's while to hire them. Unfortunately, I have to leave Nicaragua before the business experiment is finished. It seems very unlikely that the Awastara turtlemen will be able to shift from turtling to successful deep-water fishing overnight, with the meager resources the company has promised them.

The project has a fresh glow to it until I find in my fieldnotes a long conversation with a Miskitu man named George Glasgoe, from Sandy Bay, in July 1978. George told me he was negotiating with a company from California that wanted to build a lobster- and fish-processing plant in Sandy Bay and ship out the product directly from the Sandy Bay airstrip. The company promised good wages and some community benefits such as a new school. George proudly told me that he had sent a telegram directly to President Somoza about the scheme and received a favorable reply. These perennial money-making schemes on the Coast seem to pop up in every generation. They always involve local natural resources, the labor of the Miskitu men, and large profits for foreign companies and their local *costeño* collaborators. Globalization really began with the first European contacts on the Coast several centuries ago.

There are, of course, many positive human as well as natural resources in Awastara and the other Miskitu communities. Awastara men propelled their community into relative prosperity by learning to build catboats and catch green sea turtles for the local market. Men like Victor saved, took risks, and became entrepreneurs. Bright, resourceful people abound in Awastara, and we have at least one authentic genius, Casey Kingsman. In Nicaragua, however, the 1990s brought the end of social change programs and a completely laissez-faire approach to development. The decline of the Moravian Church muted a strong voice for traditional morality. Former combatants with a tough, aggressive stance toward the world found little work available. What they did find was cheap rum and a new drug of choice, cocaine.

INTOXICANTS IN AWASTARA: *GUARO* AND *CHICHA*

The ethnohistory of the Miskitu Coast reports drinking as a major feature of local life for many years, the original form being periodic *mishla* feasts with home-brewed cassava beer. European commentators from early times have interpreted drunkenness as characteristic of Native American people, in almost racist terms. "The vice of drunkenness is inherent in all Indians, and when they can get intoxicating drink they have neither the power nor the desire to abstain. Fortunately for them, they seldom have the means to buy spirits, and the intoxicating drinks made by themselves consume too much of their provisions to be indulged in frequently" (Bell 1989: 96).

Alcohol continues to affect village life. Turtle fishermen sell their turtles in Port and many succumb to the seemingly irresistible temptation to spend their earnings drinking. In February 2000 Victor's sons Hector and Lobrito brought a full boatload of turtles to Port, and Hector left Lobrito in charge of selling them. A day later the money was gone. Lobrito says that he was attacked by several men on the path up from the wharf and robbed. Others say he was drinking in a cantina, then passed out and was robbed of all the money in his pocket. Whatever the truth, he came home with no money to show for a week out on the Keys fishing. Similar stories are common in Awastara. A good percentage of the money earned by turtling simply stays in Port in bars and cantinas. An even larger percentage of the money earned by young lobster divers is spent on alcohol and cocaine.

Some men are serious workers most of the time but yield to the alcohol temptation from time to time in binge drinking. A good Awastara friend finds me in Port one day and asks to borrow 500 cordobas toward a new sail for his catboat. I loan him the money but find him drunk in the city park the following day. The 500 cordobas apparently lasted for another day or two of drinking, and the catboat never got a new sail. I found out later to my chagrin that this man is well known for these binges. His wife tells me in tears that he stays away from home for days and returns penniless, dirty, and disheveled. With money in his pocket, drink is an irresistible temptation.

I take a frightening trip from Port to Awastara in a catboat in which the captain and sailors are all drunk during the voyage. As I wait on the wharf in the evening, the captain shows up, totally inebriated, and asks for the passage money ahead of time. He disappears with the money to continue his drinking spree. By the middle of the night, the captain and sailors are back and somehow manage to get into the catboat, as it heaves up and down in the heavy swell, tied to the wharf. As we sail up the Coast the next morning, the crew continue to pass small plastic bottles (*medias*) of rum back and forth to each other. At one point the drunk steersman lets go of the tiller completely, and the boat swings instantly in a big circle. A man named Mosely, who has not been drinking, jumps up to grab the tiller, shouting, "You're crazy! Do you want us to turn over?" He tells me later about a Sandy Bay boat that recently overturned due to similar carelessness at the tiller. When we arrive at the Awastara bar, the crew is still drunk. We wait in the boat while they sleep it off and by then have missed the incoming tide to cross the bar easily. We hit hard on the sand and have to unload all the cargo and carry it, soaked, up onto the beach. During the fateful voyage, the cargo, including my plastic bags, has gotten ripped and soaked with seawater from carelessness, and I am furious with the captain. Back at the house I ask Victor how common it is for sailors and captains to be drunk at sea, and he just laughs bitterly. It turns out that part of the boat's cargo was two cases of rum, to be sold in the village. That was the cache from which those *medias* kept appearing during the voyage.

The most common drink is cheap white rum. It is called *guaro* in Nicaragua, and the most common brand, Ron Plata, is jokingly referred to as *ron pleito* or "fighting rum." Small half-liter *medias* fit easily in the pocket. They are sold on almost any street corner in Port, although none of the small stores in Awastara sell them openly. Various captains bring up cases, however, and sell out quickly from their houses, even with a steep markup.

An even cheaper drink is *chicha,* locally brewed corn beer. The traditional Miskitu word for this drink is *tualbi.* Corn is macerated in a hand grinder and then boiled, sugar is added, and the jug is left to ferment. The resulting *chicha* is white and sour tasting and leaves a residue in the bottom of the container. In 1978–79 it was brewed only around Christmas and for a few other special occasions during the year. But by 1999–2000 several households were brewing *chicha* almost every day and selling it for ten cordobas a glass. Nights are filled with the shouting and whooping of drunks from the *lalma* part of town, where most of the *chicha* is brewed. The brewers pay a local tax of thirty cordobas a gallon to the *lalma*-side *alcalde,* thus giving him a constant source of income. At one public meeting this becomes a topic of heated controversy, with some individuals standing up and vociferously denouncing the *alcalde* for selling permission to brew *chicha.*

This pattern of drinking is guaranteed to cause serious domestic problems. Women and families depend on the money that men earn for food, clothing, and other basic necessities. This fact puts in perspective Victor's comment that you can't have a woman if you don't buy her food and clothes. The strong Protestant injunction against drinking must also be seen in this light. It strongly condemns chronic binge drinking by poor working men, whose families suffer as a result of their seemingly uncontrollable behavior.

COCAINE

Cocaine and marijuana are more recent drugs that affect life in Awastara. Marijuana has been used casually in Awastara since I first arrived in 1978, but its use has increased in recent years, as marijuana bales and packets wash up on the beaches. During the 1990s, a major new development on the Coast has been the cocaine trade (Dennis 2003). The cocaine passes along Nicaragua's Atlantic Coast on its way from Colombia to market in the United States. This northbound cocaine trade has developed strongly since about 1990, coinciding with the end of the Sandinista government, reduced Nicaraguan military presence on the Coast, and consequent problems in intercepting drug shipments. Official Sandinista policy was strong disapproval of drug use. As in Fidel Castro's Cuba, drug use was regarded as a symptom of capitalist decadence. In recent years, when the few remaining patrol boats attempt to catch the drug runners, they simply throw the illegal product overboard. Large quantities of cocaine are thus washed up on the Keys or along the coastal beaches. One local theory maintains that drug runners regularly throw the expensive product overboard in order to increase the drug consumption market on the Coast. To me this seems highly improbable. Such a practice would mean abandoning high profits from U.S. sales in order to give free samples to poor Nicaraguans. Drug runners seem unlikely to ignore the high price differential for their product in the United States and in Nicaragua.

As described by Awastara people, the cocaine is packaged in one-kilo blocks, each tightly wrapped up in waterproof plastic. A box contains twenty-four kilos, and occasionally whole boxes are found on the beach. Double boxes contain forty-eight kilos. In a number of early finds in Awastara, the community shared in the cocaine bounty. Small amounts of the drug were given out to many different households to dispose of as they wished. The unit of measure is a small, empty plastic bottle, the kind in which you buy Zepol, a common Nicaraguan patent medicine similar to Vick's Vapo-Rub. In 1999 a completely full Zepol bottle was said to be worth a thousand cordobas (about eighty-five dollars). A complete kilo was worth thirty-five thousand cordobas (about three thousand dollars). The price of cocaine here is obviously a very small fraction of the street cost in the United States, since prices obey the classic laws of supply and demand. Supply difficulties resulting from the illegal nature of this agricultural product increase the price enormously in the United States. In 1999 the members of Victor's family were given a small share of the cocaine find, with Victor getting a full bottle and his eldest son getting half a bottle. After the find, for several days the Awastara landing was crowded with motorboats bringing people from other places who wanted to buy the drug from local people. Trails in the area are also said to be dangerous during such times.

In the most recent finds, however, the finder and the village authorities have kept most of the proceeds for themselves. People told me details of the disposition of the large cache found at the Keys in 1999. Two kilos were paid directly to the police, while the finder kept eleven kilos. The *lalma*-side authorities, including the *alcalde* from that side, got most of the rest of it. The *alcalde* and his subordinates were much criticized for taking so much for themselves, especially when he promptly began construction of a new house. It is said that Cornelio's long career as an Awastara political leader, which allowed him to develop and maintain political connections in Port, facilitates quick and easy sale of the cocaine. Because local authorities as well as higher officials in Puerto Cabezas receive a substantial share of any cocaine find, villagers point out that all of them have a vested interest in the cocaine trade. Antidrug programs here and elsewhere must face this simple economic fact.

There is an element of luck involved in cocaine finds. Like big wins in gambling, they seem to be random events. Apparently, the more you walk the beaches, the more you increase your chances of a find. Several local men who have made repeated finds, however, have evidently figured out where drug runners are most active or where wind and currents are most likely to have deposited cocaine. Thus there is also some degree of skill involved.

Maestro Jali tells me a sad-funny story about another man I know who received a large share of the most recent cocaine find. This man, a very pleasant fellow, has the reputation of not being particularly bright. According to Jali, he sold some of his cocaine and bought lumber for a new house. Then he took a shovel and buried the rest outside, some distance from the house, for safekeeping. We both smile at the image of the poor man, shovel in hand, burying his treasure to keep it safe. When he went back to look for it, of course it was gone. The new house still stands, half finished, when I leave months later.

The cocaine trade has also resulted in cocaine consumption in Awastara and other villages and problems of addiction among a number of young men. Up the trail from my house, one man makes cocaine into crack and sells the "rocks" to local youths for ten cordobas (a little less than one dollar) a piece. Crack is made by mixing cocaine with baking soda and then cooking it in a spoon over a candle flame until it is hard. Each spoonful of the mixture is then broken into four rocks. It is smoked in a homemade pipe made of a Zepol bottle, with a plastic ballpoint pen core used as a pipe stem. When my neighbor has a supply of crack for sale, I watch as a steady stream of young men heads up the hill toward his house to purchase it. Since he is rarely home, his wife actually sells the rocks to them, in much the same way that other households sell freshly baked bread or other homemade products.

Apparently the young men take their newly purchased rocks and consume them elsewhere. This behavior is different from local *chicha* drinkers. *Chicha* brewers, in fact, expect their customers to stay close to the house where the product is made. Customers have to be close to keep coming back for another glass of *chicha*. A cantina atmosphere thus develops around the *chicha* houses, with many drunks whooping and yelling as they consume *chicha* late into the night. In contrast, the crack vendor up the hill seemed to be providing more of a retail outlet than a "crack house" where the drug is consumed. Nonetheless, I was told that after major cocaine finds you can hear men in various parts of town whooping and hollering at the top of their lungs, just as the *chicha* drinkers do. This behavior, which sounds wild and unrestrained in the quiet calm of village evenings, is apparently a culturally patterned male response to taking mind-altering substances.

VIOLENCE AND COCAINE

As in the United States, the drug trade is dangerous and violent. Several young men have died of drug overdoses in Awastara and surrounding communities, including, most recently, a teenaged boy I knew well. He was found in the bush where he had been taking drugs with companions. In agony, he was taken by boat to the hospital in Puerto Cabezas but died before he could be treated. There are many other stories of young men who have died of overdoses in Awastara and the surrounding communities. Each case is well known and carefully noted in the local system of drug casualty reckoning. A story in the *Washington Times* (Sullivan 2002) quotes Sandy Bay elders as saying that six young men had died of overdoses in that community in recent years, and this is probably an accurate figure.

One evening nine-year-old Nena tells me the names of teenagers in Awastara who use cocaine. She describes watching one of our young neighbors as he took cocaine out of a plastic bag and snorted it up his nose. I listen with concern, realizing how common this must be, for a small girl to have seen it and describe it to me in this way.

Cocaine use has also been associated with a high level of violence toward others. In early 1999 a man I knew was killed by another who had been drinking and taking crack. I heard a detailed description from the victim's sister. He was sitting in a room full of men who had also been drinking and using drugs. Another man came to the door, very intoxicated from both drinking alcohol and taking cocaine. He pounded on the door and yelled for the victim, who got up and began arguing through the door. The man standing outside pulled out a pistol and fired a shot through the door, hitting his antagonist in the head and killing him instantly. When I visited a few weeks later, the house where the killing took place had a cross placed underneath it, and no one was living there. The killer himself stayed around the village for a week or more, until revenge seemed imminent, and then escaped to Honduras, where he remained a year later. The dead man left seventeen children by several different women, according to his sister. He was known as a good turtle fisherman and community member. The murderer, in contrast, had been violent and abusive all his life. I remember him vividly, the same man who provoked a fistfight at the Christmas dance in 1978, in which, fortunately, blood and bruises were the only result. The victim's sister told me that she had tried to find justice in Puerto Cabezas but without success, since the killer is known to be deeply involved in the cocaine trade on the Coast and to have influential friends. Authorities are reluctant to pursue someone with these kinds of connections. The murderer may remain in Honduras for some time, since the victim's relatives say that they will kill him if he comes back to the village.

Victor's cynical comment about the murder was that the killer had a gun and the victim didn't.

> If you're going to mess around, acting tough and mean, you've got to carry a gun. What sort of man gets into that kind of thing without a gun? The Spaniards [Nicaraguans] all carry them. That way, if one guy pulls a gun, the other guy does too, they both shoot each other, and done! They kill each other and no more problems from either of them.

Another violent incident in Awastara in 1997 involved four local men who were involved in finding and selling cocaine. The Moravian pastor told the men it was a sin to sell drugs. They supposedly kissed the Bible and swore they hadn't sold cocaine, when in fact everyone knew they had. Several armed drug dealers then came to the village looking for the drug and killed two young men who tried to defend the stash, riddling their bodies with bullets. One of the other Miskitu pastors in town, from the rival Church of God, told me that he stood up at the funeral and denounced the four men who had sworn on the Bible, saying it was their fault the young men had lost their lives. The killers were never apprehended. I took note of two small wooden crosses at the place on the village path where the killings took place.

Dealing in cocaine is thus dangerous business and is regarded as such by everyone. Victor's family cautions me to stay off the paths I normally walk, soon after cocaine finds, since there are so many armed and dangerous people about. They worry that I might become a victim myself. On one evening walk down to the Awastara harbor, to catch a sailboat to Puerto Cabezas, I am accompanied by Hector and Adolpo, one carrying a .22 and the other an old shotgun. I feel slightly ridiculous with such an armed escort, but I certainly appreciate the family's concern for my well-being. I make it a point never to ask direct questions about the drug trade, although most details are common knowledge and are told to me without hesitation by local people. Cocaine has become a fact of life to be dealt with here, although to me it is something new. Globalization has many faces.

One Miskitu explanation for the high level of violence is that many guns remain from the bitter conflict period of the 1980s, when Miskitu rebel groups fought a bloody war against the Sandinista army (Hale 1994). Many men have years of combat experience and are quite proficient at using automatic weapons. It is said they now have a *kupia karna* (hard heart). *Kupia karna* is also one local explanation for the increase in social strife. As ex-soldiers, many younger men won't put up with being ordered around by anyone, people say. This makes it difficult for the *alcalde* to organize people to rebuild the bridges or clean the trails, since people won't obey his orders. According to my friend Andrew Kingsman, something basic has changed in the way Miskitu people react to authority figures. Given the ferocious independence of the Miskitu character, this could certainly contribute to anarchy.

In a sobering article, Bernard Nietschmann (1987) describes the militarization of indigenous peoples around the world, fighting to defend their own lands and ways of life. Fought with modern weapons, these wars between the world's indigenous nations and the political states that seek to engulf them have been just as bloody and tragic as larger-scale wars. On the Miskitu Coast, the legacy of fear and violence left from almost ten years of fighting is still evident. With weapons available, and young men skilled in using them, the opportunities to make money through the dangerous cocaine trade make violence an ongoing part of life. The war continues, although the combatants are no longer political enemies but rather rivals in the drug trade.

COCAINE AND DEVELOPMENT: AWASTARA AND SANDY BAY

Apart from a few brightly painted new houses, there is little indication in Awastara of generalized prosperity as a result of the local cocaine finds. The money from cocaine finds seems to have disappeared like water into the sand. Things are different, however, in Sandy Bay, fifteen miles to the north. In January 2000 I am able to visit Sandy Bay with a biologist friend. During my fieldwork in 1978–79, I spent a week in Sandy Bay and considered making it my research site but eventually chose Awastara instead. In those days, Sandy Bay was a very ordinary-looking Miskitu village, a cluster of small communities around a pretty lagoon, with one-room wooden houses set on posts, just like those in Awastara. People were no more prosperous than those in Awastara.

The current reality strains the imagination. Each of the Sandy Bay communities has dozens of large new houses, made of cement block (the current preferred building material). They are brightly painted, and quite a few of them are two stories tall (photo 13). They look more like small hotels than ordinary Miskitu houses. Some have fancy grillwork, and all have bright new coats of paint. Two that I noticed have glass windows. These impressive new dwellings come in a variety of styles and designs, and efforts to build something different from the neighbors' houses are apparent. The new coats of paint and other stylish touches seem to indicate pride in ownership. All of the building materials, of course, must be transported up the Coast from Port by boat and are very expensive. Old-style wooden houses are few and far between. People have also constructed their new houses with traditional habits in mind. For instance, the elegant house in which we spent the night had no bathroom, and my companion and I had to run to the nearby bush for toilet purposes, following traditional practice. Bathrooms, which development experts would insist upon for expensive houses, are not part of Miskitu house plans.

In the Sandy Bay communities there are also brand-new school buildings, church buildings, and clinics. I visit the new Moravian church, spacious and elegant, with new wooden benches and bright new paint. It would grace any prosperous middle-class suburb in the United States and is obviously a point of community pride in Sandy Bay. In one commu-

PHOTO 13. *New house in Sandy Bay*

nity, there is even a new electric plant with street lamps. The Nicaraguan president traveled to Sandy Bay by helicopter the week before my visit, to inaugurate the electric plant. Evidently the prosperity of the community attracts a great deal of attention from the central government. The contrast with Awastara is striking. After visiting other parts of Nicaragua, it seems quite possible to me that Sandy Bay is the wealthiest town in the whole country.

The new wealth seems to have been spent in relatively traditional ways: on houses and new boats, churches, and clinics. "Luxury spending" seems to have been minor. Rather, people have invested in things that they know will be valuable far into the future. New infrastructure contributes to better educational opportunities (schools) as well as spiritual welfare (churches). More effective instruments of production (motorboats) have also been purchased. The large wooden catboats that are still the standard seagoing means of transportation in Awastara were in fact first introduced on the Coast here in Sandy Bay. The lagoon was filled with them in 1978, but they have now been almost entirely replaced by new diesel and gasoline powerboats, used for lobstering and turtling. These new boats have undoubtedly resulted in larger catches and higher incomes, an ongoing and legal contribution to the high level of prosperity enjoyed in Sandy Bay.

In terms of infrastructure, perhaps the most important point is that people have built the sorts of houses and churches that they themselves want and will use. No World Bank or USAID project could have inspired the individual creativity and pride in ownership evidenced by the houses and community buildings here. There is no doubt that the general level of wealth and prosperity in Sandy Bay has increased enormously. Thus some of the objectives of "development" are being met. Development is often defined in terms of providing greater economic participation, involving larger numbers of people in production and exchange, and giving the poorest part of the population greater access to goods and services (Rondinelli and Ruddle 1978: v). Cocaine development in Sandy Bay seems to have done most of these things. Unfortunately, however, the costs have been high: violence, theft, drug addiction, death by overdose, and involvement in a dangerous and illegal commercial system.

Cocaine is labeled as something "bad" by local people. It is condemned by the churches and is closely connected with violence. After condemning cocaine, however, Victor later mentions that he and his family haven't yet had the good fortune to find any themselves. Thus there is ambivalence regarding the drug. Even pastors from the churches are rumored to be involved. One story was told to me about a Sandy Bay pastor who found cocaine. When his church superiors condemned him for selling it, he replied, "With your salary, you can send your children to college in the United States. With this money, I can at least send *my* children to college in Managua." Large sums of money can indeed be used in productive ways, as illustrated by the current boom in Sandy Bay.

The prosperity in Sandy Bay, not shared by Awastara, just down the Coast, poses an interesting comparative problem. Cocaine finds have taken place in both communities, yet Sandy Bay is a boom town while Awastara as a whole remains quite poor. One story of which I heard several versions was that the Sandy Bay boom started in 1989, when a very large boatload of cocaine was found by local men on one of the Miskitu Keys. Thousands of kilos were said to be involved. After paying off various authorities at different levels, Sandy Bay households each got large shares, giving a real jump-start to the village economy. Whatever the truth value in this story, it seems evident that a larger volume of cocaine has indeed passed through Sandy Bay than through Awastara, thus explaining in part the differential wealth in the two nearby communities.

I suggest another hypothesis, however, to help explain the contrast. Sandy Bay is reputed to be dominated politically by a shrewd, powerful, and somewhat ruthless headman. He is said to have been involved in the 1989 find and to have controlled distribution of cocaine money ever since. Given the importance of strongmen in Miskitu political organization, the Sandy Bay headman seems to have acted quite effectively, as a man with access to a completely new, although illegal, economic resource.

Meanwhile, political factionalism in Awastara has reached the point where few community-wide decisions can be made. The three sides of town (*lalma, muna,* and *pingka*) now each have their own *alcaldes* or local headmen, and they seem able to collaborate on very few issues. Village trails and bridges go unrepaired, because no one can organize the communal work parties in which I participated twenty years ago. *Chicha* brewers, formerly licensed by the *juez de mesta* to make their product only for specific celebrations, now brew *chicha* continually with permission from their *alcaldes*. Village political meetings at which local issues are raised now dissolve into angry groups of quarreling men and women, with no one able to maintain order. The four competing churches in town seem unwilling to work toward common goals. In such an atmosphere of distrust, it is not surprising that cocaine finds are not shared among community members or that competing authorities are able to keep what cocaine has been found for themselves. One can ask: would the economic situation in Awastara today be more like that of Sandy Bay if there had been an effective strongman in Awastara?

THEFT AND SOCIAL BREAKDOWN

Accusations of theft were very common in Awastara in 1978. *Chicha* makers were accused of accepting stolen plates and kitchen utensils in payment for *chicha*. Seines and turtle nets and other personal belongings seemed to be stolen frequently. I read and wrote legal accusations, written in Miskitu, that were to be taken to the *juez de mesta* with demands for restitution. The *juez de mesta*'s only response seemed to be railing at the accused person and threatening to bring the National Guard to arrest him or her. The crime rate, as far as I could judge, was steady but fairly low.

By 1999–2000, however, things seem to be out of control. Constant petty theft is the order of the day. People tell me to be extremely careful about my belongings and recount endless stories of their own experiences. My friend Mary Kingsman, Casey's sister, lives on the far *muna* side, close to the scrub forest. The young drug addicts hide in the bush, she says, watching for a chance to come to her house and steal her things. They have taken all of her large cooking pots and pans and her radio. Stolen household goods are sold for petty cash to two men in town well known for "fencing" them to Port or elsewhere, where they exchange them for money or liquor to sell in the village. It's hard to do anything about this, because both men are prosperous and powerful. The thieves themselves convert their loot immediately into cocaine, crack, or liquor. One night, Mary tells me, while she was asleep two young men stole all her chickens, stuffing them into big bags and carrying them away. When she missed her chickens the next morning, a neighbor came over to tell her she had heard them clucking inside the bags as the thieves carried them off. "When you're taking drugs and drinking," Mary comments wryly, "you get hungry for snacks—like roasted chicken." Mary says she lives in fear of the drug addicts and worries that if she manages to buy more pots or more chickens they will just be stolen again. With very low incomes, for the poorest village families such robberies can be disastrous.

In 1999–2000 Victor's seine is stolen from underneath his house, Hector's boom and catboat tackle are stolen from the landing, floor tiles are stolen from the new clinic, and lumber is stolen from the latrine building project. *Dama* Sims's new house posts are stolen, and a big pot of beans cooking on the fire is stolen from Kilbon's widow. The stories go on and on. Everyone I talk to has been robbed of something. Awastara has rightfully earned the reputation of being a rogue community, and a spirit of fear is prevalent. "This is not the same place where you lived twenty years ago," several people tell me. Victor plants a small garden with watermelon seed behind his house. He fences it only with string, and I ask him if pigs won't eat the watermelons. "No," he replies, "pigs don't eat watermelons"—a fact I didn't know. One of the vines has a large melon on it, and Victor's ten-year-old grandson writes his name—"MELVIN"—in large letters on the skin of the melon. Watermelon is Melvin's favorite thing to eat. One night all the watermelons are stolen, including Melvin's big one. He is heartbroken. Victor comments that another neighbor found marijuana on the beach and is selling it and that the thieves probably traded the melon for marijuana.

Victor's opinions on the local theft are strong. The thing to do with the thieves, he says, is to whip them publicly, hard (*kasak wipaia*). Lecture them and whip some sense into them. *Smalkaia* at them: "You're going to die if you don't stop taking drugs." Then whip them until they behave.

And if they steal again, whip them some more! This sort of punishment seems to echo right-wing political opinion in the United States, but many traditional Miskitu would probably agree with Victor.

At the schoolhouse in the afternoon, groups of teenaged boys hang out smoking marijuana, playing cards, drinking *chicha,* and talking in loud, drunken voices. A cantina atmosphere pervades the place, offending older people who pass by the school or live nearby. They say the boys have no respect for the schoolhouse or the teachers and students. I agree with them. This just seems to be the handiest place to hang out and drink and smoke. The boys may have gone fishing in the morning, but they are free in the afternoon and choose to pass their time here. It is a very public indication of what things have come to in Awastara.

Thus the drug trade in Awastara has added drug addiction, constant theft, and violence to the town's problems, plus occasional caches of big money, most of which seems to disappear quickly, leaving behind few positive benefits. The churches are divided and squabble among themselves. Officials in Port are corrupt and cannot be counted on. Furthermore, political life in Awastara seems to parallel what's going on at the national level. The Sandinista social programs are gone, and the current government is widely recognized as corrupt and untrustworthy. Ironically enough, the former Miskitu militant organization YATAMA has now become a political party and has formed a tactical alliance with the Liberal party currently in power in the country (González Pérez and Zapata 2002). The drug trade flourishes, with newspaper estimates of three hundred thousand drug addicts within Nicaragua. Crime is rampant. An unbridled version of neoliberal capitalism lets the rich get richer and the poor sink into their misery. The newly rich park their four-wheel drive vehicles at the fancy new shopping malls in Managua, while they shop at Radio Shack and Victoria's Secret. Meanwhile, not far away, in the giant Mercado Oriental, tens of thousands of poor people bargain for food and other basic necessities. The Sandinista party has self-destructed, with former president Daniel Ortega accused of child molesting. A mood of cynicism and anarchy pervades the country. The sad state of affairs in Awastara to some extent reflects the situation in the country as a whole. Can life be different in prosperous Sandy Bay, just up the Coast?

THE TRAGEDY OF THE MISKITU COMMONS

Sociologist Christopher Kindblad, who conducted a restudy of Tasbapauni (2001), provides an interesting perspective on the current situation. Kindblad describes the coexistence of two contradictory economic systems: a traditional one based on reciprocity or gift exchange and an introduced one based on market exchange. Until about 1960, Kindblad argues, market exchange involved young men working for foreign companies away from their home communities. It was expected that they would waste some of their earnings on liquor and prostitutes, but they would also send money home. This money was used to purchase food, clothing, and other basic necessities, which were then exchanged through reciprocity within the community. Meanwhile the commons, the traditional resources of agricultural land, lagoons and rivers, and the ocean itself, remained in the hands of the local villagers. The food resources of the commons were also shared through reciprocity among all the community members.

When foreign companies began buying turtles from Tasbapauni fishermen, however, the situation changed. Young and middle-aged men were now exploiting the commons for their own individual benefit. Money obtained from turtling was used to buy food and consumer goods, which were not exchanged through reciprocity obligations. The turtle population itself began to decline, while wealth differences within the communities grew. The situation began to approximate "the tragedy of the commons" (Hardin 1968), in which the cumulative consequence of individuals' maximizing their own self-interest works to the detriment of the group as a whole. Those Tasbapauni households that were unable to participate in commercial turtle fishing, or were less successful at it, lived poorly in comparison to the emerging class of successful turtlemen.

Kindblad's work suggests that social problems on the Coast, with young men consuming drugs and alcohol and involved in violence and petty theft, are in part a generational phenomenon. He notes (2001: 37–38) that in earlier decades young men were also regarded as lazy and prone to thievery and drunkenness. Once they married and began having families, however, they were expected to become responsible providers, farming, fishing, and sharing what they produced through the reciprocity system. Today's older men were themselves irresponsible youth, to some extent.

The conflict that Kindblad describes between the long-term reciprocity system and the short-term capital accumulation system suggests another hypothesis, however. Perhaps the current delinquents are the outcasts of the new, competitive economic system, those disabled from lobster diving, or those who for one reason or another could not be successful in the small high-wage job market of recent years. Just as U.S. society has created an underclass of alienated, underemployed youths who commit crime and take drugs, so the Miskitu Coast is producing its own village underclass of thieves and drug addicts. If this hypothesis is correct, better social conditions in Awastara may not simply depend on waiting for the young drug addicts to grow up and settle down with families of their own. Traditional subsistence farming and fishing, and participation in the reciprocity-based village economy, seem to have little attraction for these alienated youths. The tragedy of the commons means that the communal resources are also diminishing.

Kinship networks with their reciprocity obligations do endure in Awastara, however, and I feel honored to be a part of Victor and Plora's large family during my last year of fieldwork. The troubling problems of alcohol and drug use and increased theft and violence are undoubtedly responses to the current economic situation; but they can also be interpreted in Miskitu terms, by referring to the rascally nature of all human beings. Part of what it means to be human, in Miskitu thought, is to seek your own advantage. The self-serving rascal par excellence is a character from the Miskitu *kisi,* Tibang the wily rabbit.

CHAPTER TWELVE

Tibang and Concepts of Personhood

The stories people tell always capture or distill, in some way, important aspects of their culture. In Awastara, when people have leisure time, they often tell *kisi,* a sort of composite traditional folktale/fable/ribald joke. What sorts of things can we learn from these *kisi* about how the Miskitu people conceive of themselves? These stories involve a picaresque sort of humor and are often quite bawdy. Crowds of children gather along with adults of both sexes to listen and giggle at them. The traditional time for telling them is after eating and before going to bed. Men are usually the *kisi* tellers, and Levi is a master of the art in Awastara. He adds appropriate sound effects and tells the *kisi* in an animated and hilarious fashion. Much of the humor comes from wordplay and from the telling itself, since the story lines are often simple and involve a few standard themes. One is a king and his unmarried daughters, and another is the search for buried treasure. The most popular stories tell about the exploits of the trickster rabbit, Tibang, as he fools his *tahti* (mother's brother), foolish Limi the jaguar. Characters such as Tibang and Limi are presented as personified animals, but they have human kinship relations and other human characteristics.

TIBANG AND THE GOLD

Tibang asked the king if he wanted a horse. "Yes!" said the king. "I'll bring you one and you can give me a fine present," replied Tibang. Tibang saw Limi coming up the road. "*Tahti,*" he said, "the king says he will give us seventy-five thousand dollars, but I am little and you are strong. Let me just put this bridle on your head and we can get to the king faster." So he put the bridle and saddle on Limi and rode him in front of the king. But Limi roared and threw him off, and Tibang ran away.

Limi was really mad. He found Tibang looking in a stream at the sparkling reflections down below. "Now I will really eat you!" he roared. "OK, OK, *tahti*, but wait a minute. First look at all the gold down below in the stream. I'm trying to drink up all the water so we can get the gold. The problem is that I am just a little man. But you are a big, strong man! Just help me suck it up." Limi looked in the water and saw that it was true. There was gold down below in the stream. "That's easy!" he roared and began to drink up the water. He drank and drank and drank. He drank so much water, it began squirting out his ass. "Wait a minute, *tahti*," said Tibang. "I'll help you." He ran and got a big stick and, whock! crammed it up Limi's ass. Limi roared in anger, but Tibang had already run off.

Along the road Tibang found a cow and, dak! chopped off its tail. He put the tail in a swampy place in the ground, with the chopped-off end down in the ground and the tail waving in the air. When Limi came running after him, panting, Tibang said, "Look, *tahti!* I know you're mad at me, but look at what I've found. It's the king's cow, who has gotten herself buried all the way underground. If we can get her out, there will be a big reward for us." Limi started to grab the tail and pull it out. Tibang said, "No, *tahti!* Don't do that! If you pull it, it will break off and we'll never get her out. You just wait here and hold onto the tail, so she doesn't bury herself any deeper. Hold on tight! Your house is just down the trail. I'll go down there and borrow a shovel from your wife. Then we can get her out." So Limi held onto the tail while Tibang went down to the house and knocked on the door. When Limi's wife answered the door, Tibang said, "Your husband says you are to have sex with me, just like you do with him." "What!" said the wife. "That can't be right. I don't believe you!" "I'll show you," replied Tibang. And he yelled as loud as he could, "*Tahti*, she says she won't give it to me!" From a distance Limi roared back, "Give it to him, woman, give it to him!" And so Tibang screwed Limi's wife, while Limi held onto the cow's tail in the ground.

TIBANG AND THE BIG FART

Limi was wondering how to catch Tibang, as usual. His wife said, "Why don't you pretend to be dead? Stretch out straight on the table, and I'll put a white sheet over you. Then I'll invite all the family over to the house, and they can stand around crying and crying because you've died. When Tibang shows up with the rest of the mourners, you can grab him and eat him." "Good!" said Limi, and so they did it. Limi was stretched out with his eyes half closed, very still under a white sheet, while the others stood around crying and looking sad. Tibang was the very last one to arrive. He came to the door and saw all the people standing around crying, and his uncle lying quite still underneath the sheet. He was suspicious. Tibang is smart, you know! He asked Limi's wife, "Did *tahti* give you the sign before he died?" "What sign?" she replied. "Well," he said, "you know that in our family there's a certain sign that someone's going to die for sure." "What is it?" asked the wife. "Well, whenever we're about to die, the dying person lets out a big fart. Did *tahti* do that before he died?" Limi was listening carefully. He promptly let out a huge, resounding fart. Tibang shouted, "Dead people don't let farts, *tahti!*" and bounded away.

♠TIBANG'S LONG EARS

Tibang went to God and said, "I want to be a big, big man." God thought about it. He really didn't want Tibang any bigger than he already was. "I'd better make this as hard as I can," he thought to himself. He said, "All right, bring me the skin of a *karas* [alligator], the skin of a *tilba* [tapir], and the *nakra laya* [tears] from Limi the jaguar." "I'll do it," replied Tibang.

Tibang thought about it for a long time. Then he went to Alligator and said, "Please help me drag my new boat from the forest down to the river [*duri raskaia*]. If you do, I'll give you a ride in it." "All right," said Alligator. So Tibang tied the rope around him and took it way back in the forest. There he found Tapir and also said to him, "Please help me drag my new boat down to the river. If you do I'll give you a ride in it." Tapir also agreed, and Tibang tied the other end of the rope around Tapir's strong shoulders. Tibang stood in the middle, where each could see him, but where they couldn't see each other. "When I count to three, start pulling!" he yelled. "One, two, three, pull!" So they pulled and pulled and pulled, one against the other. "It's coming! It's coming!" encouraged Tibang. "Pull harder!" The harder they pulled, the more Tibang shouted to keep on pulling. Finally they both just collapsed and died, from sheer exhaustion. Now Tibang had the alligator skin and the tapir skin. Only Limi's tears were left. He went to Limi and said, "*Tahti*, they've sent me to tell you something very sad. Your wife just died." Limi burst into tears on hearing the notice, crazy with grief. Tibang put a little bottle right under Limi's nose and collected all the tears.

When he got to God with the alligator skin, the tapir skin, and the jaguar tears, God thought, "What am I going to do? He's completed the hardest tasks I could think of. I have to comply with my promise. But little as he is, he's a terrible rascal. If I make him big, none of us will be able to deal with him." So God just grabbed Tibang by the ears and pulled and pulled, and his ears stretched and stretched, giving Tibang the big long ears he has today.

●TIBANG, LIMI, AND CONCEPTS OF PERSONHOOD

Structurally, many of the elements in these *kisi* come from elsewhere. The Tibang/Limi cycle of stories is quite likely from West Africa, where similar trickster tales are common. Ironically, there are no wild rabbits on the Miskitu Coast! Tibang must be an African rabbit or at least a Sambo Miskitu rabbit. Anansi or Spider stories, still told by Creole people on the Coast (see Bell 1989: 31), are definitely African in origin. The *kisi* in which suitors ask a king for his marriageable daughter are probably European in origin. At any rate, the theme is a common one in European folklore. In this as in so much of their culture, the Miskitu seem to have taken elements from disparate sources and put them together creatively, appropriating them as they continue to construct their ongoing Miskitu culture.

In recent years, CIDCA (1985a), Christian Schnarf (n.d.), and Sol Montoya and Polinario Sebastián (1990) have all published *kisi* collections. The CIDCA and Montoya and Sebastián collections are bilingual in Miskitu and Spanish and include illustrations. These books have probably had very limited circulation, but they represent a serious interest in preserving and disseminating Miskitu folklore on the part of local people and institutions. Nicaraguan scholar Adán Silva Mercado also lectures and writes about Miskitu literature, in an effort to make Spanish-speaking Nicaraguans aware that the Miskitu do have a literature of their own (Silva Mercado and Korten 1997).

In the *kisi,* Tibang's mother's brother Limi is a senior relative who should be treated with respect. Tibang's improper behavior toward him provokes laughter, probably indicating some degree of repressed hostility toward such a relative. Tibang, of course, is careful not to be openly disrespectful. His "hidden transcript" must be masked by symbolic acts of deference and the artful use of flattery (Scott 1990). In kinship relations, everyone has been in a subordinate position to elders and can identify with a clever, amoral junior kinsman who gets the best of those in control. When I ask Victor about the disrespect Tibang shows to his mother's brother, he dismisses it, saying, "They're just animals, they don't have much sense." But in fact, it is clear that Tibang has too much sense, working the kinship system very effectively to get what he wants. It is also true, of course, that Limi, so powerful and strong, is a fool, whose clever nephew can't resist taking advantage of him.

One of the key elements in the humor involves the concept of *kunin*, which means lie or falsehood. Tibang is *kuninkira* (full of lies) as he delights in making a fool of his big, strong relative, Limi. People chuckle with enjoyment, identifying with Tibang. If they were in Limi's place, however, they probably wouldn't be laughing.

*Because the *kisi* are bawdy and make fun of social rules, some missionaries have opposed them and branded them as sacrilegious. But others have taken special interest in them and tried to reinterpret them for their own purposes. The Catholic missionaries, for example, published a collection of *kisi* in mimeographed form. At the bottom of each *kisi* an explanation is given, showing how it can be reinterpreted in terms of a Christian moral. This innovation is ironic, in light of the fact that the traditional Miskitu version has no stated moral and in fact dribbles to an end once the main action is over. Instead of being morality-inspiring stories, they are really antimorality stories. They delight their audiences by showing how someone clever—a fast talker—flouts social convention but still manages to come out on top. U.S. culture, of course, has its own clever antiheroes: for example, the cartoon character Roadrunner and the fast-talking con artists often played by Eddie Murphy.

Political leaders like former Awastara headman Cornelio also act very much like Tibang, manipulating people for their own advantage, as they help resolve disputes and organize village affairs. Given strong kinship obligations, it is no surprise that leaders look out for their own relatives. Being clever and manipulative like Tibang is a trait necessary to be successful. Cornelio's enemies accuse him of theft, commenting sarcastically that his trembling right hand at his advanced age comes from using it to steal so much. Cornelio has a very modest house, just like his neighbors, however; if he has been stealing, he doesn't have much to show for it. And most tellingly, in spite of whatever suspicions they have, people still look to Cornelio for leadership.

Jaime's plan to bring development to Awastara is eventually regarded by many as simply a way for Jaime and his group to enrich themselves.

The fanfare with which his organization originated comes to be seen as a way of gaining the community's trust, in order to "tax" fishing boats offshore and keep the money. The anger that builds parallels Limi's rage at discovering that, once more, he has been tricked by Tibang.

In daily life people constantly accuse each other of being deceitful, like Tibang. One day a story circulates that Victor's son Adolpo has been thrown in jail in Bluefields for being drunk and disorderly. He won't be let out of jail until he pays for a taxi window he has smashed, say several of the young turtlemen who were also in Bluefields trying to sell their turtles. Victor throws a fit, threatening to leave Adolpo there for a few months, to teach him a lesson. Adolpo himself eventually shows up, saying it was a lie (*kunin*). Many of the other turtlemen dislike Adolpo, and perhaps they concocted the story to cause trouble in the family. Or perhaps it was true.

One day Victor and I hire a poor man named Méndez to chop down weeds around our houses. Victor tells him that the following day he can kill a pig that is rooting up the small coconut trees and take it home to eat. But by the next day Victor has reconsidered, since the pig belongs to his brother Pancho and killing it would result in a big dispute. Méndez snorts and tells me: "That Victor, he is just *kuninkira*. You can't believe anything he says. And I wouldn't have gotten in trouble with Pancho anyway, since I would have carried the dead pig way around by the boat landing, and Pancho would never have known what happened to it." In this case, Victor's reconsideration (and his change of plans) is interpreted as a *kunin*, at the same time that Méndez is planning to trick Pancho with a *kunin* of his own.

Some of the *kunin nani* played on other people can be extremely cruel and hurtful. Both radio stations in Puerto Cabezas devote several hours a day to announcements to which people in all the surrounding Miskitu communities listen attentively, to find out who is in the hospital, who has died, and what relatives are arriving from Managua or Bluefields. One morning one of the stations broadcasts an announcement that an elderly man from Awastara named Akiun has died. Akiun was in the Port hospital and later at a relative's house in the city, after a bad accident in which a horse dragged him across the ground. When the family hears the announcement, they go into mourning, preparing coffee and food for mourners who come by the house in Awastara, and begin to prepare for the funeral. The Moravian church bell tolls sorrowfully, as it does for every death in the community. School is canceled in the village that day. An *alcalde*'s representative comes around collecting ten cordobas from each household to help the bereaved family. But within a day or two the true story emerges. Someone has taken a slip of paper to the radio station in Port and paid fifteen cordobas to have the death announcement broadcast. It was a *kunin,* and in reality Akiun is still alive. I never learn who played the cruel joke; and, in fact, within a couple of months Akiun really does die. But the first death announcement was just pure *kunin.* It brought unnecessary grief to Akiun's family, apparently for the perverse pleasure of seeing them suffer or perhaps to get back at them for some wrong committed in the past. They were treated as the butt of a very cruel joke by some local Tibang. Victor explains the situation in these terms: "Those Miskitu people are all *kuninkira,* just like Tibang." From the outside, we can at least note a kind of situational ethics, in which people play *kunin* on each other, like Tibang; but, like Limi, they bitterly resent being fooled themselves.

Opposed to Tibang and his selfish manipulation of others is the Miskitu kinship ideal of living together in respect. Helms (1971: 103) points out the use of proper kinship terms of address and not indulging in gossip about others as examples of respectful behavior in Asang. Jamieson (2000b) interprets mother-in-law avoidance in terms of extreme respect. Nietschmann (1973: 61, 183) describes being thoughtful and generous toward others as the key to being a good person, pointing out that food sharing exemplifies generosity. Respect and generosity, especially toward relatives, are then the basis of Miskitu ethics. How ironic that in the *kisi* Tibang ridicules and takes advantage of his own mother's brother! Tibang is outwardly respectful, but he uses the formulas of respect to mask his true underlying nature.

The Miskitu *kisi* seem to emphasize strong, self-centered urges, a sort of powerful libido, as the underlying psychic energy motivating human beings. Resentment against the cultural requirements of respect and generosity builds through a constant chafing process and must eventually be expressed. It cannot be expressed openly, but rather takes the form of deceit and manipulation. I suggest that all Miskitu people, from young children to elderly grandparents, identify with the clever, out-for-himself rascal Tibang. This is what Victor means when he comments, "All Miskitu people are *kuninkira,* just like Tibang." Personhood here means outwardly complying with the requirements of respect and generosity, while at the same time using your wits to stay alive and get what you want.

Nevertheless, the *kuninkira* nature of the Miskitu social world can be frustrating, because it makes it difficult to find out what the truth really is. Is everyone a sort of Tibang, secretly? Or are we all both Tibang and

Limi at the same time? In this world of illusions, how are we to tell who is telling the truth and who is lying? And how on earth did the Moravians manage to implant their concepts of absolute certainty about God, sin, and salvation? At the least, Tibang shows us that authoritarian senior individuals can be manipulated and that caution in trusting others is advisable. He also makes the world a very funny place, in which we must laugh at ourselves and not take things too seriously.

CHAPTER THIRTEEN

Leaving Awastara

As I prepare to leave in 2000, I reflect on the current state of political dis-
organization in the community and on the seemingly bleak prospects for
the future. At the same time, I think how much I have enjoyed daily life
here, learning about these people and coming to have such close friends
among them. I sit in Plora's kitchen with Eliza and Maura and eat my
beans and rice with a lime squeezed on top, watching the kids playing. A
troop of little naked, uncircumcised boys runs through the house, shrieking and laughing. Melvin carries little Nachalie, who is also laughing and
screaming with delight, on his shoulders. She cries for more when he puts
her down. They run from the kitchen up the stairs into the house, out
into the yard, and back around to the kitchen. Outside Casey is working on the new catboat he is building in the shade of a huge mango tree.
The sound of his hammer blows punctuates the children's play. From the
top of the huge mango tree nearby, I can hear the low, throaty call of the
oropendula, a large oriole that makes long, swinging basket–type nests.
Occasionally a ripe mango falls with a thud from the tree. I feel very
much at home here. My Miskitu family, minus Victor, who doesn't like
pictures, poses for a group photo to take with me (photo 14) and to send
back a copy for them.

Victor tells me one day that he hopes I will continue coming to Awastara after he is dead, to see his sons and daughters and grandchildren. He
doesn't want the tie to be broken. Even Victor's nephew, who makes and
sells crack to the young men in town, comes by my house to visit and to
invite me to the World Bank meeting in Port. I realize that in spite of all
the social problems in Awastara, everyone here has treated me with courtesy and kindness, from the very beginning. For my part, I've also tried to

PHOTO 14. *My Miskitu family*

treat people in a fair, open way, and they have always responded in kind. It has made living here a very satisfying experience overall.

I have been going to Awastara for so long that it feels like one of my several homes. It is quite moving to go to the graveyard and visit the graves of old friends. For example, Bowman Hoppington is buried there, the man who first invited me to work in his cassava fields and waked me up at 3:00 A.M. to go with him. I remember wrestling the large stingray to the beach with Bowman. Gloria Renales, Victor's younger sister, is also buried there, a headstrong, sharp-tongued woman who was proud of her independence, after having five children and leaving her spouse. We spent many evenings together talking, and from Gloria I got a very liberated Miskitu woman's view of life. All of her sons have turned out badly, as she predicted they would, but they still treat me with great respect because of my friendship with their mother. My Awastara friends have insisted on showing me their way of life and on telling me their opinions in no uncertain terms, Miskitu style. They have taken it upon themselves to make sure I understand them as well as I can, during the times when I have shared their lives and struggled to learn their language.

Stories about their anthropologist undoubtedly circulate freely. Without any prompting, Wiskat draws a picture of me at work (figure 9). Using the tools of my own trade, pencil and paper, he captures the bearded, long-haired anthropologist walking around town, carrying a backpack and wearing blue jeans. I am taking a photograph of two Miskitu girls wearing identical outfits. They are standing in front of my first house in Awastara, which had a rain barrel to collect drinking water and an elevated walkway between the house and kitchen. The Adventist church at the top overlooks the whole scene, with its fruit trees planted out front. Wiskat's drawing represents a resident artist's keen observations and commentary. He puts his drawing of the anthropologist right in the middle of a large stack of drawings of life in Awastara: turtle fishing, going to the plantations, seining fish at the beach, and many other activities. Did he intend it tongue-in-cheek, or did he really think of my work as an ordinary part of daily life?

FIGURE 9. *The anthropologist at work, by Wiskat Morales*

Victor comes with me as I leave Awastara for Port, on my way back to the United States. We take the outside passage down the Coast, instead of going through the lagoon to Krukira. We leave about 5:00 P.M., sharing a ride in Jesse Kingsman's catboat with some twenty other passengers. It is a beautiful trip, with the northeast trade winds blowing steadily, the stars bright overhead, and the boat slipping along through the warm tropical sea. Farther up in the boat someone plays a guitar while people sing church hymns.

Near us a young Miskitu man I don't know begins telling *kisi*. He is a very good storyteller and soon has everyone laughing as he tells one *kisi* after another. Many involve the traditional rivals, Tibang and Limi. I listen carefully, catching some but not all of the stories. Then he starts telling one about Tibang masquerading as the Water King, at a gathering of all the other kings. My hair stands on end. Good Lord! I collected that *kisi* in 1979 from an old man now dead and published it in an article in the *American Ethnologist* in 1984. When he gets to the ending, he tells it differently. I really want to tap him on the shoulder and say, "Listen, *tuba* [sister's son], the way that *kisi* really ends is . . ." But my Miskitu isn't quite up to it, especially since I can't remember the word for "furry" in Miskitu, upon which *my* ending depends. In my version the other kings recognize Tibang because he has left his furry feet sticking out from underneath his Water King outfit. It is just as well. In these days of political correctness, how far are we allowed to intrude into the culture of the Others, anyway? But what if the Others miss us and wish we were back with them, trying to learn their language and tell their *kisi* just the way they do?

MISKITU GLOSSARY

a sla takaia   to work together.

chicha   from Spanish, home-brewed corn beer. Traditionally called *tu-albi*.

dabaia   to suck, the verb used for eating any kind of fruit.

dakakaia   to feed someone else, a verb that implies nurturance and caring.

dama   "grandfather" or any elderly man; a term of respect and affection.

dapna   son-in-law or father-in-law, used reciprocally.

diwas   the land breeze that begins to blow in the early hours of the morning.

duri raskaia   to drag a heavy boat down to the water from the place it has been constructed, which usually requires the combined strength of many people pulling.

iningka   the long, stylized but also heartfelt lament sung by close women relatives after the death of a kinsperson.

isingni   the spirit of a dead person, the phantasmagoric soul, which causes illness by returning to take away a loved one.

itimur   one of two kinds of termites that eat houses and other items made of wood, causing much destruction; the other is the *usra*.

kaisa   let's go! (a common exclamation).

kaisni   large crabs that appear on the savannah after the first rains at the end of the dry season.

kiamp   literally, "rootstock"; in social terms, a *kiamp* is a group of people descended from an important male ancestor.

kia walaia   holding one's nose to the cheek of a loved one and "smelling the skin"; the Miskitu form of kissing.

kirbaia   to stroll about having a good time, as opposed to working.

kisi   traditional Miskitu folktales, usually full of irony and salacious humor.

kral   a fenced enclosure in the river to keep turtles temporarily, until they can be taken to market in Port; from English "crawl."

kubus   a fire-hardened clay cookstove built on top of a wooden table, used in all Miskitu kitchens.

kunin   lie or falsehood or anything that turns out not to be true; Tibang in the *kisi* is constantly *kuninkira* or full of *kunin*.

kupia karna   "a hard heart," a tough, aggressive stance toward other people.

kupia kumi   "a single heart," peace, harmony, and consensus among people.

la daukaia   to lay down the law, establish rules by which people must abide.

lilka   the animating principle or soul of a human being, normally invisible; illness is often caused by supernatural beings taking away a person's *lilka*.

liwa mairin   the female spirit creature that lives in water (in the ocean, the rivers, and even in wells and creeks), who often seduces men and drowns them; a male *liwa* or *liwa waitna* also exists.

maia   mate or domestic partner or companion of either a man or a woman.

maia baikaia   the traditional procedure of asking for a woman as a mate for one's son.

mairin   woman or female.

mani taim   the dry season, from January to May.

mas mas   a small fish caught in the freshwater sloughs as they dry up from February to April.

mishla   traditional fermented beer drunk in large quantities at the *sikru*, or feast of the dead.

palaia   to speak in an angry, enraged way at a subordinate, to get him or her to do something.

pana pana laka   reciprocity: "I do something for you, you do something for me," which applies to food sharing, shared labor in the fields, and other aspects of life. It is a basic social rule in traditional Miskitu society, which has begun breaking down in modern times. Its loss is much lamented by Miskitu people.

papta   a kind of palm thatch used for roofing in earlier times.

piaia   to eat.

pri laka   freedom, the right to do whatever one wants to do.

prisku   sweetened fruit drink; from Spanish *fresco*.

rapia   father's brother.

sasmalkra   lay preacher: literally, person who preaches to or lectures others; sometimes abbreviated to *sasmal* as a more familiar term of address.

saura   bad.

sikru   traditional ceremony performed a year after someone's death to allow communication with the dead person's *isingni;* it involved consumption of large quantities of native beer and is no longer performed in Awastara.

smalkaia   to teach or preach at someone, especially a younger person, about proper behavior.

snikwaia   jealousy of an older sibling toward a new baby brother or sister who is nursing or not yet born.

sukia   shaman, curer with special spiritual powers.

swinta   "the owner of the deer" (*sula dawanka*), a short man with a broad hat and a whip, who looks after the deer and other animals of the bush and often molests women.

swira   shame, the potential for giving offense in relationships that should be governed by respect, such as that between a son-in-law and his mother-in-law (Jamieson 2000b).

tahti   mother's brother, a term of respect often used for older men in general; the older man may respond with the reciprocal term *tuba* (sister's son). In the *kisi* Tibang the trickster rabbit addresses Limi the jaguar as *tahti*.

tama   starchy vegetables, called "breadkind" in Creole English, that accompany many meals; they include cassava and plantains.

tuba   sister's son, the reciprocal term with *tahti*.

ujum   a yellow fruit from a kind of palm tree, pounded up in a mortar and eaten with sugar.

unuh   a large wooden mortar used primarily for hulling home-grown rice.

upan   meat or fish, the protein component of a meal that must accompany the *tama*.

usra   a kind of termite that makes large black nests in trees (these nests are burned and then mixed with paint to form a sticky caulk for boats).

wahmuk   a variety of native cotton, formerly woven into rope.

wahwin   a dangerous creature that roams at night and has a disagreeable smell that makes people sick. A large rock outcropping just south of Awastara is said to be a petrified *wahwin*.

waitna   man or male.

wasakia munaia   a serious and often fatal illness in a newborn infant, believed to be caused by the infant's proximity to a pregnant woman.

wita   the headman, traditionally recognized as the political authority in every village.

yabakaia   a magical incantation done in a whispered voice over an object (such as an arrow) or a sick person, which is believed to be very effective; an individual's particular form of doing *yabakaia* is secret personal property.

yaslam   very hard, cold winds out of the north that hit the Coast several times from November to January; they are especially dangerous to boats at sea.

yauhra   cassava, an important starchy vegetable, called *yuca* in Spanish.

yumuh   abdominal pains, which in Miskitu theory are related to possession by the spirit of a particular animal in the natural world. Curers who specialize in *yumuh* massage the abdomen with oil and use particular forms of *yabakaia*.

REFERENCES CITED

Adams, Richard N.
1981 The Dynamics of Societal Diversity: Notes from Nicaragua for a Sociology of Survival. *American Ethnologist* 8 (1): 1–20.

Aguirre Beltrán, Gonzalo
1967 *Regiones de refugio.* Mexico City: Instituto Indigenista Interamericano.

Archivo General de Indias
1699 Guatemala 233, folios 55–57. Seville, Spain. [I am very grateful to William V. Davidson for bringing this citation to my attention.]

Bailey, F. G.
1969 *Stratagems and Spoils: A Social Anthropology of Politics.* New York: Schocken Books.

Barrett, Bruce
1992 The Syringe and the Rooster Dance: Medical Anthropology on Nicaragua's Atlantic Coast. Ph.D. dissertation, University of Wisconsin, Madison.
1994 Salud y cultura en el Caribe Nicaragüense. *Wani: Revista del Caribe Nicaragüense* 15: 20–37.

Bastien, Joseph W.
1994 Comunicación intercultural sobre vacunación tetánica en Bolivia. *Arinsana* (Caracas) 15: 3–23.

Behar, Ruth
1993 *Translated Woman: Crossing the Border with Esperanza's Story.* Boston: Beacon Press.

Bell, C. Napier
1862 Remarks on the Mosquito Territory, Its Climate, People, Productions, etc., etc., with a Map. *Journal of the Royal Geographical Society* 32: 242–68.

1989   *Tangweera: Life and Adventures among Gentle Savages.* Austin: University of Texas Press. [First published in 1899.]

Bonfil Batalla, Guillermo

1996   *México Profundo: Reclaiming a Civilization.* Austin: University of Texas Press. [Originally published in Spanish in 1987.]

Brooks, David C.

1989   Marines, Miskitos, and the Hunt for Sandino: The Río Coco Patrol in 1928. *Journal of Latin American Studies* 21, part 2: 311–42.

1997   Revolution from Without: Culture and Politics along Nicaragua's Atlantic Coast in the Time of the Sandino Revolt, 1926–1934. Ph.D. dissertation, University of Connecticut at Storrs.

Brown, Karen McCarthy

1991   *Mama Lola: A Vodou Priestess in Brooklyn.* Berkeley, Los Angeles, and London: University of California Press.

Brown, Michael F.

1998   Dark Side of the Shaman. In *Understanding and Applying Medical Anthropology,* ed. by Peter J. Brown, pp. 170–73. Mountain View, Calif.: Mayfield Publishing Co.

Buckley, Thomas, and Alma Gottlieb, editors

1988   *Blood Magic: The Anthropology of Menstruation.* Berkeley, Los Angeles, and London: University of California Press.

Carr, Archie

1956   *The Windward Road: Adventures of a Naturalist on Remote Caribbean Shores.* New York: Alfred A. Knopf.

1967   *So Excellent a Fishe: A Natural History of Sea Turtles.* Garden City, N.Y.: Natural History Press.

Carrasco, Juan, Pablo Cuadra, Philip A. Dennis, and Morlan Muller

2000   Las maestras de Luxemburgo: ¿Una nueva cara de Grisi Siknis? Un abordaje multicultural y multidisciplinario. Occasional paper. Instituto de Medicina Tradicional y Desarrollo Comunitario, Universidad de las Regiones Autónomas de la Costa Caribe Nicaragüense (URACCAN).

CIDCA (Centro de Investigaciones y Documentación de la Costa Atlántica)

1985a   *Cuentos miskitos: Miskitu Kisi Nani.* Managua: Centro de Investigaciones y Documentación de la Costa Atlántica (CIDCA).

1985b   *Miskitu Bila Aisanka, Gramática Miskita.* Managua: Centro de Investigaciones y Documentación de la Costa Atlántica (CIDCA).

n.d.   *Trabil Nani: Historical Background and Current Situation on the Atlantic Coast of Nicaragua.* Managua: Centro de Investigaciones y Documentación de la Costa Atlántica (CIDCA).

Clifford, James

1986   Introduction: Partial Truths. In *Writing Culture: The Poetics and Politics of Ethnography,* ed. by James Clifford and George E. Marcus, pp. 1–26. Berkeley, Los Angeles, and London: University of California Press.

Comisión de Salud de la RAAN
1996   *El modelo de salud de la Región Autónoma del Atlántico Norte.* Managua: Universidad de las Regiones Autónomas de la Costa Caribe Nicaragüense (URACCAN).

Conzemius, Eduard
1932   *Ethnographical Survey of the Miskito and Sumu Indians of Honduras and Nicaragua.* Smithsonian Institution, Bureau of American Ethnology, Bulletin 106. Washington, D.C.: United States Government Printing Office.

Cox, Avelino
1998   *Cosmovisión de los pueblos de Tulu Walpa.* Managua: Universidad de las Regiones Autónomas de la Costa Caribe de Nicaragua (URACCAN).

Dampier, William
1968   *A New Voyage around the World.* New York: Dover Publications. [First published in 1697.]

Dawan Bila: La Raya Waungkataya—El Nuevo Testamento en Miskito
1974   N.p.: Sociedades Bíblicas Unidas.

Dawan Bila Aiska
1999   N.p.: Sociedades Bíblicas Unidas.

Dennis, Philip A.
1981a   The Costeños and the Revolution in Nicaragua. *Journal of Interamerican Studies and World Affairs* 23 (3): 271–96.
1981b   Grisi Siknis among the Miskito. *Medical Anthropology* 5 (4): 445–505.
1982   Coronation on the Miskito Coast. *Geographical Magazine* 54 (7) (July): 392–95.
1985   Grisi Siknis in Miskito Culture. In *The Culture-Bound Syndromes,* ed. by Ronald C. Simons and Charles C. Hughes, pp. 289–306. Dordrecht, Holland: D. Reidel Publishing Company.
1988   Herbal Medicine among the Miskito of Eastern Nicaragua. *Economic Botany* 42 (1): 16–28.
1993   The Miskito-Sandinista Conflict in Nicaragua in the 1980s. *Latin American Research Review* 28 (3): 214–34.
1999   Grisi Siknis entre los Miskitos; Grisi Siknis Miskito Nani Tilara. *Wani: Revista del Caribe Nicaragüense* 24: 5–21.
2000   Autonomy on the Miskitu Coast of Nicaragua. *Reviews in Anthropology* 29: 199–210.
2003   Cocaine in Miskitu Villages. *Ethnology* 42 (2): 161–72.

Dennis, Philip A., and Michael D. Olien
1984   Kingship among the Miskito. *American Ethnologist* 11 (4): 718–37.

Diskin, Martin, Thomas Bossert, Salomón Nahmad S., and Stéfano Varese
1986   *Peace and Autonomy on the Atlantic Coast of Nicaragua: A Report of the LASA Task Force on Human Rights and Academic Freedom.* Pittsburgh: Latin American Studies Association.

Edwards, Bryan
1819   Some Account of the British Settlements of the Musquito Shore. In *The History, Civil and Commercial of the British West Indies,* vol. 5: 202–14. 5th ed. London: T. Miller.

Evans-Pritchard, E. E.
1937   *Witchcraft, Oracles and Magic among the Azande.* Oxford: Clarendon Press.

Fagoth, Ana Rosa
1996   El ritual del isingni sakaia, Sihkru atura, El viaje del isingni. *Tininiska* 11 (June): 10–17.
1999   Poesías miskitas: Miskitu Aisanka Prana. *Tininiska* 22–23 (February–March): 1–96.

Fagoth, Ana Rosa, Fulvio Gioanetto, and Adán Silva
1998   *Armonizando con nuestro entorno.* Managua: Imprimatur Artes Gráficas.

Field, Les W.
1999   *The Grimace of Macho Ratón: Artisans, Identity, and Nation in Late-Twentieth-Century Western Nicaragua.* Durham and London: Duke University Press.

Floyd, Troy S.
1967   *The Anglo-Spanish Struggle for Mosquitia.* Albuquerque: University of New Mexico Press.

Gabbert, Wolfgang
1990   The "Kingdom of Mosquitia"—An Ethnohistorical Study of Miskito Political Organization, 1670–1821. Published in German as Das "Königreich Mosquitia"—Eine Ethnohistorische Untersuchung zur Politischen Organisation der Miskito, 1670–1821. *Wiener Ethnohistorische Blätter* 35 (1990): 45–70.
2002   Miskito Political Organization, Seventeenth to Nineteenth Centuries. Paper presented at the meetings of the American Anthropological Association, New Orleans, La., November 20–24.

García, Claudia
1996   *The Making of the Miskitu People of Nicaragua: The Social Construction of Ethnic Identity.* Uppsala, Sweden: Uppsala University.

Geertz, Clifford
1973   Thick Description: Toward an Interpretive Theory of Culture. In *The Interpretation of Cultures,* pp. 3–30. New York: Basic Books.

Goldman, Irving

1979   *The Cubeo Indians of the Northwest Amazon.* Urbana: University of Illinois Press. [First published in 1963.]

González Pérez, Miguel

1997   *Gobiernos pluriétnicos: La constitución de regiones autónomas en Nicaragua.* Mexico City: Universidad de las Regiones Autónomas de la Costa Caribe de Nicaragua (URACCAN) y Plaza y Valdés.

González Pérez, Miguel, and Yuri Zapata

2002   Miskitu Politics during the Nineties: Fragmentation or Accommodation? Paper presented at the meetings of the American Anthropological Association, New Orleans, La., November 20–24.

Gordon, Edmund T.

1998   *Disparate Diasporas: Identity and Politics in an African-Nicaraguan Community.* Austin: University of Texas Press.

Gray, Sam

n.d.   Kaisa Miskito Aisaia: An Introduction to Miskito Grammar. Mimeograph, Board of World Mission, Moravian Church, Bethlehem, Pa.

Hale, Charles R.

1987   Inter-Ethnic Relations and Class Structure in Nicaragua's Atlantic Coast: An Historical Overview. In *Ethnic Groups and the Nation State: The Case of the Atlantic Coast in Nicaragua,* pp. 33–57. Stockholm, Sweden: Department of Social Anthropology, University of Stockholm.

1994   *Resistance and Contradiction: Miskitu Indians and the Nicaraguan State, 1894–1987.* Stanford, Calif.: Stanford University Press.

Hale, Ken

1987   La naturaleza de la lengua miskita y las principales dificultades para aprenderla. *Wani: Revista del Caribe Nicaragüense* 6: 23–30.

Ham, Clifford D.

1916   Americanizing Nicaragua: How Yankee Marines, Financial Oversight and Baseball Are Stabilizing Central America. *American Review of Reviews* 53 (February): 185–90.

Hardin, Garrett

1968   The Tragedy of the Commons. *Science* 162: 1243–48.

Harris, Marvin

1979   *Cultural Materialism: The Struggle for a Science of Culture.* New York: Random House.

Hawley, Susan

1996   Does God Speak Miskitu? The Bible and Ethnic Identity among the Miskitu of Nicaragua. In *Ethnicity and the Bible,* ed. by Mark G. Brett, pp. 315–42. Leiden, New York, and Cologne: E. J. Brill.

1997   Protestantism and Indigenous Mobilisation: The Moravian Church among the Miskitu Indians of Nicaragua. *Journal of Latin American Studies* 29: 111–29.

Heath, George R.

1927 *Grammar of the Miskito Language.* Herrnhut, Saxony: F. Lindenbein. In the Moravian College Library.

1947 Miskito Lexicon. Unpublished manuscript in the Moravian Archives, Bethlehem, Pa.

1950 Miskito Glossary, with Ethnographic Commentary. *International Journal of American Linguistics* 16: 20–34.

Heath, George R., and W. G. Marx

1953 *Diccionario Miskito-Español, Español-Miskito.* Tegucigalpa, Honduras: Imprenta Calderón.

Helms, Mary W.

1968 Matrilocality and the Maintenance of Ethnic Identity: The Miskito of Eastern Nicaragua and Honduras. In *Verhandlungen des XXXVIII. Internationalen Amerikanistenkongresses,* pp. 459–64. Stuttgart and Munich, Germany: n.p.

1969 The Cultural Ecology of a Colonial Tribe. *Ethnology* 8: 76–84.

1971 *Asang: Adaptations to Culture Contact in a Miskito Community.* Gainesville: University of Florida Press.

1977 Negro or Indian? The Changing Identity of a Frontier Population. In *Old Roots in New Lands,* ed. by Ann M. Pescatello, pp. 157–72. Westport, Conn., and London: Greenwood Press.

1979 *Ancient Panama: Chiefs in Search of Power.* Austin and London: University of Texas Press.

1983 Miskito Slaving and Culture Contact: Ethnicity and Opportunity in an Expanding Population. *Journal of Anthropological Research* 39: 179–97.

1986 Of Kings and Contexts: Ethnohistorical Interpretations of Miskito Political Structure and Function. *American Ethnologist* 13 (3): 506–23.

Herlihy, Laura

2002 Ethnic and Gender Identities among the Honduran Miskitu Peoples. Paper presented at the meetings of the American Anthropological Association, New Orleans, La., November 20–24.

Hodgson, Robert

1822 *Some Account of the Mosquito Territory.* Edinburgh, Scotland: William Blackwood.

Hoskins, Janet, guest editor

2002 Blood Mysteries: Beyond Menstruation as Pollution. Special issue of *Ethnology* 41 (4).

Jamieson, Mark

1998   Linguistic Innovation and Relationship Terminology in the Pearl Lagoon Basin of Nicaragua. *Journal of the Royal Anthropological Institute* (n.s.) 4: 713–30.

1999   El inglés y la variedad de miskito en la cuenca de Laguna de Perlas. *Wani: Revista del Caribe Nicaragüense* 24: 22–32.

2000a   Compassion, Anger, and Broken Hearts: Ontology and the Role of Language in the Miskitu Lament. In *The Anthropology of Love and Anger: The Aesthetics of Conviviality in Native Amazonia*, ed. by Joanna Overing and Alan Passes, pp. 82–96. London and New York: Routledge.

2000b   It's Shame That Makes Men and Women Enemies: The Politics of Intimacy among the Miskitu of Kakabila. *Journal of the Royal Anthropological Institute* (n.s.) 6: 311–24.

2001   Masks and Madness: Ritual Expressions of the Transition to Adulthood among Miskitu Adolescents. *Social Anthropology/Anthropologie Sociale* 9: 257–72.

2002   Contracts with Satans and Relations of Production among the Miskitu. Paper presented at the meetings of the American Anthropological Association, New Orleans, La., November 20–24.

Jenkins Molieri, Jorge
1986   *El desafío indígena en Nicaragua: El caso de los miskitos.* Managua: Editorial Vanguardia.

Kindblad, Christopher
2001   *Gift and Exchange in the Reciprocal Regime of the Miskito on the Atlantic Coast of Nicaragua, Twentieth Century.* Dissertations in Sociology, 44. Lund, Sweden: Lund University.

King, F. Wayne
1995   Historical Review of the Decline of the Green Turtle and the Hawksbill. In *Biology and Conservation of Sea Turtles*, ed. by Karen A. Bjorndal, pp. 183–88. Rev. ed. Washington, D.C., and London: Smithsonian Institution Press.

Kluckhohn, Clyde
1967   *Navaho Witchcraft.* Boston: Beacon Press. [First published in 1944.]

Lagueux, Cynthia Jean
1998   Marine Turtle Fishery of Caribbean Nicaragua: Human Use Patterns and Harvest Trends. Ph.D. dissertation, University of Florida.

Lee, Richard B.
1968   What Hunters Do for a Living, or, How to Make Out on Scarce Resources. In *Man the Hunter*, ed. Richard B. Lee and Irven DeVore, pp. 30–48. Chicago: Aldine Publishing Co.

Lemley, Lynn
1981   A Grammar of Miskito. Unpublished paper written under an Under-

graduate Research Award, Office of the Vice President for Research and Graduate Studies, Texas Tech University.

LiPuma, Edward

1998   Modernity and Forms of Personhood in Melanesia. In *Bodies and Persons: Comparative Perspectives from Africa and Melanesia,* ed. by Michael Lambek and Andrew Strathern, pp. 53–79. Cambridge: Cambridge University Press.

MacAndrew, Craig, and Robert B. Edgerton

1969   *Drunken Comportment: A Social Explanation.* Chicago: Aldine Publishing Co.

Marcus, George E., and Michael M. J. Fischer

1986   *Anthropology as Cultural Critique: An Experimental Moment in the Human Sciences.* Chicago and London: University of Chicago Press.

Marriott, McKim

1976   Hindu Transaction: Diversity without Dualism. In *Transaction and Meaning: Directions in the Anthropology of Exchange and Symbolic Behavior,* ed. by Bruce Kapferer, pp. 109–42. Philadelphia: Institute for the Study of Human Issues.

Matamoros B., Jorge

1996   *Diccionario Miskitu-Español, Español-Miskitu.* Managua: Centro de Investigaciones y Documentación de la Costa Atlántica (CIDCA).

McElroy, Ann, and Patricia K. Townsend

1996   *Medical Anthropology in Ecological Perspective.* 3rd ed. Boulder, Colo.: Westview Press.

Merck Manual of Diagnosis and Therapy

1999   Whitehouse Station, N.J.: Merck Research Laboratories.

Mintz, Sidney W.

1985   *Sweetness and Power: The Place of Sugar in Modern History.* New York: Penguin Books.

1992   A Taste of History. In *Talking about People: Readings in Contemporary Cultural Anthropology,* ed. William A. Haviland and Robert J. Gordon, pp. 79–82. Mountain View, Calif.: Mayfield Publishing.

Montoya, Sol, and Polinario Sebastián

1990   *Yu Kum Kan . . . Había una vez . . .* Managua: Centro de Investigaciones y Documentación de la Costa Atlántica (CIDCA).

Moravian Church

1857–1910   Periodical Accounts Relating to the Missions of the Church of the United Brethren Established among the Heathen (September 1879, vol. 31, p. 200, "from B. Sieborger"; March 1881, p. 511, "from Br. H. Ziock"; December 1883, vol. 32, p. 546; 1890, p. 90, "Official Visitation by Br. Romig"; June 1903, "from Br. Grossman"; June 1910, pp. 562–63, "from Br. Grossman"). Yearly reports in the Moravian College Library, Bethlehem, Pa.

n.d. Documents from the archives of the Instituto Bíblico, Bilwaskarma, Nicaragua.

Mueller, Bishop Karl A.

1932 *Among Creoles, Miskitos and Sumos: Eastern Nicaragua and Its Moravian Missions.* Bethlehem, Pa.: Comenius Press.

M. W.

1732 The Mosqueto Indian and His Golden River: Being a Familiar Description of the Mosqueto Kingdom of America. In *A Collection of Voyages and Travels,* compiled by Awnsham Churchill and John Churchill, vol. 6, pp. 285–98. 6 vols. London: J. Walthoe.

Niehaus, Isak

2002 Bodies, Heat, and Taboos: Conceptualizing Modern Personhood in the South African Lowfeld. *Ethnology* 41 (3): 189–207.

Nietschmann, Bernard

1973 *Between Land and Water: The Subsistence Ecology of the Miskito Indians, Eastern Nicaragua.* New York and London: Seminar Press.

1974 When the Turtle Collapses, the World Ends. *Natural History* 83 (6) (June–July): 34–43.

1979a *Caribbean Edge: The Coming of Modern Times to Isolated People and Wildlife.* Indianapolis and New York: Bobbs-Merrill Co.

1979b Ecological Change, Inflation, and Migration in the Far Western Caribbean. *Geographical Review* 69 (1): 1–24.

1987 Militarization and Indigenous Peoples: The Third World War. *Cultural Survival Quarterly* 11 (3): 1–16.

Norwood, Susan

1997 *Gramática de la lengua Sumu.* Managua: CIDCA-UCA.

Offen, Karl Henry

1999 The Miskitu Kingdom: Landscape and the Emergence of a Miskitu Ethnic Identity, Northeastern Nicaragua and Honduras, 1600–1800. Ph.D. dissertation, University of Texas at Austin.

2002 The Sambo and Tawira Miskitu: The Colonial Origins and Geography of Intra-Miskitu Differentiation in Eastern Nicaragua and Honduras. *Ethnohistory* 49 (2): 319–72.

Ohland, Klaudine, and Robin Schneider

1983 *National Revolution and Indigenous Identity: The Conflict between Sandinists and Miskito Indians on Nicaragua's Atlantic Coast.* Copenhagen: International Work Group for Indigenous Affairs.

Olien, Michael D.

1983 The Miskito Kings and the Line of Succession. *Journal of Anthropologi-*

cal Research 39 (2): 198–241.

1985 E. G. Squier and the Miskito: Anthropological Scholarship and Political Propaganda. *Ethnohistory* 32 (1): 111–33.

1998 General, Governor and Admiral: Three Miskito Lines of Succession. *Ethnohistory* 45 (2): 277–318.

Parsons, James J.

1962 *The Green Turtle and Man.* Gainesville: University of Florida Press.

1972 The Hawksbill Turtle and the Tortoise Shell Trade. In *Etudes de géographie tropicale offertes à Pierre Gourou*, pp. 45–60. Paris: Mouton.

Peter Espinoza, Melesio

2002 Parentesco y grupo doméstico de los miskitos: Los casos de Auhya Pihni y Santa Marta. Paper presented at the meetings of the American Anthropological Association, New Orleans, La., November 20–24.

Pijoan, Michel

1944 The Miskito Indians: Some Remarks Concerning Their Health and the Lay Health Program. *América Indígena* 4: 255–63.

1946 The Health and Customs of the Miskito Indians of Northern Nicaragua: Interrelationships in a Medical Program. *América Indígena* 6 (1): 41–66 and (2): 157–83.

Pim, Captain Bedford, and Berthold Seeman

1869 *Dottings on the Roadside in Panama, Nicaragua, and Mosquito.* London: Chapman & Hall.

Pratt, Mary Louise

1986 Fieldwork in Common Places. In *Writing Culture: The Poetics and Politics of Ethnography*, ed. James Clifford and George E. Marcus, pp. 27–50. Berkeley, Los Angeles, and London: University of California Press.

Price, Richard

1983 *First-Time: The Historical Vision of an African-American People.* Baltimore and London: Johns Hopkins University Press.

1990 *Alabi's World.* Baltimore and London: Johns Hopkins University Press.

Radcliffe-Brown, A. R.

1952 On Joking Relationships. In *Structure and Function in Primitive Society*, pp. 90–104. Glencoe, Ill.: Free Press.

Reyes, Reynaldo, and J. K. Wilson

1992 *Ráfaga: The Life Story of a Nicaraguan Miskito Comandante.* Norman and London: University of Oklahoma Press.

Roberts, Orlando W.

1965 *Narrative of Voyages and Excursions on the East Coast and in the Interior of Central America. . . .* Gainesville: University of Florida Press. [First published in 1827.]

Rondinelli, Dennis A., and Kenneth Ruddle

n.d.   Miskito Grammar. Mimeograph, Board of Christian Education, Moravian Church. Moravian College Library, Bethlehem, Pa.

Vandermeer, John, Ivette Perfecto, et al.

1991   Los bosques del Caribe de Nicaragua tres años después del Huracán Joan. *Wani: Revista del Caribe Nicaragüense* 11: 78–102.

Vaughan Warman, Adolfo I.

1962   *Diccionario trilingüe, Miskito-Español-Inglés*. Managua: Talleres Nacionales.

Venezia, Paola

1996   "Didn't you say you were not going to dig us until we were all fit?": El Reto de la Educación Intercultural en Nicaragua. *Wani: Revista del Caribe Nicaragüense* 19: 3–12.

Wafer, Jim

1991   *The Taste of Blood: Spirit Possession in Brazilian Candomblé*. Philadelphia: University of Pennsylvania Press.

Weiss, Brian

1973   *The Turtle People*. 26-minute film/video. Sherman Oaks, Calif.: B & C Films.

Werner, David

1985   *Where There Is No Doctor: A Village Health Care Handbook*. Palo Alto, Calif.: Hesperian Foundation.

Wilson, John F.

1975   *Obra Morava en Nicaragua: Trasfondo y breve historia*. San José, Costa Rica: Seminario Bíblico Latinoamericano.

Wolf, Eric R.

1956   Aspects of Group Relations in a Complex Society: Mexico. *American Anthropologist* 58: 1065–78.

Wood, Corinne Shear

1979   *Human Sickness and Health: A Biocultural View*. Palo Alto, Calif.: Mayfield Publishing Co.

World Bank

1999   *The Lobster Fishery of the Honduran and Nicaraguan Moskitia: A Study of the Resource, Its Sustainable Exploitation and the Problems of the Miskito Divers Working in the Fishery*. Prepared by Arcadis Euroconsult, Arhem, Netherlands. http://wbln0018.worldbank.org/MesoAm/UnbpubHP.nsf.

Young, Thomas

1847   *Narrative of a Residence on the Mosquito Shore: With an Account of Truxillo, and the Adjacent Islands of Bonacca and Roatan; and a Vocabulary of the Mosquitian Language*. London: Smith, Elder, & Co.

INDEX

Abdominal pain (*yumuh*), 222–24

Adventists, competing denomination, 185

Aesthetics, difference in, 17–18

African origins, of *kisi*, 276

African slaves, intermarry with Miskitu, 26–28

Agriculture: decline in, 163; hours of work involved in, 162–63

Alcalde: distrusted by others, 255; settles disputes within communities, 235

Alcohol use. *See* Drinking

Amulet (*kangbaika*), as protection against sorcery, 220

Anglo affinity: Charles Hale on, 36; related to learning English, 173

Anthropologist, as visitor vs. resident, 73

Anti-heroes, and Tibang, 277

Aras Bila: bridge at, 153–54, 245; path to, 117, 221; rice plantation in, 160; rich farmland near, 156

Armadillo, edible meat of, 56

Arrival story, 42–43

Asterio, new health leader, 208–10

Attending church services: 189–91, 194–95

Attending school classes: 167–69, 173–74

Authority figures: at church congregation meetings, 243–44; in Miskitu political life, 236–37

Awastara: attacked in 1790s (Offen), 27; earliest historical mention of, 24; founding of in ancestral times, 56, 156; as rogue community, 269

Awastara and Sandy Bay, comparisons of, 267–68

"Bamboo whites," foreigners living with local women, 63–64

Bar, at Awastara River mouth, 135

Barrett, Bruce: on health care, 206; on medicinal plants, 224

Baseball: history of in Nicaragua, 65–66; Miskitu World Series, 65–68; as played in Awastara, 66–67; sorcery involved in, 68

Bathing: before entering a village, 64; pleasures of, 15–16

Bats, blood-eating, 14–15

Beans, in the diet, 156

Behar, Ruth, author of *Translated Woman*, 20

Bell, Charles Napier: on acting, Miskitu love of, 202; on affection between spouses, lack of, 87; on Anansi stories, 276; author of *Tangweera*, nineteenth-century classic, 27; on bees, varieties of, 123; on death laments, 105; on drinking *mishla*, 196, 257–58; on love songs, 93; on menstrual taboos, 226; on modesty, 95; on outspoken Miskitu character, 237; on personal names, 77; on protein hunger, 113; on *smalkaia*, concept of, 30

Bends, decompression sickness among lobster divers, 142

Berries, *biuhu*, 158

Bible: Miskitu language editions of, 29–31, 191–93; stories re-enacted in Christmas plays, 200–02

Bicycles, new phenomenon in Awastara, 44–45

Bilingual program. *See* PEBI

Binge drinking, 258

Birds, names of: 3, 120–21

Birth control, use of, 208

Boats. *See* Catboats

Bonfil Batalla, Guillermo, Mexican anthropologist, 187

Boundaries: of Awastara with Dakura and Páhara, 241; of individual property owners, 48

Boys, and independence training, 100–1

Bread, homemade, 109

Breast infections, 209

Bridge, at Aras Bila, 153–54

Brooks, David C., on "bamboo whites," 63

Brown, Karen McCarthy, author of *Mama Lola*, 20

Bushey, Fredly, on value of education, 176

Businessman from Midwest, visit of, 255–56

Captains: apprenticeship of, 140; skills of, 134–35

Cardinal directions, in Miskitu, 120

Carpenters, expert and everyday, 51

Carpentry culture, of Miskitu, 50

Carr, Archie, on sea turtles, 127–28

Casey, accident at sea of, 143–44; Victor's son-in-law, 82–83

Cashew fruit and nuts, 121–22

Cassava, 153–56; cultivation of, 154–55; season for growing, 155

Catboats: and accidents at sea, 69, 143–44; as capital investments, 140; construction of, 129–30; and deep sea fishing scheme, 254–55; history of, 130; launching of, 130–32; names of, 140; owners and captains of, 138–50; repair of, 132–33; Victor's role in developing, 130

Cattle, local herds of, 111–12

Cayman Islands, source of catboat technology, 130

CEDEHCA, Commission for Human Rights in Central America, 250–52

Cemetery, in Awastara, 106

CEPAD, Development Committee of the Moravian Church, 246, 249–50

Chicha (local corn beer): brewed in cantina-like atmosphere, 262; preparation of, 259

Child-raising, 96–102; independence emphasized in, 97

Children: as company, 13; concern for by adults, 98; and nudity, 99; power struggles with adults, 8, 97–98; rough play of, 100; running errands, 100; whipping of, 98

Christianity, 181–205; competing denominations establish themselves, 186; fundamentalist version of, 189–91; and local kinship system, 183

Christmas: as celebrated on the Miskitu Coast, 197–202; Dionysian aspects of, 196–97; plays in the churches, 200–2; residents return home at, 198

Church building, as form of economic development, 189

Church conferences, 193–95; as meeting place for young people, 194

Churches: collecting funds for new buildings, 187–88; as community centers, 204

Church funds, as carefully managed resource, 189

Church hymns, children's love of singing, 14

Church of God in Awastara, 7; founding of, 185–86; strict code of behavior in, 186

Church services, at different Awastara churches, 181

CIDCA, Centro de Investigaciones y Documentación de la Costa Atlántica, costeño research center, 19

City-village relations, 68–72

Clearing and burning farmland, 157

Clinic in Awastara, 206–10

Clothes: for dressing up, 64–65; for work in the fields, 155

Coastline, receding in Awastara, 156–57

Cocaine, 163, 251, 257; ambivalence toward, 267; distributed within community, 260–61; lobster divers and, 141; local consumption of, 261–62; prices of, 260; and prosperity in Sandy Bay, 265–68; units of measure of, 260; and violence, 263–64

Cocaine trade, beginning of, 260

Coconut milk, 160; preparation of, 119

Coconuts, husking of, 159–60

Coconut trees, 159–60; disease of, 49–50; as hazards, 50; protecting young leaves of with cow dung, 159

Coconut water, 160

Code-switching (languages), 176

Committee organization, in development projects, 250

Community breakdown, 245

Community development, principles of, 207

Community problems, discussion of, 251–52

Companies, foreign, boom periods and voracious exploitation, 32–33

Conflict resolution, in Miskitu culture, 238–40

Contraceptive herbal medicine, 208

Contributions, to local churches, 188

Conversion to Moravian Christianity, nineteenth-century, and strict conduct rules, 191

Conzemius, Eduard: on houses, old style of, 52; on intermarriage with outsiders, 28; on menstrual taboos, 226; on Miskitu kings, 233; on mother-in-law avoidance, 83; on personal names, 77; on 1641 slave shipwreck, 26; on soul (isingni) after death, 105

Co-op store in the 1970s, 246

Cornelio, as headman, 237–38

Corruption, at local and national levels, 247, 270

Courtship, Maura and Hector, 80–81

Cox, Avelino, Miskitu intellectual, 212; on conflict resolution, 239; on the prahaku, 214; on the reality of spiritual creatures, 215; on yumuh, 223

Crabs, large *kaisni* variety of, 16, 119
Crack cocaine, making of, 261–62
Credit, at Awastara stores, 150
Creole people, Miskitu Coast population of, 27–28
Crime rate, in Awastara, 268–70
Cultural appropriation, of Protestant Christianity, 187
Cultural materialism, explanation for crippled divers, 143
Culture hero in Awastara, Obediah Kingsman, 61–62

Daily routine in Awastara, 13
Dakura, early Moravian mission church at, 183–84
Dead person's spirit (*isingni*), 105
Death lament (*iningka*), 104–05
Deceit (*kunin*), in daily life, 278–79
Delinquents, as economic outcasts, 271–72
Development, in Sandy Bay, 267
Development efforts, out of cultural context, 250
Development organization in Awastara, founded by Jaime, 246–47, 277–78
Development schemes, continuity in, 256–57
Development seminars, organized by outsiders, 249–52
Diets of the world, structure of, 110
Diglossia, Miskitu-Spanish, 170–71
Discourse styles in Awastara: haranguing subordinates (*palaia*), 26; yelling questions at a distance, 45
Disputes: in Awastara, 239; in Miskitu culture, 90; typical course of, 244; within local Moravian Church, 184, 243–45
Divisions, within community, 245
Dogs and chickens, in the house, 109

Drawings of daily life. *See* Wiskat Morales
Dreams, predicting future, 218–19
Dressing up: for baseball games, 67; for church, 181; for visiting, 64–65
Drinking, 257–59; at Christmas time, 198–99; disaster for men's families, 259; in Port cantinas, 258; at traditional *sikru* feasts, 196–97; trip to Awastara with drunken crew, 258–59
Drinking water, from improved well at Victor's house, 16, 254
Drug overdoses, victims of, 262
Dual organization, of villages, 57

Education: opportunities for in Puerto Cabezas, 70; at school in Awastara, 165–70; in Spanish, 165; few tangible benefits from, 174–75
Eloquence in public speaking, 178–79, 240
English classes, in Awastara, 173
Englishmen, as kin, 84
Errands, children responsible for running, 100
Ethnic boundary marker foods, *krabu* berries, 122
Evangelists, in Port marketplace, 190
Evening routine, 13–14
Exploitation. *See* Companies
Fagoth, Ana Rosa, Miskitu intellectual, 211; on curing *yumuh*, 223–24; on *lilka* and *isingni*, 217; on soul (*isingni*) after death, 105; on *sukia*, 227–28; as tireless fieldworker, 228; on *wahwin*, 214
Farewell journey, 283–84
Farmland: at Aras Bila, 156; clearing and burning of, 157
Father-in-law/son-in-law (*dapna*) relationships, 81–82

Feast for the dead (*sikru*), 196–97
Fields as warehouse, 155
Firearms, within villages, 240
Fire danger, to houses in dry season, 55
Fireflies (*tilam*), 17–18
Firewood, 108
Fishing: commercial, for turtles, shrimp, lobsters, and fish, 32, 115–16; for *mas mas*, in creeks, 117–19; with seines, 114–16
Fishing scheme for village development, proposed by outsiders, 254–57
Fish populations, declining rapidly, 116
Food: bland, carbohydrate varieties of, 125; child's fantasies about, 125–26; as ethnic boundary marker, 114; master symbol of love, 126; traditional Miskitu varieties of, 118–19
Food sharing, as basic Miskitu value, 109, 115
Food supplies, now purchased in Port, 124
Food taboos, 56, 113, 225
Forest, virgin (*insla disang*), 157
Founding of Awastara, in ancestral times, 56
Frogs. *See* Toads
Fruit eating, 121–23; and children's nutrition, 122
Fruit trees, as signs of land ownership, 49
Fruit, wild varieties of, 122
Fundamentalist Christianity, as alternative to wasted lives, 190; strict conduct rules of, 190–91

García, Claudia: on Great Awakening, 182–83; on Moravian decline, 202–3; on *sukia*, 227–28
Generational differences, and social problems, 271–72

Generosity, as prime Miskitu value, 118
Geography, local intimate knowledge of, 241
Globalization: cocaine trade as part of, 264; and local fishing scheme, 254–57
Gold mining boom: related to silicosis and tuberculosis, 32; why Victor did not go to mines, 33
Gordon, Edmund T., on Creole population, 28
Grandchildren, raised by grandparents, 101–02
Great Awakening, 182–83
Grisi siknis, illness of young women, 216
Groom capture: historical strategy of the Miskitu, 84; Dennis's experience with, 85; and intermarriage with successful foreigners, 62–63

Hale, Charles R.: on "Anglo affinity," 36; fieldwork of in Sandy Bay Sirpi, 19; on the Great Awakening, 182; on "internalized racism," 63; on missionaries, 191–92; on MISURASATA, 34; on Sandinista conflict in the 1980s, 33–34, 264
Hale, Ken: on difficulties in learning Miskitu, 39; on Miskitu as member of the Misumalpan language family, 37
Hawksbill, turtles, 127; catching a hawksbill with Victor, 137
Hawley, Susan: on Bible as Miskitu text, 192, 214; on Moravian Church during war years, 203–04
Headmen: in Awastara, 237–38; behaving like Tibang, 277; role in dispute settlement, 239; in Sandy Bay, 268; as traditional authority figures in villages, 235–38

Healers, traditional, 224–26, 227–28; collaboration with biomedicine, 211; as colleagues, 210–11; Juan Downs in Awastara, 228–31

Health care, by Moravian missionaries, 205

Health census, by Asterio, 208

Health leader, in Awastara, 207–08

Health services, under Sandinista government, 206

Helms, Mary W.: on aboriginal Miskitu, 23; on Christmas in Asang, 198–99; on church marriage, 87; on company period, 32; on disputes within the Moravian Church, 184; on dreams, 219; ethnography of Asang, 18; on etymology of word "Miskitu," 24; on illness concepts, 211; on *kiamp* groups in Asang, 57–59, 62; on kinship terms, 77; on kitchens in Asang, 107–08; on language skills, 178; on love songs, 93; on matrilocal residence, 48; on Miskitu kings, 233, 236; on Miskitu slave raids against Mayangna, 24–25; on Moravian Christianity, 183; on phases of moon, 156; on poison, 221; on reciprocity obligations, 126; on respect behavior, 279; on trade with Mayangna, 24, 155; on women staying close to home, 86

Herbal medicine, and menstruation, 226

Hidden transcript, of Tibang, 276–77

High blood pressure, 209

Homesteading: at Cigarnaka hill, 49; at Trakis, 56

Homosexuals, male, 91–92; in community life, 131

Honey, from wild bees, 123

Hoppington *kiamp*, coconut wealth of, 58–59

Hoppington, Marcos: on competing political leaders, 235–36; and new school building for Awastara, 35

Horses, 112

House in Awastara, Dennis's, 11

House owners, both men and women, 47

House posts, both wood and cement, 54–55

Houses, 50–55; building and repair of, 50–53; earlier type of, 52; durability of, 53; fire danger to, 11, 55; portable nature of, 55; prices of, 51; roof thatching for, 52; in Sandy Bay, 265–66; scrubbing floors of, 54; sleeping arrangements in, 53–54; space underneath for sitting, 55

Humor, Miskitu sense of, 100; self-deprecating variety of, 36

Hunger, following long working hours, 125

Hurricane of 1906, in Awastara, 18

"Hysterical" behavior, among Miskitu, 216

Incantations (*yabakaia*), used in curing, 223

Individualism: in Miskitu culture, 162; and reciprocity, 97

Individuals and dividuals, 73–74

Infants: bottle feeding of, 95; illnesses of, 94–95; toilet training of, 96

Infrastructure, in Sandy Bay, 266–67

Injections, popularity of, 209–10

Intermarriage with outsiders, 62–63. *See also* Groom capture

Internalized racism, 63

Interpretive anthropology, 19–21

Invalids, care of, 111

Investments, by Awastara people, 151

Isingni: causing illness in children, 217; taken to cemetery after death, 217–18

Jamieson, Mark: on body-part metaphors, 41; on death laments, 105; on English loan words in Miskitu, 40; on groom capture, 84; on mother-in-law avoidance, 279; on *swinta*, 213; on verbs with auxiliaries, 38
Jesus, as traditional healer, 222
Jobs in the village, 149–50
Juan Downs, traditional healer, 228–30

Keys, Miskitu, days spent turtle fishing on, 136
Kiamp: in Asang (Helms), 57–59; founders of, as outsiders, 59; as localized descent groups, 57–60; as settlement groups, 58
Kindblad, Christopher, on tragedy of commons, 270–72
Kings, in the Christmas plays, 201
Kings, Miskitu, history of, 232–33
King, visits Awastara on New Year's Day, 232
Kingship: given to Miskitu by English (Victor), 234; scholarly debate about, 233
Kinship obligations: in preventing impartial decision making, 237; as top priority, 246
Kinship relations, as shared mental database, 79
Kinship system, compatible with Christianity, 183
Kinship terms in Miskitu, 74–77
Kirbaia: enjoying life as young single person, 85; strolling around at Christmastime, 199

Kisi, ribald stories or folktales, 120, 273–80
Kissing, Miskitu style of, 87
Kitchen and dining room, in Plora's house, 108
Krabu or *nancite* berries, 122
Kunin (lies), as played out in daily life, 278–79

Lagueux, Cynthia, on turtle fishing, 147
Laissez-faire development, 254–57
Land, uninhabited (Trakis), 56
Land breeze (*diwas*), 42, 114, 146
Land as free, 46
Latrines, 253–54
Laughing at ourselves, through Tibang, 280
Launching, of new catboats, 130–32
Leadership, Miskitu style of, 236–38
Leaf burning, during dry season, 50
Lemley, Lynn, on English loan words in Miskitu, 38–39
Letters, to relatives, 102
Libidinal energy, 74; exemplified by Tibang, 279
Lilka, animating principle of each human being, 217
Linguistic research, on Miskitu language, 29–30, 171–72
Literacy, as limited skill, 172–73
Liwa mairin: as cause of deformed children, 213; in drowning lobster divers, 142–43; as Juan Downs's mate, 229; as owner of all water creatures, 212–13
Lobster diving: 101, 140–43; dangers of, 142–43; squandering high wages, 141–42
Love, meaning financial support, 103
Love and affection, practical expressions

of, 87–88

Love songs: composed and sung by young men, 92–93; scholarship on, 93

Lucile, Victor's oldest daughter, 101–2

Lullabies, traditional, 14

Lumber, sawing or ripping of, 53

Luxembourg Normal School, epidemic of *grisi siknis* at, 216

Lying (*kunin*), 277–80

Magic, to keep horses from straying, 112

Mangos, importance in diet, 121–23

Manufactured goods, now necessity, 164

Manure, to protect fruit tree leaves, 49

Map of Awastara, making of, 47

Marijuana, 260

Marketplace, in Puerto Cabezas, 70

Marriages: arranged, 79; church and civil ceremonies, 86–87

Mate or domestic companion (*maia*), 87

Matrilocal residence, 48, 81; preferred Miskitu pattern, 12

Mayangna (Sumu), 24–26; capture of by Awastara people, 25–26; defensive posture of, 24, 62–63; language, 37, 178; mother-in-law taboo among, 83; trade with Miskitu villages, 155

Meals, etiquette of, 108–09

Mealtimes, 13, 109

Medicinal plants: as private property, 224–25; steaming procedure with, 225

Menstruation, 226–27

Mental database of community information, 45

MINSA, Ministry of Health, 207

Miskitu, etymology of name, 24–25

Miskitu character, arguing and squabbling, 97

Miskitu language, 37–41: body part metaphors in, 40–41; embedded cultural concepts, 40–41; ethnocentrism toward, 179–80; first grammars and dictionaries of, 29; learning of, by foreigners, 29, 39, 179–80; loan words in, 37–40; low prestige of, 171–72; nouns and verbs in, 38–39; radio broadcasts in, 71; recent linguistic work on, 171–72; relationships to other languages, 23, 37

Miskitu people: physical appearance of, 28; self-image of, 36; as tough and resilient, 18

MISURASATA, Miskitu self-determination organization, 9–10, 33–34

Modesty, about nudity, 15, 95

Money-making schemes, centuries old, 256–57

Money, small denominations of used in village, 124

Moon, phases of, related to fertility, 156

Moravian Church: in Awastara, 183–85; conflict with Sandinistas, 203–4; decline of, 202–04; disputes within, 184; history of, on Miskitu Coast, 29–32

Moravian Hospital and Bible Center, 1980s burning of, 203

Moravian missionaries: become fluent in Miskitu language, 29, 179; and health care, 205

Mortars (*unuh*), for hulling rice, 162

Mory Davis: *kiamp* of, 59; as *spirit-up-lika*, 183–84; as *sukia*, 228

Mosquito-men, parallel to Englishmen, Scotsmen (Offen), 28

Mother-in-law: avoidance pattern, 83–84; Victor, relations with, 103–4

Mother's love, 91, 93

Multilingualism, as key to success, 177–78

Murders, in Awastara, 263–64

M. W., buccaneer author, 25–26; on courtesy to Englishmen, 84; on death laments, 105; on drinking *mishla*, 197

Natural world, taxonomic interest in, 121

Neoliberal capitalism, 270

Nets, for catching turtles, 136–37

Nicaraguan Revolution, 9–10

Nietschmann, Bernard: on agriculture, 163; on beach ridge type of agriculture, 154; on beach scavenging, 144; on catboats, 130; on company period, 32; on food resources, primacy of, 107; on generosity, 279; on hurricane of 1906, 18; on illness concepts, 211; on militarization of indigenous peoples, 264–65; on older style of turtling, 136; on phases of moon, 156; on pigs in villages, 254; on protein hunger, 125; rainfall figures of, for Coast, 16; on reciprocity obligations, 126; research in Tasbapauni, 18; on system of shares, 134; on theft, 239; on turtle butchering, 111; on turtle fishing, 146–47; on turtle meat in the diet, 111; on *yumuh*, 223–24

Nursing of children, length of, 95

Obediah Kingsman: as culture hero, 61–62; as famous *kiamp* founder, 60–62; and *pingka* side settlement, 60–61

Offen, Karl: historical research of, 26–28; on introduction of rice, 160; on last Miskitu king, 233

OFPMA, Awastara development organization founded by Jaime, 246–47, 277–78

Oil exploration, near Awastara, 32–33

Old age, 102–4

Olien, Michael D.: on E. G. Squier, 227; on Miskitu kings, 232–33

On-stage behavior, 202

Outspoken character, of Miskitu, 236–37

Parson Taylor, Honduran sorcerer, 221

Paths, danger on, due to cocaine dealers, 264

Payment, to medicinal plants, 225

PEBI, Programa de Educación Bilingüe Intercultural, 166–70

Peddlers, 152

Performing, in front of others, 195, 202

Personal names, 77

Personhood: dividuals vs. individuals, 73–74; as related to Tibang, 279

Physical appearance, of Miskitu people, 28

Pigs, 112–13; role of in village hygiene, 112–13, 254; roping of by boys, 99–100

Play, of children, 100

Plays, in churches at Christmas, 200–2

Plora, head bosswoman, 86, 89

Poison beliefs, 220–22

Police, in villages, 240

Political meetings: in Awastara, 241–43; factionalism in, 242–43; in Páhara, 240–41

Population figures: Awastara, 43–44; Miskitu people, 23

Pork, not eaten by Miskitu people, 113

Postmodernism: in anthropology, 19–21; Rodrigo's version of, 215

Poverty in Awastara, in spite of cocaine money, 267–68

Prahaku, spirit of wind, 214

Pratt, Mary Louise: on arrival stories, 43; on positivistic anthropology, 21

Price, Richard, author of *First-Time* and *Alabi's World*, 20

Projects, by women, for self-sufficiency, 252

Property boundaries: of communities, 240–41; of individuals, 48

Prosperity, in Sandy Bay, 265–68

Protein: hunger for, 113–14, 125; sources of, 110–11; traded for carbohydrates, 163

Public speaking: 249; local rules about, 243. *See also* Performing

Puerto Cabezas (Port, Bilwi): alternative names for, 1; attractions of, for village people, 70; financial center for the region, 71; less desirable for living than Awastara, 72; urban power center, 68

Punishments, by Moravian Church for bad behavior, 185

Radio stations, broadcast in Miskitu language, 71

Rainfall, yearly total, 16

Rainy season, 16–18

Rascally nature, of human beings, 272

Reciprocity: and individualism, 97; the *pana pana laka*, 88, 118; in traditional economy, 271

Remittances from abroad, 71

Resolution of disputes, 244

Rice, cultivation of, 160–62

Robbery. *See* Theft

Romantic rejection, 92–93

Roof thatching, as communal task, 52

Rum, sold in Port, 259. *See also* Drinking

Sailing dories, 129–33. *See also* Catboats

Sambo and Tawira (Offen), 26–27

Sandinista government: fights drug trade, 260; health services provided by, 206

Sandinistas: battles near Páhara and Awastara, 34–35; conflict with Moravian Church, 203–4; divided loyalties toward, 35–36; and war years in Awastara, 33–36

Sandinista party, self-destruction of, 270

Sandy Bay, prosperity in, 265–68

Sasmalkra (lay pastor): conflict over in Awastara, 243–45; role in earlier times and currently, 203–4; role in Moravian Church, 30, 32

Scheper-Hughes, Nancy, author of *Death Without Weeping*, 20

School in Awastara: director faces difficult situation, 176; enrollment in, 174; history of, 165; observing bilingual classes in, 167–69; promotion rates in, 166

Schoolhouse: cantina atmosphere near, 270; new building under Sandinistas, 35; original building, 165

School textbooks in Miskitu, 167–69

Scorpius, constellation (*Yapti Misri*), 117, 218

Sea turtles: butchering of, 111; depletion of populations, 128, 147; kinds of, 127; reproduction of, 127–28. *See also* Turtle fishing

Seining, process of, 115

Settlement pattern, centripetal and centrifugal forces in, 57

Sexually transmitted diseases, 209

Shamans (*sukia*), 182–83, 227–30

Share system: in turtle fishing, 134; from seining, 115

Sibling jealousy, 96

Sikru: feast of the dead, 218; sailors vs. missionaries' attitudes toward, 197

Síndico, naming of, 241–43; new village official, 235

1978   *Urbanization and Rural Development: A Spatial Policy for Equitable Growth.* New York: Praeger.

Sahlins, Marshall
1963   Poor Man, Rich Man, Big Man, Chief: Political Types in Melanesia and Polynesia. *Comparative Studies in Society and History* 5: 285–303.

Salamanca, Danilo
1988   Elementos de gramática del miskitu. Ph.D. dissertation in Linguistics, Massachusetts Institute of Technology.

Saville-Troike, Muriel
2003   *The Ethnography of Communication: An Introduction.* London: Blackwell Publishing.

Scheper-Hughes, Nancy
1992   *Death without Weeping: The Violence of Everyday Life in Brazil.* Berkeley, Los Angeles, and London: University of California Press.

Schnarf, Christian
n.d.   *Cuentos, fábulas y leyendas de la Costa Atlántica de Nicaragua.* Puerto Cabezas, Nicaragua: URACCAN.

Scott, James C.
1990   *Domination and the Arts of Resistance: Hidden Transcripts.* New Haven and London: Yale University Press.

Silva Mercado, Adán, and Jens Uwe Korten, eds.
1997   *Miskitu Tasbaia: Aisanka Yamni bara Bila Pranakira Miskitu wih Ispailra wal Ulban/La tierra miskita: Prosa y poesía en miskito y español.* Managua: Editorial CIRA/PTEN.

Singer, Isaac Bashevis
1988   Are Children the Ultimate Literary Critics? In *Stories for Children,* pp. 332–38. New York: Farrar, Straus, Giroux. [First published in 1962.]

Siskind, Janet
1973   *To Hunt in the Morning.* London, Oxford, and New York: Oxford University Press.

Squier, Ephraim George ("Samuel A. Bard")
1965   *Waikna; or Adventures on the Mosquito Shore.* Gainesville: University of Florida Press. [First published in 1855.]

Sullivan, R. E.
2002   Miskito Tribe Finds Cocaine "No Gift of God"; As It Enriches Poor Nicaraguans, Drug Breeds Addiction, Corruption. *Washington Times,* June 11, p. A 13.

Tedlock, Barbara
1992   *The Beautiful and the Dangerous: Dialogues with the Zuni Indians.* New York: Penguin Books.

Thaeler, A. D., Jr.

Single adults, difficult situation of, 88

Sirpi Ki Mairin. See Love songs

Situational ethics, in daily life, 279

Slave trading, by the Miskitu, 25–26

Sleeping arrangements, in houses, 53–54

Smalkaia, to lecture others, 30, 176

Smell, sense of, related to health and curing, 214, 225–26

Soccer, recently introduced and played by girls, 66

Social problems, both national and local, 270

Songs: church hymns, 14, 194–95; crab song, 119–20; incantation for curing *yumuh*, 223–24; love songs, 92–93

Sorcery: cases of, in Awastara, 220–22; used in baseball, 68

Spanish language, bilingualism in, 169–70

Spiritual creatures, traditional, 212–16; abduction by, 215; explained in Biblical terms, 214–15; as protectors of the environment, 212

Spirit people (*spirit uplika*), new sort of shamans, 182–83

Starches and meat, *tama* and *upan*, 110

Stealing, of turtles at Keys, 135–36. *See also* Theft

Stolen goods, 269–70

Stores, in Awastara, 150–51

Storytelling and conversation, times for, 109

Stove (*kubus*), 108

Strongmen: and cocaine prosperity, 268; within villages, 236–37

Success in life, as related to language skills, 177–78

Sugar, and tooth decay, 123–24

Sukia, traditional shamans, 210, 227–31

Swinta: dangerous spiritual creature, 49; owner of deer, 212–13

Taxonomy of animals, in Miskitu, 121

Teachers, low salaries of, 170, 175

Tedlock, Barbara, author of *The Beautiful and the Dangerous*, 20

Teknonomy, referring to person through relationship to third person, 78–79

Termite nests, used for boat caulking, 133

Termites: flying, *usra* variety of, 17; kinds of, 51

Tetanus, neonatal, 94–95

Theft: 163, 268–70; accusations of, 239; by drug addicts, 245; at new clinic, 206–7; and social breakdown, 268–70; Victor's opinions on, 269–70

Tibang, the wily rabbit, 74, 100, 234, 272–80

Tibang and the Big Fart, 274–75

Tibang and the Gold, 273–74

Tibang's Big Ears, 275–76

Toads and frogs, repulsive to Miskitu, 113

Toilet-ification projects, 253–54

Tombs, of cement, 106

Tooth decay. *See* Sugar

Tortoiseshell, from hawksbill turtles, 127

Trade, with inland villages, 155

Tragedy of commons, 270–72

Translations into Miskitu: Bible and religious works, 29–30; scholarly work, 21

Travel, to and from Puerto Cabezas, 42–43, 69

Traveling with Miskitu companions, 64

Treasure from sea, 144–45

Triangular trade, from Awastara, 146–47

Trickster. *See* Tibang

Tuberculosis, diagnosed as *isingni siknis*, 217

Turtle crawls, 137–38

Turtle fishing: blip in Awastara's history, 148–49; captains and sailors, 134–35; mainstay of only two communities, 128–29, 147–48; near shore and on Miskitu Keys, 129; regulation of, 148; share system in, 134; traditional technique of, 136; voyage to Keys with Victor, 133–38

Turtles. *See* Sea turtles

URACCAN, Universidad de las Regiones Autónomas de la Costa Caribe de Nicaragua, new *costeño* university, 10, 176, 211

USAID, United States Agency for International Development, 206

Victor: builds first Awastara catboat, 130; demands money from World Bank, 248–49; finds treasure from sea, 144–45; household of, 12; kinship tie with, 10; life strategies of, 6–7, 124; marital dispute with Plora, 89–90; on Miskitu king, 233–34; mother-in-law of, 103–4; in old age, 104; spouses of, 88–89; on thievery, 269–70

Village layout, 43

Violence: at Christmastime, 200; and cocaine use, 263–64, 267; and weapons from war years, 264

Vitamins, in diet, 122

Wafer, Jim, author of *The Taste of Blood*, 20

Wahiwin: dangerous spiritual creature, 49, 213–14; petrified, 214

Wani, scholarly journal published by CI-DCA, 19

Wasakia munaia, illness of newborn babies, 94–95

Weapons. *See* Violence

Wells, improvements on, 254

Whipping, of children, 98

White hair, in old age, 103

Whooping and hollering behavior, and mind-altering substances, 262

Wind (*yaslam*), as danger at sea, 143–44

Winds, importance of, to sailors, 145–46

Wiskat Morales, drawings of: anthropologist at work, 283; plantation work, 158; seining at beach, 116; turtle fishing, 139

Wisconsin, University of, health program in 1970s, 205–6

Women, illnesses of, 154

Women and men: double standard at Christmas, 199–200; relationships, 90–91

Women's lives: close to their homes, 86; courtship and marriage, 79–82; *kirbaia* period when young, 85; sense of responsibility, 252; sexual relationships in, 86–89

Women's organization, in Awastara, 248, 252

Working in cassava fields, 153–55, 157–58

Working in rice fields, 160–62

World Bank scheme, 247–49

World system, ties to, 256

YATAMA, Miskitu self-determination organization, offshoot of MISURASATA, 34–36

Yumuh. *See* Abdominal pain

Zambo (Sambo), Spanish epithet for Miskitu, 28